mumiani- mummy, medicine made from
        blood.

Kuchinja- slaughter, slit throad of animal
        to drain blood.

Wazimamoto- Firemen. Those who extinguish heat-
        builds on old concepts of witchcraft

bangama- game rangers.

batumbula - butchers. Those who captured
       Africans for Europeans who ate them

Simbabulaja- Lions of Europe.

Read Ch 5 + 16
         over break
    choose 6-9 to read

Larry   910- 583- 3892
        9- 2771

STUDIES ON THE HISTORY OF SOCIETY AND CULTURE
Victoria E. Bonnell and Lynn Hunt, Editors

Speaking
with
Vampires

Speaking with Vampires

Rumor and History in Colonial Africa

Luise White

UNIVERSITY OF CALIFORNIA PRESS
Berkeley · Los Angeles · London

University of California Press
Berkeley and Los Angeles, California

University of California Press, Ltd.
London, England

© 2000 by the Regents of the University
of California

Library of Congress Cataloging-in-Publication Data

White, Luise.
  Speaking with vampires : rumor and history in
colonial Africa / Luise White.
      p.   cm. (Studies on the history of society
and culture; 37)
  Includes bibliographical references and index.
  ISBN 0-520-21703-9 (alk. paper).—
  ISBN 0-520-21704-7 (pbk. : alk paper)
    1. Vampires—Africa, East.   2. Vampires—
Africa, Central.   3. Folklore—Africa, East.
4. Folklore—Africa, Central.   5. Africa, East—
Colonial influence.   6. Africa, Central—Colonial
influence.   7. Blood—Folklore.   I. Title.
II. Series.
GR355.6.W48   2000
398.2'0967—dc21   99—36924
                                          CIP

Manufactured in the United States of America

09 08 07 06 05 04 03 02 01 00
10 9 8 7 6 5 4 3 2 1

The paper used in this publication is both acid-free
and totally chlorine-free (TCF). The paper used in
this publication meets the minimum requirements
of ANSI/NISO Z39.48-1992 (R 1997) (*Permanence
of Paper*).

Hence the historical movement which changes the producers into wage-labourers appears, on the one hand, as their emancipation from serfdom and from the fetters of the guilds, and it is this aspect of the movement which alone exists for our bourgeois historians. But on the other hand, these newly freed men become sellers of themselves only after they had been robbed of all their own means of production, and all the guarantees of existence afforded by the old feudal arrangements. And this history, the history of their expropriation, is written in the annals of mankind in letters of blood and fire.

Karl Marx, Capital: A Critique
of Political Economy, *vol.* 1

This really happened when I was back visiting the old man who lived across the road from my mother in my home town of Ninety Six, South Carolina. J. Hilton Lewis was his name. While I was there two other men, who I also knew well, drove up. As they approached us, they asked Hilton if he had heard about the murder. Hilton said he hadn't heard of it, and one of the visitors explained that it happened "on Saturday, or maybe Friday, or sometime at the weekend, maybe even late Thursday evening, but at any rate it happened in Saluda or Modoc, or maybe in Aiken or near Edgefield." It happened down the road, he was pretty sure. Hilton asked what happened, and the other visitor said that a man "was shot, or maybe stabbed to death." The other visitor disagreed: "he was clubbed to death, or maybe hit with a tire iron, it could have been a golf club . . ." Hilton interrupted: "Oh yes, I'd heard about it, I just didn't have any of the details till now."

story told by Vernon Burton, May 1995

There are vampires and vampires, and not all of them suck blood.

Fritz Leiber, "The Girl with the Hungry Eyes"

Contents

Maps

Acknowledgments

This project has been transformed by the research I did on it. I was doing the research for my dissertation—which became my first book—when I first heard stories of the firemen in colonial Nairobi who captured Africans and took their blood. Back then, I was incredulous. In fact, when I repeated this story to my research assistant's mother, I learned the word for "crazy" in Swahili in order to describe the woman who told it to me. It only struck me that this might be an interesting thing to pursue when my assistant's mother assured me that it was true, that it had happened from "the fighting of the Germans to the day Pangani was broken," from World War I to 1939. But the more questions I asked about these bloodsucking firemen, the more I learned about these stories and how different versions of them commented upon the history of which they were a part. On all the research trips that inform the bulk of this book—to western Kenya in 1986, to Zambia and Uganda in 1990, and to do archival research in England in 1991 and 1992, Italy in 1991, and Belgium in 1992 and 1993—I told myself that I needed one more piece of the puzzle, one more fragment with which to write a history and then I would be done. But I learned, quite slowly in fact, that there was no puzzle, no flat, two-dimensional representation of the world that Africans had represented in vocabularies of blood, firemen, and injections. Instead, there was a maze, almost a series of mazes, a set of meanings and messy epistemologies embodied in every fearsome hour when men and women had wondered whether it was safe to go outside and animated with every recounting of a blood accusation. Letting the maze be the maze, letting this history be as messy and meandering as it needed to be, occasioned a rethinking of the historiography that had dismissed rumor and gossip as a likely way to reconstruct the past. As this book took shape, I found myself moving from contextualizing these vampires to allowing them to comment on historiography and evidence. What better way to reexamine the way historians have thought about evidence, reliability, and truth than by studying the history of things that never happened?

The research for this book began in the 1970s. It has been funded by the Jan Smuts Fund of Cambridge University, the Division of the Humanities at Rice University, the McKnight–Land Grant Professorship at the University of Minnesota, the American Philosophical Society, the National Endowment for the Humanities, and the Wellcome Trust. That these funds became research owes much to the extraordinary generosity of those with whom I stayed while in Europe and Africa as I followed these bloodsucking firemen, and I want to thank the late Timotheo and May Omondo for my home in Yimbo, Siaya District; Jane and Opiyo Odhiambo in Alego, and Sidney Westley in Nairobi, in Kenya; Hugh and Monica Macmillan for housing in Lusaka; Megan Vaughan and Henrietta Moore and William Beinart and Troth Wells for housing in Oxford; and Robert and Helen Irwin for accommodation and friendship in London over the years. My research in Uganda would not have been possible without the generosity of Nnakanyike and Seggane Musisi. I owe a special debts to archivists: Musila Musembe at the Kenya National Archives in Nairobi; Mrs. M. N. Mutiti at the Zambian National Archives in Lusaka; Père Renault at the White Fathers Archives in Rome; Père Christian Papèians de Morchoven at Saint Andreas Abbey in Bruges; John Pinfold at Rhodes House, Oxford; and Julia Shepard at the Wellcome Trust in London.

None of this would have been possible without some extraordinary research assistants: Margaret Makuna and Paul Kakaire in Nairobi, Odhiambo Opiyo in Siaya, Fred Bukulu, Godfrey Kigozi, and Remigius Kigongo in Kampala.

This book was written during periods of unemployment and has been sustained by a number of institutions and a somewhat larger circle of friends. Fellowships at the Institute for the Humanities at the University of Michigan and the Institute for the Advanced Study and Research in the African Humanities at Northwestern University gave me the time to start two chapters. From 1993 to 1995, I had the great good fortune to be at the National Humanities Center, where fellow Fellows and staff nurtured this project: I am grateful to Robert Conner and Kent Mullikin for their generosity and to Alan Tuttle and Jean Houston for library services above and beyond the expectations of even the most pampered academics. Most of the book was finished when I was a Fellow at the Center for Folklife Programs at the Smithsonian Institution, and I am grateful to Peter Seitel for his stewardship and many discussions about orality and genre. The book was revised when I took time away from another project while at the Woodrow Wilson International Center, where Ann Sheffield's enthusiasm made a wonderful year even better. Several friends deserve special thanks. William Beinart and Troth Wells provided a respite, and a place to think about work and career, in Oxford in late 1992; David William Cohen and I have talked and written about African oral history so much that it is hard to remember who said what when, and this book owes much to his generosity; Frederick Cooper has encouraged me to let the ambiguity of African vampire stories remain ambiguous and explore the relations of power and uncertainty in which most colonized people lived; Laura Fair was my student when I began this project and is now my most astute and critical reader; Barbara Hanawalt showed me an example of unflinching professionalism, the strength of which was equal to that of her scholarship; Ivan Karp read my work with a breadth and passion of interests (and reading lists) that inspired me; Corinne Kratz helped me think about language and speech in ways that oral historians rarely do; John Lonsdale's enduring friendship and unbounded imagination has influenced this project in ways he might not recognize; David Newbury paved the way for me to teach two courses at the University of North Carolina in 1994–95; Atieno Odhaimbo saw this project at its earliest point in Nairobi and insisted that it become a book; Randall Packard talked through any number of points in medical history with me, and provided a situation at Emory University in 1995–96 that enabled me to continue my work; and Megan Vaughan has discussed many of the ideas in this book, housed me on various trips, and once suggested that I read about missionary medicine as a good way to think about blood. Throughout the time I was thinking and writing about blood, I was fortunate to have the encouragement of David Brent, Monica McCormick, and Ken Wissoker.

Earlier versions of chapters in this book were given at seminars in North America, Europe, and southern Africa. and I learned an enormous amount from the comments I received at them. Tom Beidelman,

Bill Freund, Lynn Hunt, Ivan Karp, and Tom Lacquer all read this manuscript and provided exceptionally helpful comments. As this book was revised, several friends—all on leave—took time away from their own projects to read and then reread a few of my chapters. Charles Briggs, James Ellison, David Gilmartin, Barbara Hanawalt, Laura Fair, James Hevia, Douglas Howland, and Timothy Scarnecchia were wise and careful readers, for which I am grateful.

Laura Fair, Johannes Fabian, Steven Feierman, and Peter Seitel helped me with Swahili translations; Mwelwa Musambachime and Debra Spitulnik helped me with the Bemba; and Remigius Kigongo did the Luganda for me.

A Note on Currencies and Talk

The currencies Africans allude to in the interviews quoted in this book—shillings in the sterling zone of British colonization and francs in the Belgian Congo—cover a range of values and, indeed, a range of meanings. In colonial times, East African shillings (which replaced rupees in 1921) were reckoned in pounds, shillings, and pence at the rate of 20/- = £1 and 100 cents to the shilling. In colonial Kenya or Uganda, sums of 2/50 or 15/75 were commonplace. In colonial Northern Rhodesia, however, the currency had deep ties to England (and none to India), and the currency was pounds, shillings, and pence, with £1 = 20/- and 1/- = 12 pence. Thus, in chapter 9, figures of 2/6 or 11/6 are common. At independence, East African nations retained shillings, while Northern Rhodesia's currency became Zambia's kwacha.

These interviews, however, were done between the late 1970s and the early 1990s, during which time currencies in Africa devalued drastically. It is almost impossible to tell if a reference to 50 shillings in a vampire story from Nairobi in the late 1920s told to me in 1976 by a woman who had heard it in the 1930s was 50/- at its 1976 value, its 1930s value, or its earlier value. It may also not be terribly worthwhile to try to find out the exact value of the shilling in this or any other account. What this and other speakers meant was that a specific value could be put on abduction and extraction, that that value was of an amount worth recalling, and that it was an amount of some significance. When men in Uganda asked my assistants and I if we would not be willing to secure a liter of blood for 50,000/-, they did mean present-day rates of exchange, not to fix an exact value on a liter of blood, but to show that this was a payment for which individuals might have done extraordinary things. Nowhere is this clearer than in the Congolese data made available to me through interviews conducted for Bogumil Jewsiewicki in 1991. Referring to the early 1940s—World War II—Africans spoke of the Fr 2,50 African women received for helping batumbula find victims. Whatever the value of this figure to the speaker, the reference to francs in a wartime story erased the occupation of Belgium and the use of the Reichsmark there, and gave Africans a way to speak about the continuities of Belgian rule, despite the fall of Belgium and a weak government in exile in London. The Africans who recalled the protests of the 1940s, protests fueled by the conquests of Belgium, nevertheless naturalized Belgian rule when they spoke in francs. Indeed, this particular reference to francs suggests something else, something that is a point of this book, that details and facts and figures not only describe but illustrate: they are used to get a point across, to make clear, to demonstrate, to reveal that these were specific actions done by people for specific rewards. People tell stories about bloodsucking, and they give details in shillings and francs to make their points.

PART ONE

CHAPTER I

Blood and Words

Writing History with (and about)
Vampire Stories

The name of the bloodsucker superstition is Mumiani. I understand the superstition is fairly widespread throughout Africa. The Mombasa incident took
place . . . in May or June [1947]. A man . . . started a story that the Fire Brigade were Mumiani people and had been seen walking around with buckets
filled with blood, and had taken a woman as prisoner at the Fire Station with
intent to take her blood. The man gave a good deal of detail, most of which
I forget, but the gist of it was that Fire Brigade men took this woman while she
was sleeping . . . off to the Fire Station.

The story ran round rapidly and aroused a great deal of excitement. . . .
about noon on the day the rumours got started . . . the Municipal Native
Affairs Officer heard the yarn, and . . . went to the Fire Station. . . . By that
time excitement was rapidly rising. . . . Very soon after the MNAO's arrival
at the Fire Station a larger and angry mob gathered and started to get rough.
Responsible Africans told the mob there was nothing in the story and certified
they had searched the Station and found all in order. The mob refused to believe them. The MNAO with a few African police tried first to reason with the
mob and then to disperse them. They were however heavily stoned and had
to beat a rapid retreat . . . soon after an adequate force of police came up and
after a few baton charges dispersed the crowd and made a few arrests. The excitement then rapidly subsided. The mob were roused in the first instance by
their superstitious fears, and were soon reinforced by the rowdies who are far
too numerous in Mombasa and always ready to join in any shindig.

The unfortunate Fire Brigade have I believe from time to time been suspected of Mumiani practices, because they wear black overalls, which are
reputed to be similar to the dress of the alleged Mumiani men.

George Brown (?), letter to Elspeth Huxley,
20 June 1948[1]

1. Elspeth Huxley Papers, Rhodes House, Oxford, RH MSS Afr. s. 782, box 2/2,
Kenya (1). From the level of detail in the letter both about this and issues in colonial policy and his references to Huxley's visit with him in 1947, my guess is that the writer was
George Brown, then acting provincial commissioner of Coast Province. Other accounts of
this riot are "'Human Vampire' Story Incites Mombasa Mob's Fire Station Attack," *East
African Standard*, 27 June 1947, 3; Elspeth Huxley, *The Sorcerer's Apprentice: A Journey
through East Africa* (London: Chatto & Windus, 1948), 23 n.; Kenya Colony and Protectorate, *Report on Native Affairs, 1939–47* (London: HMSO, 1948), 83.

An African politician recalled that in 1952, a man returned to his home area in central Kenya, much to the surprise of his neighbors: "He had been missing since 1927. We thought he had been slaughtered by the Nairobi Fire Brigade between 1930–1940 for his blood, which we believed was taken for use by the Medical Department for the treatment of Europeans with anaemic diseases."[2] In 1986, however, a man in western Kenya told my assistant and I that it was the police, not the firemen, who captured Africans ("ordinary people" just "associated firemen with bloodsucking because of the color of their equipment") and kept their victims in pits beneath the police station.[3]

What are historians to do with such evidence? To European officials, these stories were proof of African superstition, and of the disorder that superstition so often caused. It was yet another groundless African belief, the details of which were not worth the recall of officials and observers. But to young Africans growing up in Kenya—or Tanganyika or Northern Rhodesia—in the 1930s, such practices were terrible but matter-of-fact events, noteworthy, as in the quotations above, only when proven to be false or when the details of the story required correction. In this book, I want to study these stories both as colonial stories and for their mass of often contested details. I want to interrogate and contextualize these stories for what was in them: I want to contextualize all their power, all their loose ends, and all their complicated understandings of firemen and equipment and anemia, so that they might be used as a primary source with which to write, and sometimes rewrite, the history of colonial East and Central Africa. I argue that it is the very inaccurate jumble of events and details in these stories that makes them such accurate historical sources: it is through the convoluted array of overalls and anemia that Africans described colonial power.

These were, as officials knew, widespread stories, which showed great similarities and considerable differences over a wide geographic and cultural area. Game rangers were said to capture Africans in colonial Northern Rhodesia; mine managers captured them in the Belgian Congo and kept them in pits. Firemen subdued Africans with injections in Kenya but with masks in Uganda. Africans captured by mumiani in colonial Tanganyika were hung upside down, their throats were cut, and

2. H. K. Wachanga, *The Swords of Kirinyaga: The Fight for Land and Freedom* (Nairobi: Kenya Literature Bureau, 1975), 9.

3. Anyango Mahondo, Sigoma, west Alego, 15 August 1986. All interviews cited for 1986 were conducted by myself and Odhiambo Opiyo.

their blood drained into huge buckets. How is the historian to tease meaning out of such tales? To dismiss them as fears and superstitions simply begs the question. To reduce them to anxieties—about colonialism, about technology, about health—strips them of their intensity and their detail. Indeed, to attempt to explain these stories, to show how they made sense of the world Africans experienced, would be to turn them into mechanistic African responses: it would reduce them to African misunderstandings of colonial interventions; it would be to argue that these stories simply deformed actual events and procedures. Such an analysis would turn the resulting history away from these stories and back to the events Africans somehow misunderstood.

This book takes these stories at face value, as everyday descriptions of extraordinary occurrences. My analysis is located firmly in the stories: they are about fire stations, injections, and overalls, and they record history with descriptions of fire stations and injections. These are tools with which to write colonial history. The power and uncertainty of these stories—no one knew exactly what Europeans did with African blood, but people were convinced that they took it—makes them an especially rich historical source, I think. They report the aggressive carelessness of colonial extractions and ascribe potent and intimate meanings to them. Some of the stories in this book locate pits in the small rooms of Nairobi prostitutes in the late 1920s. Others relocate the Tanganyikan Game Department in the rural areas of Northern Rhodesia in the early 1930s. Such confusions offer historians a glimpse of the world as seen by people who saw boundaries and bodies located and penetrated. The inaccuracies in these stories make them exceptionally reliable historical sources as well: they offer historians a way to see the world the way the storytellers did, as a world of vulnerability and unreasonable relationships. These stories of bloodsucking firemen or game rangers, pits and injections, allow historians a vision of colonial worlds replete with all the messy categories and meandering epistemologies many Africans used to describe the extractions and invasions with which they lived.

This book is not simply about rumor and gossip, however: it is about the world rumor and gossip reveals. The chapters in part 2 argue that such stories perhaps articulate and contextualize experience with greater accuracy than eyewitness accounts. They explain what was fearsome and why. New technologies and procedures did not have meaning because they were new or powerful, but because of how they articulated ideas about bodies and their place in the world, and because of the ways in which they reproduced older practices. The five chapters in part 3

write colonial history with vampire stories. The result is not a history of
fears and fantasies, but a history of African cultural and intellectual life
under colonial rule, and a substantial revision of the history of urban
property in Nairobi, of wage labor in Northern Rhodesia and the Belgian Congo, of systems of sleeping-sickness control in colonial Northern Rhodesia, and of royal politics and nationalism in colonial Uganda.
In each case, evidence derived from vampire stories offered a new set of
questions, recast prevailing interpretations, and introduced analyses
that allowed for a reworking of secondary materials. Vampire stories are
like any other historical source; they change the way a historical reconstruction is done.

SITING VAMPIRES

But why have I focused on these stories of blood? There are any number
of other widespread rumors—about food additives that made men
impotent, about dreams that foretold the appearance of white men,
or dreams that foretold when they would vanish, about the origin of
AIDS—that I could have used. But they do not share the same generic
qualities and lack the similarities of plot and detail. Stories about colonial bloodsucking, in contrast, are told with—and about—a number of
overlapping details; they are identifiable over a large geographic and cultural area, both by the people who tell them and the people who hear
them, as a specific kind of story. Even people who don't believe them understand that this is a particular kind of story and often use it as an example of what Africans are willing to believe, as chapters 4 and 8 argue.
These stories are almost always taken together, so that they form a
genre, a special kind of story that, while drawing on other kinds of stories and everyday experiences in each retelling, retains a specific set of
plot and details. It is the pattern of the tale, not the circumstances of the
telling, that makes a story recognizable as belonging to a genre, different from other stories that flourish alongside reports of bloodsucking
firemen and game rangers.[4] As some of the oral material quoted in these
introductory chapters makes clear, the circulation of the genre gives
these stories their unity. These were the kinds of stories that, like some
kinds of song or praise poetry, could be extended, amended, and applied

4. Charles L. Briggs and Richard Bauman, "Genre, Intertextuality, and Social Power,"
Journal of Linguistic Anthropology 2, 2 (December 1992): 131–72.

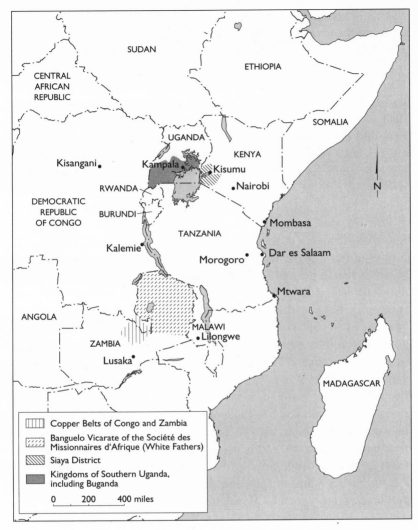

Map 1.   East and Central Africa

and reapplied to different situations in different places.[5] Listeners understand the variety of these stories as forming part of a whole: hearing a bloodsucking story from Uganda can confirm a bloodsucking story from Nairobi. When someone hears that prostitutes work for firemen in Nairobi but not in Kampala, this does not contradict the story he or she knows. Instead, it underscores the local difference that makes the stories such accurate descriptions of life in Kampala and Nairobi. The circulation, and the differences circulation reveals, makes storytellers and listeners aware of the historical location of these stories, which in turn gives the genre its authority: a story that reports so many diverse experiences from so many different places must depict elements of social life—and speech—that hearers recognize and want to repeat.

Firemen, pits, injections, game rangers, and buckets—these are the formulaic elements of these stories. The formulaic has had a troubled history in the study of oral literature. Originally thought of as a group of words that expressed an essential idea, often in meter, formulas were once considered a key tool by which Homeric bards had composed their epics. But the idea was reworked, and by the time African history emerged as an object of academic study, the very fact that formulas were an explicit tool in performance was thought to make them less reliable as historical sources.[6] The devices of storytelling were considered irrelevant to the history as a story told. Recent research, however, has argued that African oral materials never provide the same kind of stable texts that documents do and has challenged historians to unfix the boundary between the formulas used to tell a particular story and the history transmitted in that story.[7] My use of the concept of formula in this book takes up that challenge, arguing that the formulaic elements of these stories, the firemen and the pits and the injections, are simply that: terms and images into which local meanings and details are inserted by their

---

5. See Leroy Vail and Landeg White, *Power and the Praise Poem: Southern African Voices in History* (Charlottesville: University Press of Virginia, 1991), 41–44.

6. Ibid., 1–33. See also Jan Vansina, *Oral Tradition as History* (Madison: University of Wisconsin Press, 1985).

7. David William Cohen, "The Undefining of Oral Tradition," *Ethnohistory* 36, 1 (1989): 9–18; Karin Barber, *I Could Speak Until Tomorrow: Oriki, Women, and the Past in a Yoruba Town* (Washington, D.C.: Smithsonian Institution Press, 1991); Elizabeth Tonkin, *Narrating Our Past: The Social Construction of Oral History* (Cambridge: Cambridge University Press, 1992); and Isabel Hofmeyr, *"We Spend Our Years as a Tale That Is Told": Oral Historical Narratives in a South African Chiefdom* (Portsmouth, N.H.: Heinemann, 1994), and "'Wailing for Purity': Oral Studies in Southern African Studies," *African Studies* 52, 4 (1995): 16–31.

tellers. These stories say different things about injections and pits in different places because the history and the meaning of those terms is different in those places. These stories belong to a genre that is told with formulaic elements; they are about the past and can be used to recover experiences and ideas best described in terms of firemen, pits, and blood.

I call this transnational genre of African stories vampire stories, not because I want to insert a lively African oral genre into a European one, but because I want to use a widespread term that adequately conveys the mobility, the internationalism, and the economics of these colonial bloodsuckers. No other term depicts the ease with which bloodsucking beings cross boundaries, violate space, capture vulnerable men and women, and extract a precious bodily fluid from them. No other term conveys the racial differences encoded in one group's need for another's blood. Europe's literary vampires were a separate race, which fed, slept, and reproduced differently from humans.[8] Yet I worry, as historians of Africa are prone to do, that an African specificity will be lost when I invoke a dominant European term. I worry that all the regional and local history in this book will be submerged into a vision of African vampires congruent with that of European lore. But in fact, some of the very processes of storytelling that inform this book should spare me further anxieties about which term to use: in contemporary usage, "vampire" conveys little of its original meaning. Popular versions of Transylvanian counts and modernized vampires reveal how powerfully a concept— and a word—can attract and hold events and ideas that were never part of its initial construction. The issue is not so much the accuracy of terms like "game ranger" or "firemen" but how such terms can be used to describe many situations. It is not a common point of origin that gives vampire beliefs their longevity and periodicity; as Nina Auerbach points

8. David Glover, *Vampires, Mummies and Liberals: Bram Stoker and the Politics of Popular Fiction* (Durham, N.C.: Duke University Press, 1996), 22–43, argues that Count Dracula was created by the Irish Protestant Bram Stoker to show how the terrible, superstitious trappings of European Catholicism—represented in the novel by decaying castles, crosses, and terrified peasants—had harmed Irish Celts, and that *Dracula* can be read as a statement about the urgency of home rule for Ireland. For other commentaries that make the endangered culture the imperial power itself, see John Allen Stevenson, "A Vampire in the Mirror: The Sexuality of Dracula," *PMLA* 103, 2 (1988): 139–49, and Stephen D. Arata, "The Occidental Tourist: *Dracula* and the Anxiety of Reverse Colonization," *Victorian Studies* 33, 4 (1990): 621–45. Several folklorists have missed the point and claimed that vampires represent aristocratic charm and sophistication, combined with eternal life; see especially Noreen Dresser, *American Vampires: Fans, Victims and Practitioners* (New York: Norton, 1989).

out, "it is their variety that makes them survivors."[9] Indeed, I hope that the very variety of colonial vampires in this book, and the variety of colonial situations they depict, will encourage others to look more carefully at the supernatural—the very term should encourage a careful rereading of what it might mean—and at Europe's vampires. Far from being products of folk belief or a clear-cut representation of the extractions of a dominant power, vampire stories articulate relationships and offer historians a way into the disorderly terrain of life and experience in colonial societies.

TRANSLATING VAMPIRES

There are no words in the languages of the people I write about for blood-drinker or blood-taker. The words in African languages that I translate as vampire are already translations—they are words for firemen, game rangers, or animal slaughterers that had already undergone semantic shifts to mean the employees of Europeans whose job it was to capture Africans and take their blood. This of course raises another question: were the practices of firemen and game rangers and surveyors such that they encouraged stories about bloodsucking, or did these terms mean vampire before the tasks of firemen and game rangers became well known? In short, which came first, the use of a term to describe an actual thing or job, or its use to mean vampire?

There is no simple, undialogic answer. One of the oldest terms for vampire on the East African coast, *mumiani,* first appeared in Swahili dictionaries in the late nineteenth century. According to Bishop Edward Steere's dictionary of 1870, compiled on Zanzibar, *mumyani* was a mummy, but could also refer to medicine.[10] It had been a widespread belief in late nineteenth-century India, especially among plague victims on the west coast that hospitals were torture chambers designed to extract *momiai,* a medicine based on blood. The Indian Ocean trade, with African sailors coming and going between Zanzibar and India, could easily have carried the idea, as well as medicines supposedly made from blood, to East African markets.[11] Just over a decade later, Krapf's dic-

9. Nina Auerbach, *Our Vampires, Ourselves* (Chicago: University of Chicago Press, 1995), 1.

10. Edward Steere, *A Handbook of the Swahili Language, as Spoken at Zanzibar* (1870; 3d ed., London: SPCK, 1884), 349.

11. David Arnold, *Colonizing the Body: State Medicine and Epidemic Disease in Nineteenth-Century India* (Berkeley and Los Angeles: University of California Press, 1993), 220–22.

tionary, compiled near Mombasa, repeated Steere's definition of *mumiani,* as the word was transcribed, but added "a fabulous medicine which the Europeans prepare, in the opinion of the natives, from the blood of man." [12] No one I interviewed, however, said that mumiani appeared that early. Even people born in the 1890s said the practice started after World War I in Kenya and in the 1920s in Northern Rhodesia and Uganda. [13] It may be that some people on the East African coast in the late nineteenth century believed that Europeans made medicine from African blood, but their stories about it did not survive. But the term *mumiani* was in intermittent use on the coast for over a century, during which time it was given many of the contemporary meanings associated with blood accusations. In the Swahili-French dictionary of the priest Charles Sacleux, compiled on Zanzibar and published in 1941, *mumiani* is defined as mummy, and a medicine Africans believed was made from dried blood. Jews, Sacleux added, were in charge of getting the blood from people. [14] In everyday use, *mumiani* was synonymous with *kachinja* and *chinjachinja.* This Swahili term came from the verb *kuchinja,* to slaughter animals by cutting their throats and draining their blood. Doubling the root word intensified its meaning. The prefix *ka-* meant small in Kenya and gross in Tanganyika. Either or both meanings may have applied when the term was fixed in everyday use. [15] However, the term for slaughtering people, according to A. C. Madan's 1902 English-to-Swahili dictionary, was a literal translation word that meant the killing of many people (from the verb *kuua,* to kill) that did not use the root *-chinja.* [16] The use of a term specific to animals for vampires may have kept the idea of bloodsucking outside of all logic and nature. Indeed, animal butchers were not accused of bloodsucking on the East African coast: firemen were.

The word for firemen, *wazimamoto* in Swahili (*bazimamoto* in Luganda), is a literal translation: the men (*wa-*) who extinguish (from *kuzima* to put out, to extinguish) the fire or the heat (*moto*). It became

12. Rev. Dr. L. Krapf, *A Dictionary of the Swahili Language* (London: Trubner, 1882), 166–67.

13. Amina Hali, Pumwani, Kenya, 4 August 1976; Anyango Mahondo.

14. Charles Sacleux, *Dictionnaire Swahili-Français* (Paris: Institut d'ethnologie, 1941), 625.

15. Inter-Territorial Language Committee for the East African Dependencies, *Standard Swahili-English Dictionary* (Oxford: Oxford University Press, 1942), 56–57; T. O. Beidelman, personal communication, 8 September 1997.

16. A. C. Madan, *English-Swahili Dictionary* (Oxford: Oxford University Press, 1902), 371.

a generic term for vampire, always as a plural, almost as soon as it was in widespread use, well before there were formal fire brigades in most of the places where the word meant vampire. In Uganda, for example, the idea that bazimamoto took Africans' blood predated full-time firemen by thirty years. Chapters 4 and 7 explore the loose relationship between occupational practices and the social imagination, but the fact that there were no real firemen meant that the term could be applied to surveyors, yellow fever department personnel, whomever. It is not that the term had no specificity, but that its meaning was unstable enough to be made to fit any number of situations and relationships. The term *banyama* (singular, *munyama*) for game rangers in colonial Northern Rhodesia was translated by officials there as "vampire" as early as 1931. Not only did it refer to the game department in a neighboring colony, but it was another term depicting actions toward animals applied to humans. The word was never fully translated into Bemba, the local language. The prefix *ba-* means men, but *nyama* is Swahili and Nyanja for the meat of animals and quadrupeds who shed blood, either in sacrifice or as predators: cows have nyama but chickens do not. The Bemba word is *nama*.[17] Although the term does not seem to have been used in Swahili-speaking areas, *banyama* maintained its Swahili origins for Bemba speakers; it was never naturalized in the local language. Many words for vampires were never given African translations. Among the Nilotic Luo peoples of western Kenya, the word for vampire was the Swahili plural *wachinjaji,* slaughterers, and not a Luo translation. In Mozambique, the term was Portuguese, *chupa-sangue,* literally "blood drinker or blood sucker," although Swahili speakers would note the implicit pun that *chupa* means bottle in Swahili, a word derived from the Portuguese *chupar,* to suck or drain.

The pun I impute to *chupa-sangue* raises another question. When we speak of words used by people who neither read nor write, how useful are terms like "translation," and "pun," or even "multiple meanings"? Are we not better served by asking what kind of understandings speakers bring to bear on their own use of these words? The term for those who captured Africans for the Europeans who ate their flesh in colonial

17. E. Hoch, *Bemba Pocket Dictionary: Bemba-English and English-Bemba* (Abercorn: White Fathers Press, 1960), 54, 72, 107. In the mid 1930s, Africans in central Tanganyika spoke of "Bwana Nyama," the head of the game department, who went alone into the bush to look for blood, but the term *banyama* does not seem to have taken hold in Swahili (Fr. H. de Vries, Morogoro, "Superstition in Africa," *Holy Ghost Messenger* 32 [1936]: 67–69). I am grateful to Peter Pels for these notes.

Belgian Congo was *batumbula* (singular, *mutumbula*), from the Luba
-tumbula, translated in Shaba Swahili as to "butcher." [18] (Shaba Swahili
is the variant of the Swahili of the East African coast spoken in present-
day Shaba, colonial Katanga, shaped as much by work and migrancy in
the area as it was by its historical roots as a trade language.) But the
range of meanings for the root *tumbula* in the region suggest how accurately the term came to describe all the things batumbula did. In Luba,
-tumbula means "to overpower," but also "to pierce or to puncture,"
sometimes from below. [19] In many of the languages of Kenya and Tanzania, including Swahili, the meaning is "to disembowel" or "to make a
hole with a knife or sharp object." [20] *Batumbula,* a term that took hold
among the migrant labor population of the mines of colonial Katanga,
may have been heard by Swahili speakers with one set of meanings and
by Luba speakers with another set. The power and viability of the term
lay in its many meanings, which allowed the word to encompass all the
things batumbula were said to do, from digging pits, to giving their victims injections, to eating their flesh. And in colonial Belgian Congo,
batumbula was also glossed by the Shaba Swahili term *simba bulaya,*
the lion from Europe, another animal term to describe the predatory
cannibals who left their victims' clothes behind.

Why are there so many terms that could mean "bloodsucker"? And
why do so many of them describe another activity altogether? Such semantic shifts occur when existing languages do not have the words to
convey new meanings. But the fact that *wazimamoto* meant "vampire"
almost as soon as it became a word suggests that these words were se-
mantically malleable: once in everyday use, they could be taken over by
their users and given new and potent meanings. They did not simply describe firemen the way a new word might describe a streetcar or an air-

18. Johannes Fabian, *Remembering the Present: Painting and Popular History in
Zaire* (Berkeley and Los Angeles: University of California Press, 1996), 50. Sometimes
batumbula were called mitumbula, using the prefix normally given to plants, trees, and
spirits and humans involved in the spirit world (Johannes Fabian, letter to author, 22 September 1992). See also Johannes Fabian, *Language and Colonial Power: The Appropriation of Swahili in the Former Belgian Congo, 1880–1938* (Cambridge: Cambridge University Press, 1986), and id., ed. and trans., *History from Below: The Vocabulary of
Elisabethville by André Yav: Texts, Translations, and Interpretive Essay* (Amsterdam and
Philadelphia: John Benjamins, 1990), 1–3.
19. Auguste de Clercq, *Dictionnaire Tshiluba-Français* (1936; rev. ed., Leopoldville:
Impr. de la Société missionaire de St. Paul, 1960), 290; Frère Gabriel, *Dictionnaire
Tshiluba-Français* (Brussels: Librairie Albert de Witt, n.d. [1948]), 121.
20. Krapf, *Dictionary,* 384; Inter-Territorial Language Committee, *Standard Dictionary,* 478; Sacleux, *Dictionnaire,* 954; Steven Feierman, personal communication,
27 April 1998.

plane; they described firemen and what Africans thought they really did.[21] The words for firemen and game rangers and small butchers themselves were translated by Africans to describe true meanings not available in the language from which they are taken. Vampires were new. Despite scattered written references and a dictionary definition, no one I ever interviewed knew any precolonial stories about whites or Africans who took blood: "In those days there was nobody looking for blood."[22] The blood of precolonial sacrifice was bovine; the ritual killings that sometimes marked a king's death did not draw blood, and the blood of blood brotherhood was thought of as a sexual fluid, more akin to breast milk or semen than to the blood of wounds and injuries.[23] But why do some of these terms require two languages to contain their meanings? Part of the reason is again semantic: blood was not a stable enough category to allow for a local term to describe its extraction. Many African peoples do not have a specific concept for blood that matches the scientific concept of a fluid pumped by the heart into arteries and veins. Many African peoples use a word for blood broadly as a metaphor for sexual fluids, either because of symbolic systems or because of the demands of polite conversation. At the same time, many African languages distinguish between kinds of blood and the circumstances in which it leaves the body in ways that the scientific concept does not, so that the blood of childbirth and the blood of wounds are called by different terms.[24]

21. Roman Jakobson, "On Linguistic Aspects of Translation," in Rueben A. Bower, ed., *On Translation* (Cambridge, Mass.: Harvard University Press, 1959), 232–39. The Swahili for airplane is a compound word, for example: *ndege ulaya,* European bird.

22. Yonasani Kaggwa, Katwe, 27 August 1990. "Eating" and cannibalism have a wide range of meanings in East African Bantu languages that do not translate easily into English: "eating" has all the metaphorical power of "hunger" and the expressive power of "consumption." When the Kabaka, or king, of Buganda was enthroned, it was said that he had "eaten Buganda" (Benjamin Ray, *Myth, Ritual and Kingship in Buganda* [Oxford, 1991], 114).

23. See John Roscoe, *The Baganda: An Account of Their Customs and Beliefs* (London: Macmillan, 1911), 19, 268, 293; Luise White, "Blood Brotherhood Revisited: Kinship, Relationship, and the Body in East and Central Africa," *Africa* 64, 3 (1994): 359–72. The retainers of the deceased Kabaka were killed by strangulation or a blow to the head (Ray, *Myth, Ritual and Kingship,* 160–82).

24. Luc de Heusch, *The Drunken King, or, The Origin of the State,* trans. Roy Willis (Bloomington: Indiana University Press, 1982), 168–73; T. O. Beidelman, *Moral Imagination in Kaguru Modes of Thought* (Washington, D.C.: Smithsonian Institution Press, 1993), 32–35; Hugo H. Hinfelaar, "Religious Change among Bemba-Speaking Women in Zambia" (Ph.D. diss., University of London, 1989), 8; Christopher C. Taylor, *Milk, Honey, and Money: Changing Concepts in Rwandan Healing* (Washington, D.C.: Smithsonian Institution Press, 1992), 9–14, 136, 209–10; White, "Blood Brotherhood."

The red fluid circulating through the body was in some places an alien concept, best described by the Portuguese word *sangue* or by using a term derived from the verb *kuchinja*. But different conceptions of the body do not explain why some words never fully became Bemba or why Luo speakers use a Swahili word without translation. The absence of linguistic transformations, however, may be less semantic than genealogical: each plural, and each language carries a historical link to the source of the term. The term never becomes fully Bemba, or Luo, because part of its importance lies in its origin, part of its local meaning is its very foreignness.[25] And throughout this book I shall use *wazimamoto, mumiani, kachinja, banyama,* and *batumbula* as synonyms for "vampire," and vice versa: cultural literacy, like translation, is a two-way street.

Many of the published accounts of vampires have been memoirs: an author encountered the rumor, wrote about it, and theorized its meaning. Only Rik Ceyssens, in an encyclopedic article on batumbula in the Congo, argues that these stories can be traced to the sixteenth century and the slave trade. He relates stories of consumed Africans to precolonial African ideas about agricultural cycles and commodity production. According to Ceyssens, batumbula stories from World War II Kananga and Katanga, for example, were but modern versions of eighteenth-century slaves' beliefs that they were being transported to the New World to be eaten; he is more concerned with the continuity of African ideas than with the ways in which 1940s batumbula stories described the industrial spaces of the urban Congo.[26] Ceyssens flattens a variety of descriptions of consumption into ingestion and levels much of the sense of region that I try to make prominent in this book. The white cannibals of the slave trade and the white cannibals who captured the imagination of Congolese after the fall of Belgium during World War II were constructed in different social worlds. The tales told by slaves on the Atlantic coast and tales told by fishermen in the Luapula River Valley four hundred years later are not the same. While the idea of cannibalism informs these stories, the white people in each set of narratives have different meanings, different relevances, and different histories. Among Kongo-speaking people in and around Kinshasa and near the Atlantic

25. Barber, *I Could Speak,* 21.
26. Rik Ceyssens, "Mutumbula: Mythe de l'opprimé," *Cultures et développement* 7 (1975): 483–536.

coast, white people are ancestors and the Americas are the other world inhabited by the dead; the white mine supervisors and priests of Katanga batumbula stories carry quite different connotations; the Americans whose arrival was promised by the Watchtower movement in the 1930s and 1940s had different meanings still.[27] Stories of white cannibals, however similar in plot, are shaped by local concerns and local experiences; stories may travel, but they do not travel through or to passive storytellers. Interpreting stories as regional productions reveals them to be both socially constructed and socially situated; locating such stories in regional histories and regional economies yields historical evidence.[28]

Most of the people I have interviewed—and I have now interviewed about 130—say that white vampires began their work between 1918 and 1925. It seems likely that these stories were triggered by Africans' experiences during World War I, but that does not explain their meaning over the next forty years, during which time they came and went with dreadful intensity. Not every African believed these stories, of course, and many people assumed that those who did simply misunderstood Western medicine. A Ugandan politician complained that vampire beliefs were a troubling kind of popular nonsense: "My people the Baganda had strange ideas about the British. They thought they drank blood and killed children because they did not understand what happened in hospitals."[29] A Tanzanian man said that "the British government needed no blood donations because it got blood in this way, but when independence came this government stopped it. That's why hospitals always ask people to volunteer to give blood."[30] A man in western Kenya explained that once he realized that "nowadays people are required to donate blood for sick relatives," he began to "strongly be-

27. Wyatt MacGaffey, "The West in Congolese Experience," in Philip Curtin, ed., *Africa and the West: Intellectual Responses to European Culture* (Madison: University of Wisconsin Press, 1972), 49–74; Ceyssens, "Mutumbula"; Mwelwa C. Musambachime, "The Impact of Rumor: The Case of the Banyama (Vampire-Men) in Northern Rhodesia, 1930–1964," *Int. J. Afr. Hist. Studies* 21, 2 (1988): 201–15; John Higginson, *A Working Class in the Making: Belgian Colonial Labor Policy, Private Enterprise, and the African Mineworker, 1907–1951* (Madison: University of Wisconsin Press, 1989), 176.

28. Luise White, "The Traffic in Heads: Bodies, Borders, and the Articulation of Regional Histories," *J. Southern Afr. Studies* 23, 2 (1997): 325–38.

29. Paulo Kavuma, *Crisis in Buganda, 1953–55* (London: Rex Collings, 1979), 9; see also David Apter, *The Political Kingdom in Uganda: A Study in Bureaucratic Nationalism* (Princeton: Princeton University Press, 1967), 226; Lloyd A. Fallers, *Law without Precedent: Legal Ideas in Action in the Courts of Colonial Busoga* (Chicago: University of Chicago Press, 1969), 83.

30. Lloyd William Swantz, "The Role of the Medicine Man among the Zaramo of Dar es Salaam" (Ph.D. diss., University of Dar es Salaam, 1972), 336.

lieve" that wazimamoto stories actually described "the science of blood donation." [31] Misunderstandings or not, these stories presented grim ideas about knowledge, expertise, and therapeutic and political power: "These people were educated in the use of blood, they knew about the use of blood." [32] In colonial Northern Rhodesia, banyama had "white balls of drugs" that could sap their victims' wills and, a few years later, butterfly nets that could expand to capture a grown man. In Kenya, the men who worked for wazimamoto were "skilled." Jobs gave people new tools with new powers. In Uganda, some men said the bazimamoto were really health inspectors or the yellow fever department; in Tanganyika in the 1950s, others said that firemen had injections that made people "lazy and unable to do anything." [33] Not only did prostitutes in Nairobi dig pits in their small rooms in which to trap their customers for the wazimamoto, the fire station in Nairobi and the police station also had such pits, hidden from public view by clever construction.

Many authors have speculated on how these stories began. An administrator with many years experience in Tanganyika wrote that mumiani was simply the theory by which Africans explained their invasion first by Arabs and then by Europeans. It kept their dignity intact. The Arabs were said to have killed Africans for the blood, which they made into medicine that they drank or smeared on their weapons. "It was this that gave them power over Africans." [34] Stories about white people taking precious fluids from the peoples they colonized were common in the eighteenth and nineteenth centuries. Peter Pels has written an intriguing article in which he argues that mumiani stories were actually carried from India by soldiers in the 1890s, a decade after Krapf's dictionary. Drawing on David Arnold's work on epidemic disease in nineteenth-century India, Pels notes some similarities between Indian ideas about *momiyai*—a medicine made from bitumen, but said to be made from blood—and African ideas about mumiani. The similarity is too much to explain by the colonial experience, and Pels suggests that Indians' fear that sick people were brought to hospitals specifically to have momiyai removed from them was carried to East Africa by the sepoys recruited

---

31. Ofwete Muriar, Uchonja Village, Alego, Siaya District, 11 August 1986.
32. Joseph Nsubuga, Kisasi, Uganda, 22 August 1990.
33. Nechambuza Nsumba, Katwe, Uganda, 20 August 1990; Ssekajje Kasirye, Kisenyi, Uganda, 24 August 1990; Peter Kirigwa, Katwe, Uganda, 24 August 1990; Musoke Kapliamu, Katwe, Uganda, 24 August 1990; Swantz, "Role of the Medicine Man," 338.
34. Darrell Bates, *The Mango and the Palm* (London: Rupert Hart-Davis, 1962), 52.

in Delhi in the early 1890s for the East African Rifles. In 1895, the East African Rifles—700 soldiers, of whom 300 were Indian—were quartered in Mombasa; 400 Indian sepoys joined them in 1902. Pels suggests the rumor spread through conversations between these African and Indian soldiers or via the Gujurati shopkeepers he places in East Africa somewhat earlier than most sources do. A single letter to the Tanganyikan secretariat stating that the rumor began in Mombasa in 1906—at the house of a Parsee no less—was confirmation.[35] According to Pels, nothing in Africans' experience of colonial rule generated these stories.

This book argues something very different. I think there are many obvious reasons why Africans might have thought that colonial powers took precious substances from African bodies, and I doubt if Africans needed to see or hear of a specific medical procedure to imagine that white people would hang them upside down and drain their blood. I think bloodsucking by public employees is a fairly obvious metaphor for state-sponsored extractions, just as vampires are an unusually convincing modern metaphor for psychic ills and personal evil. While I think that vampire beliefs emerged out of witch beliefs—Africans, after all, did not make up these stories out of thin air—what is significant is that these particular beliefs were new. Even witchcraft did not describe what Africans were talking about when they talked about vampires. My concern is not with why the idea of bloodsucking Europeans came into being, but why it took the hold it did, and why Africans used it to depict a wide variety of situations and structures and sometimes acted upon such beliefs. As a historian, I am less concerned with the origin of vampire beliefs than I am with their power, their ability to describe and articulate African concerns over a wide cultural and geographic area.

Even if these stories were originally "brought" there by Indian soldiers garrisoned in East Africa, this does not explain the meanings they had in East Africa fifty years later. Even if these beliefs could be traced to the botched and badly done battlefield medical practices in wartime, or bismuth injections for yaws a few years later, this would not explain

---

35. Peter Pels, "Mumiani: The White Vampire. A Neo-Diffusionist Analysis of Rumour," *Ethnofoor* 5, 1–2 (1992): 166–67; the essay by Arnold has been reprinted in David Arnold, *Colonizing the Body: State Medicine and Epidemic Disease in Nineteenth-Century India* (Berkeley and Los Angeles: University of California Press, 1993). "Swahili" and "Sudanese" are almost never accurate ethnic terms, particularly in early colonial military history. Parsees are Zoroastrians; the term, which is what they call themselves in India, is from Farsi, their language.

why some Nairobi prostitutes were accused of capturing men for the firemen, and why some white doctors, some surveyors, and some policemen were accused of being vampires. The origin of the belief does not explain how these stories came and went, capable each time of describing new situations and relationships. As one Ugandan official told another, the rumor was dormant for a few years "and then something starts it off and for the next few months it's more than your life's worth to stop your car for a pee."[36] It is not a common point of origin that gives vampire beliefs their longevity and periodicity, but how elastic they are, and how broad a category "vampire" is.

The question of how and what to think about imagined events and deeds has long concerned historians. Recent debates about what constitutes "experience"—discussed below—have long genealogies: theological debates in Western Europe—including debates about witchcraft accusations and confessions—were also concerned with questions of memory, corporeality, and proof. In the next few pages I want to explore some questions of evidence raised by the literature on witch beliefs both in Europe and in Africa as a way to both suggest points of origin for African vampire rumors and the vocabularies with which vampires are described.

In a book that was far more influential to historians of Europe than it was to be to historians of Africa, E. E. Evans-Pritchard argued that witch beliefs were not superstitions, but explanations. Witch beliefs did not deny accidents or bad luck or illness, they simply explained why an accident or bad luck or an illness happened to one person and not another. His example of the granary is worth repeating: when a granary fell in the afternoon, collapsing on the men taking shade beneath it, no one questioned that this was due to the termites eating through the poles on which it stood. At the same time, however, no one thought it possible that it had fallen at the precise moment it did without some supernatural intervention: why else did it fall in the daytime, on these men and not on others? Witch beliefs explain the specificity of cause far better than Western explanations of termites do.[37] Years later, Monica Wilson noted that scientific medicine could easily be accommodated to witch

36. Christopher Harwich, *Red Dust: Memories of the Uganda Police, 1935–1955* (London: V. Stuart, 1961), 10–15. I am grateful to Michael Tuck for this reference.

37. E. E. Evans-Pritchard, *Witchcraft, Oracles and Magic among the Azande* (Oxford: Clarendon Press, 1937).

beliefs: "I know typhus is caused by lice," said her assistant, "but who sent the lice?"[38]

Fifteen years after Evans-Pritchard, anthropologists working in Africa began to argue for a sociological interpretation of witchcraft. Suspicions and gossip about witchcraft revealed social tensions, while public accusations of witchcraft revealed social conflict.[39] These anthropologists had for years focused on the way witchcraft is an idiom of intimacy: a person has another bewitched because he or she has been wronged by the other person. A brother slighted in a returned migrant's gift-giving, a co-wife insulted, or a man impoverished as his neighbor grows rich—these are the people who want to bewitch their offenders. The other horrible things witches did—going naked in daytime, consorting with hyenas and snakes, ingesting what normal people would never touch—amplified the ways that witches inverted everyday life and made it all the more appalling that they harmed those closest to them.[40] The diverse places of intimate socializing—births, for example, or beer parties—are likely to attract witches.[41] For these anthropologists, witchcraft was a way for people to articulate, and sometimes act out, the tensions inherent in specific social structures. Witchcraft was not a system of explanation or phenomenology, but embedded in social structure and social history.[42] Among the Nupe, where women were witches and a few men had the innate power to deal with witches, fatal witchcraft was attributed to the men who had betrayed their gender and failed to constrain witchcraft.[43] Sally Falk Moore argues that witchcraft accusations followed specific patterns for specific reasons, such as when the wife of a middle brother was accused of bewitching her childless sister-in-law. The weak middle brother, already working in town, could not

38. Monica Hunter Wilson, "Witch Beliefs and Social Structure," *American J. of Sociology* 41, 4 (1951): 307–13.

39. M. G. Marwick, "The Social Context of Cewa Witch Beliefs," *Africa* 22, 2 (1952): 120–35; Max Gluckman, "Moral Crises: Magical and Secular Solutions," in id., ed., *The Allocation of Responsibility* (Manchester: Manchester University Press, 1972), 1–47.

40. Godfrey Lienhardt, "Some Notions of Witchcraft among the Dinka," *Africa* 21, 4 (1951): 303–18; Beidelman, *Moral Imagination in Kaguru Modes of Thought.*

41. Ivan Karp, "Beer Drinking and Social Experience in an African Society: An Essay in Formal Sociology," in id. and Charles S. Bird, eds., *Explorations in African Systems of Thought* (Bloomington: Indiana University Press, 1980), 83–118; T. O. Beidelman, *The Cool Knife: Imagery of Gender, Sexuality, and Moral Imagination in Kaguru Initiation Ritual* (Washington, D.C.: Smithsonian Institution Press, 1997), 83, 224–25.

42. Marwick, "Cewa Witch Beliefs."

43. S. F. Nadel, "Witchcraft in Four African Societies: An Essay in Comparison," *American Anthropologist* 54, 1 (1952): 18–29.

combat the accusation; he lost use rights over his land when his wife left it. The older brother, husband of the childless woman, claimed the land for his farm.[44]

Colonial capitalism does not seem to have made witchcraft any less intimate, but there are hints from after 1920 that witch beliefs were being refashioned. Edwin Ardener's description of a world of witches and animated corpses at work in hilltop plantations in post–World War I Cameroon placed imaginary beings in the context of economic change. Witch beliefs had continuity but were not constant: a witch finder could cleanse an area of witches so that ordinary people would be safe getting rich from cash-crop production.[45] John Middleton was told that in Lugbara in northern Uganda around 1930, sorcerers who had once been migrants purchased medicines with money and "wandered aimlessly, filled with malice" killing strangers.[46] Among the Bashu in eastern Belgian Congo in the late 1950s, dispersed lineage-based villages had been consolidated just as male migrancy had coincided with the introduction of cassava, both of which increased female labor dramatically. A new kind of witch—women who taught other women to leave their bodies and punish the men with whom they were angry—became a new source of misfortune by the end of the colonial era.[47] Witches were said to be aged in postcolonial Zambia; the crones and the old men thought to be witches suggested the true burdens of kinship obligations for sons and nephews, and in postcolonial Cameroon, the victims of witches were sent to work on the invisible plantations of great men.[48]

New and improved witches did not translate into vampires, however, in either 1930s Lugbara or postcolonial Cameroon. My question, then, is why weren't the surveyors, the Parsees, or the firemen visible in East

44. Sally Falk Moore, "Selection for Failure in a Small Social Field: Ritual Concord and Fraternal Strike among the Chagga, Kilimanjaro, 1968–1969," in id. and Barbara Meyerhoff, eds., *Symbol and Politics in Communal Ideology* (Ithaca, N.Y.: Cornell University Press, 1975), 109–43.

45. Edwin Ardener, "Witchcraft, Economics and the Continuity of Belief," in Mary Douglas, ed., *Witchcraft Confessions and Accusations* (London: Tavistock, 1970): 141–60.

46. John Middleton, *Lugbara Religion: Ritual and Authority among an East African People* (1960; Washington, D.C.: Smithsonian Institution Press, 1987), 246.

47. Randall M. Packard, "Social Change and the History of Misfortune among the Bashu of Zaire," in Ivan Karp and Charles S. Bird, eds., *Explorations in African Systems of Thought* (Bloomington: Indiana University Press, 1980), 237–66.

48. Kate Creehan, *The Fractured Community: Landscapes of Power and Gender in Rural Zambia* (Berkeley and Los Angeles: University of California Press, 1997), 207–8; Peter Geschiere, *The Modernity of Witchcraft: Politics and the Occult in Postcolonial Africa* (Charlottesville: University Press of Virginia, 1997), 156–57.

Africa before 1925 called witches? They could have at least been described as these new types of witches of the post–World War I era, but
these people said to be looking for blood were called game rangers or
firemen instead. The reason in part was that they were strangers for
whom an idiom that conveyed the intimacies and the disappointments
of closeness would have been inappropriate. It would have stripped
these agents of the state of all that made them foreign and powerful. Vampires were not thought to be social problems—the result of
envy and asocial behavior; they were considered political realities. Although chapters 4 and 5 argue that vampire stories articulate new African social relations in a colonial context, when Africans spoke about
vampires—their hired agents, their cars, and the spaces in which they
worked—they described political issues in a situation that was categorically different from the tensions between siblings, co-wives, and matrilineal kin. If beer parties had been sites for witchcraft, people in Uganda
said that bazimamoto captured men after a night's drinking, as they
staggered home alone. If witches sought the intimate fluids of birth,
Congolese batumbula, at least, avoided parturient women. Vampires
were more than new imaginings for new times, they were new imaginings for new relationships.[49] I do not mean to suggest a mechanistic connection between social events and social imaginings, however; there is
another possible reason why vampire beliefs emerged out of witch beliefs, and I want to turn to European historiography to discuss it.

Europeanists have taken issues of witchcraft and witch hunting very
seriously, and in doing so, they have raised some of the questions of evidence that have informed this book. Studies of witchcraft and particularly witchcraft accusations and confessions in Europe have long noted
how similar witches' confessions were. If there was no such thing as a
devil, and if witchhunting was a crazed moment in European history,
why were the details of witchcraft—the sabbath, the spells, the familiars—so similar over a wide geographical range? Margaret Murray and
in a much more subtle way Carlo Ginzburg have argued that witches'
testimony revealed another world altogether: that not of witchcraft but
of an older religion of female and agricultural fertility, of shamans and
trances. In between Murray and Ginzburg, Norman Cohn wrote an extremely influential account of European witchhunting in which he ar-

---

49. I do not mean to suggest that Africans only experienced invasive and extractive relationships after World War I; indeed, vampire stories may well play off as yet unrecovered
imaginings about earlier extractive states.

gued that the sabbaths, trances, and familiars were the imaginings of the inquisitors, who then used torture to shape the answers they wanted and got. All these analyses are framed around either/or terms, however: the narrative of witchcraft in all its rich details either belongs to the common folk or to the inquisitors. These analyses argue that there was no shared vocabulary with which peasant women and clergymen negotiated a description of the world, no genre of talking that both parties might use to different ends.

But shared vocabulary is a tricky concept: knowing the words and using them correctly were very different things. Some vocabularies and their deployment were so far apart that confessions were difficult to obtain. Po-chia Hsia's studies of the blood libel note that the obsessions and fears of ordinary Christian folk were translated to clergymen with great speed and clarity; accusations of Jewish ritual murder began with parents telling judges that their missing children had been slaughtered by Jews. But even under torture, in trials that were conducted in two or three languages, Jews who only vaguely knew the stories Christians told about them could not always produce a description of Jewish ritual murder that satisfied their inquisitors. In late fifteenth-century Germany, tortured Jews tried in painful confusion to explain why Jews needed Christian blood—to cure epilepsy or for its healing power. To this the judges answered: "Then why is your son an epileptic?" and "we would not be satisfied." [50] Other vocabularies had to be learned and negotiated. When inquisitors in Friuli first heard people confess willingly that their spirits went out at night to guard crops from witches, they did not know what to call these *benandanti*. Were they witches or counterwitches? Inquisitors had to coin a new phrase, "*benandanti* witch," to begin to evaluate the information they heard. It took seventy years for *benandanti* to come to mean witch for both peasants and inquisitors, and even then both parties were uneasy about what kind of witch it meant. [51] In some places and instances, vocabularies were so consistent that women and theologians made concerns about the harvest, food, and nurturance central to

50. R. Po-chia Hsia, *The Myth of Ritual Murder: Jews and Magic in Reformation Germany* (New Haven: Yale University Press, 1988), passim, 21–22; the answer the judges sought was that Jews needed Christian blood for circumcision. Under torture, Jews claimed to have only heard of ritual murder from Christians; see R. Po-chia Hsia, *Trent 1475: Stories of a Ritual Murder Trial* (New Haven: Yale University Press, 1992), 37.

51. Carlo Ginzburg, *Nightbattles: Witchcraft and Agrarian Cults in the Sixteenth and Seventeenth Centuries,* trans. John and Anne Tedeschi (New York: Penguin Books, 1983), passim, and "The Inquisitor as Anthropologist," *Clues, Myths and the Historical Method,* trans. John and Anne Tedeschi (Baltimore: Johns Hopkins University Press, 1986), 160.

women's everyday lives and the most intense images of Christian piety.[52] Scholars have argued that in early modern Germany, women appropriated the inquisitors' version of witch beliefs to describe the conflicts and disappointments of their own domestic situation.[53] So shared was this vocabulary in some communities that some accused witches begged forgiveness after their confessions, and others, unrepentant in death, were said to have paralyzed the hands of the executioners attempting to carry out death sentences.[54]

It is with these varieties of vocabularies and the multiplicity of insinuated meanings that historians of witches and vampires work. It is precisely these difficulties of translation—the years when *benandanti* did not mean witch, the ignorance of Bavarian Jews of what their accusers said about them, all the men who could be called *wazimamoto*—that describe the world as people in the past saw it, with all the variations that inequalities of power and knowledge bring to such descriptions. The power relations in an interview done in rural Africa, or a judge's chamber in Friuli, may not shape the content of testimony; there may be no simple one-to-one relationship between a question asked and the answer received, let alone between the relative authorities of interrogator and speaker. Here Hayden White's analogy of the historian and the psychiatrist is useful, partly because it allows for the loose and slippery ways that information is presented, but mainly because it focuses on how historians reevaluate the information they receive. Historians foreground some meanings and submerge others to authorize an interpretation of the past. Rather than seeking a reality behind the words and images— the task of judges and inquisitors—historians' reorganization gives some meanings great and renewed power and strips others of their intensity. Ginzburg reflected on *Nightbattles* that inquisitors and ethnographers simply recoded peasant belief. But however much coding and recoding the interrogator does, the terminology remains that of the informant, and those vocabularies dominate the resulting texts. My point is not that the term *benandanti* was contested—it was, but that hardly matters for what follows—but that talk about benandanti could only be conducted by using the term. The deep cultural layers constituting the

---

52. Caroline W. Bynum, *Holy Feast and Holy Fast: The Meaning of Food to Medieval Women* (Berkeley and Los Angeles: University of California Press, 1987).

53. David Sabean, *Power in the Blood* (Cambridge: Cambridge University Press, 1984); Lyndal Roper, *Oedipus and the Devil: Witchcraft, Sexuality and Religion in Early Modern Europe* (London: Routledge, 1994).

54. Roper, *Oedipus and the Devil,* 206.

term could be maintained by the speakers even while it eluded the judges; the judges could only access the layers of historical and cultural meaning by using the term. In this way, some of the most powerful evidence in this book comes from Europeans' accounts of African vampires: they didn't believe them and often published them to show the depth of African superstition, but they presented these stories in all the rich contradictory details of the genre; they wrote with materials and constructions they themselves did not produce. Like Friulian inquisitors, historians do not reject information out of hand; rather, they rearrange it, stressing different parts according to their own interests and understandings of the world: the gap between the "spontaneous confessions" (Ginzburg's term) and interrogators expectations is never fully bridged, and terms are never fully recoded by power or culture. For fifty years the judges heard stories of benandanti and could not figure out what the term actually meant. When the confusion was over, when inquisitors and peasants began to speak the same language, *benandanti* meant witch, but inquisitors now used the term. The array of meanings of *benandante*—or *mumiani*, or *banyama*—could not be fully stifled; judges and officials could never really recode local beliefs.

In wartime colonial Northern Rhodesia, when European officials were thin on the ground, African clerks, settlers, and colonial officials sought to recode banyama into traditional African human sacrifice, which, they claimed, had gone on for centuries. "The old word used before the advent of the Europeans," *mafyeka,* which had appeared only once in official writings on banyama,[55] became the subject of memoranda in Northern Province for almost two years. A man was attacked on a path in Isoka District in 1943. When the man's assailants claimed they were only after a reward from banyama, the district commissioner, Gervas Clay, turned to Robert, the African district clerk, for clarification. Robert told him that in addition to banyama, there were mafyeka, people who sacrificed Africans at Christmas in a chief's village. The victims' blood was sprinkled on a drum used in rain-making ceremonies.[56] Africans believed that Europeans approved of this custom, Robert said.

55. Gervas Clay, district commissioner, Isoka, "Memorandum Concerning 'banyama' and 'mafyeka' with Special Reference to the Provincial Commissioner, Kasama's Confidential File on Banyama and to Incidents in the Isoka District during the Latter Part of 1943," 24 January 1944 (National Archives of Zambia [henceforth cited as NAZ], SWC2/429, Native Affairs: Banyama). Gervas Clay, interview, Taunton, Somerset, 26 August 1991.
56. Mrs. Betty Clay, reading from her diary for 13 December 1943, interview with author, Taunton, Somerset, 26 August 1991.

Clay sent for the relevant files and studied the fragments about banyama he found, recoding them with his new insider knowledge: "I would suggest the possibility that the activities of the Mafyeka . . . may not be dead and the whole banyama story may be an invention of those who wish to keep mafyeka activities alive." Most banyama incidents took place in the rainy season; those that did not were due to "the natural delay" in reports of such disappearances.[57] Although Clay and his wife had filmed the rain dance the year before and found it "completely harmless and rather dull," two African policemen were sent to observe the ceremony in 1943. They found much that was ominous: "the noise of the drum is different from an ordinary drum, and seems to be made by rubbing rather than beating" and dancers wore red and looked very serious. Clay recommended that the assailants be convicted of attempted murder, to allay African suspicions of European collusion.[58]

A few months later, R. S. Jeffreys, a retired official, wrote an unsolicited letter to the district headquarters (the boma) in Northern Province, explaining that a chance meeting had alerted him to officials' need for clarification regarding human sacrifice. Recalling that he "really knew these people" and "their dialect" when he lived in Isoka twenty years ago, he noted that kidnapping and killing by strangulation during the early rains of November was "the *observance of customary propitiary rites for the securing of an abundant harvest*." He did not use the term *mafyeka,* but assured officials that the custom still went on, albeit in great secrecy.[59] Ten days later, the provincial commissioner issued a memorandum to all DCs in which he transformed banyama into ritual murder and a harvest ritual: the word *mafyeka* had disappeared altogether, and banyama had become "the so-called banyama movement," which attempted "to obtain people for human sacrifice in connection with rain making ceremonies or to ensure good crops." A retired African clerk "of the highest integrity" had described the commonplace methods of sacrifice.[60] The letter from Jeffreys was typed (with sev-

---

57. Clay, "Memorandum Concerning 'banyama' and 'mafyeka.'"

58. Betty Clay; Gervas Clay, "Memorandum Concerning 'banyama' and 'mafyeka.'"

59. R. S. Jeffreys to Fallows, Provincial Office, Kasama, 15 April 1944 (NAZ, SEC2/429, Native Affairs: Banyama; emphasis in original). Bemba Christians reported, however, that strangulation, *ukutweka,* was the way "seriously ill" chiefs had been killed in the past. Fearing this fate, chiefs were relieved when missionaries condemned the practice. Stephen Bwalya, "Custom and Habits of the Bemba" (typescript, Mpika, 1936, Rhodes House, Oxford, RH MSS Afr. 3.1214).

60. Geoffrey Howe, provincial commissioner, Northern Province, Kasama, "Confidential Memo to All DCs," 24 April 1944 (NAZ, SEC2/429, Native Affairs: Banyama).

eral carbon copies) and filed, and, over the next few years, copies were sent around to various officials and anthropologists at the Rhodes-Livingstone Institute requesting figures on the frequency of ritual murder in the colony.[61] But mafyeka and the recoding of *banyama* were short-lived; outside of these memoranda, the term was never used. Even as officials proclaimed the new meaning of *banyama,* they forbade a London parasitologist to collect stool, blood, and skin samples for fear he would be accused of being banyama.[62] By 1945, the word *mafyeka* was gone and only the acting chief secretary, Cartmel-Robinson, himself accused of being banyama during a smallpox vaccination campaign in Isoka in 1933, defined *banyama* as meaning human sacrifice.[63] No one else did. Earlier in the year, the PC of Northern Province assured two settlers that banyama was an African superstition of no historical validity and that they should advise their laborers accordingly.[64]

But vampires, witchcraft, and ritual murder were, in Gábor Klaniczay's words, "a matter of mentality and legal practice." The place of proof in witchcraft and banyama trials and the place of popular lore in articulating that proof was not simply how the accused were convicted; it was the site in which the many meanings of terms for witch were disclosed and forced into official usage. In a very important essay, Klaniczay locates in the emergence of "vampire scandals" in the Austro-Hungarian Empire starting in the seventeenth century—"the first media event" according to Paul Barber[65]—in the decline in prosecutions for witchcraft there. The many meanings of *witch* could not survive the newly scientized appeal courts of Maria Theresa's reign, and the very facts by which vampires were separated from ordinary witches meant that vampires could never be fully investigated; they could only be

61. Elizabeth Colson, who first began research in Southern Province in 1946, recalls being asked to report on banyama when she first arrived, but she did not hear the term *banyama* used by anyone except officials until a decade later (personal communication 7, 8 August 1997).

62. G. Howe, provincial commissioner, Northern Province, to chief secretary, Lusaka, 27 March 1944 (NAZ, SEC2/429, Native Affairs: Banyama). H. F. Cartmel-Robinson, acting chief secretary, to provincial commissioner, Western Province, 20 May 1944; G. Howe to district commissioner, Kawambwa, 15 June 1944, "Survey of Helminthic Diseases" (NAZ, SEC1/1/1072). The doctor was eventually allowed to collect samples accompanied by a police escort. I am grateful to Bryan Callahan for the notes on this file.

63. Legco Debates, *Hansard,* 31 August 1945, cols. 248–49, 245–55 (NAZ, SEC2/429, Native Affairs: Banyama).

64. G. Howe to R. Hudson, district commissioner, Kawambwa, 30 April 1945 (NAZ, SEC2/429, Native Affairs: Banyama).

65. Paul Barber, *Vampires, Burial and Death: Folklore and Reality* (New Haven: Yale University Press, 1988), 5.

condemned as superstition and refuted. Vampires straddled the realms
of nocturnal bloodsucking beings and biological knowledge in which
blood was an object of investigation in and of itself. The new vampire
that emerged in the Balkans was categorically different from the bloodsucking entities that had gone before. It was dead, and in rising from the
dead, it was a dreadful parody of Christ. Vampires were a very special
kind of corpse, they never decayed; they rose from the grave only to have
carnal relations or take blood. The blood they took was not a generalized bodily fluid that might be blood, milk, or semen, however: it was a
specific red fluid that vampires took from the veins in which it circulated
in the bodies of the living. Vampires were very much a product of modern theories of the body. Prosecution of vampires raised far more problems than it would have solved; they remained outside official sanction
and in a relatively short time became a literary idiom, mixed with—then
as now—spectacular fantasies of sexuality and death.[66] However novel
eighteenth-century Balkan vampires were, they could easily be bundled
with older ideas about race and blood, so that Balkan vampires and Jewish ritual murder could sometimes be combined. Vampires troubled the
tenets of scientific humanism: a belief in vampires insisted that difference
did matter, so that the specificity of vampires could be associated with
the specificity of Jews.[67] These associations did not make vampires any
more or any less real, but it made them both a metaphor and a belief
at the same time. The accusation in 1880s London that Jack the Ripper
was a Jew in search of Christian blood must be read alongside newspaper editorials from the same year that referred to Jewish immigrant
merchants in London as vampires.[68]

I do not want to force Klaniczay's subtle analysis onto East and Central Africa, but further research might be able to look for the origin of
colonial vampires in the banning of the poison ordeal in colonial Af-

66. Gábor Klaniczay, "The Decline of Witches and the Rise of Vampires under the
Eighteenth-Century Hapsburg Monarchies," in id., *The Uses of Supernatural Power: The
Transformation of Popular Religion in Medieval and Early Modern Europe*, trans. Susan
Singerman (Princeton: Princeton University Press, 1990), 168–88. Prosecution of witches
in contemporary Africa, by contrast, strengthens ideas about witchcraft as the state and
particularly the judiciary joins popular debates about witchcraft in all their ambiguity; see
Geschiere, *Modernity of Witchcraft*, 169–97.

67. Glover, *Vampires and Liberals*, 136–52.

68. Judith R. Walkowtiz, *City of Dreadful Delight: Narratives of Sexual Danger in
Late Victorian London* (Chicago: University of Chicago Press, 1992); Colin Holmes, "The
Ritual Murder Accusation in Britain," in Alan Dundes, ed., *The Blood Libel Legend: A
Casebook in Anti-Semitic Folklore* (Madison: University of Wisconsin Press, 1991) 110–
13; Glover, *Vampires and Liberals*, 35–55.

rica.[69] I do not wish to imply that vampires rise up whenever witches go uncriminalized, but rather that without the public spectacle of ordeals—like trials—the many things witches mean are not formally debated and contested. African vampires came to be talked about differently, in different contexts: they were a synthetic image, a new idiom for new times, constructed in part from ideas about witchcraft and in part from ideas about colonialism. These vampires might move about at night, but they did not go naked: they wore identifiable uniforms and used the equipment of Western medicine. Witches and vampires were different because they operated in different historical contexts. Vampires were a discursive contradiction—firmly embedded in local beliefs and constructions but named in such a way that their outsiderness was foregrounded. Unlike witches, vampires were not deeply rooted in local society; they did not fly or travel on familiars, but had mechanized mobility. Bloodsucking firemen had none of the personal malice of witches; it was a job. As such, it did not merely imperil people in tense relationships, it imperiled everyone. Firemen and their agents were not evil but in need of money. "Wazimamoto employed prostitutes . . . they did this for the money, they needed the money, and they could do this kind of work."[70] "If somebody asked you to look for a drum or a liter of blood for 50,000/-, would you not do that?"[71] "It was not an open job for anybody, you had to be a friend of somebody in the government, and it was top secret, and it was not easy to recruit anybody . . . although it was well paid."[72] Vampires were outside the social context that witches continued to inhabit in East and Central Africa; they were seen to be internationalized, professionalized, supervised, and commodifying.

Still, why did Africans, or anyone else, articulate tensions and conflicts with stories of bloodsucking beings? Vampires, Klaniczay argues, straddle the connections between medicine and violence, between the supernatural and new scientific rationalities that were becoming naturalized. They were a way of talking about the world that both parodied the new technologies and showed the true intent behind their use. The very novelty of blood and the very detailed ways Africans said it was

---

69. Jan Vansina hints at this in "Les mouvements religieux Kuba (Kasai) à l'époque coloniale," *Etudes d'histoire africaine* 2 (1971): 155–87; on the poison ordeal, see Martin Channock, *Law, Custom and Social Order: The Colonial Experience in Malawi and Zambia* (Cambridge: Cambridge University Press, 1983).
70. Zaina Kachui, Pumwani, Nairobi, Kenya, 14 June 1976.
71. Yonasani Kaggwa, Katwe, Kampala, Uganda, 27 August 1990.
72. George W. Ggingo, Kasubi, Uganda, 15 August 1990.

extracted provide a powerful way to talk about ideas and relationships that begged description.[73] It is not that there were no other ways for Africans, or Transylvanians, to talk about wealthy men or new machines or the meaning of medical testing, but that these things were so important that they were talked about with new, specific vocabularies.

TRUTH IN VAMPIRES, TRUTH IN ORAL HISTORY

A simple premise undergirds my interpretation of vampire stories in this book: people do not speak with truth, with a concept of the accurate description of what they saw, to say what they mean, but they construct and repeat stories that carry the values and meanings that most forcibly get their points across. People do not always speak from experience— even when that is considered the most accurate kind of information— but speak with stories that circulate to explain what happened.

This is not to say that people deliberately tell false stories. The distinction between true and false stories may be an important one for historians, but for people engaged in contentious arguments, explanations, and descriptions, sometimes presenting themselves as experts, or just in the best possible light, it may not matter: people want to tell stories that work, stories that convey ideas and points. When Gregory Sseluwagi in Uganda became exasperated with my assistant and I hectoring him to admit that vampires did not exist, he said, "They existed as stories," and it was that existence with which he and his fellows were confronted daily.[74] For this man—and for historians—true and false are historical and cultural constructions. They are not absolutes but the product of lived experience, of thought and reflection, of hard evidence. "During the colonial period, I could not believe there were some people who could abduct people. I would ask myself, how could someone go missing? Could somebody disappear like a goat? But when I learned of my brother-in-law . . . taken by the Amin regime . . . then I understood. But for some of us, who did not know anybody captured by bazimamoto, it was impossible to understand it." [75]

73. I have made a similar case for North American UFO abduction narratives, which, I argue, debate race, reproduction, abortion, and the role of women in childcare. It is not that there are no other places where these issues can be talked about in contemporary American society, but that they are considered so important that they are spoken of at many sites. See Luise White, "Alien Nation: Race in Space," *Transition* 63 (1994).

74. Gregory Sseluwagi, Lubya, Uganda, 28 August 1990.

75. Ibid.

For most of the people quoted in this book, experience was true, but
not as reliable as hearsay, the circulating stories that helped a person
understand what had previously been incomprehensible. There was a
widespread belief that talk was rigorously grounded in fact. Its opposite
was the "loose talk" that characterized the Swahili-speaking people
of the East African coast.[76] Children were brought up not to speculate
idly.[77] The way to prove that vampires were real was to say so: "This is
not just a tale, nor something you gossip about," the Congolese painter
Tshibumba told Johannes Fabian.[78] Experience shaped narratives inso-
far as it was assumed that everyone spoke the truth. "If I am stealing bananas and they talk about me, they say I always steal bananas. But can
they talk about somebody they don't know, and say he is stealing? . . .
Now I have seen this recording machine. If I had not seen it, I wouldn't
be able to talk about it, but because I have seen it I can talk about it."[79]
Put simply, "people were not crazy just to start talking about something
that was not already there."[80] The issue was not how well argued a story
was—what Paul Veyne has called "rhetorical truth," established by elo-
quence and elegance[81]—but how readily and commonly a story was
told. "It was a true story because it was known by many people and
many people talked about it. Therefore it is a true story and it is wrong
to say that it is not because they would not talk about it if it was not
true."[82]

But how well can oral historians trust informants to talk about what's
true, especially if, as I argue, what is true is so historically constructed
as to be beyond generalization. Some believe that, like trial lawyers, oral
historians should not ask leading questions to elicit facts that can be
evaluated on their own terms to arrive at a single truth explaining one
version of events. Interviewers must be neutral; otherwise they risk
people telling them the stories they think the interviewers want to hear.
Jan Vansina has cautioned against leading questions with a calculus of

76. Anthony Odhiambo, Uranga, Siaya District, Kenya, 11 August 1986. According
to some old men in Siaya District, the undisciplined speech of the Swahili speakers protected them from vampires, who could not risk capturing people in Mombasa "because
people there were very wild" (Zebede Oyoyo, Yimbo, 13 August 1986).
77. Domtita Achola, Uchonga Ukudi, Alego, Siaya District, Kenya, 11 August 1986.
78. Fabian, *Remembering the Present,* 49; the word Tshibumba used for gossip is
abari, which can mean news or report (ibid., 299).
79. Julia Nakibuuka Nalongo, Lubya, Uganda, 21 August 1990.
80. Nichodamus Okumu Ogutu, Uhuyi, Siaya District, Kenya, 20 August 1986.
81. Paul Veyne, *Did the Greeks Believe in Their Myths: An Essay in Constitutive
Imagination,* trans. Paula Wissing (Chicago: University of Chicago Press, 1990), 79–93.
82. Samuel Mubiru, Lubya, Uganda, 28 August 1990.

participation and exclusion: "Any interview has two authors: the performer and the researcher. The input of the latter should be minimal. . . . Indeed, if the questions are leading questions, such as 'Is it not true that . . .' the performer's input tends to be zero."[83] This book argues something very different, that absolute notions of true and false, of interviewing technique and legalistic practices, are simply overwhelmed by local ideas about evidence, ideas that are continually negotiated and renegotiated by talking.[84] In the following exchange, who is leading whom, the way informant and interviewer toss concerns about expertise and knowledge back and forth, indicate the ways in which evidence, especially oral evidence, is produced in contentious dialogue:

Q: Some people have told us that wazimamoto kept their victims in pits. Did you ever hear this?

A: No, I never heard anything like that.

Q: Some people have said that wazimamoto used prostitutes to help them get victims. Did you hear that also?

A: Yes, I heard that wazimamoto used prostitutes for such purposes.

Q: That means these stories were true?

A: Of course they were. Who told you they weren't?

Q: Nobody told me, it was just my personal feeling that these stories were false.

A: These stories were very much true. Those stories started in Nairobi when racial segregation was there. Whites never shared anything with other races and whites were also eating in their own hotels like Muthiaga.[85]

The slippage between confirming facts, hearsay, and geographical knowledge bordering on political economy is typical of wazimamoto stories told by former migrants in western Kenya. But the slippage also poses a disjuncture between academic historians' and the speakers' no-

83. Vansina, *Oral Tradition as History*, 61, but see the appendices to this; Carlo Ginzburg, "The Inquisitor as Anthropologist," in id., *Clues*, 156–64, and "Checking the Evidence: The Judge and the Historian," in James Chandler, Arnold I. Davidson, and Harry Harootunian, eds., *Questions of Evidence: Proof, Practice and Persuasion* (Chicago: University of Chicago Press, 1994), 290–303; Susan U. Philips, "Evidentiary Standards for American Trials: Just the Facts," in Judith T. Irvine and Jane H. Hill, eds., *Responsibility and Evidence in Oral Discourse* (Cambridge: Cambridge University Press, 1992), 248–59.

84. I said as much in *The Comforts of Home: Prostitution in Colonial Nairobi* (Chicago: University of Chicago Press, 1990), 20–28. Only by "leading" informants and arguing with them does the historian learn about information important enough for informants to defend.

85. Nyakida Omolo. Kabura, Siaya District, Kenya, 19 August 1986.

tions of truth. While historians might be most concerned with which parts of the account are true and are thus useful in historical reconstruction, the speakers seem engaged in problematizing what is true, and establishing how and with what evidence a story becomes true. It is not that truth is fluid, but that it has to be established by continually listening to and evaluating new evidence. The material basis of historical truth is not eroded in such accounts, and the mediation of language is no stronger than the events it describes. Something much more subtle is going on, something oral historians may be better placed than other historians to appreciate, that the use of language is the analysis by which people ascertain what is true and what is false, what they should fear and what they can profit from. It is through talking that people learn about cause and intention. Language and event—even language and *événement*—are not opposites, but in constant dialogue and interrogation. Accounts of the past are documented with words, with descriptions of social relations and of material objects, even as the relationships between the men and women narrating these accounts are negotiated as they speak.[86] Old words, new terms and neologisms, circulating stories and eyewitness accounts, and the insights of the odd interviewer all add up to make a bedrock not of experience but of the ideas on which experience can be based. Turning those words and stories into the tools with which a historian reconstructs the past is not a matter of transforming them into something else, but of giving the words and stories the play of contradiction, of leading question, of innuendo and hearsay that they have in practice. Oral historians have not always done this well. In an early, important critique of the use of oral tradition, T. O. Beidelman complained that historians tended to make African culture static to make traditions into historical facts; finding out what really happened obscured how traditions were used on the ground, how they held "social 'truths' independent of historical facts."[87] But the line between different kinds of truth is flexible. Historical facts—like knowledge of segregation and the elite settlers' club in colonial Nairobi—emerge from

---

86. This point has been made most clearly by Ben G. Blount, "Agreeing to Disagree on Genealogy: A Luo Sociology of Knowledge," in Mary Sanchez and Ben G. Blount, eds., *Sociocultural Dimensions of Language Use* (New York: Academic Press, 1975), 117–35, but has never made a lasting impact in African history or oral history, despite David William Cohen and Atieno Odhiambo, *Siaya: The Historical Anthropology of an African Landscape* (London: James Currey, 1989).

87. Thomas O. Beidelman, "Myth, Legend and Oral History: A Kaguru Traditional Text," *Anthropos* 65, 5–6 (1970): 74–97.

social truths, just as social truths develop from readings of historical facts. Hearsay is a kind of fact when people believe it. It is impossible to say that wazimamoto stories, told and retold in East African cities, are independent of historical, or social, or sociological fact. The 1947 riot at the Mombasa fire station is but one example. In October 1958, Nusula Bua was arrested at the Kampala fire station for offering to sell them a man for 1,500/-. He told the fireman he spoke to that he had "about 100 people to sell." Bua was sentenced to three years, because it was his first offense. According to the magistrate, "People must know that the Fire Brigade is not buying people, but is intended to extinguish fires in burning buildings and vehicles." [88] It took more than officials' statements to get people to believe that firemen just put out fires, however. In 1972, the Dar es Salaam section of the Tanzania *Standard* published a half-page article, "Firemen are not 'chinja-chinja.'" [89]

Part of what made hearsay so reliable to those who repeated it was that it could resolve some of the confusions that experience actually contained. What happened to people was not always so clear and explicable that they would immediately appreciate its full import, or always have the right words to describe it at the time. Joan Scott's essay "The Evidence of Experience" (1991) and its critics have noted the limits of the project of social history. The goal of widening the range of experiences that could constitute a national, occupational, or sexual narrative simultaneously reinforced a notion of experience in which individuals are the foundation of evidence, the ultimate authorities on what they lived through. Whatever fractures and fissures in individuals' senses of themselves and their worlds that shape first-person accounts are lost: instead, Scott argues, "raw events" produce raw analyses, visual and visceral, outside language, and thus beyond the reach of historians who seek diverse experiences in order to relocate subjects in the historical records.[90] Scott's critics argue that she has gone too far, that even the most counterhegemonic of experiences are described with words borrowed for the purpose: no words are free from the materialism that gen-

88. Huxley, *Sorcerer's Apprentice*, 23n; "'Human Vampire' Story Incites Mombasa Mob's Fire Station Attack," *East African Standard*, 27 June 1947, 3; "Three Years for Attempt to Sell Man," *Uganda Argus*, 16 February 1959, 5; "'Firemen Do Not Buy People,'" *Tanganyika Standard*, 16 February 1959, 3. Bua's defense was that he had taken his friend to the fire station to get him a job, and there had been offered cash for him. While he was waiting for the money, he was arrested.
89. *The Standard*, 10 January 1972. The article was by S. Lolila.
90. Joan W. Scott, "The Evidence of Experience," *Critical Inquiry* 17 (1991): 773–97.

erates them, and words are often densely packed with historical meanings. Meanings change—like that of *benandanti*—and terms can lose one historical specificity and take on another. The use and, as chapter 4 argues, misuse, of words carries material histories of work, objects, and places. It is only when these new words are taken up and transformed into personal narratives—when circulating stories are refashioned into personal experiences and the knowledge such experiences contain— that people participate in shaping the language with which they describe the world.[91] When these new words are spoken unproblematically, as hearsay, they offer a contextualization that older terms do not provide. The repetition of hearsay provides a glimpse of the everyday talk and gossip that is a thick description of what otherwise remains as confusing as distinguishing between a wink and a twitch.[92] For example, a woman who thought she was almost captured by wazimamoto could be reassured by hearsay. Mwajuma Alexander was going to her farm late one night in 1959 after an evening's drinking with her husband and co-wife. Near a neighbor's farm, she saw a group of men, one of them white, standing around a parked vehicle. One man threw her to the ground. She ran away and hid while they searched for her. Finally, she heard one of them say, "Oh, oh, oh, the time is over," and they drove off. She fled home. The following day, her husband, on his way to a market in a nearby village, heard that the wazimamoto had caught a woman in the area; this confirmed what everyone suspected.[93] If someone told someone, who told someone, who told Mwajuma's husband, that wazimamoto were capturing women in the area, then they were.

91. See Laura Lee Downs, "If 'Woman' is Just an Empty Category, Then Why am I Afraid to Walk Alone at Night? Identity Politics Meets the Postmodern Subject," *Comparative Studies in Society and History* 35, 2 (1993): 414–37; Thomas C. Holt, "Experience and the Politics of Intellectual Inquiry," and Joan Scott, "A Rejoinder to Thomas Holt," in James Chandler, Arnold I. Davidson, and Harry Harootunian, eds., *Questions of Evidence: Proof, Practice and Persuasion* (Chicago: University of Chicago Press, 1994), 388–96, 397–400, and Kathleen Canning, "Feminist History after the Linguistic Turn: Historicizing Discourse and Experience," in Barbara Laslett et al., eds., *History and Theory: Feminist Research, Debates, Contestations* (Chicago: University of Chicago Press, 1997), 416–52. Well outside these debates, other scholars have noted that first-person accounts are often metaphors rather than descriptions; see Gyandendra Pandey, "In Defense of the Fragment: Writing about Hindu-Muslim Riots in India Today," *Representations* 37 (1992): 27–55, and Liisa H. Malkki, *Purity and Exile: Violence, Memory, and National Cosmology among Hutu Refugees in Tanzania* (Chicago: University of Chicago Press, 1995).

92. Clifford Geertz, "Thick Description: Toward an Interpretive Theory of Culture," in *The Interpretation of Cultures* (New York: Basic Books, 1973), 3–30.

93. Alexander Opaka, Mwajuma Alexander, and Helena Ogada, Ndegro Uranga Village, Siaya District, 11 August 1986.

But what constituted hearsay and circulating stories? Was the common knowledge that wazimamoto had caught a woman here or there made up from bits and pieces of the diverse experiences of many people, or was something else at play, a notion of experience that was not necessarily personal, a notion of experience that incorporated that which was heard about? If historians have worried that experience may be our own rubric for unifying diverse elements into a narrative that subsumes differences, men and women in western Kenya, at least, have suggested that diverse experiences, taken over and told as personal narratives, can reveal the power of difference and the speakers' knowledge thereof. Such domestication of circulating stories was not boastful exaggeration, or at least it was not only that. Circulating stories were told with convention and constraint. The act of making a wazimamoto story personal— adding names and places and work relations—had nothing to do with making it a better, more detailed story that explained the intricacies of bloodsucking.

The idea that a story may be true although its details are unknown to its tellers is at odds with most of the methodologies used to assess the reliability of testimony or an informant.[94] Vampire stories are neither true nor false, in the sense that they do not have to be proven beyond their being talked about; but as they are told, they contain different empirical elements that carry different weights: stories are told with truths, commentaries, and statements of ignorance. These do not make wazimamoto stories seem unlikely; it is a true story and no one would make a compositional effort to change it to make it more credible. Anyango Mahondo of Siaya, for example, explained that the police were actually the bloodsuckers, something he could neither tell his wife nor his brothers. It was "ordinary people" who could not distinguish between police and firemen. In Kampala

> When a man joined the police, he had to undergo the initial training of bloodsucking. . . . When one qualified there, he was absorbed into the police force as a constable. . . . At night we did the job of manhunting . . . from the station, we used to leave in a group of four, with one white man in charge. . . .

---

94. Indeed, Matt K. Matsuda argues that it is the evaluation of the details included in testimony—the details that locate a story in time and space—that is at the heart of the modern method of deciding whether an oral account is true or false. By the start of the twentieth century, testimonies were judged by their credibility, whether or not they sounded true to an interlocutor. Veracity became a matter of testimony, of memory and storytelling, and not a matter of the speaker's intention. Matt K. Matsuda, *The Memory of the Modern* (Oxford: Oxford University Press, 1996), 101–20.

Once in town, we would hide the vehicle somewhere that no one could see it. We would leave the vehicle and walk around in pairs. When we saw a person, we would catch him and take him to the vehicle. . . . Whites are a really bad race. . . . They used to keep victims in big pits. . . . blood would be sucked from those people until they were considered useless. . . . Inside the pits, lights were on whether it was day or night. The victims were fed really good food to make them produce more blood. . . . The job of the police recruit was to get victims and nothing else. Occasionally, we could go down in the pits, and if we are lucky, we can see the bloodsucking, but nothing else.[95]

This is presumably the account Mahondo could not tell his wife. Chapter 4 argues that this particular chunk of narrative describes on-the-job experience, supervision, promotion, and the place of race and rank therein. Now I want to examine this account as testimony, as a narrative told with different kinds of truths and frank admissions of ignorance. I am not interested in why he told this story, but in how. Mahondo has made hearsay into a narrative of personal experience: the vehicles, the nighttime abductions, the pits, the feeding of victims were all commonplace in the region's wazimamoto stories. Mahondo does not seem to be talking simply to enhance his dubious prestige;[96] instead, he seems to be establishing truth about wazimamoto—the role of the police, the evils of white people—by telling the story as personal experience and by describing his own role as a participant and a bystander. Indeed, what is important here is the way that Mahondo informs his own storytelling; the process of making a personal narrative was constrained by hearsay: if Mahondo was not speaking the truth, or claiming that he as an eyewitness knew more truth, why did he not make up a better, more elaborate story about what happened in the pits?

It is possible that it was only by conforming to the standards and conventions of hearsay that Mahondo could have been thought credible. Had he stated what actually went on in the alleged secret pits under the Kampala police station, or if he said that he knew what whites did with the blood, he might have revealed himself to be a fraud, rather than a man with insider knowledge. Performance is part of every interview, not the work of specific practitioners in specific places.[97] Speakers use a genre by giving a good example of its use shaped to meet their needs at

---

95. Anyango Mahondo, Sigoma, Siaya District, 15 August 1986.
96. This seemed to have been accomplished by the number of people in the area he had threatened to have arrested at one time or another (author's field notes, 16 August 1986).
97. Vansina, *Oral Tradition as History*, 34–41.

the moment.[98] Mahondo's eyewitness account was told the way hearsay wazimamoto stories were told. How the story was performed, and the elements with which it was performed, made it credible. Where it stood on some imaginary line between hearsay and experience had nothing to do with how accurate it was.

Zebede Oyoyo had been captured by Nairobi's fire brigade in the early 1920s. All his neighbors knew his story, which was how I came to be sent to him early on during my stay in Yimbo in 1986. My research assistant and I interviewed him twice. The first interview was a barely disguised account of his strength—"My fists were like sledgehammers." "Nobody could come near me." "When I saw the chance, I dashed out of the room . . . I outpaced them." "Those kachinjas really chased me, and when I had completely beaten them, one of them told me, 'Eh, eh you! You were really very lucky. You will stay in this world and really multiply.'"[99] The second interview, ten days later, provided a much more detailed and subtle account of his encounter in a urinal with an African man.

> I was caught near River Road. It was near the police station. I had gone for a short call in one of those town toilets. The time was before noon. . . . When I finished urinating, someone came from nowhere and grabbed my shirt collar. He started asking me funny questions, like "What are you doing here?" I told him I was urinating in a public toilet. On hearing that, the man started beating me. He slapped me several times and pulled me toward a certain room. On reaching that room, I realized that something was wrong. It was then that I started to become wild, and since I was still young . . . that man could not hold me. . . . I fought with the man until I got the chance to open the door. I shot out at terrific speed. . . . When they realized they could not catch me, one of them told me, "You, you are really lucky. You will really give birth to many children and will only die of old age. You were lucky and pray to God for that luck."[100]

I am not the first to notice that people often revise the answers they have given in a first interview when they are interviewed for a second time. Neither am I the first to find this unremarkable. Historians routinely mediate between different accounts of the same event; why should

---

98. Charles L. Briggs, *Learning How to Ask: A Sociolinguistic Appraisal of the Role of the Interview in Social Science Research* (Cambridge: Cambridge University Press, 1986), 37–38; Elizabeth Tonkin, *Narrating Our Pasts: The Social Construction of Oral History* (Cambridge: Cambridge University Press, 1992), 50–55.

99. Zebede Oyoyo, Yimbo, Kenya, 13 August 1986.

100. Zebede Oyoyo, Yimbo, Kenya, 23 August 1986.

this mediation be methodologically any different when the different accounts are provided by one person? It is only when a voice is conceived of as a single, spoken rendition of experience that contradictions become extraordinary rather than ordinary. To argue that an informant is mistaken because he or she says different things at different times, or even to argue that one account is wrong, makes linear demands on speech and self: lives and experiences are not such simple, straightforward things that they lend themselves to easy representation; people do not give testimony that fits neatly into chronological or cosmological accounts. Instead, they talk about different things in personal terms; they talk both about what happened to them and about what they did about it, but they also use themselves as a context in which to talk about other things as well.

The idea that a voice, however produced, would not change its mind or its words serves historians, not the speaker's own complicated interests. What, after all, constitutes the authority of the voice? That historians use what it says? But what happens when voices willingly speak untruths, telling stories the veracity of which they might learn, but that they do not always believe? This raises another question entirely: what makes oral evidence reliable? That it can be made to be verified just like documents, or that it is taken as a kind of evidence produced in circumstances unlike the ones in which people write diaries, reports, and memoranda? What would make oral material true: that truth is spoken during an interview or the repeated social facts and hearsay with which people talk that give us insight into local knowledge beyond one man or woman's experience? Mwajuma Alexander or Zebede Oyoyo or even Anyango Mahondo were not telling "the truth" but misrepresenting and misconstruing something that happened into vampire stories; they were constructing experience out of widespread hearsay.

Indeed, Oyoyo's second story seems to have been circulating throughout East Africa in the early 1920s. In 1923, a "Believer" wrote to the Tanganyikan Swahili-language newspaper *Mambo Leo* saying that he was now convinced that "mumiani are cruel and merciless and kill people to get their blood." He had seen this himself in Nairobi. Near the new mosque in River Road, there was a long, narrow building and a "government toilet but no permission was given for people to use these toilets. Inside the long narrow house, people stay, wear black clothes and are called Zima Moto, but the thing that is astonishing is that somebody isn't in this group and they go inside this building, they never come out again." A Luo man who worked there would not allow his brother to come near the building, not even to greet him.[101] Did Oyoyo bring this story home and craft it to depict his own strength, his own talents, and his own memories?

Zebede Oyoyo may not have been what North Americans would call henpecked, but his wives seemed dubious of his bravado. Once, visiting his compound, my research assistant overheard his senior wife asking him why he "always" spoke English to her but not with the visiting white woman. I would argue that the first version of his near-abduction was the one he wanted his wives to appreciate: it was the story of his strength and his fame. It may not have been a story Oyoyo told with any success anywhere else; we may have heard it precisely because it was received so badly at home. The narrated bravado of the first interview may have been Oyoyo's chance to get that story taken seriously. He told my assistant and me that this was, after all, a men's story: "None of my wives could realize the seriousness of these stories, but [he turned to my research assistant, a man] a man like you can realize the value and seriousness of any story."[102] The story he told us ten days later is what I like to think was the result of his reflection: having thought about the incident, he may have recalled more, and he was able to tell me this version when we returned to interview him again. While this interpretation "explains" the second interview, it is one that puts my questions at the center, just as Oyoyo's first story puts him at the center. In a provocative article, Justin Willis notes that informants may change key parts of their lives in different interviews, not because of anything the interviewer says or does, but because of other people in the room: the audience for which lives are negotiated and re-presented (as opposed to represented) is not even the interviewer.[103] Such an insight problematizes concerns about the politics of interviewing—the interview and his or her questionnaire may have little to do with what's being said or why.

My point is most emphatically not that Africans saw things in urinals and police stations that they did not understand and then told stories to explain them. My point is the opposite: that what went on in the government's strange toilets or police stations was so well known that, de-

101. "Adiyisadiki" ("Believer"), letter to the editor, Mambo Leo, November 1923, 13–14. I am grateful to Patrick Malloy for this reference and to Laura Fair and Peter Seitel for help with the translation.

102. Zebede Oyoyo, 13 August 1986.

103. Justin Willis, "Two Lives of Mpamizo: Understanding Dissonance in Oral History," History in Africa 23 (1996): 319–32.

spite attempts to conceal pits or forbid people to use toilets, it could best be described in the commonplace terms everyone used in talking about it. Telling a more unique and detailed story—describing the happenings in the pits, for example, or boasting of one's youthful strength—risked disbelief and derision.

These stories, even when told with all the conventions and constraints of hearsay, were not all received and heard the same way. Not everyone believed these stories, or believed them all the time, or believed every version a neighbor or acquaintance repeated. Nevertheless, each repetition, each repudiation, each amendment and refinement did not make a story more true or more false, but made it a more immediate way to talk about other things. Every argument or discussion a vampire story generated created a debate—stories could be evaluated on the merits of their contents, not their performance, and men and women argued over the importance of cars or men who worked only at night. Vampire stories could be refashioned and made personal or local by a few names and examples. Indeed, as part 2 argues, vampire stories are matters not so much of belief as of details: the stories are false, but the names and places and tools in them are true, and the stories are about the real fears those places and tools aroused. When men and women in Uganda recalled that bazimamoto captured people with chloroform, they were not literally describing bloodsucking or hospital practices: they were, as chapter 3 argues, talking about a European drug that had intense meaning for them because its application was similar to those of medicines used by Ugandan healers.

But did Africans believe these stories? The answer, which may not be that important to my purposes, is probably both yes and no. Or, to put it another way, Africans' understanding of these stories went beyond assessing their truth, or even the motives of those investigating these stories. In Uganda, I wrote a questionnaire that I had my research assistants give; on it, I asked about the embalasassa, a speckled lizard said to be poisonous and to have been sent by Prime Minister Milton Obote to kill Baganda in the late 1960s. It is not poisonous and was no more common in the 1960s than it had been in previous decades, as Makerere University science professors announced on the radio and stated in print.[104] But I was curious about embalasassa stories, and in one of those errors that oral historians are never supposed to admit in print, I wrote

---

104. W. B. Banage, W. N. Byarugaba, and J. D. Goodman, "The 'Embalasassa' (*Riopa fernandi*): A Story of Real and Mythical Zoology," *Uganda Journal* 36 (1972): 67–72.

the question, What is the difference between bazimamoto and embalasassa? Anyone who knows anything about a Bantu language—myself
included—would know the answer was contained in the question: humans and reptiles are different living things and belong to different noun
classes. I had not asked a stupid question to see how informants might
respond, but because I was thinking with English rather than Bantu-
language categories when I wrote it. A few of my informants corrected
my ignorance: "There is a big difference between them, bazimamoto are
people and embalasassa are lizards," [105] but many, many more ignored
the translation in my question and moved beyond it to address the history of the constructs of firemen and poisonous lizards without the
slightest hesitation. They disregarded language to engage in a discussion
of events. "Bazimamoto finished by the time of embalasassa; that was
during independence." [106] "Embalasassa came after independence, I
think in 1974, it had never happened in Uganda before." [107] In fact,
when people expressed confusion in answer to my question, it was not
about the differences between species, but between the policies of the
late colonial era and the first decade of independence: while most people
said that embalasassa came during Obote's first regime, a few said it was
"sent" by Governor Andrew Cohen in the 1950s or by Idi Amin in his
first years in power.[108] My point is not about the truth of the embalasassa story, or even the inadvertent good sense of my questionnaire, but
rather that the labeling of one thing as "true" and the other as "fictive"
or "metaphorical"—all the usual polite academic terms for false—may
eclipse all the intricate ways in which people use social truths to talk
about the past. Moreover, chronological contradictions may foreground
the fuzziness of certain ideas and policies, and that fuzziness may be
more accurate than any exact historical reconstruction.[109] Stories about
poisonous lizards, spoken to men who only came to believe in the truth
of bazimamoto stories because of the violence of Amin's Uganda, raised
questions about colonial and postcolonial states and the differences be-

---

105. Bibiana Nalwanga, Bwaise, Uganda, 24 August 1990; see also Joseph Nsubuga,
Kisasi, Uganda, 22 August 1990; Samuel Mubiru, Lubya, Uganda, 28 August 1990.
106. Daniel Sekiraata, Katwe, Uganda, 22 August 1990.
107. Ahmed Kiziri, Katwe, Uganda, 20 August 1990.
108. Gregory Sseluwagi; Samuel Mubiru; Joseph Nsubuga; Ahmed Kiziri.
109. I use this example because chronology is precisely where the most sustained and
reasonable attacks have been made on oral historiography: see, e.g., David Henige, *The
Chronology of Oral Tradition: Quest for a Chimera* (Oxford: Oxford University Press,
1974); but see also Vansina, *Oral Tradition as History*, 175–85.

tween them with each telling and retelling. Whether the story of the poisonous embalasassa was real was hardly the issue; there was a real, harmless lizard and there was a real time when people in and around Kampala feared the embalasassa. They feared it in part because of beliefs about lizards, but mainly what frightened people was their fear of their government and the lengths to which it would go to harm them. The confusions and the misunderstandings show what is important; knowledge about the actual lizard would not. Vampire stories are, then, confusions and misunderstanding of the best kind: they reveal the world of power and uncertainty in which Africans have lived in this century. Their very falseness is what gives them meaning; they are a way of talking that encourages a reassessment of everyday experience to address the workings of power and knowledge and how regimes use them.

VAMPIRES AND COLONIAL HISTORIOGRAPHY

For historians, the social imaginary in Africa carries a different history and a different weight that it does in Friuli or Augsburg. African beliefs were rarely described as the product of a cultural world that even the most rapacious colonial extractions could not stifle; more often than not, they were seen as what made Africa backward. "Believe me," wrote Frantz Fanon, "the zombies are more terrifying than the settlers; and in consequence the problem is no longer that of keeping oneself right with the colonial world . . . but of considering three times before urinating, spitting, or going out into the night." He envisioned a day when,

> After centuries of unreality, after having wallowed in the most outlandish phantoms, at long last the native, gun in hand, stands face to face with the only forces that contend for his life—the forces of colonialism. And the youth of the colonized country, growing up in an atmosphere of shot and fire . . . does not hesitate to pour scorn on the zombies of his ancestors, the horses with two heads, the djinns who rush into your body while you yawn.[110]

And even though guerrilla soldiers said they received goods from their ancestors' spirits and nationalists asked the colonial state to jail the vampire men terrorizing the town, scholars have managed to evade

110. Frantz Fanon, *The Wretched of the Earth,* trans. Constance Farrington (New York: Grove Press, 1963), 56, 58.

the phantoms with all the tools at their disposal.[111] Scholars of Latin
America have perhaps provided the best evasions. The anthropologist
Michael Taussig began his career by chiding academics for their representation of superstition: scholars wavered between "blind belief in
blind belief" and trying to explain what the belief really meant, allowing themselves the luxury of faith and skepticism at the same time.[112]
Years later, he argued that such fantasies were the distressed products
of the refractory power of colonialism. The ability to deconstruct and
distort was simply another example of colonial violence, in which the
rulers' narratives monopolized the power to imagine savagery and terror: "the colonial mode of production of reality" involved "a colonial
mirroring of otherness that reflects back onto the colonists the barbar-
ity of their own social relations, but as imputed to the savagery they
yearn to colonize." [113] Nancy Scheper-Hughes, writing of Brazil, claims
that no analyses are necessary: poor people there fear body-snatchers
because so many bodies are snatched, either by global traffickers in
adopted children and organs or by state-sponsored violence and abduction.[114] Nathan Watchel, writing of Bolivia, argues for the local logic of
beliefs in vampires and phantoms: older ideas about slaughter and sacrifice might easily settle on marginal individuals at times of social crisis.[115] All these analyses, important as they are, seek to explain belief
and the imaginary to an observer; they explain why someone might believe what is to most of the authors make-believe. I am trying to do
something different, looking not so much for the reasons behind make-
believe as for what such beliefs articulate in a given time and place. To
do this, I want to dismantle what Ann Stoler has called the "hierarchies
of credibility" so intrinsic to writings about colonial societies,[116] and
reinsert into colonial historiography the vampires and the phantoms
that are often such uninterrogated parts of colonial texts. I want to write

111. David Lan, *Guns and Rain: Guerrillas and Spirit Mediums in Zimbabwe* (London: James Currey, 1985), xv–xvii; Musambachime, "Impact of Rumor."

112. Michael T. Taussig, *The Devil and Commodity Fetishism in South America*
(Chapel Hill: University of North Carolina Press, 1980), 230.

113. Michael Taussig, *Shamanism, Colonialism and the Wild Man: A Study in Terror
and Healing* (Chicago: University of Chicago Press, 1987), 134.

114. Nancy Scheper-Hughes, *Death without Weeping: The Violence of Everyday Life
in Brazil* (Berkeley and Los Angeles: University of California Press, 1992), 233–58.

115. Nathan Watchel, *Gods and Vampires: Return to Chipaya,* trans. Carol Volk
(Chicago: University of Chicago Press, 1994), 72–89, 93–102.

116. See Ann Laura Stoler, " 'In Cold Blood': Hierarchies of Credibility and the Politics of Colonial Narratives," *Representations* 37 (1992): 140–89.

MICHAEL E. BELL

FOOD FOR THE DEAD

| On the Trail of New England's Vampires |

Appendix A: Chronology of Vampire Incidents in New England

Date	Name of Vampire	Place
1793	Rachel Harris	Manchester, Vermont
1794 or 98	Reuben or Josiah Spaulding	Dummerston, Vermont
1796	Abigail Staples	Cumberland, Rhode Island
c. 1799	Sarah Tillinghast	Exeter, Rhode Island
c. 1799	Anonymous woman	Loudon, New Hampshire
c. late 1700s to early 1800s	JB	Griswold, Connecticut
1807	Anonymous sister	Plymouth, Massachusetts
1807	Frederick Ransom	Woodstock, Vermont
1810	Janey Dennit	Barnstead, New Hampshire
1827	Nancy Young	Foster, Rhode Island
c. 1830	Corwin brother	Woodstock, Vermont
c. 1847-62	Several anonymous	Saco, Maine
1854	Lemuel and Elisha Ray	Jewett City, Connecticut
1874	Ruth Ellen Rose	Exeter, Rhode Island
1875	Anonymous woman	Chicago, Illinois*
c. 1872-88	Anonymous sister(s)	West Stafford, Connecticut
1889	Nellie Vaughn	West Greenwich, Rhode Island
1892	Mercy Brown	Exeter, Rhode Island
c. before 1893	Anonymous	Ontario, Canada*
c. before 1898	Anonymous sister(s)	Seneca Lake, New York*

* Incidents reported outside of New England

An old "witch" was dead, and his people buried him in a tree, up among the branches, in a grove that they used for a burial-place. Some time after this, in the winter, an Indian and his wife came along, looking for a good place to spend the night. They saw the grove, went in, and built their cooking fire. When the supper was over, the woman, looking up, saw long dark things hanging among the tree branches. "What are they?" she asked. "They are only the dead of long ago," said her husband, "I want to sleep." "I don't like it at all. I think we had better sit up all night," replied his wife. The man would not listen to her, but went to sleep. Soon the fire went out, and then she began to hear a gnawing sound, like an animal with a bone. She sat still, very much scared, all night long. About dawn she could stand it no longer, and reaching out, tried to wake her husband, but could not. She thought him sound asleep. The gnawing had stopped. When daylight came she went to her husband and found him dead, with his left side gnawed away, and his heart gone. She turned and ran. At last she came to a lodge where there were some people. Here she told her story, but they would not believe it, thinking that she had killed the man herself. They went with her to the place, however. There they found the man, with his heart gone, lying under the burial tree, with the dead "witch" right overhead. They took the body down and unwrapped it. The mouth and face were covered with fresh blood.

colonial history with the imaginings of the migrants, the farmers, the women who lived alone in Nairobi's townships.

In the past fifteen years, revisions of colonial history have transformed how colonial texts are read and the colonial experience is described. Topics once considered hopelessly out-of-date—missionary history, colonial law, and colonial medicine—have made powerful reappearances as studies of discourse and practice.[117] Binary categories of rulers and ruled, moribund by the late 1980s, have been all but vanquished as a more nuanced picture of colonialism—more linked to Europe than a generation of scholars had thought—produced richly detailed analyses of the structures and strategies with which colonized people sought to control their own lives.[118] Class and race have been seen as the ways in which different communities contested colonial rule and the categories it privileged: Africans refashioned the meaning of ethnicity in the colonial era as often as white communities continually healed their fractures with class-based critiques that redefined who was white and what being white entailed.[119] The historiography of Africa in

117. Channock, *Law and Social Order;* T. O. Beidelman, *Colonial Evangelism: A Socio-Historical Study of an East African Mission at the Grassroots* (Bloomington: Indiana University Press, 1982); Jean Comaroff and John L. Comaroff, *Of Revelation and Revolution,* vol. 1: *Christianity, Colonialism and Consciousness in South Africa* (Chicago: University of Chicago Press, 1991), and vol. 2, *The Dialectics of Modernity on a South African Frontier* (Chicago: University of Chicago Press, 1997); Randall Packard, *White Plague, Black Labor: Tuberculosis and the Political Economy of Heath and Disease in South Africa* (Berkeley and Los Angeles: University of California Press, 1989); Megan Vaughan, *Curing Their Ills: Colonial Power and African Illness* (Stanford: Stanford University Press, 1991); Maryinez Lyons, *The Colonial Disease: Sleeping Sickness and the Social History of Zaire, 1890–1939* (Cambridge: Cambridge University Press, 1992); Paul S. Landau, *The Realm of the World: Language, Gender and Christianity in a South African Kingdom* (Portsmouth, N.H.: Heinemann, 1995); Pier M. Larson, " 'Capacities and Modes of Thought': Intellectual Engagements and Subaltern Hegemony in the Early History of Malagasy Christianity," *Am. Hist. Rev.* 102, 4 (1997): 969–1002; Stephan F. Miescher, "Of Documents and Litigants: Disputes of Inheritance in Abetifi—a Colonial Town in Ghana," *J. of Legal Pluralism* 39 (1997): 81–119; Nancy Roe Hunt, *A Colonial Lexicon of Birth Ritual, Medicalization and Mobility in the Congo* (Durham, N.C.: Duke University Press, 1999).

118. There are two exceptionally clear summaries of this shift, Frederick Cooper, "Conflict and Connection: Rethinking Colonial African History," *Am. Hist. Rev.* 99, 5 (1994): 1516–45, and Ann Laura Stoler and Frederick Cooper, "Between Metropole and Colony: Rethinking a Research Agenda," in Cooper and Stoler, eds., *Tensions of Empire: Colonial Cultures in a Bourgeois World* (Berkeley and Los Angeles: University of California Press, 1997), 1–56.

119. On African ethnicity, see John Iliffe, *A Modern History of Tanganyika* (Cambridge: Cambridge University Press, 1979), 314–38; Charles H. Ambler, *Kenyan Communities in the Age of Imperialism* (New Haven: Yale University Press, 1987); Cohen and Atieno Odhiambo, *Siaya,* 25–35; the articles in Leroy Vail, ed., *The Creation of Tribalism in Southern Africa* (Berkeley and Los Angeles: University of California Press, 1989);

the 1980s, attentive to the struggles of African laborers, had shown that
ex-slaves struggled to control their rights to land and crops rather than
to work as free labor, while casual labor—the work men could do a few
days a week to eke out a living—might have been exploited, but it was
beyond the state's formal control.[120] Every shantytown, beggar, and
runaway wife was an affront to the ability of colonialists to control the
cities they desperately tried to plan.[121] More recent research showed
how Africans in formal employment asserted their autonomy through
the organization of work and leisure, and through the use of colonial
legislation and workers' organizations.[122] If workers' protests produced

---

John Lonsdale, "The Moral Economy of Mau Mau: Wealth, Poverty, and Civic Virtue in
Kikuyu Political Thought," in John Lonsdale and Bruce Berman, Unhappy Valley: Conflict
in Kenya and Africa (London: James Currey, 1992), 315–504; William Bravman, Making Ethnic Ways: Communities and Their Transformations in Taita, Kenya, 1800–1950
(Portsmouth, N.H.: Heinemann, 1998). On white society and how that category was
defined in relationship to African ones, see Dane Kennedy, Islands of White: Settler Society and Culture in Kenya and Southern Rhodesia, 1890–1939 (Durham, N.C.: Duke University Press, 1987); Ann Laura Stoler, "Rethinking Colonial Categories: European Communities and the Boundaries of Rule," Comparative Studies in Society and History 31, 1
(1989): 134–61; Vivian Bickford-Smith, Ethnic Pride and Racial Prejudice in Victorian
Cape Town: Group Identity and Social Practice, 1875–1902 (Cambridge: Cambridge
University Press, 1995); John L. Comaroff, "Images of Empire, Contests of Conscience:
Models of Colonial Domination in South Africa," and Lora Widenthal, "Race, Gender,
and Citizenship in the German Colonial Empire," both in Frederick Cooper and Ann
Laura Stoler, eds., Tensions of Empire: Colonial Cultures in a Bourgeois World (Berkeley
and Los Angeles: University of California Press, 1997), 163–97, 263–83; Pamela Scully,
Liberating the Family: Gender and British Slave Emancipation in the Rural Western Cape,
South Africa, 1823–1853 (Portsmouth, N.H.: Heinemann, 1997).
   120. Frederick Cooper, From Slaves to Squatters: Plantation Labor in Zanzibar and
Coastal Kenya, 1890–1925 (New Haven: Yale University Press, 1980), and On the Afri-
can Waterfront: Urban Disorder and the Transformation of Work in Colonial Mombasa
(New Haven: Yale University Press, 1987); Louise Lennihan, "Rights in Men and Rights
in Land: Slavery, Labor, and Smallholder Agriculture in Northern Nigeria," Slavery and
Abolition 3, 2 (1982): 111–39; Suzanne Miers and Richard Roberts, eds., The End of
Slavery in Africa (Madison: University of Wisconsin Press, 1988); Dipesh Chakrabarty,
"Conditions for Knowledge of Working-Class Conditions: Employers, Government and
the Jute Workers of Calcutta, 1890–1940," Subaltern Studies (Delhi) 2 (1983): 259–310.
   121. Marjorie Mbilinyi, "Runaway Wives in Colonial Tanganyika: Forced Labour
and Forced Marriage in Rungwe District 1919–1961," Int. J. of the Sociology of Law 16
(1988): 1–29; P. L. Bonner, "Family, Crime and Political Consciousness on the East Rand,
1939–1955" J. Southern Afr. Studies 14, 3 (1988): 393–420; White, Comforts of Home,
65–72, 126–46, 212–17, 221–28; Timothy Scarnecchia, "Poor Women and Nationalist
Politics: Alliances and Fissures in the Formation of a Nationalist Movement in Salisbury,
Rhodesia 1950–56," J. Afr. Hist. 37, 3 (1996): 283–310.
   122. John Higginson, A Working Class in the Making: Belgian Colonial Labor Policy,
Private Enterprise, and the African Mineworker, 1907–1951 (Madison: University of Wis-
consin Press, 1989); Keletso E. Atkins, "The Moon is Dead! Give Us Our Money": The
Cultural Origins of the African Work Ethic in Natal, 1845–1900 (Portsmouth, N.H.:
Heinemann, 1993); Patrick Harries, Work, Culture, Identity: Migrant Laborers in Mo-
zambique and South Africa, c. 1860–1910 (Portsmouth, N.H.: Heinemann, 1994);
David B. Coplan, In the Time of Cannibals: The Word Music of South Africa's Basuto

their own cycle of colonial violence in colonial reform, in which the state's terrorism imagined its victims as primitive and dangerous, innocent and in need of protection, recent scholarship—including this book—has begun to describe an imagined world of work, bodily disciplines and extractions, curing and evil that was beyond employers' control.[123]

Colonial officials had long suspected an African world that parodied their own, and revealed the contradictions of rule in documents obsessed with poor whites, Africans in clothes, and sexual morality.[124] But how did Africans articulate the contradictions of their exploitation? How did they speak about the demands of their rulers in ways that expressed their own obsessions and concerns? How could colonial sources be read so that scholars could hear the African voices silenced in the production of those same sources? This question has been central to Afri-

---

Migrants (Chicago: University of Chicago Press, 1994); Phyllis Martin, *Leisure and Society in Colonial Brazzaville* (Cambridge: Cambridge University Press, 1995); Frederick Cooper, *Decolonization and African Society: The Labor Question in French and British Africa* (Cambridge: Cambridge University Press, 1996); Laura Fair, "Identity, Difference and Dance: Female Initiation in Zanzibar, 1890–1930," *Frontiers* 17, 3 (1996): 146–72, and "Kickin' It: Leisure, Politics and Football in Zanzibar, 1900s–1950s," *Africa* 67, 2 (1997).

123. Ranajit Guha, "The Prose of Counter-Insurgency," *Subaltern Studies* (Oxford) 2 (1983): 1–42; Taussig, *Shamanism*, 2–134; Frederick Cooper, "Mau Mau and the Discourses of Decolonization," *J. Afr. History* 29, 2 (1988): 313–20, and *Decolonization and African Society* (Cambridge: Cambridge University Press, 1997). Lan, *Guns and Rain*; Phyllis Martin, *Leisure and Society in Colonial Brazzaville* (Cambridge: Cambridge University Press, 1995), and Timothy Burke, *Lifebuoy Men, Lux Women: Commodification, Consumption and Cleanliness in Modern Zimbabwe* (Durham, N.C.: Duke University Press, 1995). For gendered critiques, see Lata Mani, "Contentious Traditions: The Debate on Sati in Colonial India," *Cultural Critique* 7 (1987): 119–56, and Luise White, "Separating the Men from the Boys: The Construction of Sexuality, Gender, and Terrorism in Central Kenya 1939–59," *Int. J. Afr. Hist. Studies* 25, 1 (1990): 1–25; Lynn M. Thomas, "*Ngaitana* (I will circumcise myself): The Gender and Generational Politics of the 1956 Ban on Clitoridectomy in Meru, Kenya," *Gender and History* 8, 3 (1997): 338–63, and "Imperial Concerns and 'Women's Affairs': State Efforts to Regulate Clitoridectomy and Eradicate Abortion in Meru, Kenya c. 1910–1950," *J. Afr. Hist.* 39, 1 (1998): 121–46.

124. Randall M. Packard, "The 'Healthy Reserve' and the 'Dressed Native': Discourses on Black Health and the Language of Legitimation in South Africa," *American Ethnologist* 16, 4 (1989): 686–703; Ann Laura Stoler, "Carnal Knowledge and Imperial Power: Gender, Race, and Morality in Colonial Asia," in Micaela di Leonardo, ed., *Gender at the Crossroads of Knowledge: Feminist Anthropology in the Postmodern Era* (Berkeley and Los Angeles: University of California Press, 1991), 51–101; Nancy Rose Hunt, "Noise over Camouflaged Polygyny: Colonial Marriage Taxation and a Woman-Naming Crisis in Belgian Africa," *J. Afr. Hist.* 32, 3 (1991): 471–95; Martin, *Leisure*; Emmanuel Akyeampong, *Drink, Power, and Cultural Change: A Social History of Alcohol in Ghana, c. 1880 to Recent Times* (Portsmouth, N.H.: Heinemann, 1996). Africans were, of course, keenly aware of the nuances of dress; see Burke, *Lifebuoy Men, Lux Women*, and Laura Fair, "Dressing Up: Clothing, Class and Gender in Post-Abolition Zanzibar," *J. Afr. History* 39, 1 (1998): 63–94.

can history since its origin as an academic practice, and the question of where to find the African voices with which an academic historian might best write has concerned the field for almost forty years. The formal methodology for the study of oral tradition was to make oral history rigorous and the equal of any documentary historiography; to do so, it offered concrete guidelines for how historians might interpret accounts of a precolonial past filled with mythical heroes and mythical landscapes.[125] Scholars of twentieth-century history were not supposed to have such problems of interpretation, because oral history was declared to be categorically different from oral tradition by experts. Oral history was about things that were within living memory; facts could be checked by interviewing a number of informants, and a fantastic story could be corrected by a less imaginative informant. The emphasis was on how to verify, not how to interpret.[126] Carolyn Hamilton's protest that oral tradition and oral history have everything in common, that people draw on the forms in which the past has been presented to them to represent their own experiences and ideas,[127] did not encourage interpretive strategies for oral histories. Even a long overdue feminist critique of oral history addressed the politics of the collection of oral materials, not their interpretation.[128] But as this critique was put into scholarly practice, there were widespread concerns and critiques about ethnographic writing and the politics by which colonial peoples were made into objects.[129] In African history, academic attention shifted to

125. Jan Vansina, *Oral Tradition: A Study in Historical Methodology* (1961), trans. H. M. Wright (Chicago: Aldine, 1965), and *Oral Tradition as History;* Henige, *Chronology of Oral Tradition;* the articles in Joseph C. Miller, ed., *The African Past Speaks: Essays on Oral Tradition and History* (Hampden, Conn.: Archon Books, 1980); Heusch, *Drunken King;* V. Y. Mudimbe, *Parables and Fables: Exegesis, Textuality and Politics in Central Africa* (Madison: University of Wisconsin Press, 1991), 86–138.

126. See Vansina, *Oral Tradition as History,* 12–13; White, *Comforts of Home,* 21–28.

127. C. A. Hamilton, "Ideology and Oral Tradition: Listening to the Voices 'from Below,'" *History in Africa* 14 (1987): 67–71.

128. Claire C. Robertson, "In Pursuit of Life Histories: The Problem of Bias," *Frontiers* 7, 2 (1983): 63–69; Susan N. G. Geiger, "Women's Life Histories: Content and Method," *Signs: J. of Women in Culture and Society* 11, 2 (1986): 334–51, and "What's So Feminist about Women's Oral History?" *Journal of Women's History* 2, 1 (1990): 169–82; Marjorie Mbilinyi, "'I'd Have Been a Man': Politics and the Labor Process in Producing Personal Narratives," and Marjorie Shostak, "'What the Wind Won't Take Away': The Genesis of Nisa—the Life and Words of a !Kung Woman," in Personal Narratives Group, ed., *Interpreting Women's Lives: Feminist Theory and Personal Narratives* (Bloomington: Indiana University Press, 1989), 204–27, 228–40.

129. Johannes Fabian, *Time and the Other: How Anthropology Makes Its Object* (New York: Columbia University Press, 1983), and the articles in James Clifford and George E. Marcus, eds., *Writing Culture: The Poetics and Politics of Ethnography* (Berke

the individual, following trends in literature and anthropology. African voices were to be specific and personified, and throughout the 1980s and early 1990s, publications argued that voices should be heard and that authentic voices should be revealed in academic texts.[130] Life histories came to be synonymous with interviews; letting Africans speak for themselves became first a methodology and then a major publishing enterprise.[131]

ley and Los Angeles: University of California Press, 1986). In African history, the disaffection with the ethnographic object was as much a product of the researches of nationalist historiography as it was of debates in anthropology; see Steven Feierman, *Peasant Intellectuals: Anthropology and History in Tanzania* (Madison: University of Wisconsin Press, 1990), 13–17.

130. Nowhere is this clearer than in the reviews of Belinda Bozzoli with the assistance of Mmantho Nkotsoe, *Women of Phoeking: Consciousness, Life Strategy, and Migrancy in South Africa* (Portsmouth, N.H.: Heinemann, 1991); see esp. Elizabeth Eldridge's review in *African Economic History* 21 (1993): 191–95, but see also Vansina, *Oral Tradition as History*, 18–21; Sidney W. Mintz, "The Sensation of Moving, While Standing Still," *American Ethnologist* 16, 4 (1989): 786–96, and J. B. Peires, "Suicide or Genocide? Xhosa Perceptions of the Nongqawuse Catastrophe," *Radical History Review* 46, 7 (1990): 47–57.

131. See Mary Smith, *Baba of Karo: A Woman of the Muslim Hausa* (1954; reprint, New Haven: Yale University Press, 1981); Marjorie Shostak, *Nisa: The Life and Words of a !Kung Woman* (Cambridge, Mass.: Harvard University Press, 1983); Jean Davison with the Women of Mutira, *Voices from Mutira: Lives of Rural Gikuyu Women* (Boulder, Colo.: Lynne Rienner, 1989); Margaret Strobel and Sarah Mirzah, *Three Swahili Women: Life Histories from Mombasa, Kenya* (Bloomington: Indiana University Press, 1989), and the U.S.-produced Swahili edition, *Wanawake watatu wa Kiswahili: hadithi za maisha kutoka Mombasa, Kenya* (Bloomington: Indiana University Press, 1991); Bozzoli, *Women of Phokeng;* Kirk Hoppe, "Whose Life Is It Anyway? The Issue of Representation in Life Narratives," *Int. J. Afr. Hist. Studies* 26, 3 (1993): 623–36; Heidi Gengenbach, "Historical Truth and Life Narratives," *Int. J. Afr. Hist. Studies* 27, 3 (1994): 619–27; Susan Gieger, *TANU Women: Gender, Culture and Politics in Tanganyika, 1955–65* (Portsmouth, N.H.: Heinemann, 1997); Corinne A. Kratz, "Conversations and Lives" (forthcoming). The Swahili version of *Three Swahili Women* was published in the United States because no Kenyan publisher was interested; see Geiger, "What's So Feminist about Women's Oral History?", 182n. The life histories of women tend to proclaim their authenticity; see Domitila Barrios de Chungara and Moema Viezzer, *Let Me Speak! Testimony of Domitila, A Woman of the Bolivian Mines*, trans. Victoria Ortiz (New York: Monthly Review Press, 1978), while those of men are often summarized by scholars, without apology; see Hoyt Alverson, *Mind in the Heart of Darkness: Value and Self-Identity among the Tswana of Southern Africa* (New Haven: Yale University Press, 1978); Tim Keegan, *Facing the Storm: Portraits of Black Lives in Rural South Africa* (London: Zed Books, 1988), and Paul Lubeck, "Petroleum and Proletarianization: The Life History of a Muslim Nigerian Worker," *African Economic History* 18 (1989): 99–112; Bill Nasson, "The War of Abraham Essau: Martyrdom, Myth and Folk Memory in Calvania, South Africa," *African Affairs* 87 (1988): 239–65. But men's life histories seem to have had the space—and quite possibly the authority of a male voice—to problematize this kind of writing; see Charles van Onselen, *The Seed Is Mine: The Life of Kas Maine, A South African Sharecropper, 1894–1985* (New York: Hill & Wang, 1996), and Stephan Miescher, "Becoming a Man in Kwawu: Law, Personhood, and the Construction of Masculinities in Colonial Ghana, 1875–1957" (Ph.D. diss., Northwestern University, 1997).

But concerns about validity, authenticity, and letting Africans speak
for themselves have long and problematic histories. When the Russell
Commission was investigating the causes of the 1935 Copperbelt "disturbances," it apologized to its readers for the amount of irrelevant testimony published in *The Evidence,* but it had found that "in the case of
native witnesses, it saved time to allow witnesses to proceed with their
evidence without attempting to abbreviate it." [132] Recent versions of
this—especially Africans speaking for themselves—are concerns about
how academics can represent Africa to the wider world, the same world
that makes belief so differently valued in Africa than in Friuli. These
concerns emerged from the very academic processes by which colonial
history has been what Gyan Prakesh calls "third worlded"—made into
an object of study in the first world and given new and powerful meanings by subordinated groups there. [133] But in many cases, establishing the
authenticity of the voice—or cacophony of voices—has left it disembodied and decontextualized. Colonial subjects have been enframed as
they have been represented. Techniques of authenticating, as Timothy
Mitchell has shown, position the observer: "The world is set up before
the observing subjects as though it were a picture of something." [134]

In this book I have tried to present these vampire stories in their own
terms, not as a portrait of colonial worlds, but as a way to catch a
glimpse of the world the speakers imagined and saw. If this study has
any authority at all—indeed, if I can still use the term with a straight
face—it is not because of any particular legitimacy of the voices I quote,
but because I am writing about the colonial world with the images and
idioms produced by the colonial subjects. Like postcolonial rainmaking
or the hybrid beasts of modern bridewealth payments—like benandante
and descriptions of Jews in 1880s London—vampires are an epistemological category, with which Africans described their world, both as beliefs and metaphors. [135] This book uses the imaginary as a source for

132. Commission Appointed to Enquire into the Disturbances on the Copperbelt of
Northern Rhodesia, *Report* and *Evidence* (Lusaka: Government Printer, 1935), 2.

133. Gyan Prakesh, "Writing Post-Orientalist Histories of the Third World: Perspectives from Indian Historiography," *Comparative Studies in Society and History* 32, 2
(1990): 383–408.

134. Timothy Mitchell, *Colonizing Egypt* (Berkeley and Los Angeles: University of
California Press, 1991), 60.

135. See Feierman, *Peasant Intellectuals,* 245–64; Jean Comaroff and John L. Comaroff, "Goodly Beasts, Beastly Goods: Cattle and Commodities in a South African Context," *American Ethnologist* 17, 2 (1990): 195–216; Sharon Hutchinson, "The Cattle of
Money and the Cattle of Girls among the Nuer, 1930–83," *American Ethnologist,* 19, 2
(1992): 294–316.

colonial history; it interrogates the place of such evidence, oral and written, in historical reconstruction.

SOURCES

This book began, as an earlier section suggests, as a meditation on the uses of oral history: was it to be an additional way to establish what was true and what was false, or to add another African perspective on an event, or was it another way of obtaining evidence, a way to access a world of metaphor and belief that described and interrogated a colonial world? But the more research I did into vampire stories, the more written sources I found, and the more uneasy I became with suggesting that oral evidence and written evidence were very different, let alone opposites.

Most of the vampire stories in this book come from oral interviews conducted by myself and a variety of research assistants in Nairobi in the mid 1970s, in Siaya District in western Kenya in 1986, and in and around Kampala in 1990. Many more come from documentary accounts of vampires, including three files from the Zambian National Archives from the 1930s. Although White Fathers in Northern Rhodesia and Benedictines in the Belgian Congo were often accused of being banyama and batumbula respectively in the same period, the archives of those orders make only the most opaque allusions to those accusations, allusions that I have used in writing chapter 6. Although letters about vampires appear in the Swahili press as early as 1923, newspapers rarely mention vampire-related events until the late 1940s. Then, news items in the Kenyan press tended to explain wazimamoto to European readers, but a decade later, in Tanganyika and Uganda, mumiani stories employing local terminologies and alluding to local landmarks were commonplace, with no effort made by European authors to explain the belief to outsiders. Anecdotal accounts of vampires and the gullible Africans who believed in them were often published by administrators in the 1950s and 1960s, usually as a part of memoirs by authors who prided themselves on knowing about the African beliefs about which most Europeans were ignorant. "*Banyama! Kamupila!* Vampire-men! So the atavistic myth was going around again. . . ."[136] "Mumiani is a curious, very African thing. Africans didn't like talking about it, and when questioned

136. Peter Fraenkel, *Wayaleshi* (London: Weidenfeld & Nicholson, 1959), 200.

they would shake their heads and mumble. It wasn't new, but it was usually kept below the surface and out of sight." [137] Anthropologists working in Central Africa, however, were less smug about what they learned about banyama, and reported their own observations and confusions in letters and field notes: those who have not deposited their papers in libraries have been extremely generous with their material. Several former administrators have also been extremely helpful to me, and some of their letters inform this book. I have corresponded with several former officials to learn if there was actually a basement in the Kampala police station or any fire station in East Africa, but as the former police chief in Kampala, told me, I had "been misled" by my informants.[138]

Obviously, written accounts of vampires are no less fantastic than oral ones, but much of the other written material used in this book is fabulous as well. Missionaries claimed that Africans were eager to have surgery with chloroform in early colonial Uganda, for example, and officials in colonial Northern Rhodesia were overwrought in their eagerness to denounce the local system of slash-and-burn agriculture. The history of sleeping-sickness control policies in the pre–World War II period, which forms a large part of chapter 7, is a history of anthropomorphized flies and fictive vectors. Nowhere is a social imaginary as hard at work as when hunters attempted to protect big game from the aspersions of parasitologists. This book attempts to treat oral and written material as being equal but distinct forms of recording the past.[139] African historians have had an ambivalent relationship to orality: on the one hand, it had to be domesticated to be made the methodology by which history was written and advanced degrees were granted. On the other, the authority of the spoken word dazzled Africanists in alarming ways: it was both social and genealogical, and it could be adulterated by the written word.[140] But the value of evidence has little to do with the media in which it is available to historians. For thirty years, African historians attempted to make oral history acceptable to academic institutions by demonstrating that it was as good, and as reliable, as written

137. Bates, Mango and the Palm, 48.

138. Michael Macoun, letter to author, 18 May 1990.

139. Europeanists writing on oral history have come to this insight much more easily than Africanists; see the work of Alessandro Portelli, The Death of Luigi Trastulli and Other Stories: Form and Meaning in Oral History (Albany: State University of New York Press, 1991), and The Battle of Valle Guilia (Madison: University of Wisconsin Press, 1997).

140. Vail and White, Power and the Praise Poem, 1–39; Hofmeyr, "'Wailing for Purity.'"

documents. I argue that this argument lost sight of all the ways in which oral sources were different and contained a wealth of materials that generated different insights and visions of the past than written material would do alone. The use of oral material to add an African voice, or an African perspective, to a historical narrative derived solely from documents makes oral material an emendation to written sources. Oral sources were thus used to modify existing evidence, but they were not evidence in and of themselves. I argue that they are, of course. The oral and the written, taken together—and as the rest of this book suggests, they almost always are, or should be—add up to a vivid picture of social life and the imagination that springs from it, in part because of the ways people take circulating stories to make personal narratives both in speech and in writing. But at the same time, my use of oral and written material as equal kinds of sources complicates the evaluation of any media of sources: what, in any form, could be reliable about a vampire story? Indeed, how does history written with vampire stories, oral or written, reevaluate ideas about accuracy and chronology? My goal is not to show the irrelevance of accuracy or chronology, but to elaborate ways in which historians might find accuracy and chronologies in unexpected places.

HOW TO READ THIS BOOK

A book about accounts of colonial African vampires might not have a straightforward narrative organization. This book is organized into three sections: first; two introductory chapters that lay out the issues of evidence and method; second, two chapters that read vampire stories as a colonial genre of story in which the most general and regional reading of evidence produces glimpses of the most intimate contests of experience. The third part consists of five chapters, each of which uses vampire rumors as a primary source with which to write local histories. Each chapter in part 3 is different, mainly because history is different in each place. Some of the interview material is used in more than one—and sometimes more than two—chapters; in each case, however, it is interpreted differently. Such gerrymandering of evidence is in part my desire to reproduce rumors—they do not have the same meaning across time and space, and mean different things to different people.

Parts 2 and 3 raise another question: how do I take stories of capture and blood and claim that in some places they are about medicine and in others about labor? How can stories of wazimamoto be about property inheritance in Nairobi and twenty years later be about small-scale royal politics in Kampala? How can banyama be about sleeping-sickness control in Northern Rhodesia in the 1930s but also be about unwaged work elsewhere in that province at the same time? The answer may lie with the speakers and hearers of rumors rather than with my own methodology. Not everyone heard these rumors the same way; different speakers heard and stressed some elements and not others. The different interpretations of these rumors do not come from my own imagination but from different audiences who heard them, evaluated them, changed them, and passed them on.

But this begs another question: have I simply pulled the epistemological wool over readers' eyes in claiming that some Ugandan bazimamoto stories are about medicine while others are about royal politics? My answer, of course, is no. It is only by a close reading of these stories that I can dissaggregate those that talk about bazimamoto capturing people with chloroform—a strong indication that these stories are about medicine—from those that talk about a man found with unconscious women in his Kampala home but that never mention whether he used a drug to capture them. Nor are all vampire stories, whatever the similarities of detail, the same. The people who feared being made dull by bazimamoto used vampire stories to talk about specific drugs and techniques; the people who talked about the trial of a "well-known stupefier" in 1953 talked about royal politics at the moment of its most intense crisis using images and details of bazimamoto stories.

Vampire stories are different in different places and at different times because history is different in different places. By privileging different interpretations of rumor at different times for different reasons, I seek to convey their multiple meanings. But equally important is the fact that this book is not about speakers and their stories; it is about the elements in these stories that were used to describe different experiences in colonial Africa. As best I can, my use of evidence reproduces the way rumors were heard and the many things they meant in East and Central Africa. The five chapters in part 3 are examples of how local histories might be written with vampire stories as a primary source. Each chapter takes a series of stories from a locality—sometimes as small as an urban slum, sometimes as large as a province—and bases a historical reconstruction on it. I do not claim by my attention to regional history in part 2 and to local history in part 3 to present African epistemologies (although these parts discuss African idioms and ideas at great length); instead, I am ar-

guing for an expansion of historical epistemologies (I hesitate to call
these Western) to include rumor and gossip, to embrace the fantastic
and the scandalous, to use stories of bloodsucking firemen and well-
known stupefiers to find the very stuff of history, the categories and constructs with which people make their worlds and articulate and debate
their understandings of those worlds.

CHAPTER 2

Historicizing Rumor and Gossip

This chapter is not concerned with how Africans might have believed that Europeans hired Africans to capture their fellows and take their blood; rather, it is about how historians might use rumor and gossip as primary sources in the writing of history. But rumor and gossip have very little in common. Lumping them together is as recent as journalism and communications studies; they were put together to create a category of unreliable oral information—rumor and gossip were not thought to be substantiated like newspaper accounts. But anthropologists, in an earlier, more functionalist era, had a less romantic view of the printed word: gossip and scandal were linked together as phenomena of speech and control, while rumor was news that one later learned was false. Social psychologists and sociologists, however, who had long claimed rumor as their own, argued that falsehood was not an absolute characteristic of rumor. What characterized rumors was the intensity with which they were spread. Indeed, the more widespread and widely told a rumor was, the more it had to conform to the laws of plausibility.[1] The folklorists who struggled to disaggregate rumor from legend ended up struggling over the relative importance of the truth of stories compared to the importance of how or why they were told. Those who regarded legends as frozen rumors had not paid close enough attention to the full narra-

---

1. Tamotsu Shibutani, *Improvised News: A Sociological Study of Rumor* (Indianapolis: Bobbs-Merrill, 1966), 17–18, 76–77.

tive style of legends, and those who saw rumor and legend as unrelated tended to focus on the truth of the stories, not how they were told. But folklorists understood that what made a rumor or a legend powerful was that people believed it.[2]

But how the African peoples discussed in this book decided what was true and what was false, what was rumor and what was eyewitness account, and how much credibility to give to each is not a simple matter of how information was presented. In the case of Colonial Northern Rhodesia (Zambia), for example, the Bemba word for rumor, talk, and conversation is the same, *ilyashi*. It refers to how people exchanged information, not the credibility of that information.[3] Indeed, how rumor is distinguished from fact by Bemba speakers is not at all clear. From the 1920s on, they heard tales of a twig that could strip a man of his willpower and of Congolese cannibals who kidnapped Copperbelt workers; they heard that Catholic priests ate people; during the early years of the Depression, they heard that the king of England was in jail and that black Americans would come to replace the British.[4] This does not mean that everyone believed each and every one of these tales, or that they believed or doubted them for very long, but it does suggest that why one such story was credible while another sounded ludicrous had to do with local people's appreciation and apprehension of certain facts, not with whether a story was grandiose, frightful, and transmitted orally. But if Africans did not believe stories because they were written, nor did they doubt the rumors that were discredited in print. Published denunciations of rumor were often thought to prove its truth. The written word was as subject to debate and derision as any oral statement was. Newspapers did not underscore the truth of the printed word, but provided many contending versions of it. In the late 1940s, a Ugandan national-

---

2. These points come from the rich article by Patrick B. Mullen, "Modern Legend and Rumor Theory," *J. of the Folklore Institute* 9 (1972): 95–109.

3. On the Luapula, by the late 1940s at least, *ilyashi* meant historical knowledge; see Ian Cunnison, *History on the Luapula: An Essay on the Historical Notions of a Central African Tribe*, Rhodes-Livingstone Papers, no. 21 (Cape Town and New York: G. Cumberlege, Oxford University Press, for the Rhodes-Livingstone Institute, 1951), 3–4. Migrants to the Copperbelt from the Plateau probably understood both meanings of the word.

4. P. K. Kanosa, "Banyama—Copper Belt Myth Terrifies the Foolish," *Mutende* [Lusaka] 38 (1936) (National Archives of Zambia [henceforth cited as NAZ], SEC2/429, Native Affairs: Banyama); for published accounts, see Mwelwa C. Musambachime, "The Impact of Rumor: The Case of Banyama (Vampire-Men) in Northern Rhodesia, 1930–64," *Int. J. Afr. Hist. Studies* 21, 2 (1988): 205–09; Luise White, "Vampire Priests of Central Africa: African Debates about Labor and Religion in Colonial Northern Zambia," *Comp. Studies Soc. and Hist.*, 35, 4 (1993): 744–70.

ist—and newspaper owner—proposed a radio station, with receivers
in every chiefdom, to make sure that the correct version of events got
around. Indeed, many African oral forms that were explicitly unreliable
were known by names that played off official media—Waya Times in
Kenya's detention camps or Radio Katwe in Uganda.

Thus my concern is how to combine the insights of academics with
those of Africans in ways that might historicize rumor and gossip. Gossip and scandal served to discipline people, both those who gossiped and
those who were gossiped about; both asserted values and defined community standards. Scandal might best be historicized as accusation, a
phrase that sums up the agency and the speech act of turning ordinary
gossip into something on which action has to be taken. Rumor may simply be poised between an explanation and an assertion: it is not events
misinterpreted and deformed, but rather events analyzed and commented upon. As a result, in this book, I use the term "rumor" with as
much care and caution as my subject matter allows: it is a very poor
term with which to discuss stories that the storytellers think of as true.
Indeed, the important question may not be which phrases are gossip,
which constitute rumor, and which are accusation. Figuring out how
these labels can best be applied may not be particularly enlightening. It
may be more useful, particularly for historians, to try to find out what
these phrases meant to those who heard and repeated them, over time
and over space. Not everyone hears or appreciates or understands gossip or rumors the same way—some gossip and some rumor may be unreliable to some people while sounding perfectly reasonable to others.
Labels that foreclose this latitude of credibility may not be worthwhile.

For historians, rumor and gossip and accusation are forms of evidence we need to use with great care and caution. However much street
talk in Paris in 1750 may have resembled street talk in Kampala in 1950,
each must be examined in terms of the specificity of time and place.
Understanding gossip requires understanding social rules, values, and
conflicts; such understandings put scholars on the same ground as the
gossipers.[5] But the thorny question of how rumor and gossip make
historiography depends on the history and the historian. Georges Lefebvre's *The Great Fear of 1789* reworked secondary sources.[6] Arlette

5. John Beard Haviland, *Gossip, Reputation and Knowledge in Zincantan* (Chicago:
University of Chicago Press, 1977), 28–30.
6. Georges Lefebvre, *The Great Fear of 1789: Rural Panic in Revolutionary France,*
trans. Joan White (New York: Pantheon Books, 1973).

Farge and Jacques Revel's *The Vanishing Children of Paris* is an account of the riots of 1750 when it was said that the king abducted children either to drain their blood for his baths or to send them as colonists to New France. The authors reconstruct rumor and riot from diarists' accounts and memoirs; some sources repeat the talk of the day, others report parents' worries years after the fact.[7] In chapter 8, in discussing the trial of a "well-known stupefier" in Kampala in 1953, I have used gossip and scandal that was reported in newspapers as rumor as evidence. The high politics in which the trial took place was not reported in the press, but, I argue, it can be glimpsed through the newspaper accounts of accusations against various officials. In short, the terms "rumor," "gossip," and "accusation" are deployments, not separate and distinct categories.[8]

GOSSIP AND RESPECTABILITY

Gossip, as Max Gluckman pointed out years ago, creates ties of intimacy between those gossiping. The subject of the gossip, personal and political, is secondary to the process of creating bonds and boundaries. Scandal serves to keep an individual in line when gossip no longer does the trick. Both gossip and scandal assert social values, not as static traditions but as learned and lived practices: "outsiders cannot join in gossip," and "a most important part of gaining membership in any group is to learn its scandals."[9]

Such insights make gossip more aural than oral; the fact that it is heard is more important than the fact that it is spoken. For Gluckman, a story is credible because it sounds likely—or interesting, or worth passing on—to those who hear it, not necessarily the skill of its telling or the reliability of who tells it. A contemporary critique of Gluckman emphasized the role of "the gossiper"—the one who could manipulate information for his or her own reasons—which placed the importance

7. Arlette Farge and Jacques Revel, *The Vanishing Children of Paris: Rumor and Politics before the French Revolution,* trans. Claudia Miéville (Cambridge, Mass.: Harvard University Press, 1991).

8. For a book that uses rumor as a separate category with some success, see Patricia A. Turner, *I Heard It through the Grapevine: Rumor in African-American Culture* (Berkeley and Los Angeles: University of California Press, 1993).

9. Max Gluckman, "Gossip and Scandal," *Current Anthropology* 4, 3 (1963): 307–16.

Gossip

of gossip in speaking, rather than in listening and evaluating.[10] Such a critique, however, extracts gossip from its social context: gossip "is not only a means for an individual to assemble basic information on his peers, but it is also a technique for summarizing public opinion."[11]

How is gossip different from ordinary talking, from storytelling, or from just hanging out? Put simply, gossip is a matter of context and convention. It is talk about people when they are not present, but it is not just any kind of talk: it reports behavior; it rests on evaluating reputations. "One does not gossip about a prostitute who turns 'tricks,' but one does gossip about the respectable matron who is observed with men sneaking into her house day and night."[12] Gossip reveals contradictions. Stating that colonial states captured Africans and took their blood revealed their true nature; quoting colonialists on this issue revealed their cynicism and control. "[S]ome of the District Commissioners were announcing that 'if your goat or cow is lost—you find it, but if your relative is lost—you do not bother to find him because you will not be able to find him.'"[13]

In the Western world, the association of gossip with idle, malicious talk is relatively recent, perhaps dating from the early eighteenth century.[14] Other cultures do not see gossip as a single form of speech, however. Historicizing gossip may require using academic categories in ways that peoples in the past might not have done. The men and women quoted in chapter 1 defined gossip as "loose talk" because its subject matter was grounded in speculation, not experience; gossip was not gossip because of who told it in which context. Gossip was gossip because it was a theory, a conjecture. It might be more rewarding to abandon an-

10. Robert Paine, "What Is Gossip About? An Alternative Hypothesis," *Man*, n.s., 2, 2 (1967): 278–85.

11. John F. Szwed, "Gossip, Drinking and Social Control in a Newfoundland Parish," *Ethnology* 5 (1966): 434–41.

12. Sally Engle Merry, "Rethinking Gossip and Scandal," in Donald Black, ed., *Toward a General Theory of Social Control*, vol. 1: *The Fundamentals* (New York: Academic Press, 1984), 277–301; see also Gluckman, "Gossip and Scandal," and Szwed, "Gossip, Drinking and Social Control."

13. This was a cliché, something people in and around Dar es Salaam said about mumiami. A version of this statement appeared in letters to the editor from "Adiyisadiki" ("Believer") and "Asiyesadiki" ("Nonbeliever") in *Mambo Leo*, August and November 1923, and in an interview quoted in Lloyd William Swantz, "The Role of the Medicine Man among the Zaramo of Dar es Salaam" (Ph.D. diss., University of Dar es Salaam, 1972), 337. I am grateful to Laura Fair and Peter Seitel for assistance with translations from the Swahili.

14. Alexander Rysman, "How Gossip Became a Woman," *J. of Communication* 27, 1 (1977): 176–80; Patricia Spacks, *Gossip* (New York: Knopf, 1985).

alytical categories of "idle talk" and ask how we think about talk itself. I suggest an Africanist reading of Michel Foucault's *The History of Sexuality*, not necessarily because of what it says about sexuality, but because that is the text where Foucault develops his ideas about speaking and the voice most clearly. These are concepts Africanists hold dear.

According to Foucault, however, speaking in modern societies is far more than how individuals enter the historical record, it is how people participate in the states and civil societies that manage them. The very act of talking about oneself, or others, disciplines; the very practices of sorting out the epistemologies that shock and scandalize creates and catalogues ideas about deviance and virtue, which are enforced with each telling. Modern subjects are not only studied, counted, and classified; they speak about these things for themselves. It is how they are managed. The "task of telling everything" allocated to subjects not only "enlarged the boundaries" of the subject matter on which they might speak but "installed an apparatus" capable of producing more and more speech that eventually policed itself. Thus, the "crude," the "crass," and the "vulgar" are not distinctive forms of speech, but speech outside of that management.[15]

Does gossip police itself? Or is it too crude? Roger D. Abrahams's 1970 article "A Performance-Centered Approach to Gossip" elaborated on Gluckman and his critics, suggesting that gossip is negotiated between gossiper and audience. On the Caribbean island of St. Vincent, gossip, like story and song, is judged according "to whether it is judiciously performed in the right setting and under the properly licensed conditions." Gossip publicly condemned behavior that departed from community norms and could be used to build up the esteem of the gossiper; unsuccessful gossips were those who used the device badly, resulting in community disapprobation. Thus, unacceptable gossip is not the gossip that speaks ill of beloved persons; it is the gossip that is performed without skill or protocol.[16] In Swahili, one way to condemn gossip is to call it *takataka,* rubbish.

But what about the accusations that fall on deaf ears, the complaints that backfire and undermine the position of the accuser? Is such gossip

---

15. Michel Foucault, *The History of Sexuality,* vol. 1: *An Introduction,* trans. Robert Hurley (New York: Pantheon Books, 1978), 23–31.

16. Roger D. Abrahams, "A Performance-Centered Approach to Gossip," *Man,* n.s., 5, 2 (1970): 290–301; Sandy Yerkovitch, "Gossiping as a Way of Speaking," *J. of Communication* 27 (1977): 192–96.

invariably against well-regarded individuals? Or does it mean that some individuals are beyond reproach or that there is an ahistorical category of reputation that cannot be breached by words? Neither, I think. Unsuccessful gossip proves that gossip and accusation are negotiated, that "unimpeachable reputation" is a specific historic construct that only the most skilled and the most appropriate gossip can impeach. "Bad gossip" invades a person's privacy more than an audience will tolerate; [17] in Foucauldian terms, "bad gossip" is crude. Failed gossip backfires and causes more problems for the gossiper than for the person the gossip is about. For example, when an African man was arrested for kidnapping a small child in Northern Rhodesia in 1944—an era of many custody disputes as men returned from the mines of the Copperbelt demanding bride-wealth marriages—he stated that he was collecting blood for a white man who was banyama; after several days in jail, he changed his story, saying that he had wanted to rape the child.[18]

If I add the concepts of bad gossip and failed gossip to that of successful gossip, it is obvious why rumor and gossip are such wonderful historical sources. They occupy the interstices of respectability, exactly following the contours of local and regional concerns. Rumor and gossip allocate responsibility; they contextualize extraction. In the Northern Province of Northern Rhodesia, the provincial commissioner was said to have given the Bemba paramount chief a "large bag of money" to allow banyama into his country.[19] Rumors, more than gossip, move between ideas about the personal and the political, the local and the national. In Northern Rhodesia, it was said that African blood was made into medicine for Europeans; the long illness of King George V in 1929 was seen by many Africans as ample reason to be wary of strangers. Banyama snatched men and sold them to the Belgian Congo, where they were put to work in large secret camps not far from the border. Sometimes "they are sold to medical institutions for experiments and operations."[20] Rumors explain; they naturalize the unnatural. In the 1920s, it was said that every town in East Africa had a Parsee whose house

17. Ulf Hannerz, "Gossip, Networks and Culture in a Black American Ghetto," *Ethnos* 32 (1967): 35–60.

18. Geoffrey How, provincial commissioner, Northern Province, Kasama, to chief secretary, Lusaka, 29 January 1944 (NAZ, SEC2/429, Native Affairs: Banyama).

19. D. Willis, provincial commissioner, Kasama District, "Report on Banyama," 24 March 1931 (NAZ, ZA1/9/62/2/1).

20. Kanosa, "Banyama" (cited n. 4 above).

was equipped with pits and buckets to collect African blood.[21] In Northern Rhodesia, Africans told a district officer during the Depression that they could not go to Tanganyika Territory to look for work "because the white ants had eaten all the money, a white man told them so."[22]

Successful gossip and accusation tell us how penetrable a reputation may be, and when it is penetrable; gossip in particular discloses the boundaries of attack and subversion. In Uganda, my assistants and I asked men if they knew whether bazimamoto ever used prostitutes to help them capture men, as they were said to have done in Kenya. Many responded that they had never heard this, but that it sounded likely, since "they would do anything for money."[23] Another thought the question important: "I don't know anything about that but please, try to do research on that."[24] Successful gossip and accusation must be keenly aware of the shifts in reception and credibility of certain issues. Accusation and compliment can coexist, but they are rarely spoken to the same audience, at least not at the same time. In Uganda in 1990, many people thought that "Dr. Duke" was the man in Entebbe "who received the blood." Some people thought "he graded it and distributed it"; another thought "he was responsible for the blood transfusion at Entebbe." Many people thought he was a doctor, but one man thought he was the governor. One man did not know which department took the blood but knew the man who did: Duke. But Duke was Lyndal Duke of the Tsetse Research Department, who retired in 1934. A man described the job: "to bribe people with some little money, take them to Entebbe tse-tse areas to be bitten by the flies, something which was intended for research purposes on tse-tse victims."[25] But a few people also remembered Duke as the founder of what became the Entebbe Zoo: "Duke was a medical doctor and a fat man in size, he was working at Entebbe and he was a collector of different kinds of animals. . . . They were tamed and people could go there and see them . . . he had a pond for fish and people

21. "Asiyesadiki," cited n. 13 above.

22. J. W. Sharratt-Horne, district commissioner, tour report 6/1932 (NAZ, SEC2/767, Isoka Tour Reports, 1932–33).

23. Abdullah Sonsomola, Kisenyi, 20 August 1990; see also Adolf Namatura, Katwe, Uganda, 24 August 1990; Christopher Kawoya, Kasubi, 17 August 1990.

24. Yonasani Kaggwa, Katwe, 27 August 1990.

25. Jonah Waswa Kigozi, Katwe, 18 August 1990; George W. Ggingo, Kasubi, 15 August 1990; Joseph Nsubuga, Kisasi, 22 August 1990; Nechumbuza Nsumba, Katwe, 28 August 1990; Samuel Mubiru, Lubya, 28 August 1990; Magarita Kalule, Masanafu, 20 August 1990; Ssimbwa Jjuko, Bwase, 20 August 1990; Gregory Sseluwagi, Lubya, 28 August 1990.

could go there and see how these fish were playing."[26] "Duke had a farm for animals. . . . [H]is lions didn't kill anybody, they were for the public interest, and when you went there you would find animals well fenced in a place made of iron bars, and you would see leopards, lions, crocodiles." After such praise, gossip had to be presented with great circumspection and innuendo. "He was collecting blood, but there was a big hospital there. I don't know if he was collecting blood for bazimamoto or not."[27] A cautious accusation is far better—in terms of performance and reception—than a badly timed one, which can land the accuser in trouble. Thus, for historians at least, the power of gossip is more than a collective delight in the vices of friends and colleagues. Gossip is a reliable historical source because it traces the boundaries created by talking about someone. In that talking, a world of value and behavior is constituted: that's what Foucault's idea of discourse does; it does no more.[28]

Between Gluckman and Foucault lies, structurally and historically, communication theory. These empirical studies of rumor attempted to prove, among other things, which qualities of transmission made oral information credible—was it overheard, made authoritative by liquor, or told with greater skill and attention to detail than a true story would necessarily merit? Such surveys and quantification of how belief is articulated may have made the ambiguities of hearing and thinking too concrete and clear-cut, but they also show the skill and the discretion with which oral information is evaluated, censored, amended, and passed on or withheld.[29] They reveal how local, rather than how personal, the evaluation of gossip is.

Gossip and accusation are idioms of intimacy. How deeply do we care about the vices of people we don't know? An interpretation of gossip based solely on Gluckman would imply that we might not care about the vices of public personalities. One that combines Gluckman and Foucault would argue that there is no difference between talking about strangers or talking about our neighbors—it is the very process of gossiping that

26. Julia Nakibuuka Nalongo, Lubya, 21 August 1990.

27. Abdullah Sonsomola, Kisenyi, 28 August 1990.

28. Foucault, *History of Sexuality*, 1: 27.

29. Leon Festinger et al., "A Study of Rumor: Its Origins and Spread," *Human Relations* 1 (1948): 464–86; Gary Alan Fine, *Manufacturing Tales: Sex and Money in Contemporary Legends* (Knoxville: University of Tennessee Press, 1992), 1–42; for a survey of such studies, see Jean-Noel Kapferer, *Rumors: Uses, Interpretations, and Images* (New Brunswick, N.J.: Transaction Press, 1990), 95–105, 130–43.

creates the intimacy. In gossiping, a claim is made to knowledge and the right to speak it. How deeply we care about the vices of strangers depends in part on the meanings attached to information—how scarce, how important, and how specialized and hard to come by it is—with which the gossip gossips.[30] Gossip about people we don't know not only binds gossipers together in an imagined community of shared values, but binds gossipers to communities, states, and sanctions. Gossip about strangers may have meaning because of the very intimacy translated to daily life by the original usage of the term. But in the case of strangers, the epistemologies of our caring about the vices of strangers "percolates into formal agencies of social control" and out of them again.[31] For historians at least, this is a crucially important and theoretically rewarding place to start, because if we can historicize gossip, we look at the boundaries and bonds of a community. Who says what about whom, to whom, articulates the alliances and affiliations of the conflicts of daily life. In 1940, in colonial Elisabethville, in the Belgian Congo,

> A colonial official called a meeting with all the women . . . who made or sold beer or the local brew. The colonial official demanded of all these women the addresses of their homes, to tell the street, the number of the house and the name of the occupant. The women did this. Then, the colonial official asked that the women notify them each time a man was drunk at their houses. Then, the colonial official would send someone to arrest the drunken man. In fact, he was working for batumbula. And each time these agents arrested a drunken man they would give the woman 2,50 Fr for each person arrested.[32]

The women in Nairobi described in chapter 5 aspired to own property that could be inherited by heirs they themselves chose, without reference to blood or filiation. These women told elaborate bloodsucking stories specific to the complications and contradictions of female property-ownership. Nevertheless, some property-owning women had earned the condemnation of others; they had worked for wazimamoto and "bought their houses with the blood of somebody." Gossip was often about gossip; it criticized gossipers and their motives. A woman in Uganda said she had heard of bazimamoto, but "when anyone constructed a good house, he was suspected of being a bazimamoto, or of being involved in . . . capturing people and selling them to bazi-

30. Hannerz, "Gossip, Networks and Culture," 37–38.
31. Merry, "Rethinking Gossip," 277n., 290–94; see also Haviland, *Gossip*, 105.
32. Joseph Kabila Komba Alona, Lubumbashi, 28 March 1991. I am grateful to Bogumil Jewsiewicki for this interview.

mamoto—because he had a good house!"[33] A form of speech that actively debates and establishes and reestablishes the criteria for success and failure, for prestige and scorn, is a tool for writing the history of communities, of neighborhoods and regions, in intimate detail.

VOICES AND SUBJECTS

There are perhaps certain discomforting parallels between how modern regimes have required speaking subjects and how African historians have required them. The intellectual foundations of the oral history of living persons—the life history, or personal narrative—rest on some basic assumptions: that people are the most accurate chroniclers of their own lives, and that experience is evidence of the most reliable sort. While there have been piecemeal critiques,[34] this view dominated African history by the 1980s. And why not? The twentieth century could be best explained by those who lived through it, especially when those lives were not always deemed important enough for the historical record: African voices could fill the gaps in official documentation and provide a version of events suppressed by colonial chroniclers.[35] Voices were considered such a key tool to the reconstruction of African history that they were never problematized.

But recent work in history has queried some of the assumptions on which the oral evidence about twentieth-century Africa rests. The notion of an essential self, a persona that sees his or her life the same way over time, now seems rather quaint.[36] The idea that experience alone can provide historical evidence, on the other hand, seems far too simplistic in and of itself. What counts as experience and what counts as fantasy? How are the two to be distinguished? Can accounts of the real ever fully purge themselves of the fantastic, especially when the fantastic contains debates about the real? And how would people report things that do not

33. Bibiana Nalwanga, Bwaise, Uganda, 24 August 1990.
34. Jan Vansina, "Memory and Oral Tradition," in Joseph Miller, ed., *The African Past Speaks: Essays on Oral Tradition and History* (Hampden, Conn.: Archon Books, 1980), 262–79; Micaela di Leonardo, "Oral History as Ethnographic Encounter," *Oral History Review* 15 (1987): 1–20.
35. For a forceful statement of this position, see Luise White, *The Comforts of Home: Prostitution in Colonial Nairobi* (Chicago: University of Chicago Press, 1990), 21–28.
36. Megan Vaughan, *Curing Their Ills: Colonial Power and African Illness* (Stanford: Stanford University Press, 1991), 12–19; Ann Laura Stoler, *Race and the Education of Desire: Foucault's History of Sexuality and the Colonial Order of Things* (Durham, N.C.: Duke University Press, 1995), 7–11, 95–136.

conform to their own norms of experience? The historical reconstruction of experience is no easier. How do historians interpret things we
think our informants did not really experience?[37]

All of this should make the practice of twentieth-century oral history problematic. The question of who is reporting what experiences in
which way is crucial to our practice. Research into colonial subjectivities by historians is rare; when historians have written about African
lives, it has been to show how those lives represent colonial experiences,
or how they can be shown to illuminate and elucidate a history not discernible from the more conventional narratives of national histories.[38]
Stephan Miescher has studied men's life histories as the history of ideas
about self-presentation,[39] but there has been no formal historical inquiry into what a Bemba or Ganda self, for example, was like in 1930
and how it saw the world. Such inquiries are, or should be, crucial to
historians' work of interpretation. When people talk about what they
did in the past, are they talking about their present-day personas or
about ones from an earlier era? How can we know what someone was
like—what they felt and thought—in their twenties without rewriting
their lives for them? In some parts of Africa, we have enough information to hint at some changing notion of self, but for most places, we have
relied on vast oversimplification of personalities in order to use oral
sources. What someone says in 1990 about himself or herself in 1935
is taken to be true because the same person is doing the talking. Historians rarely ask if the experience is described with the insights of 1990
or 1935, however. Similarly, what we know about African selves in the
1980s and 1990s is applied to recorded testimonies from 1913 or 1947.

37. Joan W. Scott, "The Evidence of Experience," and Lorraine Dotson, "Marvelous
Facts and Miraculous Evidence in Early Modern Europe," in James Chandler, Arnold I.
Davidson, and Harry Harootunian, eds., *Questions of Evidence: Proof, Practice and Persuasion across the Disciplines* (Chicago: University of Chicago Press, 1994), 363–87 and
243–74; Luise White, "Alien Nation: Race in Space," *Transition* 63 (1994): 24–33; Caroline Walker Bynum, "Material Continuity, Personal Survival, and the Resurrection of the
Body: A Scholastic Discussion in Its Medieval and Modern Contexts," in *Fragmentation
and Redemption: Essays on Gender and the Human Body in Medieval Religion* (Cambridge: Zone Books, 1991), 239–97.

38. Two excellent examples are Charles van Onselen, *The Seed Is Mine: The Life of
Kas Maine, a South African Sharecropper, 1894–1985* (New York: Hill & Wang, 1996),
and Susan Geiger, *TANU Women: Gender, and Culture in the Making of Tanganyikan
Nationalism* (Portsmouth, N.H.: Heinemann, 1997).

39. Stephan Miescher, "Becoming a Man in Kwawu: Gender, Law, Personhood, and
the Construction of Masculinities in Colonial Ghana, 1875–1957" (Ph.D. diss., Northwestern University, 1997).

Such ahistorical treatment of African selves has had historiographic consequences. The absence of historicized subjectivities in colonial Africa has given scholars African voices without selves, voices in which no embodiments, interests, and powers strive to be reinvented and reinterpreted as they speak.[40] This means, in short, that the voice captured in an interview may be a risky source with which to know and understand the self of forty years before. Barbara Myerhoff has argued that much interviewing of the elderly involves their own self-conscious construction of a coherent self, whom they present "as a stable, continuous being through time, across continents and epochs." A life is reworked by the informant for very specific and personal goals: "The discovery of personal unity between the flow and flux of ordinary life is the personal counterpart of myth-making."[41] The evidence derived from people talking about their own pasts requires an understanding of who they were and how they saw themselves in their past worlds.[42]

But what about people talking about others? What about gossip? I suggest that gossip is at least as reliable as people talking about themselves. If historians have failed to historicize African selves, let alone to interpret people's words about their own lives, talk about others may be the only source left to them. Gossip, in practice, contains interests, embodiments, and local strands of power. It reveals precisely those passions, complaints, and revisions that are sometimes suppressed in the lives written about from oral interviews. In sharp contrast to the idea of Africans speaking for themselves in life histories,[43] gossip reveals motivations and interests of the gossiper at a specific moment.

40. Although courtroom testimony is outside the scope of this particular chapter, it is one of the sites in which gossip and subjectivity interrogate each other, and a site from which a subject reinvents a self with, or against, gossip; see Robert Ferguson, "Story and Transcription in the Trial of John Brown," *Yale J. of Law and the Humanities* 6, 1 (1994): 37–73. The subject need not be present to be remade in a courtroom, although when a dead subject is refashioned, the living subjects are often constrained by the positions from which they remake the dead; see David William Cohen and Atieno Odhiambo, *Burying SM: The Politics of Knowledge and the Sociology of Power in Black Africa* (Portsmouth, N.H.: Heinemann, 1992).

41. Barbara Myerhoff, *Number Our Days* (New York: Dutton, 1978), 222.

42. Scholars of early modern Europe have debated this as much as Africanists have avoided it; see, e.g., the debates generated by Natalie Zemon Davis, *The Return of Martin Guerre* (Cambridge, Mass.: Harvard University Press, 1983), including Davis's "On the Lame," *Am. Hist. Rev.* 93 (1988): 572–603; Robert Finlay, "The Refashioning of Martin Guerre," *Am. Hist. Rev.* 93 (1988): 552–71. For an excellent summary of these debates, see Lyndal Roper, *Oedipus and the Devil: Witchcraft, Sexuality and Religion in Early Modern Europe* (London: Routledge, 1994), 1–34, 225–30.

43. For Africanist examples, see Margaret Strobel and Sarah Mirzah, *Three Swahili Women* (Bloomington: Indiana University Press, 1989), and Jean Davison and the Women

Kas Maine, a black South African sharecropper, for example, presented himself as hardworking and self-righteous when he recalled turning down the invitation of his landlord for a trip to town to watch boxing: "I refused to go and told him I could not stomach that shit—sitting in a tent all day watching others do their work while we left our own unattended." [44] The recollection about another reveals a self. Indeed, in two separate interviews over a five-year period, with different interviewers, the normally laconic Maine described almost word for word his early years as an independent farmer in debt to a local shopkeeper. In each version, Maine's attempts to settle the debt earned the admiration, praise, and favor of the trader, an Australian ex-soldier named William Hambly who had stayed on in South Africa after the Anglo-Boer War of 1899–1902. [45] Do these two recollections, with their exact level of detail, reveal a terrain of memory or the strength of a performance? Such a distinction may not matter; the recollection may instead reveal the analytical possibilities of gossip, that in talking about Hambly, Maine presents himself best. Not only does Hambly become a vehicle with which Maine constructs memories of himself and his impact on others, but in recalling Hambly, Maine recalls Hambly talking about him. The line between speaking about oneself and speaking about others is hardly firm: that is precisely my point. A self is revealed in talking about others at least as much as it is revealed in introspection.

This raises another question altogether: is all talk about an absent party gossip? Most functionalists would probably say no, gossip is gossip when both parties know the absent one. Most Foucauldians would probably argue yes, but that it doesn't matter, that Maine is the real subject of this recollection. But gossip is not such an autonomous, independent part of speech that it does not slip into something else. As Ulf Hannerz notes, "the same information may be gossip or non-gossip depending on who gives it to whom." [46] A well-crafted memory may be recounted in a variety of contexts. The story of Hambly's praise of Maine may have had more pointed meanings when told to those who remem-

of Mutira, *Voices from Mutira: Lives of Rural Gikuyu Women* (Boulder, Colo.: Lynne Rienner, 1989).

44. Charles van Onselen, "Race and Class in the South African Countryside: Cultural Osmosis and Social Relations in the Sharecropping Economy of the South-Western Transvaal, 1900–1950," *Am. Hist. Rev.* 95, 1 (1990): 111–12.

45. Charles van Onselen, "The Reconstruction of a Rural Life from Oral Testimony: Critical Notes on the Methodology in the Study of a Black South African Sharecropper," *J. Peasant Studies* 20, 3 (1993): 494–514, and id., *The Seed Is Mine*.

46. Hannerz, "Gossip, Networks and Culture," 36.

bered Hambly than when told to those who did not. The appearance
of such a story in a series of interviews suggests that a way of talking
about others—whether such talking was once or still is gossip in other
venues—has become part of a repertoire of anecdotes, stories, and
memories that the speaker uses to make points about his or her life.[47]
Historicizing rumor and gossip means not only making them historical sources but utilizing the ways in which they are both historical and
intensely personal. Reading gossip, rumor, or accusation for the clues
suggested by Carlo Ginzburg allows historians to focus on the details
with which these stories are told, rather than on the truth of stories. In
his essay "Clues: Roots of an Evidential Paradigm," Ginzburg argues
that historical method was made scientific by a very specific reading of
evidence that began in the second half of the nineteenth century. Details
were to be interrogated by the trained professional; they became clues
by which a broader framework was examined and defined. The details
of the human ear, for example, reveal the authenticity of paintings and
portraits or show familial relations; a cloven hoofprint reveals a herbi-
vore. Ginzburg's own historical practice went beyond body parts, however, and he read in the witches, werewolves, and sabbats of inquisition
testimony a world of folk practices that had existed for centuries; they
were not inquisitors' fantasies.[48] But the history derived solely from
reading clues may be more linear than the personal inventions of gossip
and the periodicity of rumor would require. How people talk about
themselves and their experiences, with what words and imaginings, does
not flow directly out of a folk past; the power of those images derives
from their historical and cultural meanings, of course, but also from individuals' ability to use them to describe their lives, their conflicts, and
their fears. The power of any particular piece of gossip lies in the importance of the contradictions it reveals; the power of a rumor lies in the
contradictions it brings together and explains. What the pits in houses
or the rubber sucking tubes or cars without lights in vampire stories

47. Elizabeth Tonkin, *Narrating Our Pasts: The Social Construction of Oral History*
(Cambridge: Cambridge University Press, 1992); Isabel Hofmeyr, "*We Spend Our Year as
a Tale That Is Told*": *Oral Historical Narratives in a South African Chiefdom* (Portsmouth, N.H.: Heinemann, 1994).

48. Carlo Ginzburg, "Clues: Roots of an Evidential Paradigm," in id., *Clues, Myths
and the Historical Method* trans. John and Anne Tedeschi (Baltimore: Johns Hopkins University Press, 1988), 96–125; but see also ibid., "Witchcraft and Popular Piety: Notes on
a Modenese Trial of 1519," 1–16; "Freud, the Wolf-Man and Werewolves," 146–55; and
"The Inquisitor as Anthropologist," 156–64.

bring to personal narratives is not their fixed place in African understandings of colonial medicine or colonial technology but rather a broad genealogy of relationships of power, skill, and specialization. The tracks read to reveal the animal's habits and history, so central to Ginzburg's analysis, might get a looser reading somewhere else: the cars without lights and rubber sucking tubes in vampire stories reveal motives with as much clarity as the cloven hoofprint reveals a jawbone in natural history.

The clues and details of African vampire stories are not a special kind of thinking but a special kind of talking. They are the images and ideas and clichés that speakers reinterpret, interrogate, and problematize as they talk about themselves and others; this is the thick description provided by the use of hearsay. The power of African vampire stories lies in part in locating the similarities between a wink and a twitch in the motivations behind them; in vampire stories, there is the "thin description" of noting that twitches or winks, or rubber sucking tubes or cars without lights, are present; the thick description lies in the detailed analysis of the motivation and intent behind their presence in the African night. The cars and the tubes are not clues to a folk past or even to a recent past, but a set of meaningful images that are produced, perceived, interpreted, and parodied by the speakers themselves.[49] Indeed, Lyndal Roper has argued that such clues should be read as personal statements, and that their deployment, particularly during interrogation, reveals individual conflicts and contestations, often over what the details and clues with which they speak really mean and who controls the meaning during interrogation.[50]

If informants speak about the past and about themselves with the past, how can scholars get at African subjectivities? In most of this book, I use vampire stories as social rather than personal constructions. How might I read these stories to reveal individual histories? What if I were to read each and every vampire story as a personal statement, as evidence about a self hardly revealed in other ways? What if I were to

49. Clifford Geertz, "Thick Description: Toward an Interpretive Theory of Culture," in *The Interpretation of Cultures* (New York: Basic Books, 1973), 3–30. T. O. Beidelman makes this point somewhat differently: that Kaguru imagery is not only an analytical tool for ethnographers but the way Kaguru grasp the world about them; see *Moral Imagination in Kaguru Modes of Thought* (Washington, D.C.: Smithsonian Institution Press, 1993), 103.

50. Roper, *Oedipus and the Devil*, 225–30.

look at the specific embellishments and embroideries in each story? What if I took the way it was performed as seriously as the content? These are the things African historians are trained to weed out.[51] But looking at the ways people fashion well-known stories into their own experiences or performances may be a way to historicize an individual's own ideas about his or her self.

Zaina Kachui told me and my assistant a *wazimamoto* story about prostitutes who trapped men in pits in their rooms. It was a story common in Nairobi the 1920s and 1930s, but her version had a level of detail and commentary other stories did not have:

> A long time ago the wazimamoto was staying in Mashimoni, even those people who were staying in Mashimoni, they bought plots with the blood of somebody. I heard that in those days they used to dig the floors very deep in the house and they covered the floor with a carpet. Where it was deepest, in the center of the floor they'd put a chair and the victim would fall and be killed. Most of the women living there were prostitutes and this is how they made extra money . . . when a man came for sex, the woman would say *karibu* [welcome], and the man would go to the chair, and then he would fall into the hole in the floor, and at night the wazimamoto would come and take that man away. . . . It was easy for these women to find blood for the wazimamoto because there were so many men coming to Mashimoni for sex.[52]

In chapter 5, this story informs an analysis of property ownership and inheritance in Nairobi; but the question I want to ask now is why did Kachui tell this particular story? No other woman told it. All the other versions I heard were matter-of-fact, without this level of detail and cunning, told without so much energy, enthusiasm, and wordplay. I suggest that by contextualizing this version in terms of the life of Zaina Kachui, I can write about her life without adding emotions she herself never expressed to me in many hours of interviews and conversation. There is no possible interpretation of this material as a cautionary tale about Pumwani neighborhoods. Mashimoni—Swahili for "many in the pits"—had lost its allure as a place for prostitutes several years before Kachui came to Nairobi; besides, she made no attempt to tell this story as a contemporary witness: she was crystal clear that this was a story she had heard. But the very fact that this is not "experience" makes it even more significant that she told this particular story more than forty years after she first heard it.

51. Jan Vansina, *Oral Tradition as History* (Madison: University of Wisconsin Press, 1985), 79–82.

52. Zaina Kachui, Pumwani, 14 June 1976.

Zaina Kachui was probably born in Taveta around 1910; her father had immigrated from Kitui several years before. Her parents died when she was relatively young, leaving her and an older brother orphans in the early 1920s. Her brother encouraged her "to go with men" to support them both, but he died a year or two later, and she went to Kitui. She was not yet an adolescent: "I didn't even have breasts yet." In Kitui, she stayed with a relative of her father's, who tried to marry her to a man so many years her senior that the district commissioner stopped it. "This is a daughter," she recalled him saying, "not a wife." The DC told her to return to her father's home and, seemingly grateful for the direction, she did. But "that place was not good for me, I had to cook all the food and I hardly got any food to eat," and so she went to Thika for several years and took up prostitution there. Sometime during her years in Kitui or Thika, she had a stillborn child. She eventually came to Pumwani between 1933 and 1935. She credited an older woman with insisting that she take money from men, rather than finding a boyfriend whose own impoverished state would drain her resources, advice Kachui never fully took to heart. During World War II, a man friend offered to keep her very considerable earnings in a safe place for her, with predictable results. Nevertheless, although she never acquired property, by the time I knew her, she was living in two rooms in the house she had been living in for thirty years, supporting a younger man, who was rumored to be her lover, and selling cooked food to supplement the savings she had managed to live off for almost twenty years. Kachui died in 1981 or 1982. She would have been offended at any characterization of her life as one of failure and misery: she was very proud of her accomplishments, of the fact that in her late sixties, she did not have to ask anyone for help. The self-confident Kachui I knew in 1976 and 1977 did not reflect on the intense vulnerability, pain, and confusion of the preteen prostitute in Taveta or the thirteen-year-old almost bride in Kitui. In fact, she told me about her arranged almost-marriage in the course of explaining colonialism to me and not as a description of the exploitation of adolescents in already overburdened extended families: "In those days the government went by age, if you were young, you got a young DC to make a decision about you."

But if she did not describe her youth as one of pain and exploitation, how can I?[53] Can I accurately represent Kachui with my own interpre-

53. For Kachui's life presented as a success story, see White, *Comforts*, 88, 95, 109, 114, 117, 123–4, 147, 152, 168.

tation of what happened to her, or do I pay attention to her words, her use of language, her sense of metaphor, wordplay, and power? I suggest that her powerful fantasy of passive men, seeking only sex, falling into pits can be read to reveal her vulnerability. This is an interpretation, of course, but one that shows how gossip can be both a practical and intimate source with which to reconstruct the past. A woman passed from man to man during her adolescence might well delight in stories of men passing through property. A woman whose needs were ignored by every kinsman from whom she sought protection might well delight in a story of women's agency and men's powerlessness, a story that implied great male stupidity as well: "After a few years, men stopped coming to Mashimoni, because so many men had disappeared there." A woman who had few choices about home, about family, about men, about everything, in fact, but the remuneration men gave her, might well embellish a well-known story with details about housing, and with enormous power and control. These details of pits and prostitutes are not necessarily unproblematic clues with which historians can see the past; rather, they are the technologies of speaking with which a woman described her world in intimate terms.

GOSSIP AND SILENCE

But what about not speaking? According to Foucault, silence is an additional strategy. It is "the things one declines to say, or is forbidden to name, the discretion that is required between different speakers." Silence "functions alongside things said." Together speech and silence form discourse; speech or silence alone do not.[54] Starting in the mid 1970s, women's historians began to equate women's silence with powerlessness.[55] Within a few years, a new generation of scholars of colonialism, heavily influenced but not necessarily instructed by *Subaltern Studies,* began to look at Foucauldian silences as a point of opposition rather than a discursive strategy. The silence of omission—of colonial documents all about men, about elites, about colonized women described with all the malapropisms of white men—was read to reveal the gender

54. Foucault, *History of Sexuality,* 1: 20–27.
55. The best summary and critique of this literature is Susan Gal, "Between Speech and Silence: The Problematics of Research on Language and Gender," in Micaela di Leonardo, ed., *Gender at the Crossroads of Knowledge: Feminist Anthropology in the Postmodern Era* (Berkeley and Los Angeles: University of California Press, 1991), 175–200.

and power of colonial agendas. Reading the silences of documents was a way to see who mattered, and how they mattered, under colonial rule.[56] This insight quickly got out of hand, however: scholars of colonialism in general, and oral historians in particular, began to "listen to silences." Anyone whose voice was not included had been silenced, and any number of interviews were interpreted for what was unsaid, rather than what was said. This gave interviewers much more power than they would admit wielding. Silence in an interview, a commission of inquiry, or a courtroom, was no longer strategic, it became another site of interpretation. Not speaking was not seen as resistance but as oppression. Listening to silences collapsed the differences between speech and silence; it turned silence into a sort of interpreted speech. Interpreting silences homogenized the different cultural meanings of specific silences.[57]

I want to return here to an old-fashioned, but Foucauldian, interpretation of silences. They are neither spoken nor heard: that is their power. They evade explicit meanings. A clearly intentioned silence could elide complicity. For example, officials in colonial Northern Rhodesia regularly complained that Africans would never answer their questions about banyama. But when two men suspected of being banyama went on trial for murder in 1944, officials requested that they not be defended by the district commissioner, because that would fuel suspicions that the government was indeed behind banyama.[58] Gossip is social; no silence stands alone. In two interviews my assistant and I conducted in western Kenya, one man commented on the other's silences, not simply to comment on the other man's interview material but to assess the nature of work, migrancy, and occupational loyalty. I had gone to Goma Village in Yimbo location in western Kenya in 1986 because I knew the grand-

56. For two examples from colonial history, see Gayatri Chakrobarty Spivak, "The Rani of Sanir: An Essay on Reading the Archives," *History and Theory* 24 (1985): 247–72, and Nancy Rose Hunt, "Noise over Camouflaged Polygyny: Colonial Marriage Taxation and a Woman-Naming Crisis in Belgian Africa," *J. Afr. Hist.* 32, 3 (1991): 471–95.

57. Listening to silences has a troubling genealogy as well. In sixteenth-century Fruilian witch trials, "gestures, sudden reactions like blushing, even silences were recorded. . . . To the deeply suspicious inquisitors, every small clue could provide a breakthrough to the truth" (Ginzburg, "Inquisitor as Anthropologist," in *Clues,* 160).

58. W. V. Brelsford, tour report 1, 1939 (NAZ, SEC2/751, Chinsali Tour Reports, 1939–40); G. Kennedy-Jenkins, "The 'banyama' Scare in the Lake Chaya Area," tour report 6, 1938 (NAZ, SEC2/836, Mpika Tour Reports, 1938–40); Gervas Clay, district commissioner, Isoka District, "Memorandum Concerning 'banyama' and 'mafyeka' with Special Reference to Provincial Commissioner, Kasama's Confidential File on Banyama and to Incidents in the Isoka District during the Latter Part of 1943," and A. T. Williams, for provincial commissioner, Northern Province, Kasama, to registrar of the High Court, Livingstone, 3 April 1944 (NAZ, SEC2/429, Native Affairs: Banyama).

son of Timotheo Omondo, a Luo man who had taught at Maseno from
1924 to 1947, when he helped found the Luo Thrift and Trading Corporation.[59] Between his teaching—he taught English to perhaps three-
quarters of western Kenya's elites—and his politics, he knew almost all
his neighbors and how their experiences of wazimamoto overlapped.
Within a few hours of my and my research assistant's arrival, Omondo
told us to go to see Zebede Oyoyo, the man who had escaped the Nairobi fire brigade in 1923 and was still talking about it. We interviewed
Oyoyo twice. In the first interview, he expressed something we were to
hear again elsewhere in the district—that the policemen actively supported the fire brigade in capturing Africans. When Oyoyo was kidnapped, "policemen were right there but did absolutely nothing. In fact,
they pretended not to notice anything. . . . I concluded they too were
part of the kidnapping."[60] After our interview with Oyoyo, Omondo
suggested we go speak to Noah Asingo Olunga, who had been a Nairobi
policeman when Oyoyo was captured. After we interviewed Olunga, we
went home to Omondo's house and did a formal interview with him.

We had asked Olunga if it was true that policemen and wazimamoto
were the same. He was definite: "No. Policemen and wazimamoto were
quite different. All I know was that wazimamoto were putting on black
clothes and black caps, while policemen were wearing quite different
uniforms." He never saw any bloodsucking, although he knew people
talked about it.[61] When we interviewed Omondo, however, he did not
talk about his years in Nairobi, but about Olunga's interview, instruct-
ing us on how to interpret the silences and omission:

> Whoever worked for the police force cannot tell you much because they were
> the ones who were very much involved in these activities. In fact, policemen
> were the ones doing this work as wazimamoto agents. . . . Once one was
> a policeman he remains so even after leaving his job. Policemen are always
> careful about what they leave out. Retired policemen cannot tell you exactly
> what they were doing during their working years. . . . I think Olungu was just
> fearing to tell you what exactly they did as policemen.[62]

The silence here is not an additional, repressed version of the spoken,
but a kind of socially constituted understanding of memory, loyalty, and

59. See E. S. Atieno-Odhiambo, " 'Seek Ye First the Economic Kingdom': A History
of the Luo Thrift and Trading Corporation (LUTOCO), 1945–1956," *Hadith* 5 (1975),
221–60.
60. Zebede Oyoyo, Goma, Yimbo, 13 August 1986.
61. Noah Asingo Olunga, Goma Village, Yimbo, 22 August 1986.
62. Timotheo Omondo, Goma, Yimbo, 22 August 1986.

accountability; the silence described here is what the gossip is really about. The meaning of gossip is as social as it is personal. It is pieced together by many people exchanging information over a short period of time or by one person over a lifetime—lived experience again. When several people exchange gossip because it is exciting, what is really going on is a debate, as people argue over the details and reliability of the information, about the issues involved. Silence carries hints, allusions, references, and opinions that are not contained in the other information, but it remains silence, powerful because it is not spoken, and cannot be pulled—or decoded—into speech. Silences do not necessarily lend themselves to the same straightforward interpretation that spoken words do; they require slower or looser analyses. Indeed, a silence from one time can be disclosed at another. In the 1940s, Northern Rhodesian Africans said that it was easy to find out about banyama, because if one of their employees quit, he could talk about them.[63]

My argument here is that silences are not sites of repression but eloquent assumptions about local knowledge. They are not spoken of, not because they are unspeakable, but because they isolate fragments of powerful stories; they do not carry weight unless the gossip, to use Edgar Morin's troubling phrase, metastasizes into rumors and accusations. This brings about a "transition from the singular to the generic" in which the isolated fragments, whether barely remembered or discussed daily, were shaped into a specific kind of accusation according to specific conventions.[64] Without those conventions, without metastasis, such fragments remain the stuff of conversation, gossip, and demonstrations of common sense. "Why isn't this written about?" my assistant asked Omondo. "Here is something that happened a lot and there is no record of it in any book and in any public history. Nobody talks freely about it, why?" He replied: "Those things were mostly happening during the night and besides, I think they were taking blood to the hospitals. Nowadays we hear that such and such a blood group is needed, but in the olden days nobody was willing to donate his blood."[65]

63. Ian Cunnison, field notes, March 1949. I am grateful to Professor Cunnison for making his notes available to me.

64. Edgar Morin, *Rumor in Orleans,* trans. Peter Green (New York: Random House, 1971), 62–63; for a more historical treatment of silences and fragments, see Michel-Rolf Trouillot, *Silencing the Past: Power and the Production of History* (Boston: Beacon Press, 1995).

65. Timotheo Omondo.

The silences in gossip and the silences between gossip—even the silences in the neighborhood between Omondo and Olunga—allow gossip to be taken up anew, with new villains and new situations. The silences in gossip allow for gossip to have continued meanings to describe work and history and how old men talk; they allow old men to show off their knowledge of science and medicine in ways that public denunciations of neighbors and old friends would never do.

The full import of these silences is not always completely understood by those who speak and hear silences, let alone by a clever researcher. Like Omondo, several of the men quoted in this book claimed that, over the years, they had learned that stories about vampires were true or false. A man in Uganda never believed that people could disappear until the violence of the Amin years, but a man in Kenya said that over time, he came to realize that his friends and neighbors were actually talking about "blood donation rooms" when they told wazimamoto stories.[66]

WHO IS GOSSIP ABOUT?

If gossip is transmitted over time, how is it different from historical memory? Is lore about local heroes gossip or myth-making?[67] This raises another question: is all gossip useful for historians, or are there specific individuals about whom gossip is particularly useful for historians? Much depends on how much gossip there is, of course: the few African policemen named in official documents as vampires are not otherwise identified in written documentation; they simply became examples of an occupational category that had often been accused. The same is true of the men and women who entered the written record as victims of the vampires. But historical sources are produced in specific contexts: some gossip is foregrounded to underscore other historical concerns and constructions. In western Kenya, for example, "Oleao" was a dreaded kachinja years before he became a guard at Sakwa Prison during the Mau Mau rebellion. He had all the credentials a kachinja needed: he owned a mining company—Black Cat Prospecting—into which he conscripted prisoners; he spoke the local language well; and he drove a Landrover, but he entered the written record only as part of another

66. Gregory Sseluwagi; Ofwete Muriar.
67. Bill Nasson, "The War of Abraham Essau, 1899–1901: Myth, Martyrdom, and Folk Memory from Calvinia, South Africa," *African Affairs* 87, 347 (1988): 239–65.

man's political memoirs. Indeed, local people only knew his last name and called him "Mr. Robinson." [68] But gossip is often deployed in conversation as a way to discover whether someone is worth gossiping with. The gossip about ordinary people—people who left no paper trail—that seems to be too fragmentary to be made into history may be part of a larger framework by which informants interrogated their interlocutors. In Nairobi, for example, whenever I asked who the first women to build houses in Nairobi were, people scoffed at my question; it was too hard to answer, there were too many: no one came up with names. But when I asked about wazimamoto, I heard about Mama Amida, "the first woman to build here in Pumwani," who "sold her sister's daughter to wazimamoto." [69] She was not alone: "There was a fat woman called Halima, and she sold her sister." [70] These remarks were made almost in passing, as examples of what I was asking about. I did not realize it at the time, but these fragments were not presented as gossip but as invitations to gossip: they tested my local knowledge, to see if I knew the landscape—or at least the names and norms—well enough to join in. [71] Gossip offered to, or written to bypass, the ill-informed remains fragmentary to those who do not know enough to participate; [72] it is a strategy by which people ascertain how much someone knows and how much to reveal.

But what about gossip about extraordinary folk, famous people about whom various stories circulate and were written down? Is gossip a reliable historical source because it corrects the distortions of the written record or because it provides another dimension to official praise, or at least the writings about people clever enough not to commit their worst excesses to paper? [73] Such questions imply that written words are better and more trustworthy than gossip. Much written material is gos-

68. H. K. Wachanga, *The Swords of Kirinyaga: The Fight for Land and Freedom* (Nairobi: Kenya Literature Bureau, 1975), 143; Atieno Odhiambo, personal communication, 15 August 1997.

69. Hannah Mwikali, Kajiado, Kenya, 8 November 1976.

70. Muthoni wa Karanja, Mathare, Nairobi, 25 June 1976.

71. Jeanne Favret-Saada, *Deadly Words: Witchcraft in the Bocage*, trans. Catherine Cullen (Cambridge: Cambridge University Press, 1980), 11–13.

72. Nasson, "Abraham Essau," 257; Ann Laura Stoler, "'In Cold Blood': Hierarchies of Credibility and the Politics of Colonial Narratives," *Representations* 37 (1992): 140–89.

73. See Jeff Peires, "The Legend of Fenner-Solomon," in Belinda Bozzoli, ed., *Class, Community and Conflict: South African Perspectives* (Johannesburg: Ravan Press, 1987), 66–92. Fenner-Solomon was a lawyer who dispossessed the people of Kat River with his pen "but wasn't such a fool as to leave anything lying around on paper." The oral evidence for the man's deception and bullying is perhaps overstated, but it does represent a vision of a legal system at odds with the needs of both white and black smallholders.

sip, however. The paper trail surrounding a Scandinavian settler farming in colonial Northern Rhodesia and accused by an African in 1944 of being banyama is all fragmentary gossip. The unpublished memoirs of a district officer say that the settler was frequently involved in labor disputes on his farm, which he lost; a trader reported a well-known story that the settler had insulted the Bemba paramount chief in a retail transaction. These fragments suggest why the settler may have been known as banyama. Other fragments reveal other things, but they are nonetheless gossip. The history of the agricultural society of Zambia, for example, notes the number of leopards shot near the Scandinavian's farm but nothing else. Yengwe, Arthur Davison, another Northern Rhodesian, figured in vampire accusations for over twenty years. Davison was a labor recruiter of considerable violence. He lived in Ndola, and his private life is barely alluded to in published accounts of banyama. But when the author of one of the published accounts turned to write a history of the "characters" among Northern Rhodesia's pioneers, Davison merited his own chapter. His violence is mentioned—he had once killed eighty Africans in an attack on a stockaded village in retaliation for robbery—but most of the material is the white community's gossip: Davison had never married but had not "gone native" either and "as far as we know, left no half-caste off-spring"; he had a huge house planned in Ndola that was never finished: extensions were planned but never built, and rubble and foundation pillars dotted the landscape.[74]

But where there is more than fragmentary evidence, most of the Europeans called vampires were not those who were uniformly despised by Africans. After all, Dr. Duke was described both as a man who took blood from Africans and as a man whose animals pleased Africans. Neither the man nor his job were suspect; how he performed his job was.[75]

74. S. R. Denny, "Up and Down the Great North Road" (typescript, 1970, Rhodes House, Oxford, RH MSS Afr. r. 113). The gossipy history is W. V. Brelsford, *Generations of Men: The European Pioneers of Northern Rhodesia* (Salisbury: Stuart, Manning for the Northern Rhodesia Society, 1966), 140–43; the analytical article is id., "The 'Banyama' Myth," *NADA* 9, 4 (1967): 49–60; Dick Hobson, *Showtime: The Agricultural and Commercial Society of Zambia* (Lusaka: Agricultural and Commercial Society of Zambia, 1979), 42. See also Musambachime, "Impact of Rumor," and Kanosa, "Banyama" (both cited n. 4 above). In his study of Congolese batumbula rumors, "Mutumbula: Myth de l'opprimé," *Cultures et développement* 7, 3–4 (1975): 487–90, Rik Ceyssens claims that most of the white men so accused lived alone.

75. See Farge and Revel, *Vanishing Children*, 127–28, for a sage summary of how rumors articulated the warped and ineffectual sovereignty of the king rather than the institution of monarchy; this may be the point of every accusation of cannibalism hurled at an African president.

Time and time again the white men said to be behind vampire activities were those whose activities were all but ambiguous, the men whose deeds were a hair's breadth between the use and misuse of their authority and power, men whose actions required thick description to explain what they were doing, the twitch and the wink again. But gossip worth passing on is the gossip that reveals contradictions. Oleao, for example, was said to have spoken Luo fluently.[76] Dom Grégoire had been the subject of batumbula rumors long before he was transferred to a mission on the Luapula. When he was accused of bringing African captives to the butcheries of Elisabethville, he was actively trying to encourage the Belgian mining company, and largest single employer in all of Katanga, Union Minière du Haut Katanga to buy dried fish from the women of his mission.[77] When H. F. Cartmel-Robinson, a district commissioner in Northern Rhodesia's Western Province ordered a smallpox vaccination campaign in 1934, he was accused of collecting blood for banyama.[78] C. F. M. Swynnerton, the tsetse researcher who struggled against all odds to use African methods of tsetse control in two colonies, was known as the head banyama both in the Tanganyika Territory and Northern Rhodesia.

WHAT IS RUMOR ABOUT?

Many scholars of rumor have argued that rumor is the product of ambiguous situations: rumors resolve contradictions; they explain not only misfortune but good fortune. Rumors in Africa, Karin Barber observes, could explain how someone grew rich without working hard.[79] Tomatsu Shibutani has called rumor "collective problem-solving" in which "men caught" in ambiguous situations attempt to "construe a meaningful interpretation . . . by pooling their intellectual resources."[80] Historians have been perhaps less than eager to see rumors as explanations and collective efforts; Alain Corbin has argued that even the most contradictory rumors "revealed collective psychoses, dreams and anxieties" of a period, as when French villagers tortured and killed a harmless nobleman

---

76. Wachanga, *Swords,* 143.
77. Brelsford, "Banyama," 52; Dom Grégoire Coussement, Kasenga, to Mgsr. G. C. de Hemptinne, Elisabethville, 5 June 1948, Saint Andreas Abbey Archives.
78. Denny, "Up and Down the Great North Road."
79. Karin Barber, "Popular Reactions to the Petro-Naira," *J. Modern Afr. Studies* 20, 3 (1982): 431–50.
80. Shibutani, *Improvised News,* 17.

in 1870.[81] But suggestions of collective problem-solving and collective psychoses both make rumors the speech of unified and homogeneous populations who have no fractures in their vision of the world; such interpretations obscure the contradictory fragments of gossip that make up any rumor. Shibutani reports, for example, that during the American occupation of Japan there was a widespread rumor that General Douglas MacArthur had a Japanese grandparent. He argues that this rumor was a way for Japanese to reconcile their postwar experience of the general's reforms with their wartime belief that Americans in general and MacArthur in particular hated them.[82] But such a reading of the rumor ignores all the ways in which this particular story hints at Japanese anti-war and anti-military sentiments stifled during the war. Indeed, Farge and Revel have noted the ways in which rumor reveals wider terrains of belief and theory, of alternative visions of cause and effect, "the power of rumor meant that the whole hotchpotch of culture was in circulation in Paris, made up of snatches of knowledge, truths and half-truths, including a whole mixture of allusions which were called upon according to the needs of the moment."[83] Circulating stories are not constructed on a moment-to-moment basis; they are drawn from a store of historical allusions that have been kept alive and given new and renewed meanings by the gossip and arguments of diverse social groups.[84]

Rumors about colonial bureaucracies, corporations, events, and diseases thus are not really "about" those things at all; rather, they are narratives, explanations, and theories in which colonial bureaucracies, corporations, events, and diseases are subjects. It would be difficult to argue that rumors about clothing, food, and either deliberate or inadvertent additives—the snake in the coat, the rat in the fried chicken, the urine in Mexican beer—are about the corporations named in the stories; it would be as easy to say that these stories are about the bodily fluids contained, contaminated, or injured in these stories.[85] Arguing that these

---

81. Alain Corbin, *The Village of Cannibals: Rage and Murder in France, 1870*, trans. Arthur Goldhammer (Cambridge, Mass.: Harvard University Press, 1992), 39–48.

82. Shibutani, *Improvised News,* 79. For national interpretations of the bundled traits of many rumors, see Peter Lienhardt, "The Interpretation of Rumour," in J. H. M. Beattie and R. G. Lienhardt, eds., *Studies in Social Anthropology: Essays in Memory of E. E. Evans-Pritchard by His Former Colleagues* (Oxford: Clarendon Press, 1975), 105–31.

83. Farge and Revel, *Vanishing Children,* 117.

84. John Lonsdale, "The Prayers of Waiyaki: The Uses of the Kikuyu Past," in David M. Anderson and Douglas H. Johnson, eds., *Revealing Prophets: Prophecy in East African History* (London: James Currey, 1995), 240–91.

85. I am glossing a large literature here, so well known in professional and popular circles that it is often referred to in shorthand: rumors about rats served as Kentucky Fried

stories are about the corporations named in the stories, or about the foodstuffs contaminated, suggests that there is only one audience for a rumor, and only one possible hearing of the rumor by that audience. Are the names of companies, countries, and corporations the site of the rumor, the level of detail that makes it a better, more credible rumor, or the subject of the rumor? Do the detail and specificity of brand names make a story any more compelling or important than does the presence of any other detail? When Africans say the headquarters of bazimamoto was in the Yellow Fever Department at Entebbe, or that batumbula was headquartered at the Hotel Biano near Jadotville, are they saying that bazimamoto and batumbula stories are about these institutions or that the specificity of these institutions locates the stories in a specific region and time? The regional variations within a rumor, however fragmentary and elusive, suggest genealogies of local concerns and historical fixations that would not otherwise be apparent. During the Great Fear of 1789 in France, some regions were said to fear a British invasion; others worried that Croatian troops were massing on their borders; and still others feared Poles or Moors. These were not hysterical accusations but concerns and interests grounded in local historical experience. They do not "explain" the rumor, but they explain how it was locally credible.[86] The last five chapters of this book argue precisely that, and show how rumors can be a source for local history that reveals the passionate contradictions and anxieties of specific places with specific histories.

Asking, let alone deciphering, what a rumor is about makes a rumor about one thing. It makes rich texts of half truths and local knowledges linear and simplified. Several stories from East and Central Africa, each involving sugar, may make this point. In batumbula stories from the colonial Congo, "The captives of batumbula did not eat maize meal. They drank sugar water or they ate sugarcane. The captives who were favored this way became fat and hairy and were taken to the Hotel Biano, where they were killed and eaten. When there were enough captives, one group was transported to Belgium and another to America."[87]

Chicken; an additive in Church's Fried Chicken to sterilize black men; a snake hidden in the sleeve of a coat that bit a customer trying it on at K-Mart; and a series of tales about corporate logos and food additives are described and analyzed in Kapferer, *Rumors;* Fine, *Manufacturing Tales;* Turner, *I Heard It Through the Grapevine;* and Frederick Koenig, *Rumor in the Marketplace: The Social Psychology of Commercial Hearsay* (Dover, Mass.: Auburn House, 1985).

86. Lefebvre, *Great Fear,* 160.
87. Joseph Kabila Kiomba Alona, Lubumbashi, 28 March 1991.

A student at Makerere University College in Uganda wrote an essay about peoples' anxieties about the 1948 census: "[R]umours are being spread by ignorant people that the government wanted to know the density of the population so they could check the increase of population by giving people medicine indirectly—say mixed with sugar—for indeed when brown sugar was introduced into my country people refused to buy it because of the rumours."[88] In 1952, an anti–Central African Federation pamphlet circulating in Northern Rhodesia reported that "on 28th October the 'House of Laws' in London had decided to put poisoned sugar on sale for Africans, commencing on February 8 . . . 1953." The poisoned sugar would cause stillbirths in women and would make men impotent. "The sugar would be recognized by the letters LPS on the packets."[89]

In these stories, the level of detail and specificity about dates and locations are as great as anxieties about sugar, colonial power, and political processes. It is their ability to contain diverse elements that makes rumors powerful, or at least worth telling and retelling. Rumors contain "raw facts," Jean-Noel Kapferer insists. "Rumors do not *take off* from the truth but rather *seek out* the truth."[90] They are open to many interpretations and speak to different factions within the most homogeneous audiences. It is in their exchange and evaluation that they take on sophisticated analysis. To pull these sugar stories apart to explain the failure of brown sugar sales in one place or African conceptions of global commodity circuits in another would strip them of the rich ambivalence of the well-fed captives and the codes by which poisoned sugar was to be identified. It is the allusions and loose ends of the story that give it widespread currency and credibility. Rumors do not seek truth by themselves; the people who tell and the people who interpret rumors do. Indeed, the poisoned sugar accusations occurred shortly before Hortense Powdermaker began her fieldwork in Northern Rhodesia. She reported the stories without reference to the dates involved or the writing on the

88. J. E. Goldthorpe, "Attitudes to the Census and Vital Registration in East Africa," *Population Studies* 6, 2 (1952): 163–71. I am grateful to Lynn Thomas for this reference. As Makerere was the only university in East Africa at the time, the student may have come from either Uganda, Kenya, or Tanganyika.

89. Peter Fraenkel, *Wayaleshi* (London: Weidenfeld and Nicholson, 1959), 196.

90. Kapferer, *Rumors*, 3. Emphasis in original. Various theorists of rumors have said this various ways: Koenig, *Rumor in the Marketplace*, 19, for example, talks about the "bits of information" in rumors, whereas Festinger et al., "Study of Rumor," use the term "bundled."

packets, and she interpreted them in terms of witchcraft poisonings. For the anthropologist, this was not a rumor, but what happened when "the rational fear of Federation moved into the realm of the supernatural."[91]

There is no single correct interpretation of any single rumor; there are interpretations and contextualizations instead. If gossip reveals contradictions, rumor contains contradictions like a fishnet. Rumors rarely lose their specificity or get covered up, but once they are captured in oral or written texts, their diverse and contradictory elements become bundled together, so that teasing out a single meaning, or single hierarchy of meanings, is virtually impossible. Indeed, giving a rumor a single meaning turns rumor into something it is not, something much less rich and complex. As chapter 6 argues, the whole complicated story of a rumor is what makes it told again and again; its diverse elements are its vocabulary. These vocabularies—the details and the clues—are not unproblematic and constant; they change, are reinterpreted, and take on new and powerful meanings in large part because of the conduct and history of the rumor itself. In this way, however, pits first became associated with vampire stories in East Africa—there are published references to pits starting in 1923—and by the 1930s, surveyors, road crews, and prospectors were being suspected of being vampires because they dig pits, and by the late 1950s, white miners and geologists were being accused and sometimes attacked. Similarly, *wazimamoto* was synonymous with "vampire" in many East African cities long before they had fire brigades or any fire-fighting equipment at all; by the time there were actual, physical fire stations in Tanganyika and Uganda, Africans were said to fear Europeans driving red cars, and officials, equally attuned to the multiple meanings of rumor, used fire engines to patrol towns to discourage crime.

RUMOR, GOSSIP, AND HISTORIANS

Historicizing gossip may allow historians to access a more intimate terrain of personal experience and of thinking than other historical sources can do. The intimate anger and judgmental scorn of gossip map the changing fortunes, values, and standards of communities that other sources identify only broadly. Disembedding gossip, however, should

91. Hortense Powdermaker, *Copper Town: The Human Situation on the Rhodesian Copperbelt* (New York: Harper & Row, 1962), 64.

not entail such radical surgery that gossip is interpreted as a separate and distinct form of speech, to be segregated from the other material presented in oral interviews. Instead, historicizing gossip involves thinking about gossip as a way of talking in which people express their interests more intimately, and more personally, than they might if they were talking only about themselves. Historicizing rumor, on the other hand, may reveal little about the individual life or experiences of the speaker, but contextualized with other rumors by other speakers, it may reveal an intellectual world of fears and fantasies, ideas and claims that have not been studied before. The contradictory elements of rumors can be read to reveal the complications of everyday concerns. Chapters 3 and 4 argue that a broad interpretation of specific rumors can reveal the changing meaning of biomedical intervention or the fissures within a differentiated labor force.

PART TWO

CHAPTER 3

"Bandages on Your Mouth"

The Experience of Colonial Medicine in East and Central Africa

This chapter and the one that follows interpret vampire stories as a regional, colonial genre, the formulaic elements of which reveal an intimate history of African encounters with colonial medicine. Both chapters argue, with different but overlapping sources, that reading vampire stories as a genre—as formulaic stories told with set elements of plot and detail—encourages a historical reconstruction of specific concerns and ideas over a large geographic region. These chapters present evidence in ways that most historians of oral material would not do: I am not interested in individual testimony or the contexts of recollection or collection; I do not think it matters if one speaker is a man's third wife, another a Christian, and another a recent convert to Islam. Instead, I am interested in the elements these stories share across cultural and colonial borders. In this chapter, oral accounts are neither considered to be a spoken rendition of experience nor taken to be true. But even though they do not depict actual events, conversations, or things that really happened, they describe meanings and powers and ideas that informed how people thought and behaved. Indeed, I argue that reading evidence for its generic qualities, for the formulaic elements with which a good and thus credible story is told, reveals a level of meaning and significance that interpreting evidence as personal testimony would not do.

GENRES, VOICES, AND EVIDENCE

This chapter argues that oral African vampire rumors can be read along-side medical writings about triumphant drugs and vanquished superstitions to illuminate the context in which Western biomedicine was practiced. This chapter is not about the clash of beliefs or of technologies; it is about how technologies were believed to work, and how much power was invested in their application. It is about cures that were rubbed on the skin, or inhaled; it is about needles and scalpels that penetrated beneath the skin.

The sources I use overlap only somewhat. Missionary writings from early colonial Uganda, primarily published in the Church Missionary Society's journals, and writings by doctors and officials about medical practice in East and Central Africa provide a chronological framework that is somewhat longer than that of vampire rumors in the same region. Colonial doctors positioned themselves firmly within imperial science, and their writings describe many of the tools and technologies that figure in the vampire stories.[1] These medical writings and these oral vampire stories are not "about" the same events and experiences in any firm chronological sense. They are about the same procedures and technologies. I am not reconstructing a sequence of events and responses to them, but the vocabulary in which medical care was both negotiated and undermined. What follows is a juxtaposition of texts to get them to interrogate each other, to show how different ways of talking about colonial medicine reveals the extent of its control. This chapter, perhaps more than any other, relies on the combination of oral material and written accounts. This is not just because African anxieties about the blood taken in medical encounters are so commonplace in colonial medical writings, but because medical writing and vampire stories are so often about the same things.

1. Ann Beck, "The Problems of British Medical Administration in East Africa between 1900 and 1930," *Bull. Hist. Med.* 36 (1962): 275–83; Steven Feierman, "Struggles for Control: The Social Roots of Health and Healing in Modern Africa," *African Studies Review* 28, 2–3 (1982); 73–148; Megan Vaughan, *Curing Their Ills: Colonial Power and African Illness* (Stanford: Stanford University Press, 1991), 56; A. Chilube, "The Clash between Modern and Indigenous Medicine," *Makerere Medical Journal* 9 (1965): 36; Jean Comaroff and John L. Comaroff, *Ethnography and the Historical Imagination* (Boulder, Colo.: Westview Press, 1992), 215–34; Maryinez Lyons, "The Power to Heal: African Medical Auxiliaries in Colonial Belgian Congo and Uganda," in Dagmar Engels and Shula Marks, eds., *Contesting Colonial Hegemony: State and Society in India and Africa* (London: I. B. Taurus, 1994), 202–23.

The use of the oral and the written together, rather than as different visions, raises another question altogether: how to write history, especially colonial history? Some recent African history, some of it by me, has argued for the great reliability of oral evidence for twentieth-century Africa. Who after all was more qualified to describe colonialism than those who lived through it or under it? The words of the colonized simply describe their world with far greater detail and accuracy than any colonizer could. The voices of women, moreover, are all but absent from the colonial record; only with their own words could we reconstruct their lives. But few historians, and I include myself again, have actually relied exclusively on oral sources. Time and time again, we have used documentary material to flesh out, contextualize, and even explain the words of our informants to provide a more reliable, representative, accurate history. I have, for example, argued that a 1940s prostitute's description of male violence does not so much describe male violence as boast that a clever woman could negotiate urban life. I still think I am right, based on what I know about Nairobi prostitution and that particular informant, but nevertheless, this kind of insight comes from contextualizing testimony rather than from "letting Africans speak for themselves."[2] Most historians of colonial Africa have seen the oral and the written as two different sources with which to support their arguments. Where oral and written accounts agreed, it was proof positive. Where oral and written sources contradicted each other, this was not a problem to be resolved; instead, it proved that Africans and colonialists had vastly different opinions and memories. But simply by including the "African voice"—a term still used without irony—historians could claim that their work represented Africans' views of their experiences, even when, as was so often the case, those voices were placed in a narrative derived from colonial documents and shaped by the author's mediation.

How accurate a history, even a history of vampires, can emerge from a combination of African and colonialist voices? Doesn't the power and

2. Luise White, *The Comforts of Home: Prostitution in Colonial Nairobi* (Chicago: University of Chicago Press, 1990), 21–28, 200; Susan Geiger, *TANU Women: Gender, Culture and the Making of Tanganyikan Nationalism* (Portsmouth, N.H.: Heinemann, 1997); and Belinda Bozzoli with the assistance of Mmantho Nkotsoe, *Women of Phokeng: Consciousness, Life Strategy, and Migrancy in South Africa* (Portsmouth, N.H.: Heinemann, 1991); but see also Margaret Strobel and Sarah Mirzah, *Three Swahili Women: Life Histories from Mombasa, Kenya* (Bloomington: Indiana University Press, 1989), and Jean Davison and the Women of Mutira, *Voices from Mutira: Lives of Rural Gikuyu Women* (Boulder, Colo.: Lynne Rienner, 1989).

authority of European words invade every aspect of speech and narration? In recent years there have been a few striking colonial histories that have mediated different voices. The roughest edges of cultural contact—with Christian Maroons, for example, or black South African women in secondary schools—have been described with great power by articulating the differences between voices.[3] But separate voices make for separate pasts, each perhaps more self-contained and reified than may have been the case in actuality. Even the most effectively controlled colonial terrain was too contested, and too compromised, to allow for the disembedding of any clear "voice," colonized or colonizing. Indeed, the process of disembedding obscures the way in which voices reinvented themselves and borrowed words and images from the world around them even as it changed.[4] Ann Stoler has argued that in colonial history, the issue is not the separate voices, but the fragmentation and exclusion with which voices are generated. "We are not only piecing together fragmented stories but working from a cultural landscape in which our 'best sources' were dependent on a range of verbal and visual evidence that tapped different kinds of knowledge."[5] This chapter argues that the differences between the voices may not require rigid segregation: the voices I cite share intense ideas about the same tools and technologies. It is my goal to "listen" to these voices as different kinds of storytelling, to get them to speak about each other to tell stories about colonialism.

This chapter is not so much about comparing oral and written sources as it is about reading both sets of sources as genres. Genre does not have an either/or status but is a strategy of writing and speaking—someone goes in and out of genre to recollect, to comment, to get a point across. In the case of colonial medicine, genre is a particularly useful concept, because it accesses all the fantasies, paraphernalia, and tech-

---

3. Shula Marks, ed., "Not Either an Experimental Doll": The Separate Worlds of Three South African Women (Bloomington: Indiana University Press, 1988); Richard Price, Alabi's World (Baltimore: Johns Hopkins University Press, 1990); see also David William Cohen and Atieno Odhiambo, Burying SM: The Politics of Knowledge and the Sociology of Power in Africa (Portsmouth, N.H.: Heinemann, 1992).

4. Dipesh Chakrabarty, "Postcoloniality and the Artifice of History; Who Speaks for 'Indian' Pasts?" Representations 37 (1992): 14–19; Christopher A. Waterman, "'Our Tradition Is a Very Modern Tradition': Popular Music and the Construction of Pan-Yoruba Identity," Ethnomusicology 34, 3 (1990): 367–79; Corinne A. Kratz, "'We've Always Done It Like This': 'Tradition' and 'Innovation' in Okiek Ceremonies," Comp. Studies in Soc. and History 35, 1 (1993): 30–65.

5. Ann Laura Stoler, "'In Cold Blood': Hierarchies of Credibility and the Politics of Colonial Narratives," Representations 37 (1992): 182.

nologies with which medical power was presented and represented. Talk of vampire stories in fact often cued talk of drugs and needles.[6] The description of Western biomedicine contained in vampire accusations is substantially different from that found in doctors' and nurses' published words on the same subject, of course. What is important is that the domains of difference are the same: on the subjects of injections, anesthesia, and hospitals, Africans and medical writers both had strong opinions, but those opinions diverged totally. To use both sets of narratives to produce two narratives, or contending visions, would ignore all the ways in which the subjects of these narratives were the same. Besides, this evidence cannot be separated into discrete units; the oral invades the written too much for that. Instead, I want to suggest that they refract, that they provide ways in which to read each other, and that the formulas and the fantasies in each are in fact representations of the nature of medical care, curative therapies, and control. In both oral and written sources, the voices I quote are not presented as contextualized testimony, but as genres, formulaic stories structured by set elements and conventions. If I were to assert the authority and authenticity of the voice in this essay, I would obscure the phrases, images, attitudes, and even memories that are formulaic, that, however true and however reconstructed, are recounted as genre.

WESTERN WRITING AND WESTERN MEDICINE

The historiography of colonial medicine has changed enormously in the past twenty years. After the triumphalist narrative of the progress of

6. Elizabeth Tonkin, *Narrating Our Pasts: The Social Construction of Oral History* (Cambridge: Cambridge University Press, 1992), 50–55. By "cueing" neither Tonkin nor I mean some Pavlovian response to our questions, but rather how certain conventions of narrative and modes of talk are occasioned by cues of style and form, a point made several years ago by Robin Law, "How Truly Traditional Is Our Traditional History? The Case of Samuel Johnson and the Recording of Yoruba Oral History," *History in Africa* 11 (1984): 180–202, esp. 195–199. Cueing problematizes recent debates about the politics of interviewing; see e.g., Renato Rosaldo, "From the Door of His Tent: The Fieldworker and the Inquisitor," in James Clifford and George Marcus, eds., *Writing Culture: The Poetics and Politics of Ethnography* (Berkeley and Los Angeles: University of California Press, 1986), 77–97, Marjorie Mbilinyi, "'I'd Have Been a Man': Politics and the Labor Process in Producing Personal Narratives," in Personal Narratives Group, ed., *Interpreting Women's Lives: Feminist Theory and Personal Narratives* (Bloomington: Indiana University Press, 1989), 204–27, Lyndal Roper, *Oedipus and the Devil: Sexuality and Religion in Early Modern Europe* (London: Routledge, 1994), 199–225; and Charles van Onselen, "The Reconstruction of a Rural Life from Oral Testimony: Critical Notes on the Methodology in the Study of a Black South African Sharecropper," *J. Peasant Studies* 20, 3 (1993): 494–514.

science gave way to that of humanitarianism hindered by budgetary
constraints, colonial medical care was resoundingly condemned as an
agent of imperialism: "Apologists for colonial regimes often look my-
opically at the medical services, proclaim their humanity, and even argue that their philosophy ran counter to that of imperialism," Meredeth
Turshen writes.[7] Once medicine was seen as part of the imperial arsenal,
there were enough official statements to demonstrate that doctors were
thought to have the skills that could win the hearts and minds of subject
populations.[8] But authors writing within the medical narrative or about
it have tended, as Megan Vaughan has pointed out, to make colonial
medical history the history of colonial ideas.[9] Those writing outside of
the medical narrative, most notably John Iliffe in his study of East African doctors, have located the history of the medical profession firmly in
the colonial situation and the finances available to colonial and postcolonial states.[10] When these authors conceived of African resistance to
the drugs and needles of colonial practice, they assumed it took place
away from the clinic: "When the colonized escapes the doctor, and the
integrity of his body is preserved, he considers himself the victor by a
handsome margin," wrote Fanon.[11] Such a separation of contentious
Africans from hegemony-inducing doctors was more discursive than
anything else: when the doctor was scripted as a spokesman for empire,
he or she was not in the examination room, the operating theater, or
the laboratory.[12] Nurses, whether white women or African men, never
received the same attention: they are described neither as full-fledged
imperialists nor as devoted caregivers, as if their struggles for status
within the medical profession and within hospital regimes overshad-

7. Meredeth Turshen, *The Political Ecology of Disease in Tanzania* (New Brunswick,
N.J.: Rutgers University Press, 1984), 5; for triumphalism rampant, see Oliver Ransford,
"Bid the Sickness Cease": Disease in the History of Black Africa (London: J. Murray,
1983); on financial constraints inhibiting triumphs, see Ann Beck, *A History of British
Medical Administration in East Africa, 1900–1950* (Cambridge, Mass.: Harvard University Press, 1970), and Michael Warboys, "Science and British Colonial Imperialism,
1895–1940" (Ph.D. diss., Sussex University, 1979), ch. 2.
8. See Lyons, "Power to Heal," 202–3.
9. Megan Vaughan, "Healing and Curing: Issues in the Social History and Anthropology of Medicine in Africa," *Social History of Medicine* 7, 2 (1994): 283–95.
10. John Iliffe, *East African Doctors: A History of the Modern Profession* (Cambridge: Cambridge University Press, 1998).
11. Frantz Fanon, "Medicine and Colonization," in *Studies in a Dying Colonialism*
(New York: Grove Press, 1965), 121–45; see also Vaughan, *Curing Their Ills.*
12. But see Warwick Anderson, "'Where Every Prospect Pleases and Only Man Is
Vile': Laboratory Medicine as Colonial Discourse," *Critical Inquiry* 18 (1992): 506–28;
and my "'They Could Make their Victims Dull:' Genres and Genres, Fantasies and Cures
in Colonial Southern Uganda," *Am. Hist. Rev.* 100, 5 (1995): 1379–1402.

owed their location in the colonial project.[13] Yet in their writings, mission nurses present themselves as vulnerable to African ideas about health. They were placed in village dispensaries, where they were argued with as often as they were ignored. What made them different from the doctors who supervised them was that they published accounts of these conversations.

What happens to the history of colonial medicine when the doctor is seen in the examination room and the nurse observed dispensing drugs and ointments? The power and authority of European practitioners fractures in such encounters. Early colonial medication was as much a novelty as it was a benefit, and accounts of Africans demanding injections or tablets argue for a popularity of medication that was far beyond any embodied needs. A missionary wrote of "roaring, screaming" crowds "with noses gone, faces eaten by syphilis" demanding treatment from traveling injection clinics in the Belgian Congo in 1929,[14] but the founder of the Church Missionary Society medical mission in Uganda, A. R. Cook, observed something else in the crowds that gathered whenever he visited a rural area. "Many of course were merely drawn by curiosity, and had nothing the matter with them." They would not believe him if he told them they were well; indeed, if they were not given medicine "they would put it down to spite. . . . We consoled ourselves that they would be gradually educated up to the truth" and prepared a strong solution of liquid ammonia, and "let them have a good sniff. . . . With tears streaming down their faces, and with grateful hearts, they retired to make room for others." Powerful vapors, Cook reckoned, were considered powerful medicines; these fumes would make Africans realize "that the white man's medicine was a thing to be treated with respect."[15]

13. Carol Summers, "Intimate Colonialism: The Imperial Production of Reproduction in Uganda, 1907–1925," *Signs: J. of Women in Culture and Society* 16 (1991): 787–807; Nancy Rose Hunt, "Negotiated Colonialism: Domesticity, Hygiene and Birth Work in the Belgian Congo" (Ph.D. diss., University of Wisconsin–Madison, 1992), passim, and "Colonial Fairy Tales and the Knife and Fork Doctrine in the Heart of Africa," in Karen Tranberg Hansen, ed., *African Encounters with Domesticity* (New Brunswick, N.J.: Rutgers University Press, 1992), 143–66; Dea Birkett, "The 'White Woman's Burden' in 'The White Man's Grave': The Introduction of British Nurses in Colonial West Africa," in Nupur Chaudhuri and Margaret Strobel, eds., *Western Women and Imperialism: Complicity and Resistance* (Bloomington: University of Indiana Press, 1992), 177–88; Shula Marks, *Divided Sisterhood: The South African Nursing Profession and the Making of Apartheid* (Johannesburg: University of Witwatersrand Press, 1995).

14. Quoted in Lyons, "Power to Heal," 209.

15. Sir Albert R. Cook, *Uganda Memories (1887–1940)* (Kampala: Uganda Society, 1945), 93.

But in early colonial Africa, at least, the white man's medicine did not seem worthy of respect or even careful investigation. Africans brought their own epistemologies of causation and cure to European clinics. Ugandans, for example, doubted the efficacy of quinine tablets: "It is a little hard for them to believe a tiny pill can do them good, when they are accustomed to remedies by the pailful and are confident that the more fat they rub on their bodies the quicker will be the cure. So there really is some excuse for our black brothers and sisters." [16] Dispensary patients routinely took three days' supply of tablets at once, put ointments on body parts for which they were not intended, and argued with every nurse who offered a cure that made no sense to them. "My sickness is in my feet and . . . my wisdom tells me there is no profit in drinking medicine, but only by rubbing the mixture upon my feet can I be cured." [17] Even when ointments and tablets had meaning because they were dispensed by the skilled white doctor or nurse, that meaning was almost never the same as missionaries intended. Africans drank skin lotions and refused to return the bottles in which they came, and nurses complained that the pills they dispensed were thought of "more as charms than as physics or liniments." [18]

Even Western medicine's power to label and diagnose disease had little meaning in the first years of the encounter between Africans and Western medical expertise. In Northern Rhodesia, Africans all but mocked European treatments of sleeping sickness. [19] According to a nun in early colonial Uganda, diagnosis was "not easy. A patient will tell me 'The spirit of my ancestor kills me,' or another 'The skull keeps me from sleeping,' or 'The aches run all round me.' It needs much patience to sort out what is relevant." [20] If doctors were less patient, they were more circumspect. Privately, A. R. Cook found African ideas about illness "exceedingly exasperating" and wrote in his diary about the kind of dialogue that went on "with irritating frequency in the consulting room":

16. Kate Timpson, "Patients and Nurse at Mengo," *Mercy and Truth* 3, 36 (December 1899): 289–90.

17. Ibid.; Diane Zeller, "The Establishment of Western Medicine in Buganda" (Ph.D. diss., Columbia University, 1972), 221 ff.; 380–84.

18. Cook, *Uganda Memories,* 124; Kate Timpson, "Notes from a Nurse in Uganda," *Mercy and Truth* 3, 34 (October 1899): 245–46; see also Zeller, "Establishment of Western Medicine," 80–82, 307–8.

19. Allan Kinghorn, "Human Trypanosomiasis in the Luangwa Valley, Northern Rhodesia," *Annals of Trop. Med. and Parasitology* 19, 3 (1925): 281–300.

20. Sister M. Louis, *Love Is the Answer (The Story of Mother Kevin)* (Paterson, N.J.: Saint Anthony's Guild, 1964), 61.

DOCTOR: What is the matter with you?
PATIENT: My name is so and so.
DOCTOR: Yes, but what is your disease?
PATIENT: I want medicine to drink.
DOCTOR: Where do you hurt?
PATIENT: I don't want medicine to swallow, but to drink,
DOCTOR (sternly): WHAT IS YOUR ILLNESS?
PATIENT: Oh it goes all over me, it cries out "Ka, ka." Will you listen to the top of my head with your hearing machine (stethoscope), etc. etc.?[21]

It is difficult to read these exchanges and think that Africans came to European doctors for what we call "cures." When Africans were cured, treatment was conducted in local etiologies. Africans often came to Cook, for example, complaining of a rumbling sound in their ears. "Being now tired of explaining that this is often due to a diseased condition of the blood—for they universally put it down to insects having crawled into the ear—I now prescribe the appropriate treatment, telling them that the medicine is to kill the insects."[22] When treatments were prolonged, Africans literally unpacked their content. In early colonial Uganda, a nun had to keep careful watch on patients with skin ulcers, "otherwise well-meaning villagers, who do not approve of my remedies, will pack the clean wound with river mud or worse!"[23] Indeed, African visits to clinics may have had little to do with the quantity and quality of African suffering that missionaries wrote about daily, but with the ways in which objects and techniques of European biomedicine had become translated into African healing practices. Ointments, stethoscope, and pills may have been objects translated and substituted into local beliefs, made powerful not by their novelty or strength but because of the difficult journeys required to obtain them.[24]

21. Cook, *Uganda Memories,* 122–23, quoting his diary from 1900.
22. Ibid., 124.
23. Louis, *Love Is the Answer,* 71.
24. Terence O. Ranger, "Godly Medicine: The Ambiguities of Mission Medicine in Southeast Tanzania, 1900–1945," *Social Science and Medicine* 15B (1981): 265; Paul S. Landau, "Explaining Surgical Evangelism in Colonial Southern Africa: Teeth, Pain and Faith," *J. Afr. History* 37 (1996): 261–81; Vaughan, *Curing Their Ills,* 56–60. According to A. J. Evans, "The Ila V.D. Campaign," *Rhodes-Livingstone Journal* 9 (1944): 39–46, for example, the Ila "happily" received treatment for syphilis in wartime Northern Rhodesia. Ila came "out of the grass shelter and announce that they are 'on treatment,' each such announcement being greeted by cheers and laughter from their assembled friends awaiting their turn for examination."

Colonial medicine was configured as curative: Africans were to seek out doctors and drugs for specific conditions. By the 1920s, government-sponsored medical care in East and Central Africa was modeled on that of medical missions, with a central hospital for the seriously ill staffed by European doctors and nurses and satellite dispensaries run by African dressers who could treat wounds and minor ailments.[25] Dressers' qualifications were questioned by doctors everywhere. In Northern Rhodesia, for example, doctors demanded well-trained medical orderlies to give first aid—"The treatment of tropical sores requires both knowledge and skill, otherwise expenditure in dressings is useless"—but did not want them to perform the lumbar punctures necessary to diagnose advanced sleeping sickness. In the Belgian Congo, officials were said to give the job to "the first black who comes along," who then could not calculate dosages.[26] Yet the medicines dispensed in clinics was never fully under nurses' and dressers' control. In Kenya and Uganda, dressers were said to give whatever treatment Africans requested.[27] Well into the 1930s, mission nurses still reported that patients walked miles to a dispensary but refused treatment for "some obvious and serious condition, if it is not the particular part of the body that he wishes to bring to our notice," or rejected one kind of tablet because "I want the pink."[28] Government doctors were no less pained: in 1934, the director of medical services complained that Africans thought "Dispensaries were like shops where a man can ask for anything he likes."[29]

Demands for pink tablets or for stethoscopes on the head may not have been due to Africans' confusion over Western medicine or their

25. Marc H. Dawson, "The 1920s Anti-Yaws Campaigns and Colonial Medical Policy in Kenya," *Int. J. Afr. Hist. Studies* 20, 3 (1987): 423–24; Lyons, "Power to Heal," 109–10; Summers, "Intimate Colonialism."

26. P. H. Ward, director of medical and sanitary services, to chief secretary, Livingstone, 6 July 1932 (National Archives of Zambia [henceforth cited as NAZ], SEC2/813, Luwingu Tour Reports, 1931–32); director of medical and sanitary services, Livingstone, to chief secretary, Livingstone, 11 October 1934 (NAZ, SEC2/2/525, Tsetse Fly Control, 1932–36); Lyons, "Power to Heal," 209–10.

27. K. Ardell, "In Teso Country," *Mission Hospital* 31, 350 (1927): 62; A. T. Schofield, "Some Patients at Toro," *Mission Hospital* 31, 353 (1927): 138; Zeller, "Establishment of Western Medicine," 323–26; Dawson, "1920s Anti-Yaws Campaigns," 428.

28. Ardell, "In Teso Country"; D. A. Brewster, "A Day at the Dispensary at Ng'ora," *Mission Hospital* 36, 411 (1932): 90. These demands probably did not stop in the 1930s, but African dispensers did not write about them; see Simon Semkubuge, "The Work of an African Medical Officer," *Uganda Teachers Journal* 1 (1939): 99–101, and Lyons, "Power to Heal."

29. Quoted in Zeller, "Establishment of Western Medicine," 325.

mystification of the efficacy of various procedures. Medical anthropologists have argued that Africans chose treatments, tablets, and the placement of stethoscopes, because of their own etiologies of disease. Illnesses believed to be caused by excessive cold might best be treated by pills that were hot in color, like red or pink. These reinterpretations were debates about the nature of curing itself and reflected divergent ideas about sickness, health, and healing that did not readily conform to the dichotomies between Western and African medicine, both of which changed rapidly in the twentieth century.[30] Africans who swallowed three days' supply of tablets at once may not have misunderstood a nurse's instructions, but may have considered those instructions to be a misguided and inappropriate way to deal with disease and pain.

Africans also reinterpreted medical therapies because of how they were applied: much African curing took place above the skin. Healers used procedures of scratching the skin to produce blisters, let blood with cupping horns, and realigned broken bones. They cured many ailments by removing the alien matter introduced by supernatural means.[31] By the early 1930s, most African healing and harming took place above the skin. Sorcerers spread disease by medicines smeared on a practitioner's palm, fed to the victim, or blown with smoke from a pipe.[32]

In such a world, the ability of Western medical techniques to penetrate the skin—with injections or scalpels—seems to have had profound and contradictory meanings for Africans. Those procedures were as feared as they were welcomed. Nevertheless, injections were said to have been fully assimilated into African therapeutics: any amount of popular and professional literature about the continent proclaims injections to be the cure of choice. Whether or not this is true, or how long this has been true, or where it has been true, is something else again. Several scholars have found a wide variety of opinions about the desirability

---

30. Clark E. Cunningham, "Thai 'Injection Doctors': Antibiotic Mediators," *Social Science and Medicine* 4, 1 (1970): 1–24; Caroline H. Bledsoe and Monica F. Goubard, "The Reinterpretation of Western Pharmaceutical among the Mende of Sierra Leone," *Social Science and Medicine* 21, 3 (1985): 275–82; J.-M. Michel, "Why Do People Like Medicines? A Perspective from Africa," *Lancet* 210, 1 (1985): 210–11; Vaughan, "Healing and Curing"; Landau, "Explaining Surgical Evangelism."

31. John Roscoe, *The Baganda: An Account of Their Customs and Beliefs* (London: Macmillan, 1911), 98–101; Zeller, "Establishment of Western Medicine," 112–16; N. C. Roles, "Tribal Surgery in East Africa during the Nineteenth Century, Part 2—Therapeutic Surgery," *East Afr. Med. J.* 44, 1 (1967): 20–32, at 22.

32. L. P. Mair, *An African People in the Twentieth Century* (London: Routledge and Sons, 1934), 250.

of injections within specific areas.[33] I have argued elsewhere that injections remained so unnatural in African healing practices that they took
on topical and different meanings throughout this century.[34] Moreover,
there is some evidence that injections were preferred by clinic workers
themselves.[35] It allowed them to administer correct dosages and spared
them the demands for pink pills and stethoscopes on the head.

In the 1920s, however, the popularity of injections astonished missionary and government authors. Many scholars have argued that the
development of drugs (including the arsenic-derived Salvarsan, or "606,"
and neo-Salvarsan) for the treatment of syphilis and yaws that made injections so desired: even an incomplete course of treatment could cure
external symptoms, particularly sores.[36] Mission doctors in the 1920s
saw in Salvarsan their power to transform the African body: "Now en-
ters the doctor and the intra-muscular injection of 606 is given. Within
48 hours the change begins," wrote Cook. "To see a man admitted, his
whole body a loathsome mass of foul sores . . . and to see the same man
two or three weeks later, after one or two injections of '606', so happily
changed that his relatives hardly know him, is to behold . . . a modern
miracle."[37] In Stanleyville in the Belgian Congo, missionaries said that
it was "like magic."[38] Missionaries in Kenya and Tanganyika all noted
a new demand for injections. Prior to Salvarsan, said one, Africans
would flee hospitals rather than submit to an injection; now they
willingly paid what missionaries charged for it.[39] But as Terence Ranger
points out, the long lines of Africans seeking yaws treatment from mis-

33. "Dawa ya Sindano," *East Afr. Med. J.* 28, 11 (1951): 476; Ranger, "Godly Medi-
cine," 264–68; Maryinez Lyons, *The Colonial Disease: Sleeping Sickness and the Social
History of Zaire, 1890–1939*. Cambridge: Cambridge University Press, 1992, 188–90;
Barbara A. Bianco, "The Historical Anthropology of a Mission Hospital in Northwestern
Kenya" (Ph.D. diss., New York University, 1992), 167–78; Megan Vaughan, "Health and
Hegemony: Representation of Disease and the Creation of a Colonial Subject in Nyasa-
land," in Dagmar Engels and Shula Marks, eds., *Contesting Colonial Hegemony: State
and Society in India and Africa* (London: I. B. Taurus, 1994), 173–201.

34. Luise White, "The Needle and the State, or, The Making of Unnational Sovereignty" (paper presented to workshop on Immunization and the State, Delhi, India, 16–
17 January 1997).

35. Zeller, "Establishment of Western Medicine," 308 ff.

36. Ibid., 325 ff.; Dawson, "1920s Anti-Yaws Campaigns," 417–35; Ranger, "Godly
Medicine," 265; Lyons, "Power to Heal," 212–14.

37. Cook, *Uganda Memories,* 52.

38. Quoted in Hunt, "Negotiated Colonialism," 258.

39. R. A. B. Leakey, "At Work in Toro Hospital," *Mission Hospital,* 33 (1929): 153;
Hunt, "Negotiated Colonialism," 258; Lyons, "Power to Heal," 218–19; Dawson,
"1920s Anti-Yaws Campaigns," 228–29.

sion hospitals "resembled nothing so much as indigenous healing cults."[40] Outside of mission hospitals with lucrative private practices, however, Salvarsan was too expensive to administer on a massive scale to African subjects. It required intravenous injections, which few officials and fewer doctors thought African dressers could do without constant supervision. The development of a bismuth compound, produced in Nairobi, reduced the cost of yaws treatment by over 700 percent. Bismuth salts were injected into the muscle, so that relatively unskilled medical personnel, such as African dressers, could administer the drug.[41] Outside of mission hospitals, however, Africans problematized the course of injections far more than mission doctors did. In 1922, for example, young men in Uganda opposed the prolonged course of treatment, claiming that each injection contained\weak medicine. In 1926, officials at the government hospital noted that many Africans went from clinic to clinic in the hopes of getting oral medication but received intravenous injections instead.[42]

As a curative practice, however, injections were at once strange and familiar. Many African healing practices were no less sophisticated: a young medical missionary had observed a Caesarian section in southern Uganda in 1879, where healers also routinely restored protruding bowels, a common injury of war. Healers in Kenya and Northern Rhodesia used drugs and manual manipulation as abortifacients.[43] In the kingdoms of southern Uganda and the northern province of Northern Rho-

40. Ranger, "Godly Medicine," 265. See also H. R. A. Philip, Tumutumu Hospital Annual Report (1924), quoted in John Wilkinson, "The Origin of Infectious Disease in East Africa, with Special Reference to the Kikuyu People," *East Afr. Med. J.* 34, 10 (1957): 550. The question of the importance of where injections took place requires further investigation. In Northern Rhodesia in 1930, Africans were eager for intravenous injections that could cure sleeping sickness, but refused transport to hospitals to get them. See J. F. Gilkes, medical officer, "Report on Sleeping Sickness in the Lower End of the Luangwa Valley and Along the New and Old Great East Roads (July–August 1930)" (NAZ, SEC3/523/1, Trypanosomiasis, Sleeping Sickness in Northern Rhodesia—Luangwa Valley, 1929–30).

41. Dawson, "1920s Anti-Yaws Campaigns," 427–28. Cook's private practice—presumably like that of other mission doctors—was a major source of revenue for his mission's hospital; see Minutes of Medical Committee, 23 November 1933, Church Missionary Society Archives, University Library, University of Birmingham.

42. Zeller, "Establishment of Western Medicine," 321–27.

43. J. N. P. Davies, "The Development of 'Scientific' Medicine in the African Kingdom of Bunyoro-Kitara," *Medical History* 3, 1 (1959): 47–57. For abortionists in eastern Kenya, see Lynn M. Thomas, "Regulating Reproduction: Men, Women and the State in Kenya, 1920–1970" (Ph.D. diss., University of Michigan, 1997); in Zambia, see Bryan T. Callahan, "'Veni, VD, Vici'? Reassessing the Ila Syphilis Epidemic, 1900–1963," *J. Southern Afr. Studies* 23, 3 (1997): 421–40.

desia, practitioners attached to the royal family carried out the mutilations that were fairly common punishments for adultery, theft, and royal
disfavor.[44] Most, if not all, African peoples had practiced some form of
variolation—vaccination by scratching the skin and introducing diseased matter—both against smallpox and against what was thought by
early Western observers to be venereal syphilis but was in all likelihood
endemic syphilis or yaws.[45] In Uganda, the British were horrified to
learn that children were wrapped in bark cloth smeared with syphilitic
discharges. They blamed the epidemic that was said to infect 90 percent
of the population on this practice.[46] In smallpox variolation, the pox
was pricked with a thorn, saved on a plantain leaf and then rubbed into
the scratched area of a healthy person's arm.[47] This practice conferred
as much immunity as any vaccine therapy did in the early twentieth century. Nevertheless, early medical observers tended to ignore variolation
wherever they found evidence for its efficacy.[48] Cook's diaries present

44. Roscoe, *The Baganda,* 12, 281, 358. Adulterers lost an eye, thieves a hand; when
the king broke the foot of a tardy messenger, he often sent him to a healer to make a splint
for the bone. Bemba surgeons removed lips and noses as punishments; as late as 1930,
Audrey Richards saw the Bemba paramount chief's mutilated victims (Audrey Richards
Papers, LSE, book 2, 20 June 1930). See also A. L. Epstein, "Response to Social Crisis:
Aspects of Oral Aggression in Central Africa," *Scenes from African Urban Life* (Edinburgh: Edinburgh University Press, 1992), 166–68.

45. Roscoe, *The Baganda,* 102–3; J. N. P. Davies, "The History of Syphilis in
Uganda," *Bull. World Health Org.* 15 (1956): 1041–55, and "The Development of
'Scientific' Medicine in the African Kingdom of Bunyoro-Kitara," *Medical History* 3, 1
(1959): 47–57, at 53–54; see also Gloria Waite, "Public Health in Pre-Colonial East Central Africa," *Social Science and Medicine* 24, 3 (1987): 197–208. Yaws and syphilis are
both caused by trypanosomes, but Marc Dawson, "1920s Anti-Yaws Campaigns," 417–
35, has argued that the distinction between syphilis and yaws is not really the issue, since
the diseases provide a cross-immunity to each other. Thus anti-yaws measures increased
the incidence of syphilis by removing the immunity yaws conferred.

46. F. J. Lambkin, "An Outbreak of Syphilis in a Virgin Soil: Notes on Syphilis in the
Uganda Protectorate," in D'Arcy Power and J. Keogh Murphy, eds., *A System of Syphilis*
(London: Oxford University Press, 1914), 2: 339–54. It is noteworthy that syphilis was
blamed on indigenous medical practices, contrary to elite men's assertions that the epidemic
was the inevitable result of the emancipation of women; see Summers, "Intimate Colonialism," 787–807, and Megan Vaughan, "Syphilis in Colonial East and Central Africa:
The Social Construction of an Epidemic," in T. Ranger and P. Slack, eds., *Epidemics and
Ideas: Essays on the Historical Perception of Pestilence* (Cambridge: Cambridge University Press, 1992), 269–302.

47. Roles, "Tribal Surgery in East Africa during the Nineteenth Century," 28–29;
Davies, "Scientific Medicine," 53; Roscoe, *The Baganda,* 102–3.

48. Ronald Frankenberg and Joyce Leeson, "Disease, Illness and Sickness: Social Aspects of the choice of Healer in a Lusaka Suburb," in J. B. Loudon, ed., *Social Anthropology of Medicine* (London: Academic Press, 1976), 233–37; L. S. B. Leakey, *The Southern Kikuyu before 1903* (New York: Academic Press, 1977), 3: 889–91. I am grateful to
Charles Ambler for this reference.

the most dramatic case of observing African variolation and reinscribing it with all the violence scientific method required. During a smallpox epidemic in 1899, he and his wife drew lymph from two locally variolated Africans and eventually vaccinated perhaps 800 by the arm-to-arm method, noting only surprise at how few failures there were, "as indeed might have been surmised in an unprotected population. In their eagerness, they almost stormed the dispensary to get in."[49] Storming the dispensary can have many meanings, however. Throughout East Africa, officials noted that the communities with the most widespread variolation were those most resistant to smallpox vaccination campaigns, without drawing any inference as to why.[50] But they also noted that Africans chose which vaccinations and injections they wanted. A few weeks after healthy Africans demanded injections of Salvarsan in Uganda, for example, they rioted in opposition to plague vaccine.[51] Africans resisted vaccination campaigns in Uganda in the 1930s with a specialized needle lore. In 1936, it was said that inoculations caused leprosy because the medical officer of health used the same syringe on all patients. Some people were said to scratch their arms to give the appearance of vaccination, to fool authorities. Others rubbed the vaccination with lemon juice, dust, and other substances to prevent characteristic blisters from forming. Some claimed that inoculations made their arms sore or septic.[52] In the wartime Belgian Congo, there were barracks revolts centered around vaccination.[53] Such stories do not undermine the ways in

49. Cook, *Uganda Memories,* 52.

50. Eugenia W. Herbert, "Smallpox Inoculation in Africa," *J. Afr. Hist.* 16, 4 (1975): 539–59; Marc H. Dawson, "Socioeconomic Change and Disease: Smallpox in Colonial Kenya, 1880–1920," in Steven Feierman and John Janzen, eds., *The Social Basis of Health and Healing in Africa* (Berkeley and Los Angeles: University of California Press, 1992), 90–103; Zeller, "Establishment of Western Medicine."

51. In 1929 a European sanitation officer lost a hand, and letters were sent to the kingdom's parliament threatening to kill the king's ministers in a struggle over plague inoculations in Buganda (letter from Archdeacon G. S. Daniell, acting secretary, Church Missionary Society, to H. D. Hooper, CMS secretary, London, 23 July 1929, Church Missionary Society Archives, University Library, University of Birmingham).

52. Zeller, "Establishment of Western Medicine," 325, 339, 347n; see also Vaughan, "Health and Hegemony," for complaints about inactive vaccines, 185–86. Elsewhere in colonial Africa, vaccines were reinterpreted; see I. R. Phimister, "The 'Spanish' Influenza Pandemic of 1918 and Its Impact on the Southern Rhodesian Mining Industry," *Central Afr. J. of Medicine* 19, 7 (1973): 147.

53. Bruce Fetter, "The Lualabourg Revolt at Elisabethville," *Afr. Hist. Stud.* 2, 2 (1969): 273; J.-L. Vellut, "Le Katanga industriel en 1944: Malaises et anxiétés dans la société coloniale," in *Le Congo belge durant la Seconde Guerre mondiale* [= *Bijdragen over Belgisch-Congo tijdens de Tweede Wereldoorlog*] (Brussels: Académie royale des sciences d'outre-mer, 1983), 493–556.

which Africans assimilated European healing technologies into their own wide range of curative procedures, of course.[54] They simply re-state—in the strongest possible terms—the context in which cultural and biomedical contact took place.

Besides, that contact was made fantastic by doctors themselves. When medical missionaries introduced anesthesia, they promoted it as one of the great wonders of Western science. Even in their earliest writings, anesthesia had a fantastic quality, producing an imagined African subjectivity of awe and trust whatever the evidence. "We have no diffi-culty getting them to take chloroform," wrote CMS medical missionar-ies in 1898. When a woman was late for her operation, a nurse "found her hidden among the plantain trees praying." [55] Kings who had ordered mutilations of their subjects were among the most responsive to anes-thesia. When the CMS went to the royal court of Butoro, in southwest-ern Uganda, they spoke of the "special kind of medicine" that would "send them to sleep" without pain "while we 'cut them up,' as they term it." The king "insisted" on an operation with chloroform for himself, even though he had only an abscess on his arm. Soon "it spread over the whole country that the king had been the first to venture to take this new medicine which made him go to sleep, and the patients came to us ask-ing to be operated upon from all around the country." [56] Anesthesia might be seen to straddle African and European curative therapies: it was both inhaled and promoted cutting below the skin. For this reason, perhaps, in many parts of Africa, anesthesia was accepted without the master narrative of the good medicine and the good king and the docile kingdom, despite some horrifying descriptions of how it worked. In the

54. This question has been debated in John Janzen and William Akinstall, *The Quest for Therapy in Lower Zaire* (Berkeley and Los Angeles: University of California Press, 1978); Steven Feierman, "Change in African Therapeutic Systems," *Social Science and Medicine* 13B (1979): 277–84; Gwyn Prins, "But What Was the Disease? The Present State of Health and Healing in African Studies," *Past and Present* 124 (1989): 150–79; Jean Comaroff, "Bodily Reform as Historical Practice: The Semantics of Resistance in Modern South Africa," *Int. J. of Psychology* 20 (1985): 541–67; Mark Auslander, "'Open the Wombs!' The Symbolic Politics of Modern Ngoni Witchfinding," in Jean Comaroff and John L. Comaroff, eds., *Modernity and Its Malcontents: Ritual and Power in Postcolonial Africa* (Chicago: University of Chicago Press, 1993), 167–92; Megan Vaughan, "Healing and Curing: Issues in the Social History and Anthropology of Medi-cine in Africa," *Social History of Medicine* 7, 2 (1994): 283–95.

55. Katherine Timpson and A. R. Cook, "Mengo Hospital," *Mercy and Truth* 2, 13 (January 1898): 12.

56. Dr. A. Bond, "A Record of Medical Work at Toro," *Mercy and Truth* 11, 129 (September 1907): 274. Over the next few years, the king of Toro was keen to watch op-erations; see Vaughan, *Curing Their Ills*, 58.

Belgian Congo in the 1920s, a medical missionary instructed her assistant to explain to a chief how she would remove his ulcerated cataracts: "You will smell some cold medicine until you are quite dead . . . then she will cut the eye out, and when all the cutting is finished, she will bring you back to life again." This did not scare him, wrote the missionary, since he scheduled his surgery the next day.[57] But as with injections, government doctors told a different story. In Northern Rhodesia in 1932, officials saw little improvement in the "native prejudice against surgical operations" they had struggled against for years. "It is presumed that the DC expressed disapproval of the stupidity of the persons concerned and explained how medical treatment would benefit them."[58]

AFRICAN SPEAKING AND WESTERN MEDICINE

Throughout East and Central Africa, vampire stories and blood accusations had intensely medical meanings. Many believed that human blood was used as medicine. Whatever its Persian roots and its use in nineteenth-century Zanzibar, the word *mumiani* in modern Swahili meant a kind of medicine used externally for broken bones or cramp, or melted and drunk.[59] In Tanganyika in the 1950s, it was believed that African blood was taken to urban hospitals and there "converted into red capsules. These pills were taken on a regular basis by Europeans who . . . needed these potations to stay alive in Africa."[60] In colonial Northern Rhodesia, it was believed that African blood was necessary to cure European diseases. The illness of any well-known European, particularly the long illness of King George V in 1929, was said to be enough to spark local panics.[61] In 1932, banyama were said to "drain the victim's blood, and by making an incision behind the ear, extract a certain portion of the brain. The body is left in the bush, and the blood and brain forwarded to the Medical Department to be used as medicines in hospitals and dispensaries."[62] In Kenya, it was thought that men were taken

57. Janet Miller, *Jungles Preferred* (Boston: Houghton Mifflin, 1931), 95.
58. J. Moffatt Thomas, secretary for native affairs, Livingstone, to chief secretary, Livingstone, 4 April 1932 (NAZ, SEC2/785, Kasama Tour Reports, 1931–32).
59. "Asiyesadiki" ("Nonbeliever"), "Mumiani," *Mambo Leo*, August 1923, 4–5; E. C. Baker, "Mumiani," *Tanganyika Notes and Records* 21 (1946): 108–9.
60. W. Arens, *The Man-Eating Myth: Anthropology and Anthrophagy* (New York: Oxford University Press, 1979), 12.
61. W. V. Brelsford, "The 'Banyama' Myth," *NADA* 9, 4 (1967): 49.
62. D. Willis, provincial commissioner, Kasama, "Report on Banyama," 24 March 1931 (NAZ, ZA1/9/62/21).

by the Nairobi Fire Brigade so that their blood could be used for "the treatment of Europeans with anaemic diseases." [63] On the whole, people were vague about what was done with the blood: one man heard it was taken to America, "but I don't know what Americans did with that blood." [64] Another observed: "Whites never let out the secret of what they were doing with African blood. . . . I think the whites were using African blood to treat other Africans."

Q: But killing a person by sucking their blood in order to treat another person sounds strange. Why did they do that?
A: I don't know why the whites were doing that. [65]

Africans knew much more about how blood was extracted. In the early 1920s, in Nairobi, wazimamoto came into women's houses as they slept—"after all, these men looked like ordinary men"—carrying "a sort of sucking rubber tube that they would stick in your hands while you were asleep and draw the blood out of your body and leave you there, and eventually you would die." [66] A few years later, in the legal African settlement of Pumwani in Nairobi, a woman said that wazimamoto "used to come in the night, they would come into your room very softly and before you knew it they put something in your arm to draw out the blood, and then they would leave you and they would take your blood to the hospital and leave you for dead."

Q: Couldn't you scream for help?
A: They put bandages over your mouth, and also, these people who worked for the wazimamoto, they were skilled, so if they found you asleep they could take your blood so quietly that you would not wake up, in fact you would never wake up. [67]

A decade later, another Nairobi woman said "wazimamoto killed people, they cut their throats . . . and took the blood to people in the hospital." [68]

These accounts invert those cited in the previous section. Medical practitioners come to Africans, unannounced and unwelcomed, and do

63. H. K. Wachanga, *The Swords of Kirinyaga: The Fight for Land and Freedom*, ed. Robert Whittier (Nairobi: Kenya Literature Bureau, 1975), 9.
64. Ofwete Muriar.
65. Anyango Mahondo, Sigoma, West Alego, Siaya District, 15 August 1986.
66. Amina Hali, Pumwani, 4 August 1976. Hali explained where women might be safe by naming three African settlements that only coexisted between late 1921 and 1926.
67. Kayaya Thababu, Pumwani, Nairobi, 7 January 1977.
68. Tabitha Waweru, Mathare, Nairobi, 13 July 1976.

not heal, but silence and kill. In stark contrast to official concerns, the men were so skilled that they could take blood without waking the victim. Their technical knowledge was powerful; not only could they draw blood with something this particular woman could not name, but they could bandage her mouth to keep her from screaming. Was this a depiction of the abuse of medical technology—the use of bandages not to bind wounds but to gag—or was it a representation of chloroform, the anesthetic placed on gauze for a woman to inhale, to put her to sleep? Indeed, my allusion to "African speaking" in the title of this section is more ironic than the term's normal use as shorthand for African sources. As the next section shows, many African concerns about the power of European therapies were about what they did to African speech.

The point of this chapter is not to establish how accurate the women quoted above might be, or what these accounts really represent. Such an exercise would strip vampire stories of the rich contradictions of their details. After all, Western biomedicine takes blood and studies and interprets it. Hospitals require blood and use a number of techniques to get it from people; people need not be conscious to have their blood taken. People die in hospitals and die because they never get to hospitals. But these statements are not the facts and fantasies with which vampire stories, even the most medical ones, are told. I would suggest that these particular Nairobi accounts, with their talk of skill and how these men looked like ordinary men, observe the transition in yaws therapy, in which African dressers, at least the most reliable ones, were sent out unsupervised to give bismuth injections. They do not fully describe it, parody it, or represent it: all of these terms simply reduce the complexity of rubber sucking tubes and the drained bodies left to die to a single procedure.

For the same reason, it is almost impossible to argue that African vampire accusations misrepresent blood transfusions because of two kinds of evidence, chronological and generic. In terms of the chronological evidence, such misrepresentation seems unlikely. Until World War II, blood transfusions were rare in the tropics—without refrigeration or paraffin-lined containers, blood could not be stored long enough for a future transfusion,[69] and even when transfusion became widespread,

69. Henry M. Feinblatt, *Transfusion of Blood* (New York: Macmillan, 1926), 1–11; Alexander S. Wiener, *Blood Groups and Blood Transfusion* (Baltimore: Stratton Medical Books, 1939), 41–47, 62–66; Joseph R. Bove et al., *Practical Blood Transfusion* (Boston: Little, Brown, 1969), 4–7; Robert M. Greendyke, *Introduction to Blood Banking* (Garden City, N.Y.: Medical Examination Publishing Co., 1980), 2.

there was a perpetual shortage of donors.[70] In terms of the genre of evidence provided by bazimamoto stories, the idea of such a misrepresentation reduces the complexity of the clinic, the syringe, and "noticing" to a single medical procedure; it turns vampire stories into accounts of medical techniques, rather than stories involving medical tools and technologies. Africans did not witness strange practices and then tell fabulous stories about them. Far more goes into any story than a strange event and its oral reconstruction. When Africans saw things that were both medical and strange, they reported them as such, not as bazimamoto. During a sleeping-sickness epidemic in western Uganda in 1931, for example, one man "saw some Europeans, they came in vehicles and when they came across someone they injected him then and there. I don't know if bazimamoto could do things like that."[71]

As the following pages make clear, these stories quoted above are also about chloroform, hospitals, tools, and property. But the changes in colonial medical care and the increased use of African dressers to administer intramuscular injections outside clinics in the early 1920s figure in these stories, where the descriptions of these men's skill and stealth is in sharp contrast to the official anxieties that African dressers were unprepared for their jobs. The tellers of bazimamoto stories saw African dressers as skilled and practiced in their work, and this parodied official anxieties—which Africans may well have shared, but for different reasons—about who had the right and the power to administer medicine.

Did stories of blood rushed to hospitals from township rooms or rural airstrips invert and subvert Western biomedicine? There is no hard and fast answer, of course, and hospitals may have been a more concrete and simplistic category than bazimamoto was. Vampire accusations generally featured medicalized bureaucracies—fire brigades, medical departments, or medical department trucks on the northeast coast of postwar Kenya that "patrolled the streets in the dead of night . . . and should it come upon a straggler, draws from his veins all his blood with a rubber pump, leaving his body in the gutter limp and drained."[72] One

70. Luise White, "Cars Out of Place: Vampires, Technology and Labor in East and Central Africa," *Representations* 43 (1993): 27–50, 31–32; "Serious Lack of Blood Donors," *Uganda Argus*, 1 January 1959, 3.

71. Abdullah Sonsomola.

72. Elspeth Huxley, *The Sorcerer's Apprentice: A Journey through East Africa* (London: Chatto & Windus, 1948), 23.

Ugandan man said that people feared the Yellow Fever Department because "they were making some drugs out of blood or they were using it
with something else, that was where they were taking their victims."[73]
Indeed, well into the 1950s in most places, it was the mobility of agents
of wazimamoto that was so fearsome: they "do not walk along the paths
like honest men, but wander through the bush like outlaws."[74] In
Kenya, children had to learn "roadcrossing" in the bush to be safe from
kachinja.[75]

But in Africa as elsewhere, hospitals were unique institutions: they
claimed great expertise, they housed the living and the dead, and their
employees handled the most intimate body products. The cultural
meaning of these body products was different in different places, but
Africans were aware of how they could be used. In central Tanganyika,
for example, people complained that maternity clinics would allow
strangers to handle placenta, the stuff of the most effective witchcraft.[76]
Among many peoples in the Belgian Congo, how placenta was handled,
and by whom, proved a crucial determinant in attendance at maternity
clinics.[77] But such concerns and resistances have less to do with colonial
medicine than with common sense about taking medicines or giving
body products to strangers: in rural Africa only the very ill or the very
curious ignored the obvious dangers.[78] But hospitals could support African practices: in urban Central Africa, women used maternity hospitals to maintain seclusion better than they could in township housing.[79]

European authors, however, relished examples of Africans fearing
hospitals for reasons no more complex than white cannibals. A CMS
nurse claimed that children were disciplined in Uganda by being told

73. Peter Kirigwa, Katwe, 14 August 1990; Samuel Mubiru, Lubya, Uganda, 28 August 1990.

74. Quoted in Willis, "Report on Banyama" (cited n. 62 above).

75. D. A. Masolo, personal communication, 22 April 1997; author's field notes,
22 August 1986.

76. T. O. Beidelman, "Witchcraft in Ukaguru," in John Middleton and E. H. Winter,
eds., Witchcraft and Sorcery in East Africa (London: Routledge & Kegan Paul, 1963),
57–98.

77. Hunt, "Negotiated Colonialism," 273 ff.

78. See Bianco, "Historical Anthropology," 165–75, for specific examples. In places
where burying the dead was a specifically Christian development, hospitals may have involved people in more dealings with dead bodies than they wanted. People may have
avoided hospitals, not because people died in them, but because they were requested to
dispose of the bodies of those who died there.

79. Boris Gussman, Out in the Mid-Day Sun (London: George Allen & Unwin,
1962), 89.

that white people would eat them; hence they howled while waiting in hospitals.[80] In 1920, a missionary in the Belgian Congo terrified his house servant when he sterilized the black rubber gloves he would use in his first surgery: it looked as if he was boiling hands. All was resolved when the servant saw the missionary put on the gloves rather than eat them.[81] In the early 1960s, a European doctor told a journalist that he had trouble getting blood donors since Africans believed that he drank the blood himself.[82] Such accounts elided specific African anxieties about what happened to body parts in surgery, or during autopsy, anxieties that doctors took quite seriously in early colonial Africa: surgeons routinely allowed Africans to watch surgeries to demonstrate that body parts were neither taken nor eaten.[83] Years later, when surgery took place without observers, doctors anticipated whispered accusations that they did terrible things with the body parts they removed in operations.[84] Outside of hospitals, stories about blood-drinking were not told as racial stories: when the young T. O. Beidelman donated blood for a Maasai man in Tanganyika, a young Maasai man asked him who would drink it.[85]

Among the men and women interviewed for this project, hospitals never entered the social imagination as sites of abduction until well into the 1950s. Only then—when the larger teaching and research hospitals had been built or were in the final stages of construction—did people begin to talk about hospitals as places of great danger. Once Mulago Hospital was completed in Kampala in 1962, people claimed that skeletons were taken from the living, not the dead: when they heard sirens,

80. Timpson, "Patients and Nurse," 289–90.
81. Hunt, "Negotiated Colonialism," 223.
82. Alastair Scobie, *Murder for Magic: Witchcraft in Africa* (London: Cassell, 1965), 117.
83. Cook, *Uganda Memories,* 50–51; D. A. Bond, "A Record of Work at Toro," *Mercy and Truth* 10, 100 (1907): 103–11; R. S. T. Goodchild, "News from Kabale," *Mission Hospital* 40, 461 (1936): 137–40; Audrey Richards diaries, 20–23 June 1930, Audrey I. Richards papers, LSE; Hunt, "Negotiated Colonialism," 261–72.
84. Zeller, "Establishment of Western Medicine," 333, 116. The meaning of cutting up seems to have become increasingly menacing throughout this century. In 1900, Cook had great difficulty getting Africans to agree to postmortem examinations. Although he explained the benefits such examinations would bestow on other sick Africans, most people refused. "Slowly prejudice broke down, and one parent gave consent at once, saying, when I wished to investigate the cause of death of his son: 'Kale, ye nyama bunyama' (Why not, it is only meat)" (Cook, *Uganda Memories,* 52). No less an authority on accidental death than Idi Amin explained that one of his recently divorced wives had been found dismembered and stuffed into a gunnysack as "a result of a bungled surgical operation" (Denis Hills, *Rebel People* [London: George Allen & Unwin, 1978], 31n).
85. T. O. Beidelman, letter to author, 28 November 1994.

they knew that trucks were going to "catch people" for this purpose.[86] Hospital-based extractions were not specific and embodied, but social. In Kampala, it was said that children sold their playmates to Mulago to get bicycles.[87] At the same time that Ugandans said their blood was taken to Kenya to treat Mau Mau victims, people in Nairobi kept their children far away from King George V Hospital, where they said that white people would cut them up for blood and body parts.[88]

As hospitals began to capture the imagination of urban Africans in the late colonial era, Africans claimed that blood was being taken from welfare departments as well.[89] At the same time, however, officials became concerned about the blood accusations hurled at medical researchers in rural East Africa. In 1944, officials in Northern Rhodesia stopped a researcher from taking blood, skin, and stool samples, allowing him to do research only in the daytime, accompanied by a district officer and an African policeman.[90] In 1948, the venerable doctor Hope Trant—long considered a banyama for whatever happened in her hospital in Tuduma—was accused of drinking blood by Africans while she participated in a medical survey.[91] Medical survey teams were accused and sometimes attacked. The 1955 mediation by J. A. K. Leslie, the district

---

86. Francis Kigozi, Kasubi, 17 August 1990; Nechambuza Nsumba, Katwe, 20 August 1990; author's field notes, 15, 18 August 1990; Mulago Hospital was under construction for over a decade.

87. Julia Nalongo Nakibuuka, Lubya, 21 August 1990.

88. Peter Kirigwa, Katwe, 24 August 1990; Ahmed Kiziri, Katwe, 20 August 1990; D. A. Masolo, personal communication, 24 April 1997.

89. In Mombasa, Kenya, in 1947, and Broken Hill, Northern Rhodesia, in 1957, there were boycotts of welfare departments because they were said to be places from which Africans were abducted and their blood taken. See George [Brown] to Elspeth Huxley, 20 June 1948 (Elspeth Huxley Papers, Rhodes House, Oxford, RH MSS Afr. s. 782/2/2); Welfare Department, Broken Hill Development Corporation, January–February 1957. I am grateful to Carter Roeber for notes on this file.

90. G. Howe, provincial commissioner, Northern Province, Kasama, to chief secretary, Lusaka, 27 March 1944 (NAZ, SEC2/4/29, Native Affairs: Banyama); "Survey of Helminthic Diseases" (NAZ, SEC1/1072; I am grateful to Bryan Callahan for notes on this file).

91. On Hope Trant's reputation in Northern Rhodesia, see Gervas Clay, district commissioner, Isoka District, "Memorandum Concerning 'banyama' and 'mafyeka' with Special Reference to Provincial Commissioner, Kasama's Confidential File on Banyama and to Incidents in the Isoka District during the Latter Part of 1943," 24 January 1944 (NAZ, SEC2/429, Native Affairs: Banyama). Trant's own account of the accusations in Kigoma was that Africans had misunderstood a bottle of red wine on her dinner table; see Hope Trant, *Not Merrion Square: Anecdotes of a Woman's Medical Career in Africa* (Toronto: Thornhill Press, 1971), 127–33; a malariologist who visited her while she participated in the survey noted the caution with which she handled body products because of mumiani accusations; see Alec Smith, *Insect Man: The Fight against Malaria* (London: Radcliffe Press, 1993), 31.

commissioner near Kigoma, Tanganyika, did not establish that white
people did not drink blood, but revealed the benefits of science.

> A WHO survey party were in the area, and after the usual explanations to
> the chiefs and public, had settled in an area . . . to do a general health survey
> of the population. Unfortunately one of the assistants was seen to suck a
> blood sample into a pipette, and overnight there was panic among the popu-
> lation with the likelihood of violence, because, it was said, the Mumiani was
> at it again and Europeans were drinking blood. One of the nurses wore lip-
> stick, and this was quoted to me as evidence. I had to stop the survey and re-
> move all the staff, and I took my tent and camped in the area for a week to
> calm things down. It so happened that a separate lot of doctors, from Bur-
> roughs Wellcome, were in the District trying out a new worm drug, which
> was a great success. So for a week I carried round with me a bottle of worms
> "acquired" from local schoolboys, which was a strong argument in favor of
> medical surveys. Eventually the WHO survey was restarted a few miles
> away.[92]

SMEARING, SPRAYING, AND ORAL HISTORY

Put simply, wazimamoto used medical technologies to subdue and penetrate their victims: they "used needles which they could inject into the
hands and suck."[93] Sometimes whites used tubes, or needles connected
to tubes.[94] Such statements neither fetishized tools nor misunderstood
them but made them the marker of certain kinds of embodied extraction
and transformation. The needle itself had no power; what was fearsome
was the use to which it was put.

Patricia Turner has argued that items of material culture are sometimes misinterpreted by both sides of a racial divide, and this misinter-
pretation generates rumors.[95] I argue something quite different, that
items of material culture are spoken of specifically to mark cultural differences. When white people sucked African blood—or had it sucked
by their African employees—it could not be confused as the same kind

92. J. A. K. Leslie, letter to author, 13 March 1990. A nurse wearing lipstick and taking blood in a pipette started mumiani accusations in the Pare Mountains in Tanganyika
in 1957 (John Huddleston, interview with author, Kampala, 18 August 1990).

93. Joseph Nsubuga; Isaak Bulega.

94. Ofwete Muriar, Uchonga Village, Alego, Siaya District, 11 August 1986; Pius
Ouma Ogutu, Uhuyi Village, Alego, Siaya District, 19 August 1986.

95. Patricia A. Turner, I Heard It through the Grapevine: Rumor in African-American
Culture (Berkeley and Los Angeles: University of California Press, 1993), 15, but see also
Gladys-Marie Fry, Night Riders in Black Folk History (Knoxville: University of Tennessee
Press, 1975), 178–202.

of healing Africans did. Thus a Ugandan man assured my assistant and
I that traditional healers "were treating sick people, and although they
were sucking blood, they were sucking blood in order to relieve the pain
of the sick person . . . the blood they were sucking was not for sale as
the bazimamoto was doing." Indeed, "some people were refusing to go
to the hospitals because they feared that they might be injected without
their noticing and they were always in a panic about the bazimamoto,
and they thought that in this process of injections they might suck their
blood." [96] Another Ugandan man thought that these stories developed
because "when the Europeans were here we had a lot of diseases. . . .
They were doing research . . . and it was not easy to convince somebody
to volunteer to have research done on them so what they did was to kidnap those people." [97] In southwest Tanganyika in 1934, it was said that
the government paid to have Africans "bled with instruments," and then
a cloth was put over their faces and they were killed and their blood
taken. The anthropologist Godfrey Wilson was regarded with fear: "He
has all the instruments." [98] Vampire stories locate the tools and technologies of European medicine in ways that are different from other
narrative forms.

This very difference may require that vampire stories be read as a
genre: such a reading conflates the set elements of the clinic, the needle,
and blood much as the speaker did. What follows is an African historian's apostasy: in this and the next chapter I am interested in the
generic, the formulaic elements that make a good vampire story, rather
than in accounts of specific injections and medical conditions. This is a
writing strategy, one that enables me to use these stories to map a landscape outside of lived experience. It privileges words and images over
voices. I am trying to contextualize the genre of vampire stories, by discussing the material objects and therapeutic procedures that appear in
narratives that cross cultural and racial boundaries to disclose ideas
about colonial medicine.

And what were those ideas? Drugs, and practitioners' knowledge of
them, were powerful and disturbing, in part because of how those drugs
were applied. A man in colonial Northern Rhodesia was said to be
banyama, selling people to the Belgian Congo, and was driven out of

96. Joseph Nsubuga.
97. George W. Ggingo, Kasubi, Kampala, 15 August 1990.
98. From Godfrey Wilson's notebooks, 1935, University of Cape Town, Manuscript
and Archives Department, generously given me by James Ellison.

his village. How did people know he did it? asked Ian Cunnison: "He was seen with a man whom he had evidently doped with a needle." [99] In Uganda—and Uganda alone—the bazimamoto were said to have sprayed "some medicine directly on their victims, and afterwards they would capture them when they were nervous. It was certain they were using a medicine that no one knew about because no one knows what it was." [100] These are generic fantasies and generic proof, and they reveal the power of various drugs and the power of Europeans over their application. [101] In Uganda, such descriptions of "spraying"—fumigating— probably referred to the fumes of public health campaigns as personal attacks. Public health itself marked a shift in colonial medicine away from walk-in dispensaries to state-sponsored campaigns. [102] When they were first introduced as a plague control measure in southern Uganda in the 1930s, fumigants were hailed as an alternative to the "rat destruction drives" of the 1920s and the sometimes overzealous burning of plague victims' huts. [103] But the fumigants used were often lethal: poisonous insecticides were often used on human dwellings in the 1930s, on the grounds that the smell was so strong that the occupants would leave the house. [104] The state's use of fumigants increased the number of homes invaded and sprayed for plague fleas, but from the data I have it is not at all clear if these descriptions of spraying marked the power of drugs themselves or the invasive nature of public health campaigns.

Bazimamoto stories are those in which Europeans get the upper hand. They were not necessarily smarter than Africans, but they had better tools, more power, and, most especially, better drugs. "There

99. Ian Cunnison, field notes, September 1950. I am grateful to Professor Cunnison for making these available to me.

100. Gregory Sseluwagi, Lubya, 28 August 1990.

101. This is a deliberate allusion to the "standardized nightmare" of witch beliefs, which Africanists have also failed to historicize; see Monica Wilson, "Witch Beliefs and Social Structure," *Am. J. of Sociology* 41, 4 (1951): 307–13.

102. Zeller, "Establishment of Western Medicine," 189–220; Vaughan, "Health and Hegemony," 185–96.

103. Vaughan, *Curing Their Ills,* 40–43; Cook, *Uganda Memories,* 310; Zeller, "Establishment of Western Medicine," 339–40. But by the 1930s, the incidence of plague in southern Uganda had increased. Sporting rat-catching campaigns had reduced the population of the indigenous, disease-resistant rat and created a niche for new disease-bearing rats introduced from the East African coast by the railway (Vaughan, *Curing Their Ills,* 40). Not all diagnoses of plague were accurate, however: by the 1940s, government doctors noted a long-standing confusion of lobar pneumonia with pneumonic plague in southern Uganda (R. S. F. Hennessey papers, Rhodes House, Oxford, RH MSS Afr. s 1872 [25]).

104. Walter Ebling, *Subtropical Entomology* (San Francisco: Western Agriculture Publishing House, 1950), 5–6.

were some Europeans who would come and capture Africans." [105] "Any human being except whites could fall victim; it depended on luck. Whites never fell victim because they were the masters." [106] "They captured everybody, they did not discriminate against any race . . . but I never heard that they took Europeans." Trying to capture Indians, said a man in Uganda, "was not easy . . . you could make problems for yourself." [107] Men in Kenya said that wazimamoto tied their victims' hands and feet before they took their blood, but in Uganda, "They could give their victims some drugs to make them sleep, especially the Africans. . . . they could do this during the night . . . and take their victim to their destination when he was helpless, they could use these drugs whenever they came across their victims." [108] In Tanganyika, they used drugs that made people "unable to do anything. After this they hang you upside down and put big needles into the big veins to get blood." [109]

The issues here are far more than medicalized modes of capture located in race, but of a gendered African susceptibility to one form of medication. Men and women told similar stories, but in those stories, they described the different ways men and women responded to European drugs and technologies. Condensing several events into one scenario, even in response to a question, helps a speaker present himself or herself as a victim,[110] and being a victim was gendered. In western Kenya—on the other side of the lake from Kampala—men said victims "were injected in the head with a bloodsucking needle." [111] A man who was captured by wazimamoto on a sisal estate in Kenya in 1924 returned to Siaya District and told his friends that he and his friends "were

105. Ssimbwa Jjuko, Luwaze, 20 August 1990.

106. Zebede Oyoyo, Goma, Yimbo, Siaya District, 13 August 1986.

107. Abdullah Sonsomola; Yonasani Kaggwa. In Ankole in the 1950s, it was said that Sikhs captured Africans and took their blood (author's field notes, 20 August 1990).

108. Alexander Opaka, Ndegere Uranga, Alego, Siaya District, 11 August 1986; Ofwete Muriar; Zebede Oyoyo; Gregory Sseluwagi; Yonasani Kaggwa, Katwe, 27 August 1990; Christopher Kawoya, Kasubi, 17 August 1990.

109. Lloyd William Swantz, "The Role of the Medicine Man among the Zaramo of Dar es Salaam" (Ph.D. diss., University of Dar es Salaam, 1972), 336–37. Hanging Africans upside down seems to be a version of mumiani specific to the Tanganyikan coast; a Mr. Merrill's letter to the Tanganyikan authorities of October 1933 reported that "the victims were hung upside down over a large metal pot and the head was perforated with an iron instrument and the blood dripped into a pot." See Peter Pels, "Mumiani: The White Vampire. A Neo-Diffusionist Analysis of Rumour," Ethnofoor 5, 1–2 (1995): 165–87.

110. Amy Shuman, "'Get Outa My Face': Entitlement and Authoritative Discourse," in Jane H. Hill and Judith T. Irvine, Responsibility and Evidence in Oral Discourse (Cambridge: Cambridge University Press, 1992), 135–60.

111. Ofwete Muriar; see also Zebede Oyoyo, 23 August 1986.

taken to a small room ... their hands and legs were tied ... outside the room they were injected in the head."[112] Men in Congo recalled that batumbula had "the famous injection" that made their victims unconscious; some said it was an injection in the head.[113] In Ugandan vampire stories, Africans were made powerless by drugs administered externally to the mouth and nose: anesthesia in general and chloroform in particular had a power and meaning far beyond its use by missionaries as "a means of winning the confidence and trust of the people."[114] According to men, the bazimamoto "were capturing people and taking them someplace when they were unconscious." These drugs, "could make their victims dull." "They had something like a drug that made them unconscious ... the victims could not know where they were coming from or where they were going." "These victims would come and sniff at caliform, then they would become sleepy and taken without noticing, and they would not know where they were going or where they were coming from." When someone was given "caliform ... to sniff he could not escape, but only be unconsciously moving." Men would "become stupid." "They would bring you back when you were almost a dead person." "They collapsed on the walk back home because all their blood was taken."[115]

No one in Kenya, male or female, even those who reported their friends' recollections of wazimamoto, thought anyone survived bloodsucking. People died at once because all their blood was taken; they were "left lifeless" and "never came back to tell tales."[116] When victims were kept in pits, however, "those people whose blood was removed constantly were fed properly to make them produce more blood."[117] In the colonial Belgian Congo, victims who did not escape were eaten, but first they were fed well with sugar water and sugarcane.[118] Some men in Uganda had a different vision: "These victims were kept in a camp, and

112. Ofwete Muriar.
113. Moukadi Louis, Katuba III, Lubumbashi, 20 January 1991; Joseph Kabila Kiomba Alona, Lubumbashi, 28 March 1991. I am grateful to Bogumil Jewsiewicki for the use of these interviews.
114. Mrs. Ashton Bond, "Medical Work in Toro," Mercy and Truth 16, 189 (1912): 308.
115. Ssimbwa Jjuko; Joseph Nsubuga; Abdullah Sonsomola; Yonasani Kaggwa.
116. Alexander Opaka; Ofwete Muriar; Nyakida Omolo, Kabura, West Alego, Siaya District, 19 August 1986; Domtita Achola, Uchonga Ukudi, Alego, Siaya District, 11 August 1986.
117. Anyango Mahondo; see also George Ggingo.
118. Joseph Kabila Kiomba Alone, Lubumbashi, 28 March 1991.

they were not paid for their blood but they were captives, forced to be there." Blood was taken "every three months, every four months."[119] Some men said women were the victims bazimamoto preferred, since they had more blood than men but would not fight their captors as men did.[120] Indeed, in southwest Tanganyika in the mid 1930s, it was said that menstruating women would not go near the places where whites were said to take African blood.[121] Women in Uganda did not report long captivities, but either told of being left for dead or of being driven to a place in Entebbe, the capital, where other victims were kept, "looking dormant and still." Throughout East and Central Africa, women spoke of "bandages on your mouth" or "masks smeared with drugs" that "smelled bad." In Uganda, as in areas of Tanganyika, "They had some rooms and some instruments like masks that they used to cover your mouth." These instruments made men "dull, or impotent" but women in particular "could not shout . . . they could not talk again."[122] When a woman kidnapped by batumbula in colonial Congo in the 1940s was found, "She did not speak when they asked her questions. They brought her directly to the hospital for a few injections. They said she had been hospitalized before."[123] A dozen years later, Congolese claimed that Africans were killed in "the big hospitals in Stanleyville and Bunia. . . . Those who were kept alive were put into trances, sleeping strange sleeps, so that when they came awake they were unable to do anything except the white man's bidding."[124]

Silenced

This evidence takes my discussion of anesthesia in two directions: the drug that virtually takes on a life of its own in African popular culture and the drug as medical practice.[125] The first has to do with the quali-

119. Joseph Nsubuga; Francis Kigozi; Yonasani Kaggwa; George Ggingo, Kasubi, 15 August 1990.

120. Yonasani Kaggwa; Ssimbwa Jjuko; Anyango Mahondo.

121. From Godfrey Wilson's notebooks, 1935, University of Cape Town, Manuscript and Archives Department, again loaned me by James Ellison.

122. Bibiana Nalwanga, Bwase, 24 August 1990; Julia Nakibuuka Nalongo, Lubya, 21 August 1990; Magarita Kalule, Masanafu, 20 August 1990.

123. Kasongo Ngoiy, Cité Gécamines, Lubumbashi, 9 January 1991. I am grateful to Bogumil Jewsiewicki for letting me see this interview.

124. Colin Turnbull, The Lonely African (New York: Simon & Schuster, 1962), 226–27.

125. Starting in the 1980s at the latest, there were commonplace East African urban legends in which thieves either sprayed or injected a drug into a home so that they could steal all the contents while the occupants slept. People have told me that a syringe found in the recovered possessions was "proof" that these stores were true. Author's field notes, passim. See also Donald M. Johnson, "The 'Phantom Anesthetist' of Mattoon: A Field Study in Mass Hysteria," J. of Abnormal and Social Psychology 40 (1945): 175–86.

ties of chloroform—the drug that puts people to sleep—and its administration, which was perhaps the least professionalized aspect of medicine in colonial Uganda. The actual work of administering chloroform
was quite simple, one of the reasons it was preferred over ether in the
nineteenth century: a gauze pad was placed over a patient's nose and
drops of the drug were periodically put on the pad. In Africa's rural
hospitals, sweepers, orderlies, and European visitors were often called
upon to administer the drug during routine operations.[126] Such practices blurred otherwise well-enforced hospital hierarchies, suggesting
the generalized medicalized bureaucracies people feared. The second
question—why was the drug that put people to sleep so terrifying, and
why was that form of the terror so gendered?—cannot be answered by
asking questions solely about chloroform or its application. Such questions would shape answers that were about chloroform, not about African ideas about medical conditions or how they were caused.

What questions emerge from the formulaic quality of the evidence
presented above, the smeared and sprayed drugs and the potent masks?
I suggest these had profound meanings because these techniques of med-
icating replicated the techniques of variolation and the application of
above-the-skin cures that the peoples of southern Uganda considered
efficacious and powerful. The intensity of chloroform to terrify and stupefy came in part from its application. But the drugs and cures that had
such power could also be modified, by reconstituting a vaccination or
repacking a wound with a more familiar substance. Interpreting bazimamoto stories as individual testimony, or as memory, however fantastic, would translate these terms into individual experience and medical
history; it would not allow for this reading of "smearing" or "spraying."
But why would "injections in the head" be the form of bloodsucking
most feared by men in Siaya District in Kenya or parts of the Belgian
Congo? Given that many of these men from Siaya had been migrant laborers in the cities of the coast,[127] "injections in the head" may play on
coastal mumiani stories in which victims are hung upside down to drain

126. Mary Poovey, *Uneven Developments: The Ideological Work of Gender in Mid-
Victorian England* (Chicago: University of Chicago Press, 1988), 26–29; A. J. Boase,
"Reminiscences of Surgery in Uganda," *East Afr. Med. J.* 31 (1954): 202; see also Smith,
Insect Man, 30.

127. See K. K. Janmohammed, "African Labourers in Mombasa, c. 1895–1940," *Hadith* 5 (1972): 156–79; Frederick Cooper, *On the African Waterfront: Work and Disorder in Urban Africa* (New Haven: Yale University Press, 1987).

their blood or needles injected into the vein on their necks.[128] Other interpretations suggest themselves: the diagnosis for advanced sleeping sickness involved removing lymphatic fluid (hence the Northern Rhodesian banyama removal of "brains," for example) and local, well-defended smallpox variolation involved making incisions on the head.[129] But not being able to guess is perhaps the most reliable answer here: the specificity with which men in both Siaya and the Belgian Congo feared "injections in the head" indicates that such injections replicated another healing practice that was considered effective and strong. This particular image in particular local vampire stories does not reveal a medical misrepresentation, but local practices.

But why the particular efficacies of silenced women and sickly men? I am hardly the first to see the gendered meanings in any new medical technique, particularly chloroform, produced beyond medical control.[130] Yet East African women resisted this control. Before 1925, chloroform was rarely used in childbirth in Uganda.[131] In less than a decade, its meaning to East African women was terrifying: at Nairobi's African Maternity Hospital, women "flatly refused to inhale" chloroform at any stage in their labor or during episiotomies or the stitching that followed.[132] Did these women—who probably had heard of "bandages on your mouth"—associate inhaling chloroform with speechlessness? The meaning of speech to East African women, and their specifically medicalized understanding of how speech could be taken from them, is not something easily understood, but it does add another dimension, at least, to the feminist literature that argues that recuperating the voices of colonized women is all but impossible.[133] Rather than attempt to insert

128. Arens, *Man-Eating Myth*, 9; Swantz, "Role of the Medicine Man," 335–37; J. A. K. Leslie, letter to author.

129. Dawson, "Smallpox," 101–2.

130. Poovey, *Uneven Developments*, 50; see White, "Bodily Fluids," 425–31.

131. See Summers, "Intimate Colonialism," and Cook, *Uganda Memories*, 340.

132. M. Ross, matron, Lady Grigg Welfare League, African Maternity Hospital, Pumwani, to secretary, National Birthday Trust Fund, 3 October 1933 (Wellcome Institute for the History of Medicine Archives, S/A National Birthday Trust, F6/6, box 41). I am grateful to Lynn Thomas for these notes.

133. See esp. Gayatri Chakrobarty Spivak, "Can the Subaltern Speak?" in C. Nelson and L. Grossberg, eds., *Marxism and the Interpretation of Culture* (Urbana: University of Illinois Press, 1988), 271–313; for discussions of Victorian women silenced by the introduction of chloroform, see Poovey, *Uneven Developments*, 24–50, 164–98; for a critique, see Luise White, "Silence and Subjectivity (A Position Paper)," in Susan Hardy Aiken et al., eds., *Making Worlds: Gender, Metaphor, Materiality* (Tucson: University of Arizona Press, 1997), 243–51.

these accounts of silenced women into a secondary literature on women in the region (however provocative that literature might be),[134] I want to suggest that these accounts foreground women's own historical understanding of speaking and the ways in which it was controlled by colonial regimes; these accounts are women's own descriptions of speech and consciousness, not of the problematized ways to recuperate them. What is important here about "caliform," however, is what it does to the mind and to consciousness, and the different ways in which men and women articulate what the drug does. While injections remained an embodied practice that could cause leprosy (and much else), they were subcutaneous procedures: they may have been fearsome and fascinating because of what white people were able to take from those regions of the body. As a body of technique, injections may have been a reasonable cure for such a wide variety of maladies because of their association with the misfortunes and diseases of the modern era. Anesthesia—the drug that doctors boasted "put them to sleep"—became a medium of capture in and of itself in part because its application, like that of needles in the head, was based on older, effective local practices.

CONCLUSIONS

This chapter argues that a concept of "the voice" disembeds the speaker from social and embodied histories. Those histories might be recuperated from the words and images, wordplays and genres, with which individuals speak. Such a general reading provides a very specific history of the gendered meanings of biomedical procedures first introduced in colonial times. Those regions of the skin articulated in nuns' stories of

---

134. Royal women could use profanity in public, for example, while commoner women had to be demure; see Nakanyike Musisi, "Women, 'Elite Polygyny,' and Buganda State Formation," *Signs* 16, 4 (1991): 759. It seems unlikely that Western medical practices introduced a concept of the mouth as separate from the body in southern Uganda, as happened elsewhere; see Sarah Nettleson, "Protecting a Vulnerable Margin: Towards an Analysis of How the Mouth Came to Be Separated from the Body," *Sociology of Health and Illness* 10, 2 (1988): 156–69; Landau, "Explaining Surgical Evangelism." In Uganda, jawbones were the sacred relic of Ganda kings, although this had become contested terrain by the late nineteenth century. The role played by royal jawbones and skulls may have undergone radical transformation in the charged royal politics and regency of the colonial era; see Roscoe, *The Baganda*, 110–14, and Benjamin Ray, *Myth, Ritual and Kingship in Buganda* (Oxford: Oxford University Press, 1991), 114–23. Elsewhere in the region, commoners' mouths were sites of subcutaneous distress; see Brad Weiss, "Plastic Teeth Extraction: The Iconography of Haya Gastro-Sexual Affliction," *American Ethnologist* 19, 3 (1992): 538–52. Luo men and women did have their front teeth extracted, however.

Africans repacking ulcer treatments and of Africans' stories of Africans sniffing at chloroform were used to construct a new narrative in which ideas of curing and control were valued according to their embodied application as well as their medical results. Interpreting vampire stories across a wide cultural and geographic area for their common elements allows for a very specific history of colonial medical practices.

CHAPTER 4

"Why Is Petrol Red?"

The Experience of Skilled and Semi-Skilled Labor in East and Central Africa

This chapter is also about the interpretation of vampire stories as a genre, but relies largely on oral material to do so. Documentary evidence provides a context and a contradiction to some of the interview material, but it does not shape the chapter. In part this is because almost all the quotations come from interviews with former migrant laborers, men whose experiences of work and descriptions thereof spanned about sixty years. The rich detail of their accounts and their recollections of real or imagined training regimes, expertise, and on-the-job camaraderie provide far more data about how men performed the tasks for which they were paid than would published job descriptions and official statements about how discipline and efficiency were to be improved. Unlike in the previous chapter, I am interpreting many of these oral accounts as if they were true, or accurate. Such an interpretation allows me to examine what a man said happened at work and thus allows for a close scrutiny of the day-to-day processes of discipline and differentiation constructed there. Taking these accounts as histories of working gives me a description of a set of regional issues and concerns that I argue are best understood and interrogated on a regional, transcolonial level of generalization. This analysis is no less specific because it is based on vampire stories from Tanzania interpreted with vampire stories from Uganda

---

The title of this chapter is the title of a section of F. G. Schreerder's "Mumiani," *Book of the Holy Ghost Fathers* 44, 3 (1948). I am grateful to Peter Pels for this reference.

and Kenya; indeed, I argue that a regional reading of the genre offers much greater specificity about African concerns about technology, labor, and the various bondings of men and machines than any source read locally could do.

VAMPIRES AND WAGE LABOR

Several scholars have suggested that vampires are a perfect metaphor for capitalism. One of the things that made vampires such a powerful image in the eighteenth and nineteenth centuries was their extractive power, and how with all their distinctive clothes and equipment, they came to embody the idea of bloodsucking foreigners draining the lifeblood of humbler folk. African vampires, however, are more complex and layered. They are not generalized metaphors of extraction and oppression but ways for working men to express the subtle and contradictory anxieties that might accompany their good fortune at finding gainful employment. Historians of labor in sub-Saharan Africa have stressed the systemic nature of African participation in wage labor: the fact that the methods of recruitment and retention were as much a part of the rhythms and disciplines of the workplace as the actual labor was. As a result, work is perhaps the most neglected aspect of labor history, as Frederick Cooper has pointed out, and the ways in which workers subverted and interrogated the labor process while on the job have rarely been examined or are relegated to the marginal terrain reserved for the hidden struggles and silent resistances of a dispossessed labor force. This chapter proposes something quite different, to add to this literature the study of how working men thought about and debated the nature of their work.

The vampires in this chapter are thus a category of analysis; they are epistemological. They describe not only the extraction of blood, but how it occurs, who performs it, and under what conditions and with which inducements. I argue that it is possible to read—or more precisely, to hear—specific vampire accusations as a debate among working men about the nature of work: not its material conditions or remuneration, but how the experience of skilled or semi-skilled labor and involvement with machines could change the men who were so engaged. This is not the only possible interpretation of vampire accusations, of course, but it is the one that conforms most closely to the details and the emplotment of working men's accounts. The men quoted here were colonial policemen, firemen, health inspectors, tailors, and railway workers who rose from unskilled apprenticeship to become engine drivers. All describe these vampires in similar terms, noting the secrecy of the work, the intensity with which it was supervised, and the impossibility of knowing who exactly did it, so the vampires known to laboring men had definite characteristics. Interpreting vampires from working men's accounts does not tell us more about these vampires than other sources might, but may provide insights into the storytellers' view of the world that other sources do not: it allows us to examine differentiation in the labor process and within the labor force in the words and categories of laboring men.

Most of the data presented here come primarily from interviews with former laborers and artisans—men who were not specialized story-tellers at all—conducted in rural western Kenya in 1986 and in and around Kampala, Uganda, in 1990. These men were roughly the same age—born between 1910 and 1935—and had had overlapping life experiences: many of the Kenyans were migrants to Uganda, and many of the Ugandans had worked in supervisory positions there and in Kenya. The Kenyan material was presented to my research assistants and me as men's stories. Many of the returned migrants I interviewed in rural western Kenya claimed that once home, they never told their wives these stories, because "my wives were adults and could get the stories from other sources,"[1] or "none of my wives could realize the seriousness of these stories, but"—turning to my male research assistant—"a man like you can realize the value and seriousness of any story."[2] One man, Anyango Mahondo, who claimed to have done the work of capture himself, said that he "could not tell anyone, not even my wife" about it, even after he had told my assistant.[3] Conversely, Zebede Oyoyo, who claimed to have narrowly escaped the clutches of Nairobi firemen in a "town toilet" in 1923, told everyone about it: "Why not? I am lucky to have escaped and therefore must talk freely about it."[4] Ugandan men did not tell these stories in gendered ways that I could discern, but as stories that required the expertise of men like themselves. The two men I interviewed in En-

1. Peter Hayombe, Uhuyi Village, Alego, Siaya, Kenya, 20 August 1986; see also Menya Mauwa, Uchonga Village, Alego, Siaya, Kenya, 19 August 1986.

2. Zebede Oyoyo, Goma Village, Yimbo, Siaya, Kenya, 13 August 1986.

3. Anyango Mahondo, Sigoma Village, Alego, Siaya, Kenya, 15 August 1986. Throughout the interview, Mahondo insisted that my assistant, Odhiambo Opiyo, not tell me about his days as a policeman, despite the fact that I was sitting between them and Opiyo and I were conferring in English during the interview.

4. Oyoyo interview, cited n. 2 above.

glish noted that they too had wondered about bazimamoto and had done "research as you are doing now" many years ago.[5] Another man said he "followed it closely" since 1939 "because I did not believe it. I came to the conclusion that it was not true because I didn't find any-one claiming that one of his relatives had been taken."[6] What kind of stories were these, that were so contested, and so gendered, and that were withheld or broadcast, believed or researched according to indi-vidual experience?

Working men told stories about occupations when they told stories of vampires. If blood is taken to be a universal, ungendered, nonspecific, life-giving fluid, its removal is terrifying because of what is imagined to be removed. But if blood is thought to be gendered— and many African peoples assume that women have more blood than men—then the loss of blood is far more alarming to adult men than to adult women.[7] But in either case, blood is the most ambiguous of bodily fluids; according to context, it can signify life or death. Other bodily fluids, semen or breast milk, do not. It is possible that stories about blood, and specific forms of its removal, articulate and point out ambiguities. When the systematic removal of blood is associated with a specific occupational group, it suggests that the ambiguities have to do with certain kinds of labor.[8] Read as stories about blood, vampiric firemen represent certain reservations about specific skills and the alliances made through on-the-job training, hierarchy, and an extended working day.

In many ways, these stories fit the format of urban legends; most people believed that it was a well-established fact that firemen captured people for their blood. But the use of folkloric categories does not ade-

5. Ntale Mwene, Kasubi, 12 August 1990; George W. Ggingo, Kasubi, 15 August 1990.

6. Francis Kigozi, Kasubi, 17 August 1990.

7. Rodney Needham, "Blood, Thunder, and the Mockery of Animals," *Sociologus* 14, 2 (1964): 136–49; Victor Turner, *The Forest of Symbols: Aspects of Ndembu Ritual* (Ithaca, N.Y.: Cornell University Press, 1967), 41–42, 59–81, 249–51; Luc de Heusch, *The Drunken King, or, The Origin of the State*, trans. Roy Willis (Bloomington: Indiana University Press, 1982), 168–73; T. O. Beidelman, *Moral Imagination and Kaguru Modes of Thought* (Washington, D.C.: Smithsonian Institution Press, 1993) 35–38. See also Anyango Mahondo, interview cited in n. 3 above: "Women had the most blood. They are known to give birth many times, each time losing a lot of blood, but still they are strong."

8. The Nairobi District Annual Report, 1939 (Kenya National Archives [henceforth cited as KNA], CP4/4/1), 3, alludes to a spate of rumors in Kenya in 1939 about blankets saturated with a medicine that would make men impotent: this was a semen story, to be sure, and it involved Europeans, technology, and commodities, but it did not involve labor.

quately describe the extent to which these stories were debated and contested by their narrators with each telling and retelling. Many of my informants insisted that these stories were false because they had never met anyone who knew a victim. In Uganda, George Ggingo explained that these stories arose when Africans were unwilling to participate in colonial medical experiments and it was necessary to kidnap them.[9] Ofwete Muriar in Kenya said he was "convinced that these people came from hospitals because nowadays people are required to donate blood for their sick relatives."[10] Still others said that they had doubted these stories until postcolonial violence convinced them that anything was possible.[11] In 1923, the Tanganyikan Swahili newspaper *Mambo Leo* published letters about mumiani variously signed "Adiyisadiki" ("Believer") and "Asiyesadiki" ("Nonbeliever"). The believer knew of a long, narrow building behind a toilet in Nairobi where men called Zima Moto wore black clothes; anyone who entered the building who was not Zima Moto never came out. Women disappeared from the town as well, going to the shops in the evening and leaving their shoes there. The nonbeliever ridiculed the believer's facts: women disappeared because they were skilled at leaving their husbands, he wrote. Moreover, he had been to Nairobi and "there are two kinds of people there, those placed there by the government, their job is to be ready to put out fires in town, there are people like this in Europe, and then there are the second kind of people, who clean the toilets in town."[12] As late as 1972, a Tanzanian newspaper ran a half-page article explaining that firemen did not kill people.[13] One month later, "Nearly Victim" wrote to the editor refuting the article and asking, "Where did hospitals get their supply of blood in those grim days, before Independence? People used to disappear mysteriously in those days . . . or didn't you know that the blood was used to treat the white man only?"[14] But some people were aware of the ambiguity of these stories: "It seems these stories were true, first of all con-

9. George Ggingo, Kasubi, Uganda, 15 August 1990.
10. Ofwete Muriar, Uchonga Village, Alego, Siaya District, Kenya, 11 August 1986; see also Kersau Ntale Mwene, Kasubi, Uganda, 12 August 1990; Joseph Nsubuga, Kisati, Uganda, 22 August 1990.
11. Gregory Sseluwagi, Lubya, Uganda, 28 August 1990.
12. "Adiyisadiki" ("Believer"), letter to the editor, *Mambo Leo,* November 1923, 13–14. I am grateful to Patrick Malloy for this reference and to Laura Fair and Peter Seitel for their help in translation.
13. S. Lolila, "Firemen Are Not 'chinja-chinja,'" *The Standard* (Dar es Salaam), 10 January 1972, iii.
14. Letter, *The Standard,* 2 February 1972, 6.

sidering that they existed as stories and those who lost their relatives . . . can prove it. However, those people whose relatives were not taken can say these stories were false." [15]

VEHICLES AND VAMPIRES

Where vampires are thought to be firemen, they are called by some version of the Swahili term *wazimamoto,* the men who extinguish the fire, or heat, or light, as in brightness, but not as in lamp. Many East African vampire stories—even when told with other terms for vampire—contain generic fire brigade vehicles; many other vampire stories involve cars or vans. More often than not, captives were put into a vehicle and taken away, sometimes to be kept in a pit in the local fire station, "the property of the government." [16] There is an obvious association between the red of fire engines and the red of blood—firemen's "equipment is always red and so is blood, therefore any African in the olden days could easily conclude that they were involved in bloodsucking," Anyango Mahondo said [17]—but it should be noted that most of my informants generally did not make this association. In the late 1950s and 1960s, however, Europeans had their own set of rumors about the dangers of driving red cars and told of whites in rural East African being beaten or killed for driving in red vehicles.[18] But Africans were less concerned with color than with the characteristics of vehicles; Abdullah Sonsomola spoke of "cars which bore a cross," [19] for example, and Peter Fraenkel cites Northern Rhodesian's fears of "a grey land rover with a shiny metal back." [20] Africans were especially concerned to point out that the vehicles they described had no lights and often no windows.

Vehicles in wazimamoto stories were not only dangerous, they were found in the most unlikely places and relationships. An old man in Kampala claimed that in the days when "the only departments with cars were the police and fire brigade," the Yellow Fever Department captured people, "but since they had no motor vehicles of their own, they had to

15. Gregory Sseruwagi.
16. Anyango Mahondo, interview cited n. 3 above.
17. Ibid.
18. W. V. Brelsford, "The 'Banyama' Myth," *NADA* 9, 4 (1967): 54–56; J. A. K. Leslie, personal communication, 13 March 1990; Graham Thompson, personal communication, 28 August 1990; Atieno Odhiambo, personal communication, 31 December 1990.
19. Abdullah Sonsomola, Kisenyi, Kampala, Uganda, 28 August 1990.
20. Peter Fraenkel, *Wayaleshi* (London: Weidenfeld & Nicholson, 1959), 201.

use the fire brigade department's motor cars," which was how this rumor began.[21] In rural Tanganyika during World War II, a blood drive to
supply plasma to troops overseas failed because a fire engine was always
stationed by the small airstrip and Africans assumed that the blood was
to be drunk by Europeans. Years later, it was said that the blood of
unconscious Africans was collected in buckets and then rushed to Dar
es Salaam in fire engines.[22] In Dar es Salaam in 1947, according to a
former superintendent of police, a blood transfusion service was established, but it had no transport of its own, and so fire engines carried
blood donors to the hospital, giving rise to the rumor "that the vehicles,
usually with a European volunteer in charge, were collecting African
males for their blood and that it was a plot by Europeans to render them
impotent."[23] Officials' folklore about the fear of fire engines was such
that during Christmas 1959, police in Mbale, Uganda, patrolled the African townships in the local fire engine to keep even the criminals inside
their homes.[24]

Trucks and cars were out of bounds as well. Early in 1939, when the
governor of Northern Rhodesia visited the liberal settler Stewart Gore-
Browne at his palatial estate in Northern Province, his car was followed
by a windowless van. This caused great suspicion; it was said that Gore-
Browne and the new governor "were concocting plans for kidnapping
on a large scale."[25] Batumbula in the Belgian Congo traveled in vans
to find victims, sometimes taking men and their bicycles to their grim
destinations. In the 1940s, a Belgian priest on the Belgian side of the
Luapula River was said to imprison Africans in the belfry of his mission
church until he drove them in his van to Elisabethville, where their
brains were eaten.[26] A former miner in colonial Katanga recalled "the
last straw was that batumbula began to chase victims in an automobile
in the day time."[27] In Lamu, Kenya, in the mid 1940s, Medical Depart-

21. Samuel Mubiru, Lubya, Uganda, 28 August 1990.
22. W. Arens, The Man-Eating Myth: Anthropology and Anthrophagy (New York:
Oxford University Press, 1979), 12–13.
23. Michael Macoun, personal communication, 13 March 1990.
24. Brelsford, "'Banyama' Myth," 54.
25. Thomas Fox-Pitt, district commissioner, Mpika, to provincial commissioner,
Northern Province, Kasama, 6 March 1939 (National Archives of Zambia [henceforth
cited as NAZ], SEC2/429, Native Affairs: Banyama).
26. Rik Ceyssens, "Mutumbula: Mythe de l'opprimé," Cultures et développement 7
(1975): 483–536, esp. 490–93; Brelsford, "'Banyama' Myth," 52; Ian Cunnison's field
notes, 1949.
27. Moukadi Louis, Katuba III, Lubumbashi, 20 January 1991, interviewed for Bogumil Jewsiewicki.

ment trucks patrolled the streets, "and, should [one] come upon a strag-gler [it] draws from his veins all his blood with a rubber pump, leaving his body in the gutter."[28] In the early 1950s, in northeast Tanganyika, it was said that malaria control trucks carried bodies whose blood would be drained.[29] A few hundred miles to the south, an engineer in charge of building bridges was thought to be mumiani.[30] A few years later in west-ern Kenya, "motor vehicles painted red" drained the blood from lone pedestrians captured along the Kisumu to Busia highway; the blood was then taken to blood banks in hospitals.[31] In eastern Northern Rhodesia in 1948, children were lured to trucks on the road at nighttime, made helpless and invisible with the banyama's wands, and taken to towns across the border in Nyasaland, where they were fattened on special foods while the European employers of banyama drank their blood; they returned home "very emaciated."[32]

The intimate relations of Europeans, when enclosed in vehicles, were extremely suspicious. In rural Tanganyika in the late 1950s, a white ge-ologist was attacked; he aroused local suspicions because there were curtains on the windows of his truck.[33] In 1959, in what was then Salis-bury, Rhodesia, a "courting couple" in a parked car in an isolated spot were attacked because of "an almost firm belief" that Africans were being captured and drugged and loaded onto a Sabena aircraft, on which their bodies were "cut up and canned during the flight" to the Belgian Congo.[34] Vehicles operated by Africans were no less suspicious. Throughout the 1960s, the first African-owned bus company in western

28. Elspeth Huxley, *The Sorcerer's Apprentice: A Journey through East Africa* (Lon-don: Chatto & Windus, 1948), 23.
29. Alec Smith, *Insect Man: The Fight against Malaria* (London: Radcliffe Press, 1993), 72–73.
30. Peter Pels, "Mumiani: The White Vampire. A Neo-Diffusionist Analysis of Ru-mour," *Ethnofoor* 5, 1–2 (1995): 166–67.
31. E. S. Atieno-Odhiambo, "The Movement of Ideas: A Case Study of the Intellectual Responses to Colonialism among the Liganua Peasants," in Bethwell A. Ogot, ed., *His-tory and Social Change in East Africa*, 163–80, *Hadith* 6 (1976): 172.
32. John Barnes, Fort Jameson, Northern Rhodesia to J. Clyde Mitchell, Rhodes-Livingstone Institute, Lusaka, 10 October 1948 (J. C. Mitchell Papers, Rhodes House, Oxford, RH MSS Afr. s. 1998/4/1).
33. Darrell Bates, *The Mango and the Palm* (London: Rupert Hart-Davis, 1962), 51–53.
34. K. D. Leaver, "The 'Transformation of Men to Meat' Story," Native Affairs De-partment Information Sheet No. 20 (Salisbury, November 1960 [National Archives of Zimbabwe, No. 36413]), 2; Brelsford, "'Banyama' Myth,", 54–55. Similar stories about pigs were commonplace in the southern Belgian Congo in the 1940s; see Ceyssens, "Mutumbula," 586–87.

Kenya, Ongewe Bus, was said to carry kachinja after dusk. Passengers had to take great care not to sit beside strangers.[35] Automobiles could be transformed to perform dreadful tasks. In western Kenya in 1968, travelers were afraid to accept rides, because the wazimamoto had cars with specially designed backseats that could automatically drain the blood of whoever sat there. In 1986, this story was told as something that had happened in the past; ten years later, a researcher heard of cars with specially designed straps to keep victims still as their blood was removed.[36] Cars had become especially important in the era of AIDS: not only could they help kachinja obtain blood, they enabled them to take it across borders where cleaner, foreign blood was so desperately needed.[37]

LOCATING BUREAUCRACY

What are these stories about? They are about vehicles in unexpected places, used for unintended purposes; these are stories about borrowed transport. But was this borrowing symbolic or literal? Did it represent permeable administrative boundaries or simple lapses in colonial funding and vehicle allocations? Were the signs and symbols of bureaucratic authority being contested in a popular discourse or were official cars being appropriated by underfunded bureaucrats? While I doubt that the Ugandan Yellow Fever Department took blood samples from fire brigade vehicles—Kampala did not have a fire engine until after 1932— everywhere but in Nairobi fire fighting equipment was routinely used, by all accounts badly, by police. Dar es Salaam did not have a fire brigade until 1939; Mombasa until 1940; and Kampala until 1953. Until then, Nichodamus Okumu Ogutu said, "we only heard about wazimamoto but never saw any." [38] Officials however maintained that untrained police forces were usually unable to contain fires in those cities: "[T]he manipulation of the fire appliances in the event of emergency is left

35. Author's field notes, 20 July, 14 August 1986.
36. Author's field notes, 18 August 1986; James Giblin, personal communication, 15 August 1996.
37. Author's field notes, 20 August 1986 and 14 August 1990; Brad Weiss, *The Making and Unmaking of the Haya Lived World: Consumption, Commoditization, and Everyday Practice* (Durham, N.C.: Duke University Press, 1996), 203
38. Nichodamus Okumu Ogutu, Siaya District, Kenya, 20 August 1986.

to the unskilled, untrained, and undrilled efforts of a few African constables."[39] But where there was a formal and well-organized fire brigade, it did not do much better. Nairobi's fire brigade had its own quarters, a fire master, and two fire engines, but there was a commission of inquiry in 1926 to investigate why it was so incompetent, and nine years later it had received only forty-two fire calls and put out five fires.[40] In 1939, the Nairobi Fire Brigade failed to put out a fire in the Secretariat Building.[41] Kampala's Fire Brigade could do little about the increase in arson between 1953 and 1958, and the fire damage to stored cotton was especially severe in the dry years of 1953 and 1957.[42] But shortly after they were built, fire stations became sites of great power and significance. In 1947, a riot at the Mombasa Fire Station badly damaged a fire engine.[43] In 1958, in Kampala, a man was arrested for trying to sell his friend to the fire station; he asked for 1,500/- and was arrested while waiting for the fire master to bring his money. When he was sentenced the magistrate said, "People must know that the Fire Brigade is not buying people, but is intended to extinguish fires in burning buildings and vehicles."[44] In Dar es Salaam in 1959, William Friedland, a visiting professor at the university, observed "an occasional African crossing the street to get as far away from the fire station as possible and running when in front of the station."[45] Nevertheless, people feared the Medical

39. N. W. Cavendish, commissioner, Kenya Police, to chief secretary, Nairobi, 11 March 1939 (KNA, CS/1/19/4, Fire Fighting in East Africa, 1933–46); "The Fury of Fire," *Matalisi*, 25 March 1925, 6–7; *Uganda Herald*, 24 April 1931, 1; *Uganda Police Annual Report, 1950* (Kampala, 1951), 29–30; ibid., *1951* (Kampala, 1952), 34; ibid., *1952* (Kampala, 1953), 33–34; Works and Public Health Committee, 10 May 1938 (KNA, PC/NBI/2/53, Nairobi Municipal Council Minutes, 1938).

40. Nairobi Fire Commission, 1926 (KNA, AG4/3068); J. B. Powell, superintendent, Nairobi Fire Brigade, Annual Report, 1935 (KNA, PC/NBI2/50, Nairobi Municipal Council Minutes, January–June 1936).

41. Nairobi Municipal Council Minutes, 1939–40 (KNA, CP/NBI/2/54).

42. *Uganda Police Annual Report, 1953* (Kampala, 1954), 30–31; ibid., *1954* (Kampala, 1955), 35; ibid., *1955* (Kampala, 1965), 34; ibid., *1956* (Kampala, 1957), 37; ibid., *1957* (Kampala, 1958), 38; ibid., *1958* (Kampala, 1959), 40–41.

43. "'Human Vampire' Story Incites Mombasa Mob's Fire Station Attack," *East African Standard*, 21 June 1947, 3; Kenya Colony and Protectorate, *Report on Native Affairs, 1939–47* (London: HMSO, 1948), 83; George [Brown?] to Elspeth Huxley, 20 January 1948 (Elspeth Huxley Papers, Rhodes House, Oxford, RH MSS Afr. s. 782, box 2/2, Kenya [1]).

44. "Three Years for Attempt to Sell Man," *Uganda Argus*, 16 February 1959, 5; "Firemen Do Not Buy People" *Tanganyika Standard*, 16 February 1959, 3.

45. William H. Friedland, "Some Urban Myths of East Africa," in Allie Dubb, ed., "Myth in Modern Africa" (proceedings of the 14th Conference of the Rhodes-Livingstone Institute for Social Research, mimeographed, Lusaka, 1960), 146.

Department as well, and men and women in Kampala named various departments in Entebbe that received the blood—the Welfare Department, the Yellow Fever Department, the Veterinary Department. They may not have been confused, however. They may have been stating the problem of these stories: how do you locate extraction in bureaucracy when bureaucracy seems so fluid?

Indeed, suppose our own academic questions about narrative and bureaucracies were anticipated in, or even essential to, how these stories were told? What if the confusion of services and terrors was in fact the emplotment? What if "What were fire engines doing in the places they did not belong?" meant "What sort of society puts fire engines on runways and blood-draining vehicles on the streets at night?" Africans did not misrepresent ambulances—vans with tubes and pumps inside them—but they misrepresented their motives: the trucks did not cure sick people, but attacked those unlucky enough to be walking alone at night. These stories may be a colonial African version of a complaint one hears daily in Africa: that officials have failed to keep the streets safe. These narratives make access, mobility, and safety into issues for debate and reflection. They problematize Western technology and the vehicles in which the advantages of that technology were delivered to Africans.

The presentation of cars in stories, even stories about vampires, reveals popular ideas about the interaction between culture and technology, between bodies and machines. In many societies, automobiles generate their own folklore, becoming the vehicles of older symbols and associations, while their symbolic value is equal to their material worth. That vehicles could be controlled, modified, and transformed may have reflected the imagined powers of their manufacturers or the real needs of their owners. Cars can take people away; motoring and roads are ways of erasing boundaries and reclassifying space.[46] Such reclassifica-

46. Most of the literature is North American, with the exception of Weiss, *Making and Unmaking of the Haya Lived World*, 181–83; Eric Mottram, *Blood on the Nash Ambassador: Investigations into American Culture* (London: Hutchinson, 1983), 62ff.; Stewart Sanderson, "The Folklore of the Motor-Car," *Folklore* 80 (1969): 241–42; Jan Harold Brunvand, *The Vanishing Hitchhiker: American Urban Legends and Their Meanings* (New York: Norton, 1981), 19–46; F. H. Moorhouse, "The 'Work' Ethic and 'Leisure' Activity: The Hot Rod in Post-War America," in Patrick Joyce, ed., *The Historical Meanings of Work* (Cambridge: Cambridge University Press, 1987), 244; Warren James Belasco, *Americans on the Road: From Autocamp to Motel, 1910–1945* (Cambridge, Mass.: MIT Press, 1981), 8. It is of course possible to debate the relationship between bodies, their modifications, space, and technology without discussing cars, see, e.g., Barbara Allen, "'The Image on Glass': Technology, Tradition, and the Emergence of Folklore," *Western Folklore* 41 (1982): 85–103, and Caroline Walker Bynum, "Material Continuity, Personal Survival, and the Resurrection of the Body: A Scholastic Discussion in Its Medieval and

tions did not always seem disembodied. In 1931, in central Tanganyika, an African "agreed readily" to get into the car with the district officer and a Dr. Williamson and to give them the names of the rivers along their route, "but upon the Doctor's asking him to show his tongue, he leaped out of the car and fled in terror."[47] Cars were fearsome depending on who was in them and where they were going or where they were parked. The vanette behind the governor's car, the fire engines on the runway, and the courting couple's darkened car implied the contradiction of orderly relations: they were parked in confusing spaces that blurred boundaries.[48] But the blurred boundaries may not have been those between the Yellow Fever Department and the fire brigade; they may have been those between certain kinds of employment and machines: one man's blurred boundaries were someone else's identity. Uniforms, drills, and daily polishings of equipment made some jobs appear categorically different from the sort of casual labor a man could take up and abandon with ease. In 1935, for example, Nairobi firemen polished equipment and drilled nine and a half hours a day; the nightly lookout had to report "every fifteen minutes. . . . This is salutary from a disciplinary point of view, as well as keeping the guard awake."[49] It was a job without the boundaries of a working day. Wazimamoto "dressed in fire brigade uniforms in the daylight," but at night they were "doing this job for Europeans who were at that time their supreme commanders."[50] Such discipline and authority changed their demeanor, of course: "[T]hey are only brotherly during daylight, but at night they turn 'mumianis.' "[51] Such work paid better than the most lucrative casual labor: a woman in Tanzania was sure her husband was mumiani because he went away for weeks at a time and always returned with money: "[A] thief cannot al-

Modern Contexts," in id., *Fragmentation and Redemption: Essays on Gender and the Human Body in Medieval Religion* (New York: Zone Books, distributed by MIT Press, 1991).

47. E. E. Hutchings, district officer, Morogoro, August 1931 (Tanzania National Archives, MF 15, Morogoro District, vol. 1/A, 15–16). I am grateful to Thaddeus Sunseri for these notes. I have tried half-heartedly to find out whether this Dr. Williamson was the Williamson of Williamson Diamond Mines, who arrived in South Africa to work for De Beers in 1928. Williamson was a geologist who insisted on being called "doctor" but his Ph.D. in that field was granted in Canada in 1933; see Stefan Kanfer, *The Last Empire: De Beers, Diamonds, and the World* (New York: Farrar, Straus & Giroux, 1993), 109.

48. See Mary Douglas, *Purity and Danger: An Analysis of the Concepts of Pollution and Taboo* (London: Tavistock, 1984), 35, 85.

49. J. B. Powell, superintendent, Nairobi Municipal Fire Brigade, AR, 1935, Nairobi Municipal Council Minutes, January–June 1936 (KNA, PC/NBI2/50).

50. Daniel Sekirrata, Katwe, Uganda, 22 August 1990.

51. Abdul Baka, letter to the editor, *Tanganyika Standard*, 14 July 1969, 4.

ways be lucky. One day he might miss or be caught. But my husband always comes back with money so I am sure he is mumiani." [52]

CONCEALING MEN

These stories do not tell us anything about the living African men inside the vehicles.[53] Cars without windows cannot reveal the men inside; they were known to be hidden, or at least undetectable. One man said he could not be sure of the race of bazimamoto in Kampala because they always did their work at night.[54] Another claimed that they were chosen for their jobs with great secrecy and caution. "It was not an open job for anybody, you had to be a friend of somebody in the government, and it was top secret, so it was not easy to recruit anybody to begin there, although it was well paid." [55]

If vehicles without windows or lights concealed their occupants, they also hid the work of fighting fires, and the labor process of capturing people: "I only heard that wazimamoto sucked blood from people but I never heard how they got those people." [56] "The act was confidential." [57] The relationship of the vehicles—and their specific sounds—obscured the work. In Nairobi in the 1940s, Peter Hayombe recalled, "Their actual job was not known to us. All we were told was that they were supposed to put out burning fires. Whenever there was a burning fire we would hear bell noises and we were told that the wazimamoto were on their way to put it out." [58] But many people also heard that the wazimamoto "ambushed people and threw them in a waiting vehicle," [59] and

52. Quoted in Lloyd William Swantz, "The Role of the Medicine Man among the Zaramo of Dar es Salaam" (Ph.D. diss., University of Dar es Salaam, 1972), 337.

53. Dead bodies transported in vehicles were another matter, however. Corpses were said to be purchased from hospitals and driven to the Congo. Several men "transported dead bodies in the backseat of his car. These bodies were always smartly dressed." A few others sold corpses "to Senegalese who used them to safely transport their gold in. These dead bodies were cut through the skin, opened inside, and then gold could be dumped there. If the authorities tried to arrest them, these people could claim they were taking sick relatives for treatment." Ahmed Kiziri, Katwe, Uganda, 20 August 1990. Similar stories were told by Musoke Kopliumu, Katwe, Uganda, 22 August 1990; Daniel Sekirrata, Katwe, Uganda, 22 August 1990; Gregory Sseruwagi, Lubya, Uganda, 28 August 1990.

54. Sepirya Kasule, Kisenyi, Uganda, 28 August 1990.

55. George Ggingo, Kasubi, Uganda, 15 August 1990.

56. Noah Asingo Olungu, Goma Village, Yimbo, Siaya, Kenya, 22 August 1986.

57. Simbwa Jjuko, Bwaize, Uganda, 20 August 1990.

58. Peter Hayombe, interview cited in n. 1 above.

59. Domtila Achola, Uchonga Ukudi Village, Alego, Siaya, Kenya, 11 August 1986; Alozius Kironde, Kasubi, Uganda, 17 August 1990.

"the victims used to call out for help when they were being taken in the vehicle,"[60] but even men and women who had narrowly escaped capture did not know much more. Late one night in western Kenya in 1959, a woman "found a group of men hiding behind a vehicle that had no lights of any sort." She ran and hid, but they looked for her until "the first cock crowed and one of them said 'Oh, oh, oh, the time is over.'"[61] In rural Uganda that same year—across eastern Africa, 1959 was a year of widespread blood accusations[62]—a man was awakened by villagers "saying that the place had been invaded by bazimamoto." He hid behind a large tree and "narrowly evaded capture." In the full moon's light, he could see their car and their clothes—"black trousers and white coats"—but could not describe what they did: "Afterwards I heard that several people had lost their blood."[63]

Even men who claimed to have done this work, either as firemen or policemen, described a labor process that had more to do with hierarchies and automobiles than with co-workers. Anyango Mahondo said that capturing Africans was essential to discipline, rank, and on-the-job seniority, and he described the organization of work as a relationship to a white man and a waiting vehicle.

> When one joined the police force [in Kampala] in those olden days, he would undergo the initial training of bloodsucking. . . . When he qualified there, he was then absorbed into the police force as a constable. This particular training was designed to give the would-be policeman overwhelming guts and courage to execute his duties effectively. . . . During the day, we were police recruits. Immediately after sunset, we started the job of manhunting . . . we would leave the station in a group of four and one white man, who was in charge. Once in town, we would leave the vehicle and walk around in pairs. When we saw a person, we would lie down and ambush him. We would then take the captured person back to the waiting vehicle. . . . We used to hide vehicles by parking them behind buildings or parking a reasonable distance from our manhunt . . . the precautions we took were to switch off the engine and the lights.[64]

Here, knowledge of the vehicle is described in much greater detail than is knowledge of the white man. The extension of the working day

60. Alozius Kironde, Kasubi, Uganda, 17 August 1990.
61. Margaret Mwajuma, Ndegro Uranga Village, Alego, Siaya, Kenya, 11 August 1986.
62. Brelsford, "'Banyama' Myth,", 54–56.
63. Gregory Sseruwagi, Lubya, Uganda, 28 August 1990.
64. Anyango Mahondo, interview cited n. 3 above.

is taken for granted in this account. What does it mean when people describe technology, equipment, and modified vehicles in ways that obscure descriptions of work and the time the work takes? The absence of light and useful windows, the "shiny metal back" made these vehicles closed, protected, and opaque. Their insides were not known. Men who could describe the insides of pits could not describe the insides of trucks. Dangerous vehicles and the modifications specific to them made the men who performed the work of capture safe, secluded, and anonymous; even they could not describe what they did. But veiling labor with different mechanisms—curtains, no lights, shiny metal backs—kept it secret and indicated that something the public should not see was going on inside. Veiling labor focused attention on it, and on the need to maintain secrecy, and made it the object of scrutiny and speculation.[65] Making certain jobs hidden relocated them in the realm of the imagination; while certain kinds of workers might complain about a lack of public awareness of their jobs, that lack of awareness gave the public enormous control: their description of what went on in the hidden vehicle went unchallenged by the men in the cars.[66] When Africans asserted what went on inside these vehicles, they were imagined as places of the most frightening productions: the Sabena aircraft on which Africans recently turned into pigs were canned. To counter the fears of what was inside a curtained van, a district officer in Tanganyika gave villagers a tour of the inside of a white geologist's van; he thought that if they saw what the curtains actually hid—a bed, a table and chairs, and a photograph of a fiancée—he could guarantee the young man's safety.[67] When the anthropology student John Middleton first came to northern Uganda in 1950, his funders had given him a bright red van, closed in the back, "and the rumor had gone round among the Lugbara that he used it to go out and steal babies to eat before touching up the paintwork with their blood." But a local mechanic was able to install rear windows "so that all and sundry could more easily inspect his possessions."[68]

65. Ludmilla Jordanova, *Sexual Visions: Images of Gender in Science and Medicine between the Eighteenth and Twentieth Centuries* (Madison: University of Wisconsin Press, 1989), 92–93.
66. Robert McCarl, *The District of Columbia Fire Fighters' Project: A Case Study in Occupational Folklore* (Washington, D.C.: Smithsonian Institution Press, 1985), 131–36, reports that Washington, D.C., firefighters routinely complained that the public's ignorance of firefighting increased the likelihood of fires while maintaining that the techniques and challenges of their work made it too esoteric to make public.
67. Bates, *Mango and the Palm*, 53–54.
68. Roland Oliver, *In the Realms of Gold* (Madison: University of Wisconsin Press, 1997), 117.

REVEALING LABOR

The veiling of labor was frequently done with metal and electrical equipment. In Kampala, it was commonplace to explain that the term *bazimamoto* referred to the use of automotive equipment, not to firefighting. "These people did their job at night, so when they approached somebody they would switch off the lights and in Kiswahili to switch off is *kuzima* and the light is *moto*."[69] This translation of Kiswahili into Luganda is wrong; *kuzima taa* means "to put out the light"; *kuzima moto* means "to put out the fire." But it is a mistranslation that reflects the importance of automobile equipment in Ugandan vampire stories.

And what is that importance? It seems to be a knowledge of the mechanics of engine sounds and electrical systems. It was a technical knowledge known only to a privileged few, whose specialized skills then concealed the labor process by which it was acquired. A labor process, according to Marx, is the "hidden abode of production," discernible only when one leaves the noise of the factory floor.[70] Elsewhere, a trade unionist's description of the labor process collapses the boundaries between bodies: "The brains of the foreman are under the worker's cap," said Big Bill Haywood, one of the founders of the Industrial Workers of the World.[71] Some of the material presented here, however, suggests that the secrecy of the labor process may have been concealed by laborers themselves. Work routines learned on the job may have produced an unexpected camaraderie. A man who was a railway fireman in Nairobi from 1936 to 1958 described a fabulous subterranean system of technical sophistication:

> Pipes were installed all over the town. People never used to know the exact place where the pipes were, but us, we used to know. Whites were very clever. They used to cover the pipes and taps with some form of iron sheets. When a fire was burning anywhere we would go locate the tap and fix our hoses up. . . . Running water was there throughout the year, therefore we never experienced any shortage of water at anytime of the year.[72]

69. George Ggingo; also Mangarita Kalule, Masanafu, Uganda, 20 August 1990; Juliana Nakibuuka Nalongo, Lubaga, Uganda, 21 August 1990; Joseph Nsubuge, Kisati, Kampala, Uganda, 22 August 1990; Musoke Kopliumu, Katwe, Kampala, Uganda, 22 August 1990; Gregory Sseruwagi, Lubya, Uganda, 28 August 1990.

70. Karl Marx, *Capital, A Critique of Political Economy*, vol. 1 (1867; reprint, Harmondsworth: Penguin Books, 1976), 279–80.

71. William "Big Bill" Haywood, 1914, quoted in John Higginson, *A Working Class in the Making: Belgian Colonial Labor Policy, Private Enterprise, and the African Mineworker, 1907–51* (Madison: University of Wisconsin Press, 1989), 86.

72. Alec Okaro, Mahero Village, Alego, Siaya, Kenya, 12 August 1986.

To understand is to exert powers [handwritten]

Nairobi in the mid 1930s had two fire engines and 508 hydrants, and virtually no funds for hydrant or water distribution system repair.[73] Nevertheless, this fireman's account praises informal knowledge, which could only be learned on the job, or from co-workers' conversations and anecdotes, especially in places where recruits were hired off the street and did not graduate from training programs.[74] In this account, the informal expertise of firefighting—passed from white man to black man—was knowing where the pipes were hidden, not putting out fires. A Holy Ghost Father in Tanganyika complained about a young African whose informal knowledge dominated a conversation about machines. The priest was explaining to a few Africans that "the driving power" in cars and airplanes was petrol, when a well-traveled African remarked that he had once seen a car filled with petrol and had seen that the petrol was "reddish . . . according to him the power of the petrol was derived from the fact that there was human blood in it! And his opinion met with general support."[75] Understanding the technology of how things worked was part of the experience of African migrancy, as was talking about what they were not allowed to fully understand. In 1923, a man wrote to a Tanganyikan newspaper that wazimamoto worked near the toilets the government built in Nairobi "but afterwards gave no permission for people to use those toilets."[76] In Kampala, it was said,

They kept victims in big pits. Those pits were made in such a way that no one would notice them. Whites are very bad people. They are so cunning and clever. . . . The job of police recruits was to get victims and nothing else. Occasionally, we went down the pits, and if we were lucky saw bloodsucking in progress but nothing more. . . . Those pits were really hidden, and even those working within the police station could not notice them. The pits were built horizontally, and at the entrance they built a small room. To hide the whole thing from everyone the entrances were covered with carpets. . . . The blood was sucked from the victims until they were considered useless. When that day came, they would die and then be buried in a more secret place, known only to the government. . . . people were buried at night to keep the secret.[77]

73. J. B. Powell, superintendent, Nairobi Municipal Fire Brigade, AR, 1935, Nairobi Municipal Council Minutes, January–June 1936 (KNA, PC/NBI 2/50).

74. McCarl, *District of Columbia Fire Fighters' Project,* 136–40. Apprenticeship, however, was often parodied by religious movements in the colonial Congo; see Edouard Bustin, "Government Policy toward African Cult Movements: The Cases of Katanga," in Mark Karp, ed., *African Dimensions: Essays in Honor of William O. Brown* (Boston: African Studies Center, Boston University, 1975), 117.

75. Schreerder, "Mumiani" (cited n. 1 above).

76. "Adiyisadiki" (cited n. 12 above).

77. Anyango Mahondo, interview cited n. 3 above.

My point is not that the knowledge of technologies, times and places was more important than the work itself, but that the knowledge that was otherwise secret bonded a few select Africans to specialized procedures. In November 1934, Godfrey Wilson's assistants told him of the "highly" paid African men "sent out by the government" to kill other Africans and take their blood, which hospitalized Europeans required. "The Government says to them 'if you are caught, we will not be responsible, you will be killed.'"[78] In 1958, in eastern Northern Rhodesia, prison warders overheard rumors that the local station of the Société des Missionnaires d'Afrique, called the White Fathers, were about to kidnap Africans and had already marked their victims with "the Sign of the Cross which was not visible to the intended victim or to his fellows but only to the Europeans and their African henchmen."[79] The invisible signs, the secrets of the pipes and the pits, the allocation of responsibility, reveal another dimension to workers' own and popular perceptions of the advantages—technological and social—of semi-skilled labor. Those popular perceptions underscored the bonds between wazimamoto and the men they employed. In Tanganyika in the early 1930s, a chief complained that "tricksters" extorted money by carrying "bottles of red ink" that spilled when they deliberately bumped into passers-by. Claiming that "they were servants of 'mumiani'" who had just spilled the bottles of blood they were taking to their "masters," they then told these strangers they now needed more blood. The frightened strangers gave them money to get rid of them.[80] Europeans' anecdotes had it that after the riots at the Mombasa Fire Station in 1947, whites in a wealthy suburb ended their dinner parties "sharp at eight" so that the servants who lived in town could "march together" home, carrying "spears and other warlike gear" to fight off mumiani.[81] Bonds between workers and employers were different from those of blood. According to a Tanganyikan man, when a man came to greet his brother who worked for wazimamoto in Nairobi, his brother quickly sent him away: "[L]eave right now, if my friends see you here you are dead. Let me ask you," wrote

---

78. Godfrey Wilson's notebooks, 1935, University of Cape Town, Manuscript and Archives Department.

79. Brelford, "'Banyama' Myth," 55.

80. E. E. Hutchings, district officer, Morogoro, "'Mumiani' or 'Chinjachinja,'" (Tanzania National Archives, film no. MF 15, Morogoro District, vol. 1, part A, sheets 25–26, August 1931, but inserted into file marked 1938).

81. Edward Rodwell, *Coast Causerie 2: Columns from the Mombasa Times* (Nairobi: Heinemann, 1973), 21.

a believer, "someone who comes to see his brother at work, should he die?" [82]

Occupational folklorists have described how technical expertise is parodied by those so skilled—the airplane pilots who board a plane with a white cane and dark glasses to frighten their passengers—as a challenge to managerial authority.[83] Bolivian tin miners performed ceremonies that denied the importance of skill, "to make the tools help us in our work." [84] African historians who have been able to compare oral and written accounts of the same skilled labor have shown how specialized, skilled labor portrays itself and is portrayed in words of privilege and superiority. Mine managers' views of Basotho shaft sinkers in South Africa, for example, encouraged their sense of superiority but also praised their camaraderie; Basotho shaft sinkers spoke of their favored status in the mine compounds and of the high wages their specialization offered.[85] Workers' narratives may reveal the tensions and conflicts at the workplace that managerial accounts omit. Workers' oral narratives about technology, however imprecise and inaccurate they are, are a way to foreground ambiguities and conflicts about the work itself. The man who boasted of the knowledge of hidden pipes he shared with "clever whites" was proud of his on-the-job training. He also insisted that in his twenty-two years as a railway fireman, he never saw anyone captured, although he admitted that "on seeing us people used to run in all directions." [86]

But other men saw certain kinds of skills as courting danger. A Ugandan man said that bazimamoto "operated in villages during the night. A bell would be tied up to an electricity pole and when it was rung, immediately a vehicle would drive by to pick victims. Once a man was captured near my home. He was one of the Uganda Electricity Board workers." [87] African concerns about mechanization, about the technological nature of skilled jobs may have been expressed in vampire stories: the

82. "Adiyisadiki" (cited n. 12 above).

83. Jack Santino, "'Flew the Ocean in a Plane': An Investigation of Airline Occupation Narrative," *Journal of the Folklore Institute* 15, 3 (1978): 202–7.

84. A miner quoted in June Nash, "The Devil in Bolivia's Nationalized Tin Mines," *Science and Society* 36, 2 (1972): 227; for another interpretation, see Michael Taussig, *The Devil and Commodity Fetishism in South America* (Chapel Hill: University of North Carolina Press), 1980, 207–13.

85. Jeff Guy, "Technology, Ethnicity, and Ideology: Basotho Miners and Shaft Sinking on the South African Gold Mines," *J. Southern Afr. Studies* 14, 2 (1988): 260–69.

86. Alec Okaro.

87. Sepirya Kasule.

physical conditions of workers on the job—the subject of so much
investigation by employers and scientists—were also debated by the
workers themselves.[88] These concerns do not seem to have been about
the societal impact of mechanization, but about a gendered boundary
between men and machines that could refashion potency and performance.[89] Blood accusations were most public in the mines of colonial
Katanga after mechanized shovels were timed and tested against a team
of pick-and-shovel men.[90] People in Dar es Salaam in the late 1950s and
1960s feared for the potency of men who went to give blood in fire engines, or thought that firemen had injections that made men "lazy and
unable to do anything."[91] Twenty years later, Tanzanians claimed that
certain houses in Mwanza, on the eastern shore of Lake Victoria, stole
peoples' blood. "The front door is made of wood, and they have written 'Danger, Electricity' on it. But if you touch it, straight away the electricity catches you and your blood is sucked out."[92]

Vampire stories were most private when occupations were neither
challenged nor explained. The return home leveled the distinctiveness of
the most extraordinary careers: "All policemen in those olden days were
the agents of wazimamoto." But "when someone was a policeman he
remains so even after leaving his job. Policemen are always careful what
they leave out. Retired policemen cannot tell you what they were doing
during their working time."[93] The same man who described how best to
park a car when capturing unwary Africans said he could not tell anyone about it. "How could I do that after swearing to keep secrets? The
works of policemen were very hard and involved so many awful things
some of which cannot be revealed to anyone. Because of the nature of
my work I could not tell anyone even my wife . . . even my brothers I
could not tell."[94] Storytelling both presents personal identity and allows
it to be negotiated and redefined by the audience; withholding sto-

88. Anson Rabinbach, *The Human Motor: Energy, Fatigue, and the Origins of
Modernity* (Berkeley and Los Angeles: University of California Press, 1992); for examples
of the frequency with which scientists botched attempts to ameliorate health hazards in
the workplace, see Donald Reid, *Paris Sewers and Sewermen: Realities and Representations* (Cambridge, Mass.: Harvard University Press, 1991).
89. Guy, "Technology, Ethnicity, and Ideology," 269, gives a particularly graphic example of this point.
90. John Higginson, "Steam without a Piston Box: Strikes and Popular Unrest in
Katanga, 1943–1945," *Int. J. Afr. Hist. Studies* 21, 1 (1988): 101–2.
91. Quoted in Swantz, "Role of the Medicine Man," 336.
92. Weiss, *Making and Unmaking of the Haya Lived World,* 203.
93. Timotheo Omondo, Goma Village, Yimbo, Siaya, Kenya, 22 August 1986.
94. Anyango Mahondo, interview cited n. 3 above.

ries may permit personal and professional identity to be rigidly maintained.[95] These stories were not explanations; they were accusations:
they did not explain misfortune, but imputed work, identity, and loyalty.

TOOLS OF EMPIRE

When studying narratives about vampiric firemen in Africa, it is important that we identify what was weird and unnatural in these stories
to their tellers and not become overly concerned with what seems that
weird and unnatural to ourselves. It is easy for Western scholars to get
bogged down in the issue of blood-drinking Europeans, but that is in
fact the most natural part of the story, demonstrated over and over by
community and common sense: "Of course the stories were true. . . .
People used to warn each other not to walk at night." [96] But what was
unnatural and weird to the people who told these stories may well have
been those things that were rare and unnatural in their daily lives—cars
and electricity.

But these stories are not simple condemnations of technological
change and motor transport; medical technology and cars and electrical
equipment were, in narrative and in daily life, mediated through a very
African medium—working men. Specialized equipment was used by
small specialized occupational groups, and for these men, technology
had an intense meaning: they talked about it in interviews more than
they talked about work. For the most part, technical knowledge was ap-
portioned so sparingly and so slowly that it began to defy natural laws:
in this way, railway firemen could claim that they had water even in the
dry season. In reality, the allocation of specialized tools and tasks to a
few skilled laborers kept most people in ignorance of how automobiles
or electricity poles actually worked; on a symbolic level, this kept technology from becoming naturalized in any way.

The very peculiarity of cars, lights, and mirrors made the men who
could use them a little peculiar as well. The new tools not only bonded
men to machines in odd ways—whatever went on inside the curtained
truck?—but bound men to mechanization. Marxist theorists of the la-

95. This point comes from two articles by Jack Santino, "Miles of Smiles, Years of
Struggle: The Negotiation of Black Occupational Identity through the Personal Experience
Narrative," *J. American Folklore* 96, 382 (1983): 394–412, and "Occupational Ghostlore: Social Context and the Expression of Belief," *J. American Folklore* 101, 400 (1988):
207–18.
96. Nyakida Omolo, Kabura, West Alego, Siaya, Kenya, 19 August 1986.

bor aristocracy have described how the work rhythms required by the technological demands of new industries identified skilled workers with management in nineteenth-century England.[97] Although the same processes did not take place in non-industrialized Africa, it is likely that their specialized tools and techniques placed skilled laborers under their employers' control in ways that unskilled laborers had never been managed. Such a man might know where "the clever whites" hid their pipes, or pits, or signs, or have had the on-the-job training "to execute his duties effectively," but he was, in the process, never insulated from his employer's supervision and commands, or the vulnerability these commands brought him.

Tools and technology have recently been studied as one of the ways in which Europeans dominated the colonized world; they were supposed to overpower Africans or to mystify them.[98] But the contradictory meanings of tools in these stories is too intricate, and too dense, to be explained in any single way. The tools in these stories have been assimilated; to some extent, they were already familiar objects, whatever their origin.[99] What made them fearsome was how and why they were used — both in narrative and as narrative. On the Northern Rhodesian Copperbelt, there were *mupila,* "white balls of drugs," thrown into the path of a lone traveler, to whom the banyama then spoke. "If he answered all his power left him, his clothes fell off, and he no longer had a memory or a will."[100] In the southeastern Belgian Congo in the 1940s, flashlights had the same effect.[101] In Dar es Salaam, thirty years later, "They use many things to catch people. Sometimes they use a mirror . . . your mind changes and you just follow to any place they go."[102] Tools themselves, properly used, could disempower ordinary Africans. Those who were skilled enough to use them lost something too — not their sense of direction, but their identity: they became invisible.

97. F. H. Moorhouse, "The Marxist Theory of the Labour Aristocracy," *Social History* 3, 1 (1978): 64–66.

98. Daniel R. Headrick, *The Tools of Empire: Technology and European Imperialism in the Nineteenth Century* (Oxford: Oxford University Press, 1981), and Michael Adas, *Machines as the Measures of Men: Science, Technology, and Ideologies of Western Dominance* (Ithaca, N.Y.: Cornell University Press, 1989).

99. See Ivan Karp, "Other Cultures in Museum Perspective," in id., and Steven D. Levine, eds., *Exhibiting Cultures: The Poetics and Politics of Museum Displays* (Washington, D.C.: Smithsonian Institution Press, 1991), 373–85.

100. P. K. Kanosa, "Banyama—Copper Belt Myth Terrifies the Foolish," *Mutende* [Lusaka] 38 (1936) (NAZ, SEC2/429, Native Affairs: Banyama); Eustace Njbovu, Kapani, Luangwa, Zambia, 22 July 1990.

101. Ceyssens, "Mutumbula," 491.

102. Quoted in Swantz, "Role of the Medicine Man," 336.

In these narratives, technology reveals unnatural acts—not blood-sucking or odd behavior in parked cars, but the regimented labor process required by technology: on-the-job training, rank, time discipline, and intense supervision, even after hours. The cars and lights and mirrors in these stories were not the only Western, specialized tools introduced into colonial Africa, but they are the only such equipment that regularly appears in vampire stories over a wide geographic and cultural area. These technologies did not arouse accusations about the forcible removal of blood because they were foreign or even because they were associated with a dominant power; they feature in these stories because they aroused the greatest anxieties.[103] But they did not arouse anxieties because they were imperfectly understood or imperfectly assimilated or because automobile lights had not become a "natural" African symbol; they aroused the greatest anxiety because these were technologies that exposed other kinds of relationships. The presence of bells or cars without lights in so many personal narratives about vampires reveals the extent to which these new tools and technologies meant something terrifying to individual Africans. They were not terrifying in and of themselves, but because of how they were used and by whom. The relationships of hardened control over a few privileged workers revealed by the new technologies of cars and bells and lights were intrusive to the point of extracting blood, intensive to the point of supervising skilled labor on the job or after hours. Men and women in Uganda who translated *bazimamoto* as "the men who turn off the light" had a powerful, mechanical term to describe the work that extracted blood, the skilled Africans who carried it out, and the whites who supervised them. Naming the vampires after what they did to a car pronounced their work unnatural; it made it clear that these tasks were performed at night, well beyond the standards and the norms of the working day. Thus the term captured the distinctions between the skilled workers, the European overseers, and the population whom it was their job to abduct.[104]

But how are we to make sense of these particular arrangements of metal and electric lights and blood? Which was most horrible, the drain-

103. Gary Allen Fine, "The Kentucky Fried Rat: Legends and Modern Society," *J. of the Folklore Institute* 17, 2–3 (1980): 237; Allen, "'Image on Glass,'" 103; Bynum, "Material Continuity," 64.

104. Franco Moretti, *Signs Taken for Wonders: Essays in the Sociology of Literary Forms,* trans. Susan Fischer, David Fragacs, and David Miller (London: Verso, 1983), makes a similar point about horror literature, particularly *Frankenstein* and *Dracula:* both represent the extremes of a society, he argues; "The literature of terror is born *precisely out of the terror of a split society,* and out of the desire to heal it" (83).

ing of blood or the use and abuse of familiar tools and trucks? Certainly, assertions about the nature of work, wages, and progress are made by the vehicles without lights, rubber pumps, and bells in these stories,[105] but these images were always animated by employed Africans. In Kampala, the bazimamoto "employed agents who lived among the people and had cars."[106] But was it the owners, the drivers, or the cars that took the blood? Such a question may make distinctions that the storytellers I have quoted studiously avoided. While my informants were crystal clear that the bazimamoto were humans, most described the technological aspects of human agency. They did not distinguish a clear-cut boundary between man and machine, and if we attempt to impose such a line, we may lose sight of the questions and anxieties that made the line between man and machine so blurred: if someone works with specific tools in a specific mechanized space, or even when he is taken to donate blood in a fire engine, how can he retain his masculinity, his humanity? What kind of being lives in a truck with curtained windows, and what kind of beings reproduce in the backseats of parked cars?[107] Indeed, did the men who worked closely with machines—drivers, passengers, men who worked with electricity or mechanical shovels—rehearse biological or mechanical reproduction?[108]

But if African workers were concerned about what happened to men who got too close to machines, employers and officials favored the idea that Africans could be dazzled by technology. In 1933, for example, a European wrote to the Tanganyikan government explaining the origins of mumiani: a Parsee who lived near Mombasa in 1906 who "would attract natives to his house by means of a magnetic glass."[109] If Africans imagined that these technologies sucked blood or made men impotent, officials explained them as simple misunderstandings. The Tanganyikan

105. See Jordanova, *Sexual Visions,* 111.

106. Samuel Mubiru, interview cited n. 21 above.

107. *Embalasassa,* the mythical "poisonous reptiles which politicians never wanted to talk about publicly" were said to have been sent by Obote during his first regime to kill Baganda; they could also breed in machines, claimed Jonah Waswa Kigozi, Katwe, Uganda, 16 August 1990. "Somewhere . . . near Kaziba market [on the Tanzanian border] there was something made out of an old army tank which the villagers broke into only to discover embalasassa eggs inside." Alozios Matovu, Uganda, Kasubi, 17 August 1990, among others, concurred. See also W. B. Banage, W. N. Byarugaba, and J. D. Goodman, "The Embalasassa (*Riopa fernandi*): A Story of Real and Mythical Zoology," *Uganda Journal* 36 (1972): 67–72.

108. Mark Seltzer, *Bodies and Machines* (New York: Routledge, 1992), 13, 25–41.

109. Mr. Merrill, to colonial secretary, Tanganyika Territory, 19 October 1933. I am grateful to Thaddeus Sunseri and Laura Fair for these notes.

African who told his fellows that petrol was red because of blood simply misunderstood the additives in British army petrol, wrote the priest; other Africans were said to have misunderstood roofing tar, bottles of red wine, or why fire engines were red.[110] But employers and officials wanted tools and structures that would impress Africans. The same year that the Nairobi Fire Brigade put out five fires, the fire master complained that he had no sliding pole to help him get to fire engines quickly: as it was he had to dash through his sitting room and down a narrow flight of stairs; he wanted a pole placed outside his bedroom window. "My desire is the efficiency of the brigade."[111] Many years later, when Indian merchants gave Uganda the gift of a large clocktower to be erected on the roundabout of the Kampala Fire Station in 1954, they installed two loudspeakers to amplify the chimes. One faced the town and the other the suburb of Katwe—so well known for rumor that the popular term for street talk was "Radio Katwe." It was hoped that these chimes would wake up workers in Katwe and that eventually the loudspeakers could be used to broadcast announcements there.[112]

CONCLUSIONS

Why did African men represent the conflicts and problematics of the new skills and economic regimes in stories about public employees who sucked blood? The simplest answer is perhaps best: no other idea could carry the weight of the complications of work, identities, and machines. First, it is a metaphor of colonial origin; despite official attempts to link it to "traditional" practices, most African informants said bazimamoto emerged in the late teens and early 1920s. Second, these vampires were described with all the tools and technologies, all the uniforms, titles, and rank and authority of colonial bureaucracies: vampires were encumbered with all the formalities and inefficiencies of colonial public services. Their dreadful night duties explained the senseless routine and the discipline of their daytime jobs. That capturing Africans was a job for

110. Schreerder, "Mumiani" (cited above); Hutchings, "'Mumiani' or 'Chinja-chinja,'" (cited n. 80 above); Bates, *Mango and the Palm,* 54–55; Hope Trant, *Not Merrion Square: Anecdotes of a Woman's Medical Career in Africa* (Toronto: Thornhill Press, 1970), 127–44.

111. J. B. Powell, Nairobi Municipal Fire Brigade, AR, 1935, Nairobi Municipal Council Minutes, January–June 1936 (KNA, CP/NBI/2/50).

112. "Kampala's New Clock Tower," *Uganda Herald,* 29 May 1954, 1. I am grateful to Timothy Scarnecchia for these notes.

some Africans, requiring intense secrecy, organization, and supervision, made vampires uniquely well suited to represent the conflicts and ambiguities of labor, because vampiric firemen were not an established fact: many people doubted their existence, and insisted that the rumors began when Africans misconstrued European actions. The debate was not merely about whether or not colonial vampires existed, but about the nature and the attributes of certain kinds of labor. The disputable character of wazimamoto was part of its significance; such disagreements continually posed the questions, did an identifiably separate group of skilled laborers exist and, if they did, what was their impact on the wider society?

PART THREE

CHAPTER 5

"A Special Danger"

Gender, Property, and Blood in Nairobi,
1919–1939

This chapter is about local meanings, local usages, and local concerns. The vampire stories told in the legal African locations of Nairobi were not very different from those told elsewhere in East Africa, but they had a markedly different time frame, and, I argue, markedly different meanings. The vampire stories and the gossip about who worked for *wazimamoto* did more than identify unpopular accumulators or explain how bad people became rich. This chapter argues that local versions of rumor and gossip provided some of the images, metaphors, and vocabularies that created new cosmologies, new moral constructs in which new rights and obligations were invented, made concrete, and passed on. Women maintained their fragile hold on durable property rights by all the strategies colonial societies made available; they described these rights as perhaps more distinct and solid than they actually were: as this chapter shows, some of the most vocal advocates of women's property rights were women who had never owned homes themselves. But at the same time, propertied and unpropertied women told stories about skilled wazimamoto who crept silently about women's rooms with tubes and bandages in the night, and with stories about individual women who sold their sisters and their friends to the wazimamoto. For some women, wazimamoto stories were a way to describe the vulnerability of propertied women, the "special danger" faced by those women who lived alone. Most vampire stories were about extraction and agency; they showed the grim and mercenary motives of the colonial state, but

in Nairobi these stories added another layer of agency and work to wazimamoto—women who worked for the firemen, capturing victims for
them. They described a world in which relations of blood were easily ex-
propriated and just as easily kept at bay.

URBANIZATION IN KENYA

Perhaps the most significant way in which urban Kenya differed from
rural Kenya even at the turn of the century was that women could own
huts in the former but not in the latter. The degree of that ownership was
often compromised by a variety of factors, such as the undermining of
women's Koranic inheritance in early colonial Mombasa by an amicable
combination of their relatives and the colonial state, but wherever wom-
en's property ownership was allowed to occur, women clung to it by
whatever means were at their disposal.[1] Women's property ownership
under colonialism was markedly different from what they had had before: in the "house property complex" of South and North-east Africa,
the land a women farmed was distributed to her sons and she had cus-
todial rights over the livestock destined for them as well.[2] But as early as
1899 in eastern Kenya, when no legal system actually governed the area,
twenty-five Maasai "loose women" built huts and were taxed on them
by the Imperial British East Africa Company.[3] A few years later in Nairobi, women built huts, divided them into rooms, and lived in one and
let the others at high rents. Within a few years, women were speculating
in the city's burgeoning property market.[4]

1. Margaret Strobel, *Muslim Women in Mombasa* (New Haven: Yale University Press,
1979), 58–69; Greet Kershaw, *Mau Mau from Below* (Oxford: James Currey 1997), 59,
126–27; provincial commissioner, Coast Province, to colonial secretary, Nairobi, "Legal
Ownership of Huts by Independent Women," 23 June 1930 (Kenya National Archives
[henceforth cited as KNA], PC/Coast/59/4).

2. Jack Goody and Joan Buckley, "Inheritance and Women's Labour in Africa," *Africa*
43, 2 (1973): 108–20; Godfrey Muriuki, *A History of the Kikuyu, 1500–1900* (Nairobi:
Oxford University Press, 1974), 75–76; Achola Pala Okeyo, "Daughters of the Lakes and
Rivers: Colonization and Land Rights of Luo Women," in Mona Etienne and Eleanor Leacock, *Women and Colonization: Anthropological Perspectives* (New York: Praeger, 1980),
186–213; Margaret Jean Hay, "Women as Owners, Occupants, and Managers of Property in Colonial Western Kenya," in id. and Marcia Wright, eds., *African Women and the
Law: Historical Perspectives* (Boston: African Studies Center, Boston University, 1982),
110–23.

3. Harold Mackinder Papers, 20 July 1899, Rhodes House, Oxford, RH MSS
Afr. r. 29.

4. Janet M. Bujra, "Pumwani: The Politics of Property" (mimeographed SSRC [U.K.]
report, 1972), 9–13, 51–54, and "Women 'Entrepreneurs' of Early Nairobi," *Canadian
J. of African Studies* 9, 2 (1975): 213–34; Charles H. Ambler, *Kenyan Communities in the
Age of Imperialism* (New Haven: Yale University Press, 1988), 139–40; Luise White, *The*

The question this chapter addresses is not how women achieved this, but how women talked about it, and how they constructed a world of fears and fantasies that imagined the possibility of women's property ownership. Indeed, this is the only chapter in which all the vampire stories are taken from oral interviews. Stories about blood, about who had it and who wanted it, and how it was obtained and purchased, were stories about concrete relationships; the fluidity and intimacy of blood meant that fluid relationships could be made solid when expressed in its vocabulary.

Historically, women had a variety of strategies for controlling and directing the flow of resources— woman-to-woman marriage, the allocation of use rights from their matrimonial parcels of land, or using house property cattle for bridewealth to marry another woman.[5] Our knowledge of these strategies is severely limited because researchers have rarely inquired about them; no one seemed to wonder how sixty-year-old childless women managed their wealth. But colonial urban life offered the legal mechanisms—and the legal space—by which these strategies could become durable. Colonial courts, land offices, and arbitrary systems of land tenure provided rights that were not under the control of fathers and husbands and brothers. "At home, what could I do? Grow crops for my husband and father. In Nairobi, I can earn my own money, for myself," said Kayaya Thababu, who went there in the mid 1920s.[6] Within the constraints of urban land tenure, women constructed rights for themselves and their heirs far beyond what they had been able to do previously.

But urban women's property rights, delicate as they were, did not come about in a political vacuum. By the mid 1920s, half of Nairobi's African property owners were women, almost all said to be prostitutes

---

Comforts of Home: Prostitution in Colonial Nairobi (Chicago: University of Chicago Press, 1990).

5. Christine Obbo, "Dominant Male Ideology and Female Options: Three East African Case Studies," *Africa* 46, 4 (1976): 371–88; L. S. B. Leakey, *The Southern Kikuyu before 1903* (London: Academic Press, 1977), 800–801; Regina Smith Oboler, "Is the Female Husband a Man? Woman/Woman Marriage among the Nandi of Kenya," *Ethnology* 19, 1 (1980): 69–88; Patricia Stamp, "Kikuyu Women's Self Help Groups," in Claire Roberstson and Iris Berger, eds., *Women and Class in Africa* (New York: Holmes & Meier, 1986), 27–44; Fiona MacKenzie, "Land and Territory: The Interface between Two Systems of Land Tenure, Murang'a District," *Africa* 59, 1 (1989): 91–109; Ivan Karp, "Laughter at Marriage: Subversion in Performance," in David Parkin and David Nyamwaya, eds., *The Transformation of African Marriage* (Manchester: Manchester University Press, 1987), 137–54.

6. Kayaya Thababu, Pumwani, 7 January 1977.

who had bought or built their houses with earnings from such work. Although the colonial state recognized the value of landlords who were also prostitutes—they had every reason to keep the peace, and their acquisitiveness kept labor circulating faster than pass laws did—officials were ambivalent about the social life that had emerged outside of colonial control, and the sense of community and stability it imparted to urban Africans in a city designed for European residence. The solution, worked out in committees between 1912 and 1915, was to allow Europeans freehold throughout the city and Africans usufruct in one small and poorly drained portion of it. In the official African location, Pumwani, finally established in 1921, plots could be transmitted to heirs but not bought and sold. The creation of one legal settlement made the two remaining African settlements illegal and had the effect of making housing in both places functionally usufruct, as few people were willing to buy houses that could be demolished at a moment's notice. The threat of removal in Kileleshwa (demolished in 1926) and Pangani (demolished in 1939) meant that few Africans would be willing to buy houses there. The state's ambivalence did not stop at usufruct, however: between 1912 and 1939, it made several attempts at landlordism, housing railway and municipal employees on their own estates, which rapidly became slums. Finally, the state borrowed the money to build an extension to Pumwani in 1939.[7]

The registration of land titles, even for usufruct housing in a city, offered new opportunities for women. Generally, in rural East Africa, husbands could negotiate their control over land whether or not they themselves farmed on it.[8] To give the Kikuyu example, men gave their wives gardens, from which their wives were obliged to feed them; children could take crops from their mothers' gardens without permission, but not from their fathers'; men controlled the disposal of their own crops but not their wives' surplus production. Fathers might give daughters a plot of land upon marriage, but they had to relinquish it to their brothers on demand. At marriage a man acquired for his wife a portion of his mother's cultivated land. Men's prestige—what John Lonsdale has called "civic virtue"—was based on how generous they were with land.

7. White, *Comforts of Home*, 45–48, 51–78, 80–83, 126–46.
8. Okeyo, "Daughters of the Lakes"; Hay, "Women as Owners"; Henrietta Moore, *Space, Text, and Gender: An Anthropological Study of the Markawet of Kenya* (Cambridge: Cambridge University Press, 1986), 65–71.

Women essentially had usufruct rights to all the land they farmed, which they could extend to other women.[9]

Usufruct was thus nothing new to East African women. What became new, after 1921, was women's ability to control usufruct rights through registration. Colonial legislation allowed for the ungendered registration of land. In rural East Africa, land registration was to become a specific political response to adult *men's* vulnerabilities in land rights; it usually followed intense land speculation.[10] But the very fact of registration gave to local practices and strategies the power to name, and to mobilize, diverse social relations: in Nairobi in 1921, it allowed for durable rights of female inheritance and filiation.

How did women articulate their newfound control? They recounted the paperwork matter-of-factly, but they reported an anthropology of imaginary relations among themselves, townsmen, and firemen with passion and detail. Women told stories about how blood—sometimes their own, sometimes men's—was redirected. Women in Nairobi described a natural history of new urban property rights with their own versions of stories about capture, penetration, and extraction—stories in which the men of the Nairobi Fire Brigade, black men employed by white men, captured people and removed their blood.

Stories about the wazimamoto began in Nairobi at the end of World War I. Most people said the practice ceased by the end of World War II. On the whole, men told stories about being captured, or almost captured, when they were out alone, and women told stories about the particular vulnerability they faced when they lived alone. These stories

9. Gretha Kershaw, "The Land Is the People: A Study in Kikuyu Social Organization in Historical Perspective" (Ph.D. diss., University of Chicago, 1972), 54–55; Peter Rogers, "The British and the Kikuyu, 1890–1905: A Reassessment," *J. African Hist.* 20, 2 (1979): 255–69; Fiona MacKenzie, "Local Initiatives and National Policy: Gender and Agricultural Change in Murang'a District, Kenya," *Canadian J. of African Studies* 20, 3 (1986): 377–401; John Lonsdale, "The Moral Economy of Mau Mau: Wealth, Poverty and Civic Virtue in Kikuyu Political Thought," in id. and Bruce Berman, *Unhappy Valley: Conflict in Kenya and Africa,* bk. 2, "Violence and Ethnicity" (Athens: Ohio University Press, 1992), 315–504; Carolyn Martin Shaw, *Colonial Inscriptions: Race, Sex and Class in Kenya* (Minneapolis: University of Minnesota Press, 1995), 28–59; Claire E. Robertson, "*Trouble Showed Me the Way": Women, Men, and Trade in the Nairobi Area, 1890–1990* (Bloomington: Indiana University Press, 1997).

10. M. P. K. Sorrenson, *Land Reform in Kikuyu Country* (Nairobi: Oxford University Press, 1967), 52–71; Robert Bates, "The Agrarian Origins of Mau Mau: A Structural Account," *Agricultural History* 61, 1 (1987): 1–28. Gretha Kershaw, "The Land Is the People," notes that land consolidation in Kiambu was not a reform of land tenure "but has become a statement about who had tenure and to what extent" (61n).

survived thirty and forty years after the events they described; indeed, in the late 1970s, these stories were told with excitement, enthusiasm, and care. Other rumors were not that important, and they did not last. A cursory reading of police informers' reports from the 1930s and 1940s reveals some of the rumors no one remembered in the mid 1970s and 1980s: from 1939, that blankets were treated with a mysterious substance that would render men impotent, or that European doctors had perfected injections that would produce "bottled babies" without women.[11] Informers' reports never mention wazimamoto, perhaps because informers did not believe these stories were rumors or loose talk. But vampire stories had their own histories in Nairobi, and died out there even as they were being told and retold in other parts of the country. Most of people said that the wazimamoto stopped taking blood in 1939, when Pangani, the oldest African settlement in Nairobi "was broken." A few said it continued into the early 1940s and died out by 1942 or 1943.[12] Women who came to Nairobi during World War II heard that the wazimamoto sucked African blood; "but later I learned that they just put out fires," Sara Waigo said. This chapter asks what was specific about Nairobi that generated such stories bound with such temporality and how women's versions of these stories might disclose their conceptualization of urban space and its security and possession. For many years, oral historians have worried about the difficulty of establishing chronology from oral sources.[13] In part, I hope this chapter will interrogate that concern: does a distinct chronology alert researchers to local events and their sequence, or does it disclose local ideas and ideologies in precise ways?

When and where were women safe from vampires? Amina Hali, born in what was to become Nairobi in the 1890s, spoke of the time between 1921 and 1926, when the three settlements she names coexisted:

> Things were alright here in Pumwani but Pangani and Kileleshwa were dangerous places for a woman to live alone because she was in danger of being attacked by men from the wazimamoto. . . . they would come to Pangani and Kileleshwa in the afternoon and they would go with a woman, and pay her, and this way they would find out which woman lived alone and which ones

11. Central Province District Annual Report, 1939–41, 3 (KNA, PC/CP 4/4/1).

12. Celestina Mahina, Mathare, 14 March 1976; Esther Kimombo, Mathare, 9 June 1976; Sara Waigo, Mathare, 1 July 1976; Amina Hali, Pumwani, 4 August 1976; Salim Hamisi, Pumwani, 29 March 1977.

13. The classic critique is David Henige, *The Chronology of Oral Tradition: Quest for a Chimera* (Oxford: Oxford University Press, 1974).

did not, and they would come back at night and do their work. . . . these people carried sort of a rubber sucking tube that they would stick into your hands while you were asleep and draw the blood out of your body and leave you there, and eventually you would die.[14]

Not every woman who lived in the legal location of Pumwani thought it safe, however. Kayaya Thababu came to Pumwani in 1926. She described the skills and strategies of wazimamoto and how defenseless women were:

Q: Did you ever hear stories about wazimamoto?

A: Yes, they used to come in the night, they were a special danger to women who stayed alone, they would come into the room very softly and before you knew it they put something on your arm to draw out the blood, and then they would leave you and they would take your blood to the hospital and leave you for dead.

Q: Couldn't you scream for help?

A: They put bandages over your mouth, and also, these people who worked for wazimamoto, they were skilled, so if they found you asleep they could take your blood so quietly that you would not wake up, in fact you would never wake up.

Q: Did this ever happen to you or one of your neighbors?

A: No but I heard about it a lot.

Q: When?

A: Before the coming of the Italians [i.e., before 1940].

Q: Were you frightened of them? How did you make sure they didn't come to your room at night?

A: I was very frightened and there was no way to be sure they would not come, but when the fighting of the Italians ended they stopped coming for blood. But if you had a boyfriend staying with you at night you were safe, because they were afraid of waking two people.[15]

Other women simply negotiated with the wazimamoto: "They came when I was all alone and I told them there were people outside I lived with. I could not have told them I lived alone, otherwise they would have taken my blood and left me to die," said Kibibi Ali.[16]

Nevertheless, living alone, especially in the legal location, gave some women some specific advantages. By the 1930s, many childless prosti-

14. Amina Hali, interview cited n. 12 above.
15. Kayaya Thababu, Pumwani, 7 January 1977. The "coming of the Italians" refers to the 20,000 Italian prisoners of war captured in Ethiopia in 1940 and marched to Kenya, and to World War II, called in Swahili "the fighting of the Italians."
16. Kibibi Ali, Pumwani, 21 June 1976.

tutes—women who had lived alone—designated heirs to houses they had purchased or built in Pumwani. Usufruct gave to urban mud huts the same qualities as land: access to ownership could be secured through an intimate relationship. But even in Nairobi, women's property rights were more problematic than men's. According to a Muslim woman, Tamima binti Saidi, "It has always been difficult for women to inherit property, even in Pumwani the district commissioner had to be called in when a woman left everything to her daughter, even if she had no sons." [17] Nevertheless, women in Nairobi utilized unwieldy state intervention to control their properties. For example, if a childless woman did not formally designate an heir "on the paper that allowed her to own the building," then the Nairobi Municipal Council would "take over the building" when she died, becoming the owner and letting the rooms.[18] Yet many women did just that, bluntly rejecting kinship ties: it was by careful deliberation that they guaranteed that their property would not go to the families into which they had been born. Childless women most often designated as their heirs young women they had sheltered in town or brought from their rural homes. They were almost never blood kin, and to the best of my knowledge, the designated heirs were never males.[19] These relationships, between women of different generations, had specified rights and obligations and conferred specified duties and privileges. According to Tabitha Waweru, born in Pumwani in 1925:

> Some women were really rich, and when they became old, because they didn't have any family living around Nairobi, that old woman could chose another woman and tell everyone "This is my heir." She would have to love you, really, to do that for you, but it happened a lot. To become an old woman's heir, you would have to cook for her, clean for her, wash her clothes for her, everything. Then one day this old woman will take the young woman to the DC's office and say, "This is my daughter, I want her to get my property when I die" . . . and the DC would write it down; that's how a lot of women got plots in Pumwani. A lot of women in Pumwani did this, they befriended old women, and they got property this way.[20]

Such filiations were as binding as ties of birth. But the various strategies by which such filiations were achieved were as dangerous as they were empowering. In the same interview Tabitha Waweru said that the wazi-

17. Tamima binti Saidi, Pumwani, 15 March 1977; Thomas Colchester, former municipal native affairs officer, Nairobi, London, 8 August 1977.
18. Sara Waigo, Mathare, 1 July 1976.
19. White, *Comforts of Home,* 119–22.
20. Tabitha Waweru, Mathare, 13 July 1976.

mamoto employed prostitutes to find victims: "They didn't just take blood from men; sometimes a prostitute would invite another woman to spend the night, and then the wazimamoto would come for her, for her friend."[21]

How could a young woman know why an older woman befriended her? Would she be made an heir, or would she be sold to wazimamoto? The fact that both kinds of stories coexisted was not a contradiction; it was what was crucially important about them—both sorts of stories, frequently heard, depicted the complications of being female, alone, and propertyless in colonial Nairobi and the contradictory nature of any relationship that could bestow property within the law in the city. Indeed, these stories also reflected the contradiction by which filiation worked: in rural, patrilineal East Africa, mother-child ties could only be strengthened within the bonds of marriage, not outside them.[22] In Nairobi, mother-child ties were invented and inscribed without matrimony and very often without biological ties. Virtually all of these householders came from patrilineal societies; they were creating new relationships in a hard parody of uterine rights without marriages but with the equivocal support of the colonial state. Stories about the wazimamoto, with their formulaic Nairobi themes of tubes to extract blood, the invasion of space, and betrayal may have been more than cautionary tales of the perils of urban life. These stories may have provided a biological rationale for property inheritance that was not based on birth but superseded kinship ties. Stories about blood and the colonial state's role in its removal may have made usufruct and the designation of heirs natural and legitimate.

BLOOD AND BONE IN EAST AFRICA

The blood of rubber sucking tubes, the blood drawn from the arm of sleeping women was perhaps a more specific bodily fluid than many East African peoples recognized, at least in the 1920s. As many chapters in this book argue, blood—the red fluid that flows through the body—was one of many fluids that Africans had, reproduced with, and shed in biological systems in which their circulation through the body was not a given. East African blood was the stuff of matrilineal inheritance; it was

21. Ibid.
22. Ivan Karp, *Fields of Change among the Iteso of Kenya* (London: Routledge & Kegan Paul, 1978), 87–88.

not specifically female, but it was thought of in opposition to semen, which was the stuff of male inheritance. The terminology is tricky, as semen itself was sometimes talked about as a kind of blood specific to men. But theories of gender and gestation explained how babies were made; they do not provide an exact gendered identity of fluids: among the patrilineal Teso, blood and bone are opposites; fathers contribute form to the fetus. But among the patrilineal Zande, a child is formed from its mother's blood, as are children among the matrilineal Kaguru.[23] This is not to say that East African peoples make the same associations between blood and maternal inheritance; instead, it may be more accurate to say that some systems of kinship foreground this idea, while it is in the background of other systems of kinship. But systems of kinship were not the only systems of blood ties. Mixing male blood with another man's blood could create intimate relationships among men: blood brotherhood signified intimacy both where blood was a metaphor for kinship and where it was not.[24] In Bunyoro, it was said that men achieved with blood pacts what women achieved through marriage; an Ankole ceremony announced: "Your blood brother cuts your nails."[25] Nineteenth-century blood brotherhood ceremonies in East Africa collapsed boundaries between races and represented instant milk kinship. An 1894 ceremony between a European hunter and a Meru elder pantomimed that they had been nursed by one mother; in Bunyoro, the name for the ceremony of blood brotherhood was literally "drinking at the same place."[26]

In nineteenth-century Kenya, exchanges of blood facilitated land sales. Litigants before the Kenya Land Commission testified that when

23. Ivan Karp, "New Guinea Models in the African Savannah," *Africa* 48, 1 (1978): 1–16; E. E. Evans-Pritchard, "Zande Blood Brotherhood," *Africa* 6, 4 (1933): 469–501; T. O. Beidelman, "The Blood Covenant and the Concept of Blood in Ukaguru," *Africa* 33, 4 (1963): 321–42.

24. Evans-Pritchard, "Zande Blood Brotherhood," 397; Beidelman, "Blood Covenant," 328; I have argued that blood brotherhood creates an idealized version of kinship between men; see Luise White, "Blood Brotherhood Revisited: Kinship, Relationship and the Body in East and Central Africa," *Africa* 64, 3 (1994): 359–72. Mixing men's blood and women's menstrual blood was very risky, however: "When you have your monthly period and after you bleed for three days you then urinate a lot, and if during those days after you go with a man whose blood does not match yours then you will develop *kisonono* [gonorrhea]," Amina Hali said (cited n. 12 above).

25. J. M. Beattie, "The Blood Pact in Bunyoro," *African Studies* 17, 4 (1958): 198–203; F. Lukyn Williams, "Blood Brotherhood in Ankole (Omukago)," *Uganda Journal* 2, 1 (1934): 33–41; White, "Blood Brotherhood Revisited."

26. Ambler, *Kenyan Communities,* 83; see also Williams, "Blood Brotherhood in Ankole," 40–41; Beattie, "Blood Pact in Bunyoro," 198.

Dorobo sold land to Kikuyu in the nineteenth century, the principals frequently became blood brothers. When they did not, the number of goats, rams, and steel tools exchanged increased substantially. Moreover, "when a man becomes the blood brother of another, and is given a piece of land, that means that he is liable to protect him against anyone wanting to rob his land or his properties."[27] Blood exchange thus secured property transfers that were not inherited and gave the participants a degree of responsibility and continued involvement that outright sale did not have. The penetration of body boundaries enforced land boundaries.

Blood brotherhood was men's business; what women—who shed another kind of blood regularly—thought of the institution has not been of much concern to a century of foreign participants and observers. But in many parts of East Africa, the power of women's blood, in menstruation and childbirth, was fearsome, while the impact of men's blood was considerably tamer—it made business transactions more personal and made men intimates. If blood brotherhood did indeed wane in the colonial era—and the evidence for this is anything but conclusive—it was not for lack of business transactions. Men reported entering into blood brotherhood to secure commodities, safe passage, and the like. The ceremonies may have lost their bodily specificity and imagery, but they were no less binding. Indeed, blood brotherhood became the domain of healers and contractual relationships.[28]

The biological assumptions on which blood brotherhood rested, the metaphors and beliefs that made it a rational way for men to conduct their business, were based on ideas that explained the relationships and biologies people saw every day. When Africans began to initiate other relationships of body, inheritance, and place, new metaphors and beliefs emerged. Put somewhat differently, the ways in which Africans de-

27. Kenya Land Commission, *Evidence and Memoranda*, (London: HMSO, 1934), 1: 285, 271, 329. It is unlikely that these Dorobo were Okiek misnamed by colonial authorities, inasmuch as the term incorporated a number of peoples living in the area; see Corinne A. Kratz, "Are the Okiek Really Maasai? or Kipsigis? or Kikuyu?" *Cahiers d'études africaines* 79, 20 (1981): 355–85, and *Affecting Performance: Meaning, Movement, and Experience in Okiek Women's Initiation* (Washington, D.C.: Smithsonian Institution Press, 1994), 60; J. E. G. Sutton, "Becoming Maasailand," in Thomas Spear and Thomas Waller, eds., *Being Maasai*, 38–60 (London: James Currey, 1993); and John G. Galaty, "'The Eye That Wants a Person, Where Can It Not See?': Inclusion, Exclusion, and Boundary Shifters in Maasai Identity," in ibid., 174–94.

28. White, "Blood Brotherhood Revisted," 268–39; Steven Feierman, *Peasant Intellectuals: History and Anthropology in Tanzania* (Madison: University of Wisconsin Press, 1990), 174.

scribed their ability to manage blood and control its flow—and the tense biology of relationships and possessions that blood represents—shifted in the colonial era.

PITS AND PLACE IN PUMWANI

When Pumwani was, after much fanfare, established in 1921 as the only legal place Africans could live in Nairobi, plots were allotted to those Africans who could build huts on them within two months. Such a policy favored those who had owned property in the older settlements; they were allowed to own shops; others were not. All new householders paid an annual plot-holding fee. The earliest wazimamoto stories I have collected come either from the villages that were not demolished to populate Pumwani or from the streets of the city best known to workingmen. Before 1925, River Road—the street that linked central Nairobi to the African areas—was said to be the most dangerous place for men, "especially the job seekers." [29]

Well into the 1930s, forest separated the nascent white suburbs from the central city, in which specific areas zoned for Indian residential and commercial use were established in the early 1920s only after Africans had been driven out of them. Men knew the spatial arrangements of the city and why they were in place: "These stories started in Nairobi when racial segregation was also there." [30] Indeed, the legal status of land formed the background to 1920s wazimamoto stories from Nairobi: Kileleshwa, built on crown land—which legally belonged to the king, not the colony—and was demolished to make an arboretum in 1926, was one of the places where women were most vulnerable, while others said that victims' bodies were buried in Kibera, a settlement of Nubian soldiers also on crown land. According to Timotheo Omondo, *kibera* was a Luo word for people who were "silenced in a sad manner"; the Nubian community were "not required to express their opinions" about who might be buried in there.[31]

But Nairobi in the early 1920s was also a city with a severe labor shortage. Men looking for work were free to traverse the city: "In the olden days there was no helping someone find a job. People used to

29. Timotheo Omondo, Goma Village, Yimbo, Siaya District, 22 August 1986.
30. Nyakida Omolo, West Alego, Siaya District, 19 August 1986.
31. Ibid.

go anywhere to ask for jobs."[32] Despite the pass laws introduced in 1919, working men claimed they feared only agents of the wazimamoto who would lead them "to somewhere nobody knew," where the wazimamoto would suck their blood.[33] The idea of specific places that were beyond African control, or sometimes beyond African knowledge, figured prominently in men's vampire stories from the 1920s: a "town toilet" in River Road was notorious for wazimamoto abductions and known to migrants throughout the region. A man who worked in Nairobi was said to have seen a small room next to the toilet to which captives were taken.[34] A man in Dar es Salaam gave its exact location: on River Road near the Bohora Mosque, behind where the "Zima Moto" stayed, was a toilet men could only use with permission, but where a man from Kavirondo disappeared; even his brother could not find him.[35] Others said captured Africans were "driven to a secret place" where their blood was sucked with rubber tubes.[36] No woman my research assistants or I spoke to knew of such places; women in Pumwani only began to fear public toilets in the late 1930s. After 1937 or 1938, the toilets women feared were a generalized site of vulnerability, without location or specificity or even very detailed description: "The wazimomoto would come at night and climb over the wall and pounce on you if you were alone," Hadija bint Nasolo said.

Q: What wall?

A: The wall of the toilets, the wall of your room, any wall. If they found you alone they would draw your blood and leave you dying, even if you screamed there was nothing that could save you once they started to draw your blood. . . . Once when I and two friends entered a latrine, I was the first to finish . . . and came out first, alone. Just five yards away was the wazimomoto car with some men standing beside it, and when they saw me they started calling me and I started screaming . . . my friends came out at once and the wazimomoto men went away.[37]

Prostitutes did not speak of the wazimamoto lurking in "places that looked empty" until the early 1940s.[38] Before the late 1930s, however,

---

32. Ibid.
33. Ibid.
34. Zebede Oyoyo, Goma, Yimbo, Siaya District, 13, 23 August 1986.
35. "Adiyisadiki" ("Believer"), letter to the editor, *Mambo Leo,* November 1923, 13–14.
36. Pius Ouma Ogutu, Uhuyi Village, West Alego, Siaya District, 19 August 1986.
37. Hadija bint Nasolo, Pumwani, 3 and 8 March 1977.
38. Gathiro wa Chege, Mathare, 9 July 1976.

women's wazimamoto stories described the mastery of space and time and the ambiguity of personal relationships.

In the 1920s and 1930s, women in Pumwani and Pangani lived with an anxious geography of hours and habits. Only Timotheo Omondo reported that he had been accosted by the wazimamoto "at roughly nine o'clock at night." Not only did he recall the imprecision of his memory, but he described a near-capture, not his knowledge of how to outwit the firemen. Careful women could learn to avoid dangerous situations, which were animated at specific hours. Women who were prostitutes claimed that it was dangerous to go out after 6:30 at night, 8 at night, or 10 at night. They claimed that certain shops—owned in both Pangani and Pumwani by plot-holders until the mid 1930s—were dangerous. In Pangani, where a milk merchant was said to work for the wazimamoto "we would never send children to the shops after 6:30 at night." [39] But in Pumwani in the 1920s, "from 8 o'clock in the evening nobody could go out for fear of meeting them." [40] By the late 1930s, according to Miriam Musale, "In Nairobi the government used to tell people not to go out after 10 o'clock at night and if you didn't listen it meant you didn't care if you lived or died." [41]

What are all these references to time about? Precise attention to time discipline does not usually characterize colonial African social life; indeed, without clocks how did Africans in an urban location tell time at night? Were these women simply observing that the wazimamoto operated in a world defined by the specifics of employment—a world of hierarchy, uniforms, and hours? Nairobi's firemen may have straddled the boundaries between formal and informal work, however: on the one hand, firemen were put to the most routine work, polishing equipment and standing watch. On the other, they responded—at least in theory— to emergencies and put out fires, work that was different—and at a different time—each time they did it.

Nevertheless, exact timekeeping was a characteristic of urban wage labor, and the formalized ways in which men's days were subdivided and

---

39. Fatuma Ali, Pumwani, 21 June 1976; see also Bujra, Pumwani, 28–29.

40. Chepkitai Mbwana, Pumwani, 1 and 2 February 1977. Being late for work often maintained alternate systems of time-keeping and work discipline; see E. P. Thompson, "Time, Work Discipline, and Industrial Capitalism." *Past and Present* 38 (1968): 56–97, and Keletso E. Atkins, "'Kaffir Time': Preindustrial Temporal Concepts and Labor Discipline in Nineteenth-Century Natal," *J. African Hist.* 29, 2 (1988): 229–44.

41. Miriam Musale, Pumwani, 18 June 1976. Some women said it was 8 o'clock (e.g., Elizabeth Kaya, Pumwani, 17 August 1976).

controlled would have influenced how women organized the domestic tasks that reproduced wage labor. But many men resisted the precision of labor discipline and did not show up for work at the hour specified by their employers. Most women interviewed in Pumwani described men's employment as a general condition of the male life cycle, not of hours, at least until the early 1940s: men "used to work, except for the young boys who couldn't find work."[42] When women had been formally employed, primarily during World War II, they were paid by the task, not by the hour.[43] It is possible that these references to hours may have represented colonial curfews—10 P.M. in Pumwani—but it is unlikely: while most prostitutes acknowledged the dangers of arrest, none mentioned the curfew, which seems to have existed only on paper. The only curfews that were enforced were those of wartime, which applied to men as well as to women.[44] It is altogether possible that the specificity of hours was an aspect of these women's recent lives that they simply fed back into their memories, or that these women may have been illustrating the "islands of timekeeping" that distinguished Nairobi from rural East Africa and subjected it to new rules and imagined events.[45] In that case it would be important to ask why they associated precise hours with wazimamoto and not with other activities, such as cooking or their own prostitution? It is possible that many of these women simply used specific hours as a way to make sure that an otherwise naive researcher understood their point, that the wazimamoto operated after dark. They were using the specificity of time to describe urban life. But then, why did some women identify the dangerous hour as 6:30 and others as 8 or 10, and why did others describe wazimamoto activities in terms of minutes?

These references to time in Pumwani wazimamoto stories may not simply be about time discipline and the place of wage labor therein; they may allude to menstruation, or at least women's blood. Many thought that the wazimamoto preferred women victims: "Women had the most blood. They give birth many times, each time losing a lot of blood, but

---

42. Chepkitai Mbwana.
43. Zaina Kachui, Pumwani, 14 June 1976.
44. Chepkitai Mbwana; Kayaya Thababu; Miriam Musale; Zaina Kachui.
45. These points come from two very different studies of time-keeping, Pierre Bourdieu, "The Attitude of the Algerian Peasant toward Time," in J. Pitt-Rivers, ed., *Mediterranean Countrymen* (Paris: Mouton, 1963), 55–72, and Nigel Thrift, "Owners' Time and Own Time: The Making of a Capitalist Time Consciousness, 1300–1880," *Lund Studies in Geography*, ser. B, 48 (1981): 56–84.

still they are strong," said Anyango Mahondo.[46] What is constant in
these accounts is an hour, not any specific hour, indicating that periodicity was important: the wazimamoto was predictable. These women
may not have been describing the time discipline of firemen, but that the
firemen wanted women's time-disciplined blood in particular. For most
women in early colonial East Africa, menstruation had been an asocial
experience. Many women claimed to have been surprised by menarche.[47]
Adult women maintained some version of seclusion during menstruation: "During your periods you were not allowed out of the house for
three days."[48] "You took care to see that a man could never see anything; we took care ourselves."[49] When childless women owned property and chose their heirs, menstruation may have lost some of its mys-
tical significance, and it became subject to the same mundane laws that
had come to govern everything else in Nairobi. "When prostitutes were
menstruating . . . they would take the money they had saved from selling their bodies and buy this cotton. . . . At that time they would only sit
and the money which they had saved would keep on feeding them until
their period ended," Margaret Githeka said.[50] Vampire stories that
claim knowledge of timekeeping may assert that women could keep
their blood safe from expropriation if they stayed indoors at specific
hours of the night. If some spaces were beyond Africans' knowledge,
time did not have to be unmanageable as well.

Spaces, however, were unpredictable and appeared in unlikely places.
Pits were commonplace in East African vampire stories. In Uganda, even
an educated modernizer like E. M. K. Mulira knew about Mika, for
example:

> He had a big house and in one room was a big pit and on the pit there was a
> mat and on the mat there was a chair. He would take his friends and say,
> 'You're my special friend and I want to show you this wonderful thing I have,
> go into that room and sit on the chair, I'll be right there.' The man would go
> sit on the chair and fall straight into the pit, and then the bazimamoto would
> come and take his friend.[51]

46. Anyango Mahondo, Sigoma, West Alego, Siaya District, 15 August 1986.
47. Zaina Kachui; Christina Cheplimo, Pumwani, 17 March 1977. "In Pumwani, you
women were taken to a friend of their mother's to explain menstruation" (Zaina binti Ali,
Calyfonia, 21 February 1977).
48. Wangui Fatuma, Pumwani, 29 December 1976.
49. Asha Wanjiru, Pumwani, 23 December 1976.
50. Margaret Githeka, Mathare, 2 March 1976; Mary Salehe Nyazura, Pumwani,
13 January 1977.
51. E. M. K. Mulira, Mengo, Uganda, 13 August 1990.

Women knew about the shopkeeper in western Kenya who had a pit behind his premises.[52] Men knew about a farmer who trapped victims in pits until the wazimamoto could come and get them.[53] Anyango Mahondo described the pits beneath the Kampala Police Station, where captured Africans were kept "just like dairy cattle." The pits had been domesticated to hide their dreadful purpose: "To hide the whole thing from everyone the entrances were covered with a carpet . . . even those working within the police station could not notice them. All they could see were only small but separate houses. . . . Inside the pits, lights were always on whether it was daytime or night." The Nairobi Fire Station and the Dar es Salaam Fire Station were said have pits: "Whoever was inside the pits was never allowed to see the sun shine."[54] Between the 1930s and 1960s, white prospectors, surveyors, and geologists—men who dug pits—were accused of being agents of wazimamoto; most were feared and some were attacked.[55] In 1920s Nairobi, pits were a social phenomenon. One part of Pumwani was known as Mashimoni, meaning "many in the pits" from *shimo*, the Swahili term for pits, hole, or quarry. It was said Mashimoni got its name because so many of the men who went there in the 1920s were never seen again. In a 1976 interview, Zaina Kachui, who arrived in Pumwani in 1930, explained why:

I heard that a long time ago the wazimamoto was in Mashimoni, even those people who were staying there bought plots with the blood of somebody. I heard that in those days they used to dig the floors very deep in the house and they covered the floor with a carpet. Where it was deepest, in the center of the floor, they'd put a chair and the victim would fall and be killed. Most of the women living there were prostitutes and this is how they made extra money, from the wazimamoto. So when a man came for sex, the woman would say, "Karibu, karibu," and the man would go to the chair, and then he would fall into the hole in the floor, then at night the wazimamoto would

52. Domtita Achola, Uchonga. West Alego, Siaya, 11 August 1986.
53. Nyakida Omolo; Nichodamus Okumu-Ogutu Uhuyi, Alego, 20 August 1986; Raphael Oyoo Muriar, Uchonga Village, Alego, 21 August 1986.
54. Salim Hamisi, Pumwani, 29 March 1977; Raphael Oyoo Muriar, Uchonga Village, West Alego, Siaya District, 20 August 1986.
55. E. E. Hutchins, DO, Morogoro, Morogoro District Book, vol. 1, August 1931. I am grateful to Thaddeus Sunseri for taking notes on this file for me. Darrell Bates, *The Mango and the Palm* (London: Rupert Hart-Davis, 1962), 47–55; "'Witchcraft' Murder of Geologist," *Tanganyika Standard* 2 April 1960, 1; William Friedland Collection, Hoover Institution, Stanford University, Summary of Vernacular Press, *Ngwumo*, 4 October 1960; H. K. Wachanga, *The Swords of Kirinyaga: The Fight for Land and Freedom,* ed. Robert Whittier (Nairobi: Kenya Literature Bureau, 1975), 143; Peter Pels, "Mumiani: The White Vampire. A Neo-Diffusionist Analysis of Rumour," *Ethnofoor* 5, 1–2 (1995): 166.

come and take that man away. When they fell down they couldn't get up again. . . . The wazimamoto were white people, but the people who worked to kill people, these were African, but wazimamoto employed the prostitutes who lived in Mashimoni because it was easy for these women to find blood for the wazimamoto because there were so many men going to Mashimoni for sex. They did this for the money, they needed the money, and they could do this kind of work.

Even if this was a story she told with equal conviction in the 1930s, it is unlikely that she told it to discourage men from frequenting Mashimoni: Kachui made it clear she was repeating hearsay. Besides "after a while men stopped going to Mashimoni because the wazimamoto worked there," and by 1931 or 1932, Mashimoni had been eclipsed by the new "market for prostitutes" of Danguroni.[56] It seems more likely that this story reveals more about strategies of blood and filiation than it does about prostitutes' strategies. The carpet—called by the most commonplace word for a woven mat (*mkeka,* for sleeping or prayer) represents the extent of a woman's control over space, its possession, and how space is hidden, and privatized. Indeed, the woman who digs a deep hole in a small rented room and covers it with a man-made fiber is literally undermining the limits of rented accommodation; she is subverting her legal relationship to property as she alters it to appropriate men's blood. The chair on the carpet covering the pit remains suspended, but when the man falls into the hole "he cannot get up again": women have mastered these spaces and men have not. Indeed, women could do something with this space that men could not do.

Women could dig pits. The holes in prostitutes' rooms articulate not only the women's awesome control over their own residences but the fact that the differences between urban men and urban women—or working men and working women—were such that they could not be contained or depicted on one level. The construction of a literal spatial hierarchy articulated new relationships. Such a construction is even more significant for anyone concerned with blood, which flows downward: in many parts of East Africa, from the western Rift Valley to the plains of Tanzania, women were forbidden to climb on a house or step over a man, for if men were beneath women's genitals, blood could fall on them.[57] What can it mean in another context, where space and in-

---

56. White, *Comforts of Home,* 86–93, 116–24.
57. T. O. Beidelman, *Moral Imagination in Kaguru Modes of Thought* (Bloomington: Indiana University Press, 1986), 35; Moore, *Space, Text, and Gender,* 181

timacy are managed differently, for a woman to stand above a trapped and doomed man? In East and Central Africa, menstrual blood was thought to pollute the homestead.[58] When women control their own homes—at the very least, to the extent of excavating them—how then can a home be protected and be made safe for those who are female? What ideas about blood have to change for women and property to be safe in homesteads owned by women? Stories about pits in Mashimoni, where women "bought plots with the blood of somebody," assert that a woman *can* be above a man, that menstrual blood does not pollute homesteads, but in fact gives women unique and specific ways to possess real property.

This is more than an account of the alteration of space, however; it depicts the alteration of space for a specific purpose—to drain men's blood. The context is sexual; indeed, it is the availability of sexual relations for money that brings men to Mashimoni. These particular pits reverse the connotations of sexuality; they make men penetrable and unable to acquire property; pits indicate that in Pumwani inheritance could be separated from biological reproduction. In Mashimoni, property did not pass from males or to males; men passed through property and into the structural oblivion of pits. If blood—male and female—refers to maternal inheritance, then motherhood was redefined in Mashimoni: there, property did not pass through women to men, and women did not protect men's property. Women used their property to dispossess men.

The pits in small Pumwani rooms, like the pits in colonial buildings and stations, did not exist. It is therefore important to note how differently they are described by men and women. Women described pits as places and sites; men's descriptions of pits tended to have an extraordinary level of detail and commentary. The pits beneath the Kampala Police Station were so intricate because "whites are very bad people. They are so cunning and clever." The subterranean pipes and taps were known only to Nairobi's firemen: "Whites were very clever. They used to cover the pipes and taps with some form of iron sheets."[59] The covered pits—

58. Jean S. LaFontaine, "The Ritualization of Women's Life-Crises in Bugisu," in id., ed., *The Interpretation of Ritual: Essays in Honour of A. I. Richards* (London: Tavistock, 1972), 159–86; Leakey, *Southern Kikuyu,* 1: 163–66; 3: 1241; Thomas Buckley and Alma Gottlieb, "A Critical Appraisal of Theories of Menstrual Symbolism," in Buckley and Gottlieb, *Blood Magic: The Anthropology of Menstruation* (Berkeley and Los Angeles: University of California Press, 1988), 3–40.

59. Anyango Mahondo; Alec Okaro, Mahero Village, West Alego, Siaya District, 12 August 1986.

covered with mats, huts, whatever—were subterranean systems that could be entirely closed off from the world above. This in turn suggested what was below the surface, suggestions animated by local connotations of what knowledge was hidden and suppressed.[60]

Time, property, and social reproduction were reversed in these pits. The many references to how the pits were illuminated suggest more than the deprivations faced by the victims of wazimamoto; in these accounts, working men described places where the ability to reckon time was taken from them.[61] Pits commoditized men; they became "just like dairy cattle." In each of these examples, the site of underground production was made familiar by making it horrific, intricate, and timeless. Throughout the 1920s, "the place nobody knew" was no less fearsome, but it was made familiar by these repeated descriptions. The clever whites may have been able to hide fantastic spaces, but Africans—particularly those in secure occupations—could find out about them and talk about them.

In central Kenya, however, pits were not merely symbolic spaces, they were boundaries: they marked the limits of acquired property, and they made it private, or they separated one family's territory from another's. The social and physical imaginings pits animated came in part from their historical meaning in land transactions. According to Dorobo elders, the same men who sealed land transfers with blood brotherhood in the nineteenth century, "the general way of marking out a boundary was to show the purchaser our game pits and tell him which ones he could not pass."[62] To the north of Dorobo country, Kikuyu marked boundaries with streams and valleys. Where the landscape had no distinguishing features, the landscape could be altered or body products used to mark boundaries: people planted trees, heaped stones, or buried human hair. As late as the mid 1950s, boundary-making was men's work.[63] When Africans told stories about clever white men digging pits in public places or African women digging pits in their rented rooms, they were not only describing the expropriation of land by Europeans

60. Peter Stallybrass and Alon White, *The Politics and Poetics of Transgression* (Ithaca, N.Y.: Cornell University Press, 1986), 140–51; Rosalind Williams, *Notes on the Underground, An Essay on Technology, Society, and the Imagination* (Cambridge, Mass.: MIT Press, 1992).

61. This is E. P. Thompson's point about factory design in the eighteenth century in "Time, Work Discipline, and Industrial Capitalism."

62. Kenya Land Commission, *Evidence*, 1: 222.

63. Muriuki, *History of the Kikuyu*, 76; MacKenzie, "Land and Territory," 99.

and women, but their expropriation of African men's rights to limit that expropriation. If rights over land can only be maintained with a distinct vocabulary of technical sophistication, as H. W. Okoth-Ogendo argues,[64] then pits and blood would seem to have become part of a specialized East African vocabulary in which rights to land were debated and defined. Without pits, women luring men or women to their rooms were simply working for wazimamoto, not asserting rights over land and its transmission.[65]

DISCARDING BLOOD

Many prostitutes, including property owners, did not tell stories in which men were the victims of the wazimamoto; they told stories in which women were. Just as single women's property in Pumwani was transmitted to adopted daughters, sisters, and sisters' children, single women told stories in which young girl visitors, friends, and sisters were sold to the wazimamoto by prostitutes. Just as I know of no case where a prostitute designated a man as the heir of her house, I know of no case where a woman was said to have sold brothers, brothers' sons, or male friends to the fire brigade. Many prostitutes did sell their customers, of course, but that was part of their work: according to Tabitha Waweru, sometimes a prostitute "would see a man, invite him in, feed him, sleep with him, and when he's asleep the wazimamoto would come and take him." Women sold women with as many courtesies, but they described the process and its emotional content with considerably greater detail.

Why were women both agents and victims? Why did women's stories make female friendship, even female kinship, not only terrifying, but lethal? In a place where women befriended each other and passed property to each other, and sometimes to sisters or sisters' children, why did women tell stories in which women sold their women friends, their sisters, and their sisters' children to the wazimamoto? The question implies that Pumwani prostitutes should identify either with the agents or the victims, that they should tell stories that were much less ambiguous

64. H. W. O. Okoth-Ogendo, "Some Issues of Theory in the Study of Tenure Relations in African Agriculture," *Africa* 59, 1 (1989): 6–17.

65. In 1950s Dar es Salaam, according to Lloyd William Swantz, "The Role of the Medicine Man among the Zaramo of Dar es Salaam" (Ph.D. diss., University of Dar es Salaam, 1972), 337, it was said that several women of the Tanganyikan African National Union's Women's League would entice men to their rooms and take their blood; they were said to be employees of the fire brigade.

than their urban social and property relations were. Storytellers reshape hearsay into what is familiar; popular stories reflect the contradictory nature of relationships and the possibilities that constitute those relationships.[66] Sisters' daughters and close friends—all potential heirs in interwar Nairobi—were powerful relationships in Pumwani. Relations with male friends, brothers, and to a lesser extent sisters' sons, did not convey the same power, the same kind of inheritance, or the same degree of social reproduction. It is entirely possible that these stories survived because the tellers and the listeners acknowledged the ambiguities of kinship and friendship. Women in Pumwani in the 1970s articulated the strains and contradictions of those relationships with each retelling of these stories.

These contradictions were lived, and they were remembered with a specificity of names and durations and rewards. Hannah Mwikali, who came to Pumwani in the mid 1920s, identified one Mama Amida, "the first woman to build a brick house in Majengo," who "sold her sister's daughter to the wazimamoto for money although later they came for her too."[67] According to Mwana Himani bint Ramadhani, who came to Nairobi in 1930, prostitutes sold each other:

> When I first came to Nairobi . . . I used to fear to go visit my friend, a woman like me, because the wazimamoto would hire a black woman and when her friend came to visit she would find out if she was married or not, or if her family came to visit her, and then she would tell the wazimamoto when her friend would be coming again, and then, during that visit, maybe after ten minutes, thirty minutes, the wazimamoto would come and kill you.[68]

Muthoni wa Karanja, who lived in an illegal settlement, but who visited Pumwani regularly between 1935 and 1939, said "there was a fat woman named Halima and this woman sold her sister to these people but she was lucky enough to escape . . . before they finally captured her. They used to sell people for 50/- a person; no wonder these women could afford to build houses in Pumwani." She claimed that the firemen themselves were very selective about their victims: "At 10 o'clock at night the wazimamoto came and looked for victims. They would throw rocks at doors until someone opened and then they would take whoever opened

66. Janice Radway, *Reading the Romance: Women, Patriarchy, and Popular Literature* (Chapel Hill, N.C.: University of North Carolina Press, 1984), 119–45; see also Beidelman, *Moral Imagination*, 102–3, 116–9.

67. Hannah Mwikali, Kajiado, 8 November 1976.

68. Mwana Himani bint Ramadhani, Pumwani, 4 June 1976.

the door, unless it was a child, because children do not have much blood, not as much as an adult."[69]

This specificity of detail is more than a devastating critique of the plotholders some of these women despised. These accusations are hurled at women who seemed to commoditize not only sexual relations but kinship relations and, almost as frequently, those of friendship. As such, however, these accusations are also descriptions, however violent and bloody, of the construction of families and the hierarchy of relationships and obligations that families represented. Firemen would not take a child, for example, because that child was evidence that its mother did not live alone. A woman would be called Mama Amida because she was someone's mother; she would not leave her stone house to her sisters' daughter.

The abandonment of kin and friends, the failure to animate the new relationships that Nairobi offered, became the focus of women's disgust and disappointment. Years later, women conflated the disregard for blood ties with the disregard for the proper handling of menstrual blood. According to Zaina Kachui, who so forcefully described the pits in Mashimoni, "In the old days you wouldn't let anyone see your blood, even if you had a boyfriend living in your room, he could not be allowed to see your blood, or bloody clothes. In these days you see bloody rags everywhere, in the streets and in the toilets; it's the way I used to see dead babies in the toilets all the time."

It was not only prostitutes who commoditized kin and discarded children and siblings. Between 1936 and 1939, the colonial state, after much hesitation, demolished Pangani and replaced it with an estate of its own devising: it offered former Pangani landlords lifetime leases on cement-block four- and six-room houses. The conditions of these lifetime leases allowed landlords to select tenants and charge rents competitive with those in Pumwani, but they could not pass on their property when they died, when their houses would revert to the City Council. The Pangani householders' decision to accept the state's offer was painful—the estate was called Shauri Moyo, literally "matter of the heart," before it opened—but 90 percent of Pangani's woman landlords accepted it, thus ending usufruct in one settlement and leaving landlords in Pumwani decidedly wary.[70] It is altogether possible that more women landlords would have gone to Shauri Moyo, but women who owned property as

69. Muthoni wa Karanja, Mathare, 25 June 1976.
70. White, *Comforts of Home*, 132–46.

designated heirs were not eligible for relocation there.[71] Although some women landlords in Shauri Moyo tried to pass their houses on to their daughters or their designated heirs, their wills were rejected by the state, while popular history in Pumwani had it that the "rich women of Pangani" built houses in Shauri Moyo for themselves.[72] This local revisionist history of African housing in Nairobi held that Pangani's women landlords *voluntarily* abandoned usufruct, thus abandoning not only their children but sisters, sisters' daughters, and a whole network of friends and potential friends whose entitlement to property and access to land was all but curtailed in Nairobi after 1939.

Many women in Nairobi said that the wazimamoto stopped capturing people when Pangani was finally demolished. This may have been a convenient marker, but other events, such as talk of war with the Italians over the border, or the fire that destroyed the colonial secretariat buildings in town,[73] might also have been what was memorable about 1939 for prostitutes. It would seem that as the new, social meaning of Nairobi usufruct was effectively dislodged in 1939, stories about the wazimamoto removing the blood from women who stayed alone began to die out.

CONCLUSIONS

Stories about the removal of precious bodily fluids by some agency of the colonial state provided vivid examples of rapacious imperial extractions, should any have been needed in colonial Nairobi. But this chapter argues that when told, these stories did not describe Europeans' unchecked power but Europeans' weakness and dependence on the cooperation of African prostitutes. It is possible that the colonial state, with its "rubber sucking tubes" and its electric lights in pits, was the background for these stories, not the subject matter. The disdain with which the "clever whites" were condemned was part of the construction of an urban social world, but beyond the contempt and dislike were subtle and nuanced imaginings that described new orderings of household, gender, and property relations. Through the construction of a fantastic vision of European violence, Africans reported changes in their social life, their concepts of pollution and vulnerability, and their land tenure.

71. Miriam binti Omari, Pumwani, 25 March 1977.
72. Hadija Njeri, Eastleigh, 5 May 1976; Sara Waigo, Mathare, 1 July 1976.
73. Nairobi Municipal Council Minutes, 18 September 1939 (KNA/PC/NBI/2/54).

CHAPTER 6

"Roast Mutton Captivity"

Labor, Trade, and Catholic Missions
in Colonial Northern Rhodesia

This chapter and the one that follows are based exclusively on written evidence. Rather than suggesting that written accounts of oral phenomena lose a great deal in transcription and translation, I argue that the very messiness of documentary evidence allows for an analysis of bundled ideas, of the contradictions and confusions of colonial thinking, and the economies, justifications, and policies that thinking created. Unlike chapters 5 and 8, in which oral evidence provides a sequence of who knew what about whom, and where they knew it, in these chapters there are no layers to unravel, no final insights that stripping away images and ideas can promise. Indeed, the written evidence used here is dense and disorganized—priests' accounts of African ideas about coins and their value follow reports of a strike by catechists, for example. For all the chronological clarity of written sources, the very density of these accounts suggests relationships that, taken together, show what rumors meant on the ground in the colonial Northern Rhodesia.

GOSSIP AND AUTHORITY

When I was a girl I was taught not to gossip by a school game: we would sit in a circle and someone would whisper a phrase into the ear of the person sitting next to her. By the time the phrase was returned to the first speaker, it was totally deformed—hilarious proof that hearsay distorted facts. I had already published a book based extensively on oral inter-

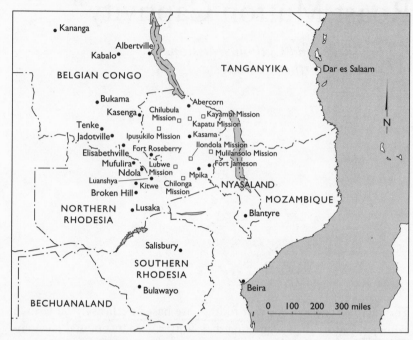

Map 2.   The Belgian Congo and Northern Rhodesia

views when I realized how insidious this game was, that it rested on two extremely authoritarian principles: that information should be transmitted passively, and that no one has the right to alter or amend received statements.

Real life and real gossip and rumormongering are substantially different, however. The purpose of gossiping, rumormongering, and even talking is not to deliver information but to discuss it. Stories transmitted without regard for official versions, stories that are amended and corrected and altered with every retelling, are indeed rumors, but they are also a means by which people debate the issues and concerns embodied in those stories. In a historiography based on such stories, then, there is no one true or accurate version. It is precisely the fact of many variants that is crucial to our understanding the meaning of these stories. Each one, taken on its own, may be interesting and suitable for analysis, but taken together, they form a debate, public discussions and arguments about the issues with which ordinary people are concerned. And, more important, these stories *were* taken together: they were neither told in isolation nor recounted without contradiction or correction.

There was no single established version; there was no single accurate account. Instead, these stories were told, exchanged, criticized, refined, and laughed at—they were part of public knowledge, a way to argue and complain and worry. Taken together, the stories I shall discuss articulated why Africans should have been concerned about the motives and activities of certain groups, whether firemen, tsetse-fly pickets, game scouts, or Catholic priests.

This chapter explores why one congregation of Catholic missionaries was accused of drinking Africans' blood. It is not a conventional historical narrative. Not only will it lack a beginning, middle, and an end, it will not attempt to tell a coherent story. If vampire accusations have multiple meanings, one chapter in this book should have multiple endings. What follows are three sets of evidence—some historiography, the accusations, and the economics of the missions—and four separate interpretations of the accusations. My goal is not to explain these particular vampire accusations, but to contextualize them, and show how they might be interpreted to form a debate about the priests' ritual and daily practices. My concerns are not about popular culture as most twentieth-century African historians understand it—music, oral literature, and street wisdoms of various sorts—but about popular debates about ideas: the meaning of sacrifice, food, and blood, and tensions over work and its remuneration.[1] These questions were engendered in the most formal of settings—in schools, during Communion, and in the workplace—but they were debated in a popular form, rumor and gossip.

EVIDENCE: ZAMBIAN HISTORIOGRAPHY

This chapter is part of a revision, or at least erosion, of the conventional wisdoms of the history of Zambia that has been going on for a decade. The Northern Province of Zambia (colonial Northern Rhodesia) was historically the catchment area for the mines of Katanga in the then Belgian Congo, the Zambian Copperbelt, and the Lupa Goldfields in southeast Tanganyika. It has been considered a classic labor reserve: rural poverty sent men to the mines, from which they returned when they had earned some money. Copper had been smelted from malachite in the region long before European rule, but new industrial technologies made the copper sulfides found far below the surface accessible. The first mine

---

1. I take this point from a somewhat different study of Catholicism in Central Africa, Terence O. Ranger, "Taking Hold of the Land: Holy Places and Pilgrimages in Twentieth-Century Zimbabwe," *Past and Present* 117 (1987): 159–90.

in Katanga opened in 1906;[2] well into the 1920s, a large proportion of the migrant labor force was from Northern Province.[3] In colonial Northern Rhodesia, there were mines owned by European prospectors as early as 1902, but the development of the Copperbelt there did not begin until 1922 and did not take off until 1927, when there were about 9,000 men employed there. By late 1930, however, there were almost 32,000 Africans working on the Copperbelt.[4] Starting in the 1920s, labor from Northern Province was recruited for both mining and plantation work in Tanganyika; because sisal wages were higher and more reliable, workers tended to stay three years on the sisal plantations of Tanga but an average of six months in the Lupa Goldfields.[5]

Africans' rural experience was represented by Europeans as one of intense demands for African labor. The diaries of the White Fathers (the Société des Missionnaires d'Afrique) are filled with references to visits by labor recruiters from the Lupa Goldfields, from Copperbelt mines, and from the Union Minière d'Haute Katanga, asserting the inexorable attraction of wage labor: "Recruiters come by car from Ndola and with their promises entice them, hiring a number of workers, whom they transport without charge to the mine. How can the blacks, like big children, resist this?"[6] Men did stay away from the countryside. Even during the Depression—when the number of workers on the Copperbelt dropped from 31,941 to 19,313 by late 1931 and to 6,667 by the end of 1932—many men did not return home, although some went to look

2. Daniel R. Headrick, *The Tentacles of Progress: Technology Transfer in the Age of Imperialism, 1850–1940* (Oxford: Oxford University Press, 1988), 269–76.

3. Johannes Fabian, *Language and Colonial Power: The Appropriation of Swahili in the Former Belgian Congo, 1880–1938* (Cambridge: Cambridge University Press, 1986), 82, 86; John Higginson, *A Working Class in the Making: Belgian Colonial Labor Policy, Private Enterprise, and the African Mineworker, 1907–1951* (Madison: University of Wisconsin Press, 1989), 80.

4. Headrick, *Tentacles of Progress,* 270; Charles Perrings, *Black Mineworkers in Central Africa: Industrial Strategies and the Evolution of the African Proletariat in the Copperbelt, 1911–1941* (London: Heinemann, 1979), 47; James Ferguson, "Mobile Workers, Modernist Narratives: A Critique of the Historiography of Transition on the Zambian Copperbelt [Part One]," *J. Southern Afr. Studies* 16, 3 (September 1990): 395; Arthur Copman Papers, National Archives of Zambia (henceforth cited as NAZ), HM6/CO3/4/2.

5. E. H. Jalland, provincial commissioner, Abercorn, comments on tour report 3/1936; R. L. Parr, district officer, Abercorn, tour report 4/1936; A. F. B. Glennie, district commissioner, Abercorn, tour report 1/1937 (NAZ, SEC2/819, Tour Reports: Abercorn, 1932–36).

6. Société des Missionnaires d'Afrique, *Rapports annuels,* no. 25 (Algiers: Maison-Carrée, 1929–30), 206, quoting the monsignor of Chilubula Mission. Société des Missionnaires d'Afrique, Rome, Diaire de Chilubula, 22 February 1929, 18 April 1931; and for sisal plantations in Tanganyika, Diaire de Kayambi, 13 June 1922.

for work in Katanga or South Africa.[7] Audrey Richards claims that 40 to 60 percent of Northern Province men were absent from their villages in the early 1930s, although these men were not all working; many were looking for work.[8] James Ferguson, following A. L. Epstein, has challenged the picture of male migrants temporarily working in towns but without urban ties, and has argued that between the 1930s and the 1950s, workers' movements between urban jobs, and between jobs at a single mine, were at least as commonplace as were workers' periodic returns to the countryside.[9] Those men who stayed on the Copperbelt during the Depression looked for work and articulated their need for employment in terms of status and community, not just livelihoods. In 1933, the leader of a Bemba workers' association went to the capital to protest unemployment and low wages: "People like me can't go home," he said. "We have settled in the towns, adopted Europeans' ways, and no longer know village life." [10] It was not only European ways that made the Copperbelt attractive to Africans; Africans could be hired as skilled labor there as well. By 1935, a white South African trade unionist worried that Copperbelt Africans were already breaching "the sacrosanct line" between unskilled and skilled mine labor.[11] Wage labor seems to have had some advantages for colonial Northern Rhodesians; there was the possibility of advancement, and when there was no work, men could go to Lusaka or Southern Rhodesia and work as domestics.[12]

7. Ferguson, "Mobile Workers," 397.

8. Audrey I. Richards, *Land, Labour and Diet in Northern Rhodesia: An Economic Study of the Bemba Tribe* (London: Oxford University Press, 1939), 23. Men often tried to shirk their marital obligations, saying they were "resting after their work in the mines" or "about to take other jobs 'soon,'" thus placing a heavy strain on the resources of the matrifocal group (172). Thus migrant labor and participation therein was a social strategy both for household accumulation and household domestic struggles. See also Henrietta L. Moore and Megan Vaughan, *Cutting Down Trees: Gender, Nutrition, and Agricultural Change in the Northern Province of Zambia, 1890–1990* (Portsmouth, N.H.: Heinemann, 1994), 47–49.

9. Ferguson, "Mobile Workers," 402–3; see also A. L. Epstein, *Politics in an Urban African Community* (Manchester: Manchester University Press, 1958), 5–15.

10. Lewis H. Gann, *A History of Northern Rhodesia: Early Days to 1953* (London: Chatto & Windus, 1964), 254, quoted in Ferguson, "Mobile Workers," 398. This was the description of wage labor that officials seemed to like most: "[T]hose who go further afield are for the most part . . . those whom the 'glitter' of life in the large industrial areas attracts, and those who have tasted the luxuries of life . . . and have developed a taste for such things" (E. Bolton, district commissioner, Mpika, tour report 2/1938, NAZ, SEC2/836, Mpika Tour Reports, 1933–38).

11. Michael Burawoy, *The Colour of Class on the Copper Mines: From African Advancement to Zambianization* (Lusaka: Institute for African Studies, 1972), 13.

12. Karen Tranberg Hansen, *Distant Companions: Servants and Employers in Zambia, 1900–1985* (Ithaca, N.Y.: Cornell University Press, 1989), 52–54, 75–79; Eustace Njbovu, Luangwa, Zambia, 22 July 1990.

The peoples of Northern Province, primarily Bemba, practice a slash-and-burn agriculture called *citemene*. According to Audrey Richards's painstaking research in the early 1930s, the sexual division of labor of men cutting down trees and clearing land and women planting and harvesting crops and preparing food was disrupted by the demand for male labor on the Copperbelt and in Katanga, and this created "the hungry months" of February, March, and April: there were not enough men to clear fields sufficient for their families' needs. But Henrietta Moore and Megan Vaughan have argued that citemene was not the main food-producing system among the Bemba; hoed mound gardens were, although tending them was "considered hard and unromantic work by the Bemba." [13] Indeed, the White Fathers raised tribute for boarding school students based on the number of mound gardens a village had. [14] According to Vaughan and Moore, seasonal food shortages were due, not to the size of women's citemene gardens, but to the combination of women's domestic and agricultural tasks at certain times of the year. Women would have faced this seasonal burden whether men were present or not. [15] In the village of Kasaka in 1933, for example, Richards found a ratio of 19 men to 23 women, in her opinion enough men to clear adequate citemene gardens. Food supply was not an issue in Kasaka; women's work was: Richards's daily records show that when women's agricultural labor was particularly heavy, they neglected some time-consuming domestic tasks, such as gathering and cooking, so that "the natives' diet may be inadequate in certain seasons of the year because the housewife is too busy to provide proper meals." [16] It would seem that absent men shaped their families' needs and expectations and ideas about work and money, not their food supply. But the extent of a sexual division of labor in which men migrated and women farmed became the lens through which officials and academics saw Bemba society.

This chapter explores African ideas about the meaning of work, money, food, and to a lesser extent, religion, through vampire accusa-

---

13. Richards, *Land, Labour and Diet,* 304. This may have been because mound gardens were "considered unglamorous and hard work"; see Moore and Vaughan, *Cutting Down Trees,* 41, and Jane I. Guyer, "Female Farming in Anthropology and African History," in Micaela di Leonardo, *Gender at the Crossroads of Knowledge: Feminist Anthropology in the Postmodern Era* (Berkeley and Los Angeles: University of California Press, 1991), 257–77.
14. Société des Missionnaires d'Afrique, Rome, Diaire de Chilubula, 14 July 1927; Diaire de Kapatu, 31 March 1933.
15. Moore and Vaughan, *Cutting Down Trees,* 46–60, 104–12.
16. Richards, *Land, Labour and Diet,* 176; for an unpacking of this statement, see Moore and Vaughan, *Cutting Down Trees,* 50–60.

tions. In doing so, I use European sources almost exclusively—the diaries of Catholic missions and district officers' reports. These texts were not produced in identical circumstances, however. The priests produced two kinds of documentation, the Annual Reports of their order, published by the Mother House in Algeria and the daily diary of each mission station. The Annual Reports are straightforward, if somewhat anguished, records of African affairs—labor recruitment or religious revivals—while the diaries provide a remarkable chronicle of the daily life of the mission. Like many diaries, these record everyday events, and they do not always elaborate on what was well known to the priests themselves. The diarists were more concerned about official support for Protestant missionaries than they were, for example, about the anti-Catholicism of Watchtower after 1920, of which the priests were fairly tolerant.[17] I do not claim to ferret African voices out of these texts, however. I simply use European sources about vampiric priests to reveal African ideas about blood and the issues for which blood was a potent metaphor in the Northern Province of Northern Rhodesia.

EVIDENCE: VAMPIRE ACCUSATIONS

Between the mid 1920s and the mid 1950s, charges that Africans working for Europeans captured other Africans for their blood were commonplace in Northern Rhodesia's Northern Province. In almost all the accusations, these African vampires went by the generic name *banyama*. But in almost every outbreak of these accusations that came to the attention of colonial officials, one order of Catholic priests—the Société des Missionnaires d'Afrique, known in Africa and among themselves as the White Fathers, because of their robes— were identified as some of the Europeans behind the banyama.

Between 1928 and 1931, there were periodic panics over banyama in the Kasama District of Northern Province. In some areas it is said, probably with great exaggeration, that no African would go out alone. It was frequently said that the provincial commissioner had met with the Chitimukulu, paramount of the Bemba, to pay him to allow banyama into his country. The White Fathers claimed that "the natives believe that there

17. Société des Missionnaires d'Afrique, Rome, Diaire de Chilubula, 18 June 1924, 6 September 1926; Diaire de Kapatu, 9 June 1925; Diaire de Ipusukilo, 14 January 1928, 30 April 1935; Diaire de St. Mary's, 7 March 1938; Diaire de Mulilansolo, 11 May 1942; see also Karen Fields, *Revival and Rebellion in Colonial Central Africa* (Princeton: Princeton University Press, 1985), 3–13, 129–34.

are two Banyama at Chilubula [their station in Kasama District] whose names are unknown, and that anyone from the mission is accordingly treated with suspicion." White Fathers both at Chilubula and Ipusukilo, in Luwingu, advocated "strong repressive measures."[18] In 1932, the monsignor of Chilubula received a handwritten letter in poor English— the White Fathers were a French-speaking order, whose priests spoke Bemba well—which "made gross insults not to be repeated" and called the monsignor "a prince of demons, a serpent, and a sorcerer." Apparently the work of an African Protestant, it demanded that the White Fathers return to Europe, where God would punish them. It was signed "your good roast mutton captivity, imprisonment, and bandages."[19] Although it is difficult to surmise very much from the recipient's summary of such a letter, the transformation of captured Africans into animals or, sometimes, cooked meat is a common feature of Central African vampire stories, and bandages figure prominently in vampire accusations in East and Central Africa.[20]

Although White Fathers were named as banyama during almost every outbreak of these rumors,[21] very little entered the written record, other than that fat priests—like fat administrators—or those with long beards were particularly suspect.[22] By the 1920s and 1930s, Watchtower openly accused Catholics of cannibalism, saying, "bakatolika balaya abantu" ("Catholics eat people"), but it is not clear whether this reflected or encouraged local opinions.[23] More specific accusations against

---

18. D. Willis, provincial commissioner, Kasama District, "Report on Banyama," 24 March 1931 (NAZ, ZA1/9/62/2/1); see also Gann, *History of Northern Rhodesia,* 1964, 321; Mwelwa C. Musambachime, "The Impact of Rumor: The Case of the Banyama (Vampire-Men) in Northern Rhodesia, 1930–1964," *Int. J. Afr. Hist. Studies* 21, 2 (1988): 205–9. Willis had the confidence of the White Fathers more than any official who came after him, and he and his French wife were regular visitors at Chilubula; see Diaire de Chilubula, *passim.*

19. Société des Missionnaires d'Afrique, Rome, Diaire de Chilubula, 18 March 1932.

20. In many vampire accusations, the technologies of Western biomedicine, especially injections and bandages, were used to subdue victims. See K. D. Leaver, "The 'Transformation of Men to Meat' Story," Native Affairs Department Information Sheet No. 20 (Salisbury, November 1960 [National Archives of Zimbabwe, No. 36413]); George Shepperson, *Myth and Reality in Malawi* (Evanston, Ill.: Northwestern University Press, 1966), 7–8; W. V. Brelsford, "The 'Banyama' Myth," *NADA* 9, 4 (1967): 54–55; Rik Ceyssens, "Mutumbula: Mythe de l'opprimé," *Cultures et développement* 7 (1975): 483–536; Musambachime, "Impact of Rumor," 207; and esp. chapter 3 above.

21. Gervas Clay, Taunton, Somerset, England, 26 August 1991.

22. Musambachime, "Impact of Rumor," 208, 211.

23. Mwelwa C. Musambachime, personal communication, 29 January 1992; Fields, *Revival and Rebellion,* 131–34.

White Fathers appear in a 1967 article by Vernon Brelsford, the former district commissioner of Chinsali, than there were in his official reports. When he first encountered these rumors in Chinsali in 1939, Brelsford was, if anything, discreet, writing only about Africans' relative unwillingness to talk about them in any detail.[24] Two decades later, after independence, however, Brelsford recounted anecdotes about the Belgian priest Dom Grégoire Coussement, the most notable banyama in the Luapula Valley. Dom Grégoire was said to be a White Father but was placed by Brelsford at the Dominican mission at Chibondo.[25] Accusations against Dom Grégoire abounded. It was said that a man with two wives, presumably wanting to convert, offered the older one to Dom Grégoire to give to the banyama to be killed, but Dom Grégoire demanded the younger one, and that he "and his minions" kidnapped Africans and imprisoned them in the belfry of his church until he had time to drive them to Elisabethville in his closed van.[26] In the late 1940s, it was said that Dom Grégoire worked for the Belgian government and crossed the Luapula into colonial Northern Rhodesia to capture people there.[27] In 1958, in Northern Rhodesia's Eastern Province, banyama victims were chosen in advance and "marked in some occult fashion by the White Fathers concerned with the Sign of the Cross which was not visible either to the intended victim or to his fellows but only to the Europeans and their African henchmen." After enough people were marked, the "victims of the Cross" were collected, taken away, and killed.[28] In 1960, just across the Zambezi River, farm workers believed that on a certain day a whistle would blow and those people who had a cross marked on their clothing would, "acting under an irresistible impulse," rush to a lorry parked in the nearby veld, which would take them somewhere to be drained of their blood or to be turned into pork or beef.[29]

24. V. W. Brelsford, tour report 1, 1939 (NAZ, SEC2/751: Chinsali District Tour Reports, 1939–40).

25. Brelsford, "'Banyama' Myth," 54–55. The mission at Kasenga had been Benedictine—like Dom Grégoire—in the 1940s, but by the time Brelsford wrote his article, the mission had been taken over by the Salesians. The reinscription of both Dom Grégoire and several local missions as White Fathers probably reflects their reputation in Northern Rhodesia. Ian Cunnison, personal communication, 4 February 1992.

26. Brelsford, "'Banyama' Myth," 54–55.

27. Ian Cunnison, field notes from Luapula, March 1949.

28. Brelsford, "'Banyama' Myth," 49–60.

29. Leaver, "'Men to Meat.'"

EVIDENCE: MISSIONS AND EXTRACTIONS

There were White Fathers in Northern Rhodesia thirty years before
there were banyama accusations. Missions were founded at Mambwe
in 1895, Kayambi in 1896, and Chilubula in 1902. The founder of these
stations, Père Dupont, had a fearsome local reputation as a sorcerer who
shot lions and healed the sick, but he was not very different from other
missionaries who established themselves in Africa at the turn of the century.[30] Once the missions were established, however, the White Fathers
relied on African catechists to proselytize the countryside—not because
the territory of their vicariate was so vast, according to the White Fathers'
historians, but because the competition from the London Missionary
Society and Livingstonia Mission was so intense, according to historians
of Protestant missions and independent churches.[31] As a result, White
Fathers' missions typically had a few priests for spiritual work—three
in Chilubula in the 1920s, but only one at smaller stations like Kapatu
or Chilonga—and at least as many "coadjuteurs," religious brothers
who worked to supplement the material well-being of the mission either
by supervising construction or making furniture. A very few worked
closely with private enterprises.[32] Most of the stations had been founded
before 1915; Mulilansolo and Ilondola were founded in the 1930s with
the patronage of a French countess. Aside from Chilubula, none of the
missions were terribly well-off. (Chilubula was by all accounts the best-
provisioned place in Northern Rhodesia: it had wheat fields, herds of
pigs, and a talent for *charcuterie*.) Other stations never managed to
grow all their own food, even with student labor, and they frequently
had to trade with the countryside. Their schools never had strong government support, and never attracted many students, since, as a French-
speaking order, their instruction in English was sometimes poor.[33]

30. Andrew Roberts, *A History of the Bemba: Political Growth and Change in North-
eastern Zambia before 1900* (Madison: University of Wisconsin Press, 1973), 259–69;
Brian Garvey, "The Development of the White Fathers' Mission among the Bemba-Speaking Peoples, 1891–1964" (Ph.D. diss., University of London, 1974), 149–53; Michael
O'Shea, *Missionaries and Miners: A History of the Beginnings of the Catholic Church
in Zambia with Particular Reference to the Copperbelt* (Ndola: Mission Press, 1984),
20–25.
    31. Garvey, "Development of the White Fathers' Mission," 153; Fields, *Revival and
Rebellion*, 129–34; Arie N. Ipenburg, *Lubwa: The Presbyterian Mission and the Eastern
Bemba* (Lusaka: Teresianum Press, 1984), 26–28.
    32. Société des Missionnaires d'Afrique, *Rapports annuels*, no. 19 (1923–24), 189,
206; "Development of the White Fathers' Mission," 149ff.
    33. Société des Missionnaires d'Afrique, Rome, Diaire de Ilondola, 15 January 1934;
Diaire de Kapatu, 7, 12, 18 January 1938; Diaire de Chilubula, 8 June 1931; Hugo H.

Indeed, White Fathers were accused, not only of vampirism, but of violating the conventions of retail trade. On the Luapula, at least, the White Fathers operated barter stores that did not take money and sometimes exchanged goods for farm labor. At Ipusukilo, one priest rhapsodized about their new barter store

> built of bricks . . . open all day long, and the Africans are ready to use it. In it one finds stationery, basic materials, and a wide variety of clothes, for which those who do not have money exchange foodstuffs or work. There are many reasons for the store's appeal: beads, stamps, paper, envelopes—the things one buys in a store. I have no money. Contribute flour or firewood. I have neither. You are a lazy person, cultivate: on your farm, you will find everything with which to purchase all that you desire. The manager is prevented by an infirmity from hard work, but if you work here and nowhere else, these goods will be given to you.[34]

In July 1932, L. G. Mee, a trader, complained to the boma that the White Fathers at Lubwe and Ipusukilo had for some time been selling calico to Africans as well as paying wages in calico.[35] The secretary for native affairs replied that the priests had already been warned about this.[36] The White Fathers at Ipusukilo had been trading cloth for salt, which they then exchanged for grain locally. In August 1932, the boma informed them that trading in salt and cloth was illegal without a general trader's licence, which they could purchase for 50/- for six months— "an absurd regulation," the priests complained.[37]

At Chilubula and other missions, the economics of boarding schools had long disrupted the priests' relations with the countryside. Money for boarding school students' clothes had to be raised from tributes from the countryside. But "some parents did not understand that their children in catechism classes must work free on mission farms; recalcitrant students make work impossible." These students were dismissed

---

Hinfelaar, "Religious Change among Bemba-Speaking Women in Zambia" (Ph.D. diss., University of London, 1989), 111–12.

34. Société des Missionnaires d'Afrique, Rome, Diaire de Chifobwe-Ipusukilo, 11 December 1926.

35. P. W. M. Jelf, district officer, Tour Report, Fort Roseberry, June–July 1932 (NAZ, SEC2/888). Mee was with Thom Stores, a manager of which figured in vampire accusations in Northern Province in the mid 1940s. Geoffrey Howe, provincial commissioner, Northern Province to chief secretary, Lusaka, 29 January 1944 (NAZ, SEC2/429, Native Affairs: Banyama); Hugh Macmillan, personal communication, 21 August 1991.

36. J. Moffatt Thomas, secretary for native affairs, 18 August 1932, Tour Reports, Fort Roseberry, June–July 1932 (NAZ, SEC2/888).

37. Société des Missionnaires d'Afrique, Rome, Diaire de Chifobwe-Ipusukilo, 9 August 1932.

"to seek their fortunes elsewhere." [38] In 1936, boarding school students had to work for the mission for three weeks.[39] In 1939, catechists and students returned to Chilubula without the expected tribute for their up-keep; parents claimed that there were now so many students attending school that it was impossible to subsidize them all. Père Reuter—who had only returned to Chilubula in 1937 after years of supervising the diggers at the Lupa Goldfields in Tanganyika—made a speech to the students. "You have neither paid nor done work," he said. "If each of you works six days a month, we shall have enough revenue for fifty-four students. Please remember that there are many children in the villages between 10 and 12 years of age who no longer study here. Why?"[40] At Kapatu, eight students ran away because they were asked to work five days a month to pay their school fees.[41] At Ilondola, in 1948, classes were suspended because there was no food for the students. Never-theless, students were asked to stay at the mission and work for three weeks, "a good occasion to see their spiritual and moral progress."[42]

Catechists' wages also caused dissent. In 1906, in Chilubula, cate-chists demanded that their pay be increased from one shilling a week to one shilling for three days' work; a few catechists were dismissed, but they did receive a slight increase. In 1931, a group of catechists at Ipusu-kilo threatened not to hold classes unless their wages were increased; they received a stern lecture, and a few were dismissed.[43] Catechists de-manded a tribute of flour in the villages they visited—which they fre-quently did not receive. During the Depression, catechists were known as *kupula,* meaning "those who beg for food," according to the priests, but according to Richards, a derisive term applied to the casual labor that Bemba offered to wealthier households during harvest times, work that was generally spoken of with great contempt.[44] By 1934, catechists

38. Société des Missionnaires d'Afrique, Rome, Diaire de Chilubula, 27 Decem-ber 1931.
39. Ibid., 22 February 1936.
40. Ibid., 27 July 1937, 15 May 1939.
41. Société des Missionnaires d'Afrique, Rome, Diaire de Kapatu, 31 March 1933.
42. Société des Missionnaires d'Afrique, Rome, Diaire de Ilondola, 27 April 1948.
43. Société des Missionnaires d'Afrique, Rome, Diaire de Cibofwe-Ipusukilo, 15–19 April 1931.
44. Société des Missionnaires d'Afrique, Rome, Diaire de Chilubula, 23 February 1927; 14 July 1927; 22 July 1927; 1 May 1928; 16 November 1933; Richards, *Land, Labour and Diet,* 145. "Only an absolutely destitute person or an imbecile would reckon to subsist in this way as a regular thing," Richards writes, but she notes that *ukupula* had become very common in the early 1930s as one of the survival strategies available to "de-serted wives . . . during the bad times of the year," and a footnote on the same page clari-fies the use of the term: "*Ukupula* is loosely applied to all forms of scrounging, but tech-

earned two shillings a week, the same as unskilled agricultural laborers earned and far less than the 22/- paid surface workers on the Copperbelt. When not working, catechists lived at the mission and grew their own food.[45] In 1940, the White Fathers Mission at Mulilansolo did not have enough money to pay catechists regularly for their tours, which, the father superior lamented, "caused them to do the work of God very quickly."[46] In 1943, catechists returned from their tour and returned their books, demanding an increase in salary, "A real revolt!"[47]

In 1938, a European in Fort Jameson, in Eastern Province, complained to the boma that the White Fathers at St. Mary's refused to allow their converts to work for him. The White Fathers insisted that these accusations were false. They claimed that this man ("a Jew") had "debauched" the women who worked on his farm, and in protest they had prevented Catholics from working there. Nevertheless, the district commissioner called all the local chiefs to the boma and said, "Be on your guard against this mission, you are not their slaves, missionaries should have no say in this matter."[48] Two years later, the priests at St. Mary's complained that wartime economies had caused them to enlist reluctant porters. "We do not have enough money for paying porters, so we request that our Christians carry our luggage. Some are strong and good at heart about this, but others need a little prayer and even then will say they are sick just at the moment of departure."[49] In 1948, the father superior of St. Mary's complained that there seemed no end to wartime and even postwar economies: "The salary of unskilled workers is more than three times that of our catechists . . . they are leaving us, the best ones especially, and it is this continual change in personnel that makes our mission seem secular."[50] In 1958, the priests were unable to pay

---

nically speaking means labour in return for food only" (Richards, *Land, Labour and Diet,* 145 and n). *The White Fathers' Bemba-English Dictionary* broadly accepts this translation, defining *kapula* as meaning a person who earns a living helping others (Cape Town: Longmans, Green for Northern Rhodesia and Nyasaland Joint Publications Bureau, 1954), 246.

45. Garvey, "Development of the White Fathers' Mission," 155, 157–58. This comparison might have been lost on Africans themselves, since in 1934 there were not many jobs on the Copperbelt; see Moore and Vaughan, *Cutting Down Trees,* 48–49, 168–70.

46. Société des Missionaires d'Afrique, Rome, Diaire de Mulilansolo, 21 June 1940.

47. Ibid., 24 December 1943.

48. Société des Missionaires d'Afrique, Rome, Diaire de St. Mary's, Fort Jameson, 7 March 1938.

49. Ibid., 2 January 1940.

50. Société des Missionaires d'Afrique, *Rapports annuels,* no. 39 (1948–49), 39, 212–13.

their catechists at all, because most of the money for wages had been stolen from a priest's house.[51]

❧ DETAILS: BLOOD AND THE EUCHARIST

How do we link these disparate sets of evidence together? I don't think it is possible, or even worthwhile. If I argue that vampire accusations mean one thing and not another, it would imply that all the ambiguities meant by blood and priests and the tangled associations of crosses and cars were incidental to these stories. If symbols and metaphors and meanings are indeed complex, layered, and polysemic, how do we write about them? As a rule, historians "prove" things. We argue that one line of reasoning, backed up by evidence, is correct in part by our arrangement of details and data, but also by showing how other lines of reasoning are flawed. If I were to do this now, I might prove that these accusations were indeed about the White Fathers' labor practices and not about the Mass, blood, or retail trade. This would make for a tight and well-reasoned essay, but it would deform the substance of these accusations. Finding the single "correct" reason for vampire accusations against White Fathers would privilege certain details over others in a way that I have no evidence that the rumormongers actually did. It would, in Hayden White's ungainly term, "detraumatize" some elements of these stories, and the emplotment of the resulting chapter would have been governed by my narrative strategy, not one grounded in these accusations themselves.[52]

But how do we arrange evidence according to specifications other than our own? As historians, we want to tell stories that have some accuracy, even when they are about things that never happened. We want—or at least I want—to reflect actual events and processes, not just to emplot. The issue is not merely one of interpretation, but of how interpretation might best be done. In the absence of actual, detailed accusations against specific priests or missions, we have no shape or struc-

51. Société des Missionnaires d'Afrique, Rome, Diaire de St. Mary's, Fort Jameson, 25 February 1958, 28 April 1958.

52. Hayden White, "Historical Text as Literary Artifact," in *Tropics of Discourse: Essays in Cultural Criticism* (Baltimore: Johns Hopkins University Press, 1978), 86–87, and "Interpretation in History," in ibid., esp. 51–58; see also Peter Lienhardt, "The Interpretation of Rumour," in J. H. Beattie and R. G. Lienhardt, eds., *Studies in Social Anthropology: Essays in Memory of E. E. Evans-Pritchard by his Former Oxford Colleagues* (Oxford: Clarendon Press, 1975), 105–31.

ture of stories to examine. Instead, we must look at details, at ideas about blood, and ingestion, as well as the objects and the images that figure in rumors about blood-drinking priests. We need to scrutinize mission activities closely as well, and look at how daily mission life was conceived, conducted, and paid for. But finding such details, whether about blood or rates of pay, requires that we read missionary and colonialist documents to uncover African categories. This is contradictory; these are not African sources. But these are documents about something Africans believed in and Europeans did not. They are the comments of missionaries and officials on other people's images, ideas, and notions about bodily fluids. Such readings require that I read European sources exactly as I read oral materials: not for their "truths" but for their details, large and small.[53]

My interpretation therefore begins with a large detail, the Mass, which is not mentioned in banyama accusations. After all, Catholic priests do announce that they drink blood regularly, and they frequently tried to impress that idea on their African converts. "The idea that the Cross is associated with the Eucharist is henceforth stamped clearly in the eyes of the believers. The Father Superior has made a fresco in the church with examples of the proper faith: the luminous cross now dominates the altar where each day we consume the eucharistic sacrifice," the White Fathers at Kapatu noted with delight at Easter 1929.[54]

Thomas Fox-Pitt, formerly district commissioner in Ndola and Mpika, but later secretary of the Anti-Slavery Society in London, argued in his 1953 essay, "Cannibalism and Christianity," which the *Manchester Guardian* refused to publish, that African misunderstandings of European actions led to the vampire accusations against missionaries in Central Africa. It was not the Mass in and of itself that gave rise to certain fears, but the social context in which the Mass took place. From the start, Fox-Pitt wrote, missionaries claimed that accepting their faith would protect Africans from witchcraft. To fearful Africans, "It did not seem unreasonable that the eating of the body and the drinking of the blood of the all powerful man-God should be an antidote to the less

---

53. See Carlo Ginzburg, *Clues, Myths and Historical Method*, trans. John and Anne Tedeschi (Baltimore: Johns Hopkins University Press, 1988). For all my criticisms of Ginzburg's use of clues in chapter 2, I am indebted to him on this point and, indeed, in much of this chapter.

54. Société des Missionnaires d'Afrique, Rome, Diaire de Kapatu (Saint-Leon de Kaliminwa), 29 March 1929.

powerful magic of the witch who had eaten the flesh of an ordinary person." He noted that the popular witch-finding movement of the mid 1930s, *mucape,* used a red liquid "like wine" to identify and kill sorcerers who had not surrendered their amulets; it was an inversion of the Mass. But

> [p]arallel with this idea ran the dreadful suspicion that the Europeans who would eat the flesh and drink the blood of their revered leader would feel no compunction about eating Africans if they thought it would benefit them.
>
> As long as the mission churches were open to both Africans and Europeans this suspicion had little to support it for all could see that the Europeans were drinking wine and eating bread like themselves but when the Europeans in the towns began to gather in separate churches and exclude Africans from their services the suspicion grew that the ceremonies performed were different and far more menacing.
>
> It was about at the time of the imposition of the first colour bar churches that Africans began among themselves to accuse Europeans of being "banyama," the meat men, who capture Africans and eat them or drink their blood.[55]

Did Protestant administrators overestimate the power of the Eucharist, or did they conceptualize banyama as an African discourse about food? Despite the fact that there were medical elements in most banyama accusations—in 1929, blood was said to be needed to cure King George V's illness, for example, and in 1931, blood was to be forwarded to the Medical Department[56]—in their official and in later academic interpretations, these stories became food stories. Officials blamed

55. Thomas Fox-Pitt, "Cannibalism and Christianity" (1953), Thomas Fox-Pitt Papers, School of Oriental and African Studies, London, MS 6/5, Correspondence, 1952–53. Fox-Pitt came to Northern Rhodesia in 1923 and served as a district officer first in Ndola on the Copperbelt, then at Mpika, and, after World War II, in Kitwe. There he encouraged the emerging trade union movement and taught English two evenings a week in an African night school. He was quickly transferred, first to Barotseland in 1948 and then to Fort Jameson in Eastern Province in 1949, but again championed the cause of African labor. In 1951, he was put on the retired list, and he returned to England in 1952, where he became secretary of the Anti-Slavery Society and was closely involved with the nationalist movements of Central Africa. In 1960, he began working for the London Committee of Kenneth Kaunda's United National Independence Party. He returned to Zambia at independence and was awarded the Order of Freedom medal; for the next two years, he served in Zambia's Ministry of Local Government. He retired to England in the late 1960s and died in 1989. Colonel Bray in Nadine Gordimer's novel *The Guest of Honor* is loosely modeled on Fox-Pitt.

56. Brelsford, "'Banyama' Myth," 49; D. Willis, provincial commissioner, Kasama District, 24 March 1931 (NAZ, ZA1/9/62/2/1); Musambachime, "Impact of Rumor," 205–7; Wim M. J. van Binsbergen, *Religious Change in Zambia* (London: Kegan Paul, 1981), 349n.

banyama on African ideas about the Mass, or on the migrant labor system that left women farmers alone and vulnerable. Even a hastily concocted indigenous origin for the rumors from the mid 1940s was based on the food supply: an aged settler informed officials that whenever the rains were late, Bemba chiefs kidnapped and sacrificed innocent Africans to ensure a bumper harvest.[57] Read individually, these explanations for banyama are all credible, but, as I shall show, taken together they are part of a larger colonial discourse about the food supply in Northern Rhodesia.

In Christian countries the importance of the Eucharist was the miracle of transubstantiation. The eating of Christ had a magical significance that the eating of ordinary people—or ordinary food—lacked.[58] Viewed in its own context, the Eucharist was as horrifying as it was divine: even some of the disciples left Jesus over the prospect of eating his flesh—especially in a way that mocked Passover—but the bread of the Eucharist was not like other bread.[59]

The view from Northern Rhodesia may have lacked many of these connotations. That Catholic priests ate flesh and drank blood may have seemed an unpleasant but plausible boast, and especially since only priests drank the wine, it put them in a new category altogether. Bemba sorcerers, in contrast, began their otherwise mundane careers with an outrage, usually father-daughter incest or intra-clan infanticide.[60] If we understand banyama accusations as popular debates about Catholicism, then the issue here is the literal interpretation of the Mass; transubstantiation does not seem to have taken hold in the popular imagination of

57. Gervas Clay, district commissioner, Isoka, "Memorandum Concerning 'banyama' and 'mafyeka' with Special Reference to the Provincial Commissioner, Kasama's Confidential File on Banyama and to Incidents in the Isoka District during the Latter Part of 1943" (NAZ, SEC2/429, Native Affairs: Banyama, 24 January 1944); R. S. Jeffries to secretary for native affairs, 24 April 1944; LegCo Debates, *Hansard,* 31 August 1945, cols. 221–22, 248–49, 254–55, in NAZ, SEC2/429, Native Affairs: Banyama. These ideas were based on genuine customs of human sacrifice—to honor departed royalty, not to feed commoners—and a 1920s Bemba bogeyman, Ne Koroma, and some well-placed anti-royalist feeling among educated Bemba; see Société des Missionnaires d'Afrique, *Rapports annuels,* no. 24 (1924–25), 293–94; Stephen Bwalya, "Customs and Habits of the Bemba" (typescript, Mpika, 1936, Rhodes House, Oxford, RH MSS Afr. s. 1214); and Clay's memorandum cited above.

58. Caroline Walker Bynum, "Women Mystics and Eucharistic Devotion in the Thirteenth Century," *Women's Studies* 11 (1984): 179–214.

59. Gillian Feeley-Harnik, *The Lord's Table: Eucharist and Passover in Early Christianity* (Philadelphia: University of Pennsylvania Press, 1981), 66–67.

60. Richards, *Land, Labour and Diet,* 456.

the Bemba in the 1930s.[61] The problem for residents of Northern Province was that Catholic priests ate flesh and drank blood, not that bread and wine sometimes became flesh and blood.[62] Indeed, across the border in colonial Katanga, Africans accused white mine compound managers of eating women and the occasional man. People were eaten instead of bread; they were not transformed into bread.[63]

But even with a culturally specific notion of the Eucharist for Northern Rhodesia, we should take Caroline Bynum's point about medieval women and food seriously: that where food is regularly in short supply and where feeding is an exclusively female domain, the Eucharist takes on a special meaning, the specific form of which is control over food, not people.[64] This is of course not wholly applicable to Central Africa, but the relationship between deforestation, food, and women's work was a colonial obsession in Northern Rhodesia by the mid 1930s,[65] and administrators tended to contextualize African ideas in those terms. Thus, when Fox-Pitt first encountered rumors about banyama he saw them not as a political issue, but as evidence of the perils of the widespread male migrancy that left women alone, defenseless, and overworked. Chiefs told him that

women everywhere are very nervous about working alone in their gardens far from villages and often run back to the villages in panic because they have

61. There is a literature that suggests that "the person of Jesus Christ" is difficult for Africans to incorporate in their belief systems, partly because of his association with a colonial past, and partly because his power is both divine and ancestral; see Mathew Schoffeleers, "Folk Christology in Africa: The Dialectics of the Nganga Paradigm," *Journal of Religion in Africa* 19, 2 (1988): 157–83.

62. Where transubstantiation was taken seriously, blood accusations frequently involved the host. European accusations of Jewish ritual murder often included the theft of the host, which was said to turn into a bleeding baby Jesus once outside a church; see R. Po-chia Hsia, *The Myth of Ritual Murder: Jews and Magic in Reformation Germany* (New Haven: Yale University Press, 1988), 10–12, 50–51, 54–56, 128, 131, 222. Other accusations of ritual murder in Christian times conflated blood and bread: early Christians in Rome were accused of hiding the infants they were about to eat in dough, and a thousand years later, it was said that Jews needed the blood of Christian children to make matzoh; see Bill Ellis, "De Legendis Urbis: Modern Legends in Ancient Rome," *J. of American Folklore* 96, 380 (1983): 200–208, and Alan Dundes, "The Ritual Murder or Blood Libel Legend: A Study of Anti-Semitic Victimization through Projective Inversion," in id., ed., *The Blood Libel Legend: A Casebook in Anti-Semitic Folklore* (Madison: University of Wisconsin Press, 1991), 337.

63. "Note pour Monsieur Toussaint, Département MOI, Elisabethville, 15 février 1943," Archives du personnel, Gécamines, Lubumbashi, Democratic Republic of the Congo, loaned me by T. K. Biaya.

64. Caroline Walker Bynum, *Holy Feast and Holy Fast: The Religious Significance of Food to Medieval Women* (Berkeley and Los Angeles: University of California Press, 1987), 31–112.

65. See Moore and Vaughan, *Cutting Down Trees*, 33–50.

seen someone near them in the bush. I have no doubt that this "banyama" story that has been going round the country for the last few years is due to the large number of lonely and unprotected women now in the country. It will go on . . . as long as the social system of the villages is upset as it has been for the past 15 or 20 years.[66]

But if the flesh of the Eucharist was food, what was the blood? The most commonplace preindustrial assumption in which blood became food was that breast milk was blood transformed by biological and social processes.[67] But the relationship of blood to breast milk, and the qualities of breast milk itself, were not at all clear in Northern Rhodesia. In *Land, Labour and Diet in Northern Rhodesia,* Richards states emphatically that the Bemba did not consider breast milk food; it was a source of comfort: infants were force-fed gruel from the age of three or four weeks to nourish them.[68] Her earlier work, however, suggests that the Bemba understood that breast milk nourished. One of the apocryphal visions of mucape was a "mythical woman with one breast in front and one behind. The good she would suckle in front, while the wicked would find themselves following willynilly behind."[69]

If the blood of the Eucharist was food, then the interpretation of banyama becomes another argument—and another popular statement—about the Bemba food supply. Many interpretations of banyama phenomena have rested, not on hunger or food in and of themselves, but in the season of planting and rains, hunger and harvest. Some officials in the 1940s who experienced banyama as a political threat tried to show that banyama was simply a modern-day cover for the human sacrifices that supposedly took place whenever the rains were late.[70] A. L. Ep-

66. Thomas Fox-Pitt, district commissioner, Mpika, to provincial commissioner, Northern Province, Kasama, 6 March 1939, "Re: Banyama Rumors" (NAZ, SEC2/429, Native Affairs: Banyama).

67. For diverse examples, see Caroline Walker Bynum, "The Body of Christ in the Later Middle Ages: A Reply to Leo Steinberg," *Renaissance Quarterly* 39, 3 (1986): 399–439; Paul Farmer, "Bad Blood, Spoiled Milk: Bodily Fluids as Moral Barometers in Rural Haiti," *American Ethnologist* 15, 1 (1988): 62–83; and Caroline H. Bledsoe, "Side-Stepping the Postpartum Sex Taboo: Mende Cultural Perceptions of Tinned Milk in Sierra Leone" (MS).

68. Richards, *Land, Labour and Diet,* 69.

69. Audrey I. Richards, "A Modern Movement of Witchfinders." *Africa* 8, 4 (1935): 449. Indeed, children could not suckle from women who had not gone through initiation (Audrey Richards Diaries, 6 March 1931, Audrey Richards Papers, London School of Economics, London).

70. Geoffrey Howe, provincial commissioner, Northern Province, Kasama, to chief secretary, Lusaka, 29 January 1944; Cantrel-Robinson, chief secretary, LegCo Debates 31 August 1945, *Hansard,* cols. 221–22 (NAZ, SEC2/429 Native Affairs: Banyama); Gervas Clay, interview with the author, Taunton, Somerset, England, 26 August 1991.

stein's 1979 psychoanalytic interpretation of banyama replicates some of the colonial discourse about the agricultural cycle in Bemba country. The trauma of weaning was intensified by the seasonal cycle of hunger and plenty in Northern Rhodesia, and this caused "the oral aggression" of beliefs about colonialists who sucked their victims' blood.[71] In this analysis, blood and breast milk need not be the same substance; the anxiety results from the ways that sucking has become culturally charged.[72] In 1992, Epstein elaborated his analysis of banyama, locating it in Bemba concepts of the body and wholeness.[73] Interpreted in this way, banyama accusations against White Fathers may have reflected what Hugo Hinfelaar, himself a White Father, has seen as Bemba beliefs that priests monopolized concepts of the body and of blood.[74] Accusations against priests may have parodied invasive Catholic dogma—fat priests and fat administrators, men actively engaged in changing what Africans did to their bodies, were particularly suspect.[75] Such accusations also represented elaborate ideas about bodies, both African and European. Indeed, Fox-Pitt placed the origin of banyama rumors in events of 1930, when Africans believed that white men entered the compounds of the Copperbelt and captured Africans by striking each one with "a stick of rubber—mupila—which paralysed him"; Africans were then thrown into a lorry and driven off. "It was thought by authorities that this scare originated from the visits of a feeble minded European youth to the compounds where he frightened African women by sticking them with a blind worm."[76] The conflation, by administrators or Africans, of body

71. A. L. Epstein, "Unconscious Factors in the Response to Social Crisis: A Case Study from Central Africa," *Psychoanalytic Study of Society* 8 (1979): 3–39; see also Alphonse Gintzburger, "Accommodation to Poverty: The Case of Malagasy Peasant Communities," *Cahiers d'études africaines* 92, 23–4 (1983): 419–42. Locating active, "irrational" beliefs in hunger or tainted food supplies is not unique to African studies, however; see Georges Lefebvre, *The Great Fear of 1789: Rural Panic in Revolutionary France*, trans. Joan White (New York: Schocken Books, 1973), and Mary Kilbourne Matossian, *Poisons of the Past: Molds, Epidemics, and History* (New Haven: Yale University Press, 1989).
72. See Joan Copjec, "Vampires, Breast-Feeding, and Anxiety," *October* 58 (1991): 25–43.
73. A. L. Epstein, "Response to Social Crisis: Aspects of Oral Aggression in Central Africa," in *Scenes from African Urban Life: Collected Copperbelt Essays* (Edinburgh: Edinburgh University Press, 1992), 158–207.
74. Hinfelaar, "Religious Change," 90.
75. Musambachime, "Impact of Rumour," 208; see also Epstein, "Response to Social Crisis," 167–69.
76. Fox-Pitt, "Cannibalism and Christianity" (cited n. 55 above). A government-owned newspaper sold to Africans described *mupila* as "white balls of drugs" used by Africans to capture Africans by paralyzing them, causing them to lose their memories, and making their clothes fall off; see P. K. Kanosa, "Banyama—Copper Belt Myth Terrifies the Foolish," *Mutende* [Lusaka] 38 (1936) (NAZ, SEC2/429, Native Affairs: Banyama).

parts and bodily failures—paralysis, feeble-mindedness, genitals and sight—suggests that banyama not be located in beliefs about food but in beliefs about the body and the fluids and functions of which it is comprised.

Was blood a drink in Bemba communities in the 1930s? If so, what kind of drink? According to Brelsford, it was medicinal; Africans believed that their blood and internal organs were needed to cure European diseases. The illness of any well-known European was reason enough for a banyama panic.[77] According to Hinfelaar, the Bemba word *umulopa* means not only blood but all the fluids that transfer life: vaginal secretions, semen, and blood.[78] In the Bemba theory of procreation, only women passed blood on to their children; men's blood was not inherited by their children.[79] This theory was beginning to be questioned in the early 1930s when men returned from the Copperbelt demanding bridewealth marriages and rights over children, but the impact of these new ideas on ideas about blood is difficult to ascertain. In both the old and new ideas, however, marriage made blood somewhat magical and very private but still largely female: according to Richards, adultery was said to "mix blood," and if the wife of an adulterer saw the blood of her husband's lover, the wife would die.[80] But the blood women shed and the blood men shed were not the same thing in the minds of many Central African peoples.[81] The special, well-publicized attention given to Christ's blood—or even the blood banyama took (and mixed) indiscriminately from men and women—may have indicated a degree of specificity that was absent in local concepts. The blood of male missionaries—and of anti-European fantasies—may have represented ideas about commodities and the sale of labor power, as well as ideas about nurturance and colors.

It is important here that we look at systems of color classification, both as it applies to the red of blood and to the red or white of wine

---

77. Brelsford, "'Banyama' Myth," 49.

78. Hinfelaar, "Religious Change," 8.

79. Audrey I. Richards, "Mother-Right among the Central Bantu," in E. E. Evans-Pritchard, ed., *Essays Presented to C. G. Seligman* (1934; reprint, Westport, Conn.: Negro Universities Press, 1970). 276; Hinfelaar, "Religious Change," 322.

80. Audrey I. Richards, *Chisungu: A Girl's Initiation Ceremony among the Bemba of Zambia* (London and New York: Routledge, 1982), 34; Hinfelaar, "Religious Change," 32.

81. Luc de Heusch, *The Drunken King, or, The Origin of the State,* trans. Roy Willis (Bloomington: Indiana University Press, 1982), 168–70; Victor Turner, "Color Classification in Ndembu Ritual: A Problem of Primitive Classification," in *The Forest of Symbols: Aspects of Ndembu Rituals* (Ithaca, N.Y.: Cornell University Press, 1967), 59–92.

(a drink forbidden to Africans in the colony).[82] In the West, blood and wine, both as fluids and as metaphors, carried exceptional powers that could make rituals ambiguous and their use in everyday problematic: without the mediation of another liquid or specific meals, they could make miraculous rituals exceptionally complex and layered.[83] But in Northern Rhodesia, wine as an intoxicating liquid seems to have been far less important to Africans than beer was.[84] Wine seems to have been most meaningful when it was red and bottled and drunk by Europeans. A generic red liquid in bottles took on immense power in ways that clerics and administrators could never have anticipated. The bottled red liquid of mucape could kill an unrepentant sorcerer years after he or she had drunk it,[85] and during the banyama scares in Tanganyika in 1931, according to E. E. Hutchins, "bad characters" spilled the contents of "bottles of red ink" bumping into passers-by and then claimed that "they were servants of 'mumiani' and now their master's medicine was lost. Considerable sums as compensation have been extorted from ignorant natives by this old ruse." Hutchins also reported that a group of European surveyors were accused of being mumiami and threatened so often that they had to be withdrawn from the area because, missionaries told him, "some of them were seen to drink red wine." [86] In the late 1940s in Tanganyika, the doctor Hope Trant was accused of being banyama by the people who saw her drink red wine with her dinner.[87]

Most Central African matrilineal peoples have a tripartite system of classification based on red, white, and black; these are the only colors for which they possess "names." Of these colors, red represents life and

82. In much of British colonial Africa, including Northern Rhodesia, Africans were forbidden to consume "European-type" bottled beers and wine; see Charles Ambler, "Alcohol, Racial Segregation and Popular Politics in Northern Rhodesia," *J. African History* 31, 2 (1990): 295–313, and Michael O. West, "'Equal Rights for All Civilized Men': Elite Africans and the Quest for 'European' Liquor in Colonial Zimbabwe, 1924–1961," *Int. Rev. of Social History* 37, 3 (1992): 376–97.

83. Feeley-Harnik, *The Lord's Table,* 155–56.

84. Richards, *Land, Labour and Diet,* 77–81; Ambler, "Alcohol," 295–305; West, "'Equal Rights.'"

85. Richards, "Modern Movement of Witchfinders," 449; Société des Missionnaires d'Afrique, Rome, Diaire de Chilubula, 29 June 1934; Diaire de Kayambi, 5 June 1934.

86. E. E. Hutchins, district officer, Morogoro, "Report on 'Mumiani' or 'Chinja-chinja,'" (Tanzania National Archives, film no. MF 15, Morogoro District, vol. 1, part A, sheets 25–26, August 1931, but inserted into file marked 1938). Hutchins believed that European surveyors drinking bottled red wine were one reason the rumor spread through Morogoro. I am grateful to Thaddeus Sunseri for taking notes on this file for me.

87. Hope Trant, *Not Merrion Square: Anecdotes of a Woman's Medical Career in Africa* (Toronto: Thornhill Press, 1970), 127–44. I am grateful to Megan Vaughan for this reference.

death, depending on context, while white represents purity and health; black is the color of disease, witchcraft, and death. Because of black's straightforward qualities and its power, tripartite systems tend to give way to binary systems in which red and white become binary opposites. In ritual practice and daily life, red absorbs some of the qualities of black, and red and white can be seen to contradict each other. Thus, the Ndembu of western Zambia say that semen is blood "purified by water," while among the Bemba, white paint on a hut washed away the pollution of menstrual blood.[88] In colonial Northern Rhodesia, the contradiction of priests in white robes said to be drinking African blood may have been difficult to tolerate: it announced that the priests were free of any taint that might result from such an action. But Europeans' power over African blood was not only their real and metaphoric ability to extract it and openly consume it; it was their ability to take it and bottle it and transport it throughout the world.

But what about Fox-Pitt's second point, that it was not merely Africans beliefs' about the Mass but racial segregation that left Africans free to imagine such things about the Mass? There were no racially segregated churches in Northern Province, where, as administrators were quick to point out, there were not enough Europeans even to fill all the available government positions.[89] Segregated Masses took place on the Copperbelt, however, performed not by White Fathers but by Jesuits, who arrived at Broken Hill in 1927, or Franciscans, who moved from Broken Hill to Ndola in 1931. The fact that in rumor most priests were known as White Fathers may have referred generically to the color of priests' robes, and it may also have represented what the color of those robes and the priests who wore them meant to the peoples of Northern Rhodesia.

But if banyama is a literal, local reading of the Mass, how do we account for the time lag between the first Catholic missions among the Bemba in the late 1890s and the first banyama accusations in the late 1920s? The question suggests a mechanical relationship between Catholic practices and African responses; the issue may not be the Mass, but what the Mass meant to Africans at a given time. Thus, it may be more useful to suggest, as Fox-Pitt asserted, that the idea of blood-drinking priests became a powerful source of anxiety because of the political contexts in which those and other practices were thought to take place.

88. Turner, "Color Classification in Ndembu Ritual," 59–92; Richards, *Chisungu*, 81.
89. NAZ, SEC2/1297, Northern Province Annual Report, Native Affairs, 1937.

Africans were among the first Protestants to evangelize the Bemba, and the heritage of revivalist movements, especially those of John Chilembwe in Nyasaland and Mwana Lesa in Northern Rhodesia, was strong.[90] But after the strike on the Copperbelt in 1935, relations between Christian missionaries and Africans became quite tense. At Luanshya, along with other Europeans, Protestant missionaries had been protected from strikers by machine-guns.[91] Officials later criticized White Fathers for how they had educated the Bemba. White Fathers responded that officials had not done enough to counter Watchtower propaganda—which called the disturbances a "pre-arranged Catholic riot"—but after that, in their churches, White Fathers urged converts to join Catholic Action groups on the Copperbelt and avoid trade unions.[92] The social context of Christian practices and teachings were those of labor, and any explanation of banyama that does not consider labor relations is flawed.

DETAILS: WORK AND PAY

Banyama stories were about Africans who were employed by Europeans to capture other Africans. If we locate vampire accusations against White Fathers in the labor relations of each mission and the wider colony, we get a very different picture, one that may link ideas about the alienation of labor power with those about the circulation of money and commodities and the commoditization of blood. Men from the Northern Province of Northern Rhodesia had been migrant laborers for years—men went to Katanga, the Lupa Goldfields, and the Copperbelt; during the sisal boom of the 1920s, they went to the plantations of Tanganyika Territory—so that the sale of labor power for money was commonplace by the 1930s. What made it remarkable, apparently, was how it was remunerated.

According to Audrey Richards, money had been circulating in the region since the turn of the century, when administrators were charged with encouraging the payment of wages and taxes in cash, rather than

90. Ipenburg, *Lubwa*, 5–7; Fields, *Revival and Rebellion*, 114–23, 163–74, 179–85.
91. Sean Morrow, "'On the Side of the Robbed': R. J. B. Moore, Missionary on the Copperbelt, 1933–1941," *J. of Religion in Africa* 19, 3 (1989): 249–50.
92. *The Golden Age*, quoted in Henry S. Meebelo, *Reaction to Colonialism: A Prelude to the Politics of Independence in Northern Zambia, 1893–1939* (Manchester: Manchester University Press, 1971), 175; Société des Missionnaires d'Afrique, *Rapports annuels*, no. 30 (1934–35), 328; ibid., no. 39 (1938–39), 257; Société des Missionnaires d'Afrique, Rome, Diaire de Kapatu, 12 June 1940, 7 October 1940.

in kind. European-owned stores, mainly those of Thom and the African Lakes Company, also encouraged cash transactions. Although Richards insists that, despite the number of men away, the actual use of money in everyday life was limited, her evidence is contradictory. Many Bemba regarded money as a medium for specific transactions. In the late 1920s, for example, a woman on her way to visit her son on the Copperbelt was found dying of starvation with 2/- tied in a cloth: "It had apparently never occurred to her to use the money to buy supplies," Richards wrote.[93] But within a few years, Richards observed, the use of money created new ties of rights and obligations: if a woman who lived alone, or with one or two married daughters, purchased food with money, she was not obligated to share it. Richards saw "a young couple eat meat alone while almost starving neighbors looked on. They shrugged their shoulders when questioned, and said 'We bought this meat with money.'"[94] By the early 1930s, money seems to have become a fairly commonplace medium to exchange for male labor. A small brideprice was creeping into Kasama District, and the 10/- given to fathers instead of service was "money to cut trees," which according to Richards was "the wage for a month's work at European rates."[95] My point here is not about the monetization of suitor service, which is part of larger struggles over bridewealth and contested systems of marriage taking place in Bemba country, but that a ritual payment was now reckoned in the language of the labor market, with remuneration measured by time, not work, and at European rates. In this the Bemba were not fetishizing money, giving it properties above and beyond exchange; they were standardizing the relationship of labor power to money. Africans who worked for Europeans for free were ridiculed. At Kayambi in the late 1920s, for example, priests designated two girls to bring reeds to the station for Easter. Although the mission had no authority over them, they seemed willing to do this. Only when they were "abused and insulted" in their villages did the mission agree to pay each girl's father 2/- for their work.[96]

But how money was used and how money was talked about may have been different in colonial Northern Rhodesia. When talked about, money is an international language that transcends ethnic and political

93. Richards, *Land, Labour and Diet*, 220.
94. Ibid., 153.
95. Ibid., 218–20.
96. Société des Missionnaires d'Afrique, Rome, Diaire de Kayambi, 23 January 1927.

frontiers and proclaims the sophistication of the speaker.[97] Debates and
rumors about how money is to be used, however, reveal local concerns
about the value of money both as a medium of exchange and as a token
of political authority.[98] During the time Richards did her fieldwork, the
demand for mine labor dropped precipitously; there was a shortage of
money throughout Northern Province, and there were widespread rumors that unemployed copper miners had been promised exemptions
from their 1932 taxes.[99] In Isoka District, returning migrants told the
district commissioner that "it was no good looking for work in the Tanganyika Territory because the white ants had eaten all the money." [100] As
the suspension of the gold standard came into effect, rumors about the
value of currencies circulated. Africans parodied the idea of "face value"
amid the dire conditions on the Copperbelt. Men who did not have the
money to buy firewood or food claimed that the king of England had
been jailed for one month because he demanded "too many taxes" and
that the coins with his face on them had lost their value.[101] In 1933, the
rumor circulated that British rule was about to end, and that Englishmen would be replaced by black Americans, who would bring American
currency; a year later, the gradual withdrawal of South African silver
coins from circulation was said to herald the closing of Chinsali boma.[102]
Taken together, these rumors reflect the importance of money. Stephen
Gudeman's reworking of Richards has characterized the Bemba village
economy as one in which commodities and services circulated among
villagers, headmen, chiefs, and ancestors according to customary rules
of allocation and distribution.[103] But in the wider, industrialized econ-

97. Olivia Harris, "The Earth and the State: The Sources and the Meanings of Money
in North Potosi, Bolivia," in J. Parry and M. Bloch, eds., *Money and the Morality of Exchange* (Cambridge: Cambridge University Press, 1989), 233–34; Keith Breckenridge,
"'Money with Dignity': Migrants, Minelords, and the Cultural Politics of the South African Gold Standard Crisis, 1920–33," *J. African History* 36 (1995): 271–304.

98. See Keith Hart, "Heads or Tails? Two Sides of the Coin," *Man*, n.s., 21 (1986):
367–86.

99. H. A. Watmore, Tour Report 3/1932 (NAZ, SEC2/835, Tour Reports, Mpika,
1931–33); Breckenridge, "'Money with Dignity.'"

100. J. W. Sharratt-Horne, district commissioner, tour report, 6/1932 (NAZ, SEC2/
767, Isoka Tour Reports, 1932–33). White ants do eat paper money; see Sharon Hutchinson, "The Cattle of Money and the Cattle of Girls among the Nuer, 1930–83," *American
Ethnologist*, 19, 2 (1992): 294–316.

101. Société des Missionnaires d'Afrique, Rome, Diaire de Chilubula, 10, 14, and
24 February 1932.

102. Musambachime, "Impact of Rumour," 204; Annual Report on Native Affairs,
Chinsali, 1935 (NAZ, SEC2/1298, Annual Report on Native Affairs, Chinsali, 1935–37).

103. Stephen Gudeman, *Economics as Culture* (London: Routledge, 1986), 100–101.

omy of Northern Rhodesia—at least from the vantage point of Bemba laborers in the 1930s—money did not circulate through commodities but from wage labor to taxation. Money defined the relationship between Africans, Europeans, and the state. The ruptures in these relationships were described in rumors of ingestion, imprisonment, and blood.

What kinds of work relationships obtained at White Fathers' missions? The priests were not exchanging goods and services for money, or when they were, the amount of money was pathetically small. The barter stores of the Luapula missions, the heavy-handed methods of making Christian men porters—all these contradicted the economic world of which most Bemba had experience. Even boarding schools were subsidized, not by parents' fees, but by children's labor. Where the White Fathers did pay in money, those small sums were often contested and sometimes withheld.

The accusations that deformed and parodied conversions, church belfries, and priests' insistence on monogamy were not popular religion, they were popular economics. Outbreaks of banyama accusations often corresponded with incidents involving unpaid or underpaid catechists. There was a catechists' strike at Ipusukilo at about the same time that there was an outbreak of banyama rumors in the district; a few months later, the accusations reached Kasama District headquarters at the same time that boarding school students refused to work; banyama accusations came forcibly to the attention of the boma within a week of the threatened strike by catechists at Mulilansolo in 1943;[104] in 1958, the catechists of St. Mary's were said to mark victims with the sign of the cross the same year that they were not paid at all. This is not to claim that there is a mechanical relationship between banyama accusations and catechists' wages. The process by which bloodsucking becomes a powerful and credible metaphor is far too complex for that. But I want to suggest that vampire accusations may have taken hold when relations of work and remuneration were severely disfigured. Accusations that the White Fathers sucked African blood may have described a specific labor market.[105]

104. I have taken the chronology of banyama scares from Clay, "Memorandum" (cited n. 57 above).

105. Most of the Europeans accused of being banyama are not mentioned in the written record. The most notorious one was Arthur Davison, a labor recruiter based at Ndola. Musambachime, "Impact of Rumor," 206; S. R. Denny, "Up and Down the Great North Road" (typescript, 1970, Rhodes House, Oxford, RH MSS Afr. r. 113).

Stories about vampire priests were an idiom—like strikes and slow-downs—with which labor was debated. Vampire accusations did not just debate the nature of the work catechists and Christians did for White Fathers, they debated the specific form of remuneration. The low and frequently nonexistent salaries paid catechists, the White Fathers' numerous attempts to monopolize local labor, raised the question, why are these people working? These stories explain—or, if that is too strong a term, account for—why catechists might work without pay, why people might trade at the barter stores. The frequent references to the "minions" of the priests as the true agents of banyama sought to understand and give meaning to work relationships that were unwaged.

But the idea of wage rates, commodity prices, and local labor markets may have been abstractions in rural Northern Rhodesia. During the Depression, at least, the competitive labor markets were hundreds of miles away (and rumored to have no money), and there was no agreed upon social necessity by which wages were set. Barter stores and anxieties about the value of money had seriously distorted the value of commodities and wages. Wages had been set by employers; commodity prices had been set by shopkeepers; sometimes commodities and wages were one and the same. If banyama accusations are to be located in labor relations, it is necessary to look as closely as the sources allow at their generic employers and shopkeepers, the Europeans accused.

DETAILS: WHITE MEN

How do we read the lack of specificity about the White Fathers in banyama accusations? They were, after all, just a few of the many Europeans who were said to take Africans' blood. Suppose I suggest that the White Fathers were merely stock characters, like villains in melodrama, in these complex and layered stories, some of many diverse individuals called banyama and made important only by the garbled evidence presented in archives and documents? Suppose I suggest that the real issues in banyama stories were the economic relationships—or un-economic relationships—that gave rise to vampire accusations? What if I locate these accusations in relationships, not events, facts, or figures? In that case the relationship between the catechists' threatened strikes and banyama accusations of 1943 would be obvious, if mechanistic: the real cause triggered an outburst against imagined practices. What if I locate vampire accusations not only in a parsimonious priesthood but in relations between merchants and patrons? We get the same level of detail about white people—which is not very much—but an accusation firmly rooted in retail trade.

Let me introduce evidence about a white man who was not a priest. Early in January 1944, "a strange man" ran off with a small child in the southern part of Kasama district. "On being arrested this man stated that he belonged to the 'banyama' and that he had been sent out by Mr. Glieman (an Abercorn settler) to collect blood." By late January, he had "changed his story and now states that he ran off with the child as he wished to rape her." [106]

Unpacking such a story is a challenge. Kidnapped or missing children—singly and in groups—figure in many banyama accusations and Northern Province memoranda of the 1940s. This may have been due to child custody disputes, inasmuch as men who had worked on the Copperbelt increasingly insisted on bridewealth marriages and control over children, or to disputes over pawning.[107] In the early 1930s, for the first time, fathers began pawning their children, the White Fathers noted.[108] In both cases, mother's brothers might have taken children back to their homes.

But what do we make of the man's saying that he belonged to the banyama and had been sent to collect blood for a specific white man, Orne Glieman? I assume the man gave what he thought to be the right answer, the answer that he thought would set him free. If he believed, in the words of the parliamentary member for native interests in 1945, the "popular misconception that the Government knows all about what is going on and is conniving in the practices," [109] claiming that he worked for the European known locally as a banyama may have seemed the wisest possible answer. I cannot assess his second answer nearly as well, because we do not know the circumstances in which it was induced. We

106. Geoffrey Howe, provincial commissioner, Northern Province, Kasama, to chief secretary, Lusaka, 29 January 1944 (NAZ, SEC2/429, Native Affairs: Banyama).

107. Clay, "Memorandum" (cited n. 57 above); John Barnes, Fort Jameson, to J. Clyde Mitchell, 10 October 1948, J. Clyde Mitchell Papers, Rhodes House, Oxford, RH MSS Afr. s. 1998/4/1; John V. Taylor amd Dorothea A. Lehmann, *Christians of the Copperbelt: The Growth of the Church in Northern Rhodesia* (London: SCM Press, 1961), 114–16; Jane L. Parpart, "Sexuality and Power on the Zambian Copperbelt, 1926–54," in Norman R. Bennett, ed., *Discovering the African Past: Essays in Honor of Daniel F. McCall* (Boston: African Studies Center, Boston University, 1987), 57–64. I am grateful to Megan Vaughan for suggesting this line of inquiry to me.

108. Société des Missionnaires d'Afrique, Rome, Diaire de Chilubula, 10 February 1932, 24 June 1932.

109. Bishop of Northern Rhodesia, member for native interests, LegCo Debates, 31 August 1945, *Hansard*, cols. 221–22 (NAZ, SEC2/429, Native Affairs: Banyama).

can be reasonably certain that this was an answer acceptable to his interrogators, but the first answer took hold locally, and when the man
was brought to trial, it was recommended that he not be defended by a
district officer—the usual practice—"in view of the widespread suspicion amongst Africans . . . that the Government in general and the District Commissioner in particular are sympathetic toward the 'banyama'
cult and are responsible for recent disappearances." [110]

Why Orne Glieman? There are in fact several reasons why he might
have been considered banyama. He was shadowy even by the standards
of white settlers in Northern Rhodesia. A Scandinavian, he is remembered as having claimed to be the illegitimate son of the king of Sweden
or Denmark, and had come from the Congo to a farm in the Siasi Valley, near Abercorn, in 1927. There his oldest son accidentally shot two
Africans, killing one. Glieman senior was involved in "the usual labor
disputes in which he was not infrequently defeated, much to his cha-
grin." [111] But Glieman was accused of drinking blood, not in Abercorn,
but in Kasama, where he worked as a manager for Thom Stores; there
he was known as a man who did not treat Africans very well. In 1939
or 1940, he gravely insulted the Chitimukulu, the paramount of the
Bemba. The Chitimukulu wanted to buy a length of valve tubing from
Glieman for his bicycle. Glieman rudely asked him why he wanted valve
tubing when there were plenty of rats' tails that could be used for the
purpose. This caused great offense; there was a boycott of the store, and
Glieman was forced to retire to his farm in Abercorn. [112]

Without any oral versions of the Glieman-as-banyama story it is almost impossible to get very much out of this account, but the basics are
nonetheless compelling. Here not only was an ordinary economic transaction—the purchase of a commodity with money—refused, but the of-
fensive shopkeeper suggested the transaction be replaced by foraging. [113]

---

110. G. Howe, provincial commissioner, Northern Province, to chief secretary,
Lusaka, 29 January 1944; A. T. Williams, for provincial commissioner, Northern Prov-
ince, Kasama, to registrar of High Court, Livingstone, confidential, 30 April 1944 (NAZ,
SEC2/429, Native Affairs: Banyama).

111. Denny, "Up and Down the Great North Road"; Dick Hobson, *Showtime: The
Agricultural and Commercial Society of Zambia* (Lusaka: Agricultural and Commercial
Society of Zambia, 1979), 42; Richard Hobson, personal communication, 7 July 1991.

112. Geoffrey Mee, son of L. G. Mee, manager of Thom Stores in Fort Roseberry,
1940–54,, interviewed by Hugh Macmillan, Lusaka, 10 August 1991.

113. Rat tails themselves were a medical metaphor even in such unsophisticated hands
as Glieman's: anti-rat and anti-plague campaigns in East and Central Africa rewarded
Africans who brought rat tails to their chiefs, but most of the rat hunting in Central Africa
was done by young boys or, less commonly, women; see Megan Vaughan, *Curing Their Ills:
Colonial Power and African Illness* (Stanford: Stanford University Press, 1991), 40–43.

The issue was not only that the Chitimukulu was insulted, but how he was insulted: Glieman deformed relationships grounded in money; indeed, he refused them. Vampire accusations not only described unfair extractions, they identified those Europeans who did not participate in the circulation of money. Elsewhere in Southern Africa, blood became a metaphor for money; the difficulties men face in accumulating money—that it burns a hole in their pockets—in so many cultures reflects not only the heat generated by monetary transactions, but the fluidity of cash.[114] Sharon Hutchinson's work on the Nuer, however, maintains that in actual practice people do not stress the analogy between blood and money, in order to make the differences between money and people clear.[115] But the banyama accusations against the missions, their barter stores, and Orne Glieman suggest that money and blood are situational similes, deployed in very specific instances: when people spoke of blood to describe what money was like, they were defining how money functioned in specific relationships, how it in fact circulated.

There is, however, another reason why Glieman might have been known as banyama—he said he was. Such a terrifying boast would not have been out of character for the man described above, and another European in Northern Rhodesia known as banyama—Arthur Davison, a labor recruiter based at Ndola—was said to have encouraged the rumor, enjoying the celebrity it gave him.[116] But white people do not spread banyama stories; Africans do. Rumors do not take hold because of the credibility of any one person doing the telling, but because of how they articulate and embody the concerns of the people spreading and hearing the rumor.[117] Understanding banyama requires understanding why these beliefs made so much sense to those who believed them.

114. Jean Comaroff and John L. Comaroff, "Goodly Beasts, Beastly Goods: Cattle and Commodities in a South African Context," *American Ethnologist* 17, 2 (1990): 209.
115. Hutchinson, "Cattle of Money," 302–3.
116. V. Y. Mudimbe, personal communication, 10 January 1992; "Banyama—Copper Belt Myth Terrifies the Foolish" (cited n. 76 above); "Five Years for African Who Threatened to Kill Broadcasters," *Central African Post* [Lusaka], 27 January 1953, 1; W. V. Brelsford, *Generations of Men: The European Pioneers of Northern Rhodesia* (Salisbury: Stuart, Manning for the Northern Rhodesia Society, 1966), 140–41; Musambachime, "Impact of Rumor," 206–7. Similarly, according to Anthony Oliver-Smith, "The Pishtaco: Institutionalized Fear in the Peruvian Highlands," *J. American Folklore* 82, 326 (1969): 363–68. Peruvian mestizos reported "with much hilarity" that they would kill a pig or a dog and leave its entrails beside blood-drenched clothing to convince Indians that the fat-extracting phantom mestizo of the Highlands was nearby and would punish them for not working harder.
117. See, e.g., Patricia A. Turner, "Church's Fried Chicken and the Klan: A Rhetorical Analysis of Rumor in the Black Community," *Western Folklore* 46, 4 (1987): 294–

DETAILS: TALK

I want to propose a fourth interpretation, one that returns us to the issues raised in the first part of this chapter. What if I were to argue that each outbreak of banyama rumors was part of a transcolonial movement of vampire accusations, and that the form these accusations took in Northern Rhodesia or Katanga had to do with how local events and actors were inserted into widely told border-crossing stories? What if no specific event or action caused a specific banyama accusation? What if specific events and actions were used to make a transcolonial narrative local? Just as mucape and Watchtower crossed ethnic and colonial frontiers, from Nyasaland to Northern Rhodesia and Katanga and northwest to Tanganyika, vampire accusations also swept the countryside "like the Charleston or mah jong in England some years ago."[118] But unlike mucape and Watchtower, banyama rumors were an oral genre. Ideas and images were exchanged and amended, and in each new place, they were literally inscribed with characters and actors and equipment specific to local concerns: ideas and images were embodied and emplotted. Thus, in 1931, banyama accusations ranged from Northern Rhodesia to central Tanganyika; in 1943, there were charges that white men drank African blood from Kananga in the lower Congo region through Katanga to Northern Rhodesia's Northern Province. Across the copperbelts of the colonial Belgian Congo and Northern Rhodesia, different images had different meanings and connotations—white compound managers were the cannibals who terrified African mineworkers in Katanga, while priests and shopkeepers and labor recruiters were said to suck African blood a few hundred miles away. The local Northern Rhodesian meanings of banyama accusations—whether about labor practices or the Mass—are no less clear, however, because these movements were transnational. Vampire accusations were specifically African ways of talking that identified new forms of violence and extraction; the actual description of these forms took place in the new technologies and teleologies of colonial economies: with their Catholic priests, white men with beards, and game rangers, banyama stories foregrounded what was both different and dangerous.

306; Gary Alan Fine, *Manufacturing Tales: Sex and Money in Contemporary Legends* (Knoxville: University of Tennessee Press, 1992); Jean-Noël Kapferer, *Rumors: Uses, Interpretations, and Images* (New Brunswick, N.J.: Transaction Publishers, 1990), 50–51.

118. District officer, Abercorn, 16 June 1934, quoted in Fields, *Revival and Rebellion,* 87.

Many of the vampire accusations described in this chapter seem to have taken elements from the Book of Revelations—the invisible mark that identifies victims, the final sound that compels its listeners to follow. These were not only new images but ones specific to religious teachings; their power came from the catechism classes and sermons and readings of which they were a part. Rearranged as the props and ideas in terrifying stories, they may have had different meanings in different places, but they brought priests and mission practices into each retelling.

Vampire accusations were the rumors that debated rates of pay, the currency in which payment took place, and the ways in which Europeans articulated relationships reckoned in money; they debated the new medical and religious meanings of blood, and the importance of customary systems of color classification. Vampire accusations debated these issues with each addition of a new character or a new image. These images and characters had the power to terrify and explain because they touched on so many Northern Rhodesian—or Congolese, or Tanganyikan—experiences and concerns. They had intense meaning because they were told and retold in the vocabularies of people's daily lives and conflicts. For this reason, there is no one interpretation that fits all banyama rumors, no single analysis that can explain how banyama accusations developed and then faded. Like the blood extracted and abstracted in them, banyama rumors had the fluidity to describe many situations.

CHAPTER 7

Blood, Bugs,
and Archives

*Debates over Sleeping-Sickness
Control in Colonial Northern Rhodesia,
1931–1939*

This chapter is about the interaction of African ideas and imperial science. It argues that the very specific vampire accusations that emerged in the Northern Province of Northern Rhodesia in the 1930s involved local and colonial ideas about the relationship between wild animals, tsetse flies, authority, and *citemene*, the form of shifting cultivation specific to the poor soils of the Congo-Zambezi watershed. Neither African nor European ideas on these subjects were fixed, nor was one untouched by the other. Although I shall present European ideas and African ideas in sequence, I do not see them as separate and distinct. African experience with tsetse flies shaped European ideas about control of such insects, which were necessarily tailored to fit African realities.[1] Indeed, it may be more useful to think of what follows as a presentation of scientific evidence (i.e., the kind of evidence we expect to find in essays about shifting cultivation) followed by a presentation of evidence of a very different sort (i.e., the kind usually considered inappropriate for historiography).

1. Michael Worboys, "Science and British Colonial Imperialism, 1895–1940" (Ph.D. thesis, Sussex University, 1979), ch. 2; John M. MacKenzie, "Experts and Amateurs: Tsetse, Nagana, and Sleeping Sickness in East and Central Africa," in J. Mackenzie, ed., *Imperialism and the Natural World* (Manchester: Manchester University Press, 1990), 187–212; Maryinez Lyons, *The Colonial Disease: A Social History of Sleeping Sickness in Northern Zaire, 1900–1940* (Cambridge: Cambridge University Press, 1992).

This chapter also suggests, with some trepidation, that the African ecological nightmare, whether disease or overpopulation, is in part a trope.[2] Over the past 100 years, "science" and "medicine" have become ways of talking about Africa that embody ideas about disaster and renewal. The ecological history of Africa needs to incorporate data that will move scholars away from this paradigm. Sleeping sickness is a real and virulent disease, and my task here is not merely to identify a discourse but to describe and elaborate other visions in which sleeping sickness was seen as a manageable disease in Northern Rhodesia. The other visions are not expressed in the language of germs, parasites, or apocalyptic epidemics; they are expressed in the language of colonial departments, officials and assistants, and blood. There is a body of thought in cultural studies that claims that people not only debate the changes taking place around them, they debate the terms in which those changes are described.[3] But to label either of these constructions "African" or "European" would be a mistake, I think, and I suggest that readers think of both of these as colonial constructions, in which the project and the materials are the same, but the position of the narrator is different.

But where are these narrators found? The sources I use here are from European archives: all the descriptions of vampires here have been mediated through the writings of colonial officials, colonial doctors, and the like. Over the past two decades, African historians have regarded such mediations with grave suspicions; the historian's task was to find ways to hear the African voices submerged in such archives and to unveil the processes of inscription and recoding that constituted each mediation. In this chapter I look directly at the mediations, at the African ideas distorted in the sources, so that I can relocate African voices—and the vampires they talk about—in those archives. Archives, James Hevia and Gayatri Spivak remind us, do not merely report colonial activities, they report the elaborate colonial attempts to recode local space, local property, and local ideas into imperial terms. The making of a colony out of a variety of African landscapes and disorderly states required that it be reterritorialized, made into a new unit, with new maps and rules to

2. Richard Waller, "Tsetse Fly in Western Narok, Kenya," *J. African History* 31, 1 (1990): 71–90, has argued that most recent studies of tsetse use the fly as a trope with which to study the progressive decline of Africa.

3. See, e.g., Stephen William Foster, *The Past Is Another Country: Representation, Historical Consciousness, and Resistance in the Blue Ridge* (Berkeley and Los Angeles: University of California Press, 1988).

fit the British empire.[4] The official recoding of African spaces and ideas was as partial as it was elaborate. No land, no population, and no institution was ever made fully identical to the imperial categories in which it was placed, and no imperial codes were ever completely adopted by farmers, chiefs, and porters. The inability of the colonial state to fully recode and reterritorialize is revealed in colonial archives. Reading colonial archives to tease out African voices suggests layers of domination that can be stripped away to reveal a colonial subject buried beneath the imperial project. Another kind of reading might reveal intense struggles over domination in each archival reference to an incomplete recoding, or to another bungled reterritorialization. In such a reading, archives report the struggles, imperial and local, over the vocabularies and tools of domination. Evidence such as vampire rumors opens a space in which historians can accurately see the failures of recoding and the incomplete reterritorialization that was the practice of colonial rule.

But what kind of evidence is rumor, and how can I use it to move from the politics of representation to the politics of tsetse control? In its most positivist form, *rumor* is the officials' term for information they have not engendered, shaped, or controlled. It is a category that simultaneously reveals popular conceptions about the actions and ideas of those in authority and declares the weakness of official channels of information and education. But what happens when I read rumors alongside naturalists' studies and colonial biomedicine? I want to suggest that for academics at the end of the twentieth century, the differences between rumor and research reports are great; they are recounted in different media and they have completely different levels of credibility. But for the subjects of the research and of colonial biomedicine, rumor and our own notions of fact may not have been all that different. The Bemba language does not have separate words for rumor, talk, and conversation. Indeed, how rumor was distinguished from fact in the 1930s is not at all clear.[5] Both covered the same ground, both contained the same actors and

4. Gayatri Chakrobarty Spivak, "The Rani of Sanir: An Essay on Reading the Archives," *History and Theory* 24 (1985): 247–72; James L. Hevia, "The Archive State and the Fear of Pollution: From the Opium Wars to Fu-Manchu," *Cultural Studies* 12, 2 (1998): 234–64.

5. On the Luapula, by the late 1940s at least, *ilyashi* meant historical knowledge; see Ian Cunnison, *History on the Luapula: An Essay on the Historical Notions of a Central African Tribe*, Rhodes-Livingstone Papers, no. 21 (Cape Town and New York: G. Cumberlege, Oxford University Press, for the Rhodes-Livingstone Institute, 1951), 3–4. Migrants to the Copperbelt from the plateau may have well understood both meanings of the word.

issues, but the rumor—at least as it was told and retold in colonial Northern Rhodesia in the 1930s—was often presented as a personal narrative. Rumors were not thought to be less believable if they were not first-person accounts, however: no one thought something untrue because it was said to have happened to a friend of a friend. Scientific knowledge, however, could be and frequently was disseminated in fragments, without the very frameworks that made it make sense.[6] The vampire accusations of the early 1930s, for example, referred to activities in Tanganyika Territory that were said to be about to shift to Northern Rhodesia's Northern Province, but were no less apparent—or frightening—to officials because of that.[7] Official arguments about citemene, cassava, and deforestation, on the other hand, were often made without reference to African ideas about tsetse flies, ecology, and wildlife. Moreover, officials frequently anticipated that their arguments would be ignored.

The world in which black Northern Rhodesians lived seems to have had more varied forms of information than that of their British counterparts. Starting at least in the 1920s, Bemba-speaking peoples heard tales of a twig that could strip a man of his willpower and of "Kasai cannibals" who kidnapped African mineworkers. They heard that Catholic priests ate people. During the early years of the Depression, they heard that the king of England was in jail and that black Americans would come to replace the British. They heard that Europeans hired Africans to capture other Africans and take their blood; they heard the dangers of citemene.[8] This is not to say everyone believed everything they heard. People believed stories—even if belief was not a constant state—

6. I take these points from two diverse studies of American culture, Gary Alan Fine, *Manufacturing Tales: Sex and Money in Contemporary Legends* (Knoxville: University of Tennessee Press, 1992), 83, 174–75, and John C. Burnham, *How Superstition Won and Science Lost: Popularizing Science and Health in the United States* (New Brunswick, N.J.: Rutgers University Press, 1987).

7. D. Willis, PC, Kasama, "Report on Banyama," 24 March 1931 (National Archives of Zambia [henceforth cited as NAZ], ZA1/9/62/2/1).

8. P. K. Kanosa, "Banyama—Copper Belt Myth Terrifies the Foolish," *Mutende* [Lusaka] 38 (1936) (NAZ, SEC2/429, Native Affairs: Banyama). For published accounts, see W. V. Brelsford, "The 'Banyama' Myth," *NADA* 9, 4 (1967): 52–58; George Shepperson, *Myth and Reality in Malawi* (Evanston, Ill.: Northwestern University Press, 1966), 3–9; Karen E. Fields, *Revival and Rebellion in Colonial Central Africa* (1985; reprint, Portsmouth, N.H.: Heinemann, 1997); Mwelwa C. Musambachime, "The Impact of Rumor: The Case of the Banyama (Vampire-Men) in Northern Rhodesia, 1930–1964," *Int. J. Afr. Hist. Studies* 21, 2 (1988): 205–9; Luise White, "Vampire Priests of Central Africa: African Debates about Labor and Religion in Colonial Northern Zambia," *Comparative Studies in Society and History* 35, 4 (1993): 744–70; and see chapter 6 above.

because of how they appreciated and apprehended certain facts, not because a story was grandiose, frightful, or told orally. From the vantage
point of a Bemba village, belief in "rumors" and "facts" appeared to
be equally tentative. Audrey Richards dismissed muchape, the transnational witch-finding movement of the early 1930s, as precisely the
kind of novelty the Bemba took up and quickly abandoned.[9]

But colonial science was not the mirror image of an African intellectual faddishness. Colonial science was anything but a monolith; officials
continually argued with the state and one another about forests, wild
animals, and African agriculture. "Scientific research" had a credibility
in colonial circles that the eyewitness accounts of naturalists did not
have. But rather than evaluate various trends in colonial thinking, I want
to find a way to interpret them all, as representing different visions of the
world and ways to understand it that changed over time. Recent trends
in literary criticism have argued that it is worthwhile to read scientific
texts the way we read novels, as cultural products that reveal the concerns and anxieties of a specific milieu.[10] In this chapter I suggest that it
is possible to read the fictive as the same kind of historical source as scientific texts.

This chapter is about the mosaic of colonial beliefs, African and European, the supposedly superstitious and the supposedly scientific,
about sleeping-sickness control. It argues that these beliefs, like so many
tiles, can be placed alongside one another so that an observer can discern the different narratives of science, land use, and medicine and see
how no single vision of fact and consequence ever fully dominates another. What follows are two discrete histories, one of pathogens, the
other of vampires. Without oral evidence, this may be the only way I can
proceed. The questions of who is saying what, when, and of who repeats
which rumor with intense belief and who argues against it with equal
passion—the very evidence that makes rumors form a debate rather
than a monolith—is not discernible from archival sources. Where individual African viewpoints appear, they do so at the behest of colonial
authorities, so that I am hesitant to read the words of an African writing for a government newspaper or a district clerk's words as anything

9. Audrey I. Richards, "A Modern Movement of Witchfinders," *Africa* 8, 4
(1935): 448.
10. See Gillian Beer, *Darwin's Plots: Evolutionary Narrative in Darwin, George Eliot,
and Nineteenth Century Fiction* (Boston: Routledge & Kegan Paul, 1983), and Ludmilla
Jordanova, ed., *Languages of Nature: Critical Essays on Science and Literature* (London:
Free Association Books, 1986).

more than those of a man doing his job. What follows, I hasten to point out, is a very conservative interpretation, in which I have stayed very close to my documents. This exegesis is based on a reading that could best be called vampire-driven: the questions I have asked and the files in which I have sought answer to them have all been determined by my reading of the Northern Rhodesian vampire accusations of 1931.

BUG STORIES

Tsetse flies carry the protozoa, called trypanosomes, that cause sleeping sickness (trypanosomiasis) in humans and domestic livestock. There are two kinds of trypanosome and two kinds of sleeping sickness, the origins and nature of which are by no means agreed upon: some think these are different environmental responses, others that the structure of the trypanosomes differs. Thus, the two kinds are either called by the names of the protozoa—*Trypanosoma gambiense* and *Trypanosoma rhodesiense*—or by the environments in which they occur, riverain and savannah. The terminologies of both types of sleeping sickness involve hosts (sometimes called the reservoir), vectors, and ecologies. The vector is the only method of disease transmission, as the trypanosome transforms in the fly's body over several days to become infectious. In *T. gambiense*, infected flies live in the shade on riverbanks and feed off humans, or occasionally reptiles, and infect them; because the disease can be transmitted from human to human, it can be spread by relatively small numbers of flies. Humans are the hosts, flies the vector. In *T. rhodesiense*, tsetses live in wooded areas—the bush—and feed off wild animals, which do not become infected, but they can also feed off humans or domestic ungulates when they are available: wild animals are the hosts, and the flies are the vector. Entomologists—amateur and professional—have tended to ignore the protozoon for the fly and studied the behavior of various species of tsetse in order to show how different varieties of trypanosomiasis are spread and how different ecosystems encourage that spread. Sleeping-sickness control organizations in British Africa invariably included entomologists.[11] Protozoologists, who seem to have been more influential in francophone Africa, regarded the dif-

---

11. A. J. Duggan, "An Historical Perspective" (typescript on trypanosomiasis, Wellcome Institute for the History of Medicine, Centre for Contemporary Archives, London [henceforth cited as WCCA], WTI/TRY/C1/3).

ferences between the trypanosomes as crucial and saw *T. gambiense* as an entirely different disease from *T. rhodesiense.*[12]

The "discovery" of sleeping sickness was truly a colonial phenomenon. While the disease had been known in West Africa for centuries, its spread in the havoc of colonial conquest to previously uninfected regions—the Congo River basin and Busoga in Uganda are perhaps the most dramatic examples—created epidemics of apocalyptic proportions. The other discovery, of the cause and etiology of the disease, is one of the great stories of tropical medicine, combining all that was exotic about epidemics in Africa with all that was memorable about scientists' and explorers' egos.[13] It was a discovery that would not have been possible without the scientific advances of the late nineteenth century, particularly germ theory. Germ theory made the debilitating diseases of the tropics avoidable; they were not caused by the gaseous matter of climate and decaying organisms (miasma), as had been previously thought, but by protozoa and bacteria, which could be conquered as they had been conquered in Europe.[14] But as Maryinez Lyons has argued, germ theory had its drawbacks. If the miasma theory had related tropical diseases to their geographical location, the bacteriology and protozoology of tropical medicine alienated disease from the landscape.[15]

But the sleeping sickness of this grand tradition was *T. gambiense;* the discovery—or invention, depending on whether one stands with the protozoologists or the entomologists—of *T. rhodesiense* was pursued with far less excitement and even some trepidation, as researchers con-

12. John Ford, *The Role of Trypanosomiasis in African Ecology: A Study of the Tsetse Fly Problem* (Oxford: Oxford University Press, 1971), 255–57; James Giblin, "Trypanosomiasis Control in African History: An Evaded Issue," *J. Afr. Hist.* 31, 1 (1990): 59–70; Lyons, *Colonial Disease,* 48–53.

13. "As far as David Bruce is concerned—in his first 24 hours in Uganda he was shown a case of trypanosome fever and saw slides of the parasite and was handed a collection of biting flies amongst which he recognized a tsetse fly. . . . Rarely can the investigator of the cause of an obscure disease be handed quite so much immediately relevant information in so short a time . . . and one does not have to be a microbiologist or a genius, or even a Fellow of the Royal Society to realize that here were immediate leads" (J. N. P. Davies, "Informed Speculation on the Cause of Sleeping Sickness, 1898–1903," *Medical History* 12 [1968]: 200–204). See also Lyons, *Colonial Disease,* 64–101; J. N. P. Davies, "The Cause of Sleeping Sickness: Entebbe 1902–03," *E. A. Medical J.* 39, 3 and 4 (1962): 81–99, 145–60; Oliver Ransford, *"Bid the Sickness Cease": Disease in the History of Black Africa* (London: J. Murray, 1983), 109–32.

14. John Farley, *Bilharzia: A History of Imperial Tropical Medicine* (Cambridge: Cambridge University Press, 1991), 14–15.

15. Lyons, *Colonial Disease,* 37–39, see also William Coleman, *Yellow Fever in the North: The Methods of Early Epidemiology* (Madison: University of Wisconsin Press, 1987), 97–100, 111–12, 131–34, 187–93.

cerned themselves with identifying an etiology and relating its cause to the trypanosomiasis of domestic stock, called *nagana*. *T. rhodesiense* was difficult to identify in part because local doctors expected humans to develop *T. gambiense* and in part because victims sickened and died so rapidly that Africans only identified the last stages of the disease, and then only for adults; presumably children succumbed so rapidly that sleeping sickness was confused with other afflictions. It was only in 1912 that the Luangwa Sleeping Sickness Commission, headed by investigators from the Liverpool School of Hygiene, demonstrated that the trypanosome carried by *Glossina morsitans* could feed off wild animals and humans alike.[16] Research in Nyasaland and South Africa in 1913 showed that *T. rhodesiense* was identical to *T. brucei*, discovered by David Bruce in Natal in 1894, the cause of nagana.[17] Not everyone accepted the idea that *T. rhodesiense* was caused by the trypanosome of wild animals and domestic livestock, but the fact shaped sleeping-sickness and tsetse-control policies in the 1930s.

In areas where *T. gambiense* was prevalent, attempts to control sleeping sickness became attempts to control populations—either by restricting their movements, by isolating the sick, or by removing whole villages.[18] But areas where *T. rhodesiense* was prevalent were, according to the thinking of the times, areas where cattle keeping was impossible, so that attempts to control sleeping sickness became attempts to control land use and relations between humans and wild animals. There were never as many cases of *T. rhodesiense* in East Africa as there were of *T. gambiense* on the riverbanks and lake shores of East and Central

16. G. W. Ellacomben, "Notes on a Case of Sleeping Sickness Treated at Livingstone Hospital during 1911" (WCCA, WTI/TRY/C21/1); A. May, *Report on Sleeping Sickness in Northern Rhodesia to February 1912* (Livingstone: Government Printer, 1912), 9, 10–13; Leroy Vail, "Ecology and History: The Example of Eastern Zambia," *J. Southern Afr. St.* 3, 2 (1977): 141.

17. D. Bruce, D. Harvey et al. "The Trypanosomes Found in the Blood of Wild Animals Living in the Sleeping Sickness Area, Nyasaland," *J. of the R.A.M.C.* 21 (1913): 566; David Bruce Collected Papers, WCCA, RAMC/1675/1; David Bruce, "Trypanosomes Causing Disease in Man and Domestic Animals" (Croonian Lecture, 22 June 1915, WCCA, WTI/RSTMH.G3/3/8); C. A. Hoare, "History of *Trypanosoma brucei gambiense*" (MS, 1968, WCCA, WTI/TRY/C1/9). John Ford calls the debates about the relationship between the various trypanosomes "prolonged and not very productive" (Ford, *Role of Trypanosomiasis*, 71).

18. Maryinez Lyons, "From 'Death Camps' to *Cordon Sanitaire:* The Development of Sleeping Sickness Policy in the Uele District of the Belgian Congo, 1903–14," *J. Afr. Hist.* 26 (1985), 69–91, and id., *Colonial Disease*, 199–222; Mwelwa C. Musambachime, "The Social and Economic Effects of Sleeping Sickness in Mweru-Luapula, 1906–22," *Afr. Econ. Hist.* 10 (1981): 151–73.

Africa. *T. rhodesiense* was more virulent, but since it was carried from animal to human, rather than from human to human, it was far less contagious. For that and for economic reasons, there was far more concern about nagana in East and Central Africa than there was about human sleeping sickness. Studies of *T. rhodesiense* tended to be centered on cattle rather than people. As late as the 1950s, when livestock losses from trypanosomiasis were less than those from rinderpest, tsetse flies and the fear thereof prevented profitable land use.[19]

In the case of sleeping sickness, the politics of land use was mediated through the new discipline of tropical medicine. In his history of yellow fever, François Delaporte charts the origins of the field. It mapped the interactions of living things to arrive at pathologies and in doing so, imbued insect vectors not only with the power of life and death, but the power of science: they could be controlled by knowledge about them. Tropical medicine drained one ancient symbol of its meaning and replaced it with another: "[D]eath came not now in the form of a man with a scythe but of a biting insect."[20] But if germ theory simply swept the miasma-ists away, along with their intimate sense of peopled locations, parasitologists swept the bacteriologists out of British tropical medicine. "Non-tropical" bacteriological diseases were ignored, and tropical medicine concentrated on worms, insects, and protozoa. The link between parasitology and tropical health convinced experts that these diseases could be prevented without studying how local populations became ill. Much colonial health policy focused on protozoa and vectors. Insect vectors and animal hosts were where protozoa spent part of their lifecycles, and killing the insect or animal could kill the protozoa.[21]

In the case of *T. rhodesiense* and *G. morsitans,* this pitted tsetse control against a vocal hunting lobby and one faction of imperial science. When in 1913, for example, David Bruce was convinced that *T. rhode-*

19. Edward A. Lewis, "The Objects of EATTRRO" (typescript, 1953, Edward Aneurin Lewis Papers, WCCA, WTI/EAL/16).

20. François Delaporte, *The History of Yellow Fever: An Essay on the Birth of Tropical Medicine,* trans. Arthur Goldhammer (Cambridge, Mass.: MIT Press, 1991), 147.

21. Michael Worboys, "Manson, Ross, and Colonial Medical Policy: Tropical Medicine in London and Liverpool, 1899–1914," in Roy MacLeod and Milton Lewis, eds., *Disease, Medicine, and Empire: Perspectives on Western Medicine and the Experience of European Expansion* (London: Routledge, 1988), 21–37; Farley, *Bilharzia,* 27–29; Randall M. Packard, "The Invention of the 'Tropical Worker': Medical Research and the Quest for Central African Labor on the South African Gold Mines, 1903–36," *J. Afr. Hist.* 34, 2 (1993): 271–92.

siense and the trypanosome that caused nagana were identical, he became an even stronger advocate of the extermination of wild animals than he had been previously. His reasoning had to do with ideas about what formed an infectious reservoir and how best to control it. Questioned before a 1913 Colonial Office Sleeping Sickness Committee that had many hunters on it, Bruce was asked why wild animals were the host for infectious *T. rhodesiense,* rather than birds, immune herds of cattle, or even people. The birds in *G. morsitans* country were too small and too mobile to be a good source of food for tsetse flies, there were no herds of cattle in *G. morsitans* country, and humans made poor hosts for *T. rhodesiense,* because only a few were infected and those were too sick to travel about and spread the disease, he responded.[22] He strenuously opposed the preservation of big game in "fly country": "It would be as reasonable to allow mad dogs to live and be protected by law in our English towns and villages."[23]

Although some suggested localized experiments in game eradication,[24] few of Bruce's contemporaries agreed with him about the relationship of *T. rhodesiense* to wild animals. German scholars disputed his findings; Alward May, Northern Rhodesia's medical officer, disregarded the findings of the Luangwa Sleeping Sickness Commission and claimed that man was the principle reservoir for *T. rhodesiense;* E. E. Austen of London's Natural History Museum argued that tsetse were specific to certain habitats: these could be emptied of people and left to game, inasmuch as tsetse flies did not follow game.[25]

Such debates about vectors and hosts, about flies and buffalo, were debates about how to classify and categorize animals. Such classifications were and are as much a part of scientific research about animals as they are artifacts of "traditional" society.[26] In the 1920s and 1930s,

22. Bruce believed that the course of colonial exploitation would rid most areas of *G. morsitans:* "a short time" after "a few thousands of natives and a few hundreds of white men" came to work in a fly-infested area, "you will not find a big mammal, as they are all shot, and you will not find a fly either" (Minutes of Evidence, Dept. Comm. on Sleeping Sickness, Colonial Office, 10 October 1913, 3, 5, WCCA/WTI/TRY/CI/2).
23. Bruce, "Trypanosomiasis Causing Disease."
24. Rupert Jack, "Tsetse Fly and Big Game in Southern Rhodesia," *Bull. Ent. Res.* 1 (1914): 97–110; Sir William Leishman Collected Papers, "The Suggested Experiment of Game-Destruction in a Localised Area" (1915; WCCA, RAMC/563).
25. John M. MacKenzie, *The Empire of Nature: Hunting, Conservation, and British Imperialism* (Manchester: Manchester University Press, 1988), 236; May, *Report on Sleeping Sickness,* 24–25.
26. See Donna Haraway, *Primate Visions: Gender, Race, and Nature in the World of Modern Science* (London: Routledge, 1989).

what was known about *T. rhodesiense* was the supposedly contagious relationship between reservoir, vector, and victim. Attempts to study the specific relationships—human to landscape, human to animal—that might cause or limit the disease gave way to the study of a vector abstracted into "the fly." While it is tempting to suspect that this was the result of pressure by the hunting lobby, it seems more likely that it was part of the intense focus on vectors and pathogens that characterized early research in tropical medicine.[27] Thus, the very people studying fly-human or fly-animal interactions anthropomorphized tsetses—saying, "The Tsetse fly loathes the presence of man,"[28] for example—and the fly became as important in research as was the disease. By 1935, there was a Parliamentary Tsetse Fly Committee.

C. F. M. Swynnerton, the most important tsetse researcher in this story, understood that fly behavior was based on human observations. A naturalist of extraordinary capability, Swynnerton had come to Africa as a nineteen-year-old farm manager and first attracted attention with his study of a mixed fly belt in North Mossurise, on the Southern Rhodesia–Mozambique border, in 1921, in which he noted, among other things, that male flies sometimes traveled on humans, causing some observers to think they were attacking.[29]

Swynnerton's studies of the tsetse fly's ecological niches, including his 580-page monograph *The Tsetse Flies of East Africa* (1936), which catalogued the various species' eating, breeding, and resting habits, put the fly in the foreground. Swynnerton read the landscape to show how tsetse could be limited without the wholesale slaughtering of game. Knowledge of the fly, Swynnerton argued, would allow science to combat the vector without significantly disrupting the reservoir or destroying the hosts—a method of disease control that David Bruce had characterized twenty years before as "a nice pious wish."[30]

27. Michael Worboys, "Manson, Ross and Colonial Medical Policy"; Megan Vaughan, *Curing Their Ills: Colonial Power and African Illness* (Stanford: Stanford University Press, 1991), 37, but see MacKenzie, "Experts and Amateurs."

28. *Report . . . on the Trade . . . of the British Central African Protectorate* (London, 1896), 12, quoted in Vail, "Ecology and History," 139.

29. John J. McKelvey, Jr., *Man against Tsetse: Struggle for Africa* (Ithaca, N.Y.: Cornell University Press, 1973); C. F. M. Swynnerton, "An Examination of the Tsetse Problem in North Mossurise, Portuguese East Africa," *Bull. Ent. Res.* 11 (1921): 304–30.

30. Interdepartmental Committee on Sleeping Sickness, *Report,* Cd. 7349 (London, 1914), 11. It took until 1953 for the fly to return to its status as an insect vector, rather than a source of disease itself. Edward A. Lewis, director of the East African Tsetse and Trypanosomiasis Research and Reclamation Organization, likened sleeping sickness in East Africa to malaria in medieval England, noting that tsetse were only dangerous be-

LAND, FLIES, AND SCIENCE

Different varieties of tsetse fly live in different places. In East and Central Africa, the colonial concern was about G. *morsitans,* the fly that carried the trypanosome fatal to domestic livestock, and, to a lesser extent, humans. While the riverbank-dwelling T. *gambiense* could be transmitted from human to human, the trypanosome carried by T. *morsitans* required an animal host, so that methods of describing and of preventing one kind of sleeping sickness came to be about the relations between humans and animals. If sleeping sickness of the savannah was carried by wild animals, then the goal of biomedical policies was to separate humans and wild animals, big and small.

From these policies came studies of "the fly." By the 1930s, most scientific knowledge of G. *morsitans* was based largely on Swynnerton's research, which demonstrated the viability of African methods of tsetse control. Nevertheless, the major impact of Swynnerton's work both on his own career and on the shape of tsetse research was to suggest an either/or paradigm in which centralized settlements and tsetse flies were inexorably opposed.

Swynnerton showed how knowledge of various tsetse flies' behavior could be used to control their numbers and habitats. G. *morsitans,* for example, breeds on barren ground toward the end of the rainy season; G. *brevipalis* lives in wooded undergrowth that remains in leaf throughout the year; all tsetse flies need shade. Well-timed grass burning could therefore limit the habitats of two species of *Glossina.* Ngoni in North Mossurise had burned grass late in the dry season, when leaves had fallen and the grass was at its driest, so that the fires would be intense enough to draw a wind. Such a fire would not only destroy the grass but much of the young growth and some high shade; with sufficient rain, however, the grass would rapidly grow back. Swynnerton became a proponent of late burning, a method of tsetse control that he believed white settlement had greatly disrupted: "Under the white man everyone burns as he pleases." White farmers' uncoordinated grass burning failed to check tsetse populations, and different species of fly flourished.[31]

The behavior of wild animals, according to Swynnerton, was shaped by human intervention as well. Under Ngoni domination, large parts of

---

cause of "the diseases they carry. . . . The object must be to rid the country of trypanosomiasis . . . not rid Africa of tsetse fly" (typescript cited n. 19 above).

31. Swynnerton, "Examination of the Tsetse Problem in North Mossurise," 323–25.

the Central African countryside had centralized states with concentrated populations. Densely populated areas and mile after mile of cultivated fields surrounded by deforested areas allowed Africans to live and keep cattle in health.[32] When the population decreased, or when an area was raided and the population scattered, the land reverted to bush and game, and tsetse became widespread—a medicalized version of tribal warfare. Swynnerton had been very impressed by Ngoni accounts of methods of tsetse control. When Umzila conquered North Mossurise in the 1860s, the somewhat scattered population lived near belts infested by *G. morsitans*; cattle had to be sent to highlands or they died. But Umzila ordered his population to draw near the king, moving villages and settlements to the lower altitudes of the territory. "Every one of my informants has described most graphically the result of this concentration," wrote Swynnerton. "The bush simply disappeared and the country became bare, except for the numberless native villages . . . and gardens." All that was left of the woodlands was an uncleared and uninhabited "Oblong," virtually a game reserve for Ngoni hunting parties. Outside the Oblong, hunters tracked wild pigs and buffalo herds whenever they appeared.[33]

It was on the strength of this research that Swynnerton was appointed the game warden of Tanganyika Territory in 1921; his goal was to control tsetse flies without the wholesale slaughter of game, the policy already in sporadic operation in Southern Rhodesia. In 1923, he chose Shinyanga for the site of his research, where he was to experiment with ideas about competing ecosystems, bush and wild animals, and cattle and cultivation—mainly through bush clearing and centralized settlements.[34] Shinyanga had been the site of a major epidemic in 1923, but Swynnerton had selected it because of its particular cycle of retreat and advance of tsetse flies: cleared land was free of tsetse, but when the population declined or moved on, the tree roots sent up shoots on which tsetse flies from adjacent infested bush alighted and then traveled to human settlements on passersby.[35] In practice, however, Swynnerton's subtle analysis of the local landscape was overwhelmed by the sheer scope of widespread bush clearing, which by the mid 1920s required a levy of

32. Vail, "Ecology and History," 132.
33. Swynnerton, "Examination of the Tsetse Problem in North Mossurise," 332–33.
34. Ford, *Role of Trypanosomiasis*, 183.
35. Ibid., 196.

almost 8,000 men.[36] Swynnerton has been contested academic terrain in recent years. Although John Ford praises his attention to seasonal details, John Iliffe sees him as a harbinger of soil erosion, and John MacKenzie as an agent of the hunting lobby.[37] A close reading of Swynnerton's work reveals the complexities of daily life in sleeping-sickness areas, however, rather than an ignorance of rainfall patterns or apologies for bushpig and buffalo. During the Mwanza epidemic of 1922, for example, he suggested that *T. rhodesiense* could be transmitted by man-to-man contact, based on his observations of the division of labor between sick and well Sukuma in their households. The absence of animal vectors, however specific, was taken up by the hunting lobby, but not because Swynnerton was their mouthpiece. He was a keen hunter and very close to the hunting lobby, but, as we shall see, from 1923 until his death in 1938, he proposed a variety of methods of tsetse control, including the seasonal and the agricultural. Time after time, however, the proposals that were implemented were those that conformed most closely to official agricultural policies.

The importance of the landscape to the location of tsetse flies made epidemiology and land use overlap. A new dimension, population density per square mile, one of the most important markers of scientific discourse in this story, became the cause and cure of sleeping sickness. There might be tsetse flies in areas with population densities as low as one person per square mile, but that was not sufficient to sustain an epidemic of sleeping sickness. Areas with population densities of five per square mile would not have enough cleared land to prevent tsetse flies, and they would have epidemics. Where there were twenty-five people per square mile, there would be enough cultivation and tillage to prevent tsetse advance. Best of all would be a hundred people per square mile, a population density that could crop and clear a fly-free area in which Africans and cattle could live in health.[38] In 1930—a year after Swynner-

---

36. John J. McKelvey, Jr., *Man against Tsetse: Struggle for Africa* (Ithaca, N.Y.: Cornell University Press, 1973), 150; W. H. Potts, "Tsetse Fly and Trypanosomiasis" (MS, 6 December 1947, WCCA, WTI/TRY/C18/1).

37. Ford, *Role of Trypanosomiasis,* 182–85; MacKenzie, "Experts and Amateurs," 204–8; John Iliffe, *A Modern History of Tanganyika* (Cambridge: Cambridge University Press, 1979), 270–72.

38. McKelvey, *Man against Tsetse,* 151; G. Maclean, "Memorandum on Sleeping Sickness Measures" (Tanganyika Territory Medical Department, Dar es Salaam, 1933), 4; H. M. O. Lester, "Sleeping Sickness Concentrations in Tanganyika Territory" (typescript, 14 December 1938, WCCA, WTI/TRY/C18/4).

ton had resigned to start the Department of Tsetse Research—Tanganyika Territory attempted to establish large, compact settlements, as if population density, in and of itself, could combat tsetse flies and sleeping sickness.[39] Concentrated villages, like tracts of cleared bush, encouraged soil erosion, however; Swynnerton's biomedical theories of the 1920s became the environmental terrors of the 1930s and 1940s.[40]

In tsetse research, the science enshrined in population ratios was translated to tsetse populations, which were measured according to the numbers Swynnerton's African assistants could catch. In the early 1920s, the "fly boys" of Tanganyika Territory stood still in the bush and recorded the number of flies each caught per hour. The resulting figure— flies per boy/hour—was later rejected by two of Swynnerton's entomologists, W. H. Potts and T. A. M. Nash, as unscientific.[41] To time discipline, they added the discipline of distance. Potts divided the Shinyanga bush into sections according to vegetation; each fly boy was assigned a section and would then walk along a path, stopping to collect flies every twenty or hundred yards, to establish the density of flies per boy 100 yards or, where flies were densest, flies per boy/yard. These fly rounds became increasingly complex, precisely laid out in grids or octagonal spirals to compensate for seasonal variations in flies' whereabouts or the number of flies scared away by these activities. Even so, in 1930 a zoologist, C. H. N. Jackson, published a critique of the flies per boy/mile measurements, writing that they did not systematically accommodate flies' eating habits.[42] By the early 1930s, if not before, the very extent of fly rounds—in some areas there were thirty miles of paths— was thought to have disturbed mammalian hosts, so that tsetse and an-

39. McKelvey, *Man against Tsetse*, 151; Ford, *Role of Trypanosomiasis*, 196.

40. Iliffe, *Modern History of Tanganyika*, 271–72; Duggan, "Historical Perspective"; Lester, "Sleeping Sickness Concentrations"; for anxieties about soil erosion, see David Anderson, "Depression, Dust Bowl, Demography, and Drought: The Colonial State and Soil Conservation in East Africa during the 1930s," *African Affairs* 83, 322 (1984): 321–43; William Beinart, "Soil Erosion, Conservation, and Ideas about Development: A Southern African Exploration," *J. Southern Afr. Studies* 11, 1 (1984): 52–83; Ian Phimister, "Discourse and the Discipline of Historical Context: Conservation and Ideas about Development in Southern Rhodesia 1930–1950," *J. Southern Afr. Studies* 12, 2 (1986): 263–75; Kate B. Showers, "Soil Erosion in the Kingdom of Lesotho: Origins and Colonial Response, 1830s–1950s," *J. Southern Afr. Studies* 15, 2 (1989): 263–86.

41. T. A. M. Nash, "A Contribution to the Bionomics of *Glossina morsitans*," *Bull. Ent. Res.* 21, 2 (1930): 205–8; Potts, "Tsetse Fly and Trypanosomiasis"; McKelvey, *Man against Tsetse*, 175.

42. C. H. N. Jackson, "Contribution to the Bionomics of *Glossina morsitans*," *Bull. Ent. Res.* 21, 4 (1930): 493.

imal populations moved elsewhere.[43] In Northern Rhodesia, which had no official tsetse-control organization comparable to that of Tanganyika Territory, fly rounds were considered a viable research method by district officers well into the 1930s: "In order to survey the density of the fly an African (immunized by injection, of course) walked along the bush path with a white cloth pinned to the back of his shirt. A man with a notebook walked behind him and counted the flies which settled on the cloth. The result was later recorded in a graph as 'Density of fly per boy mile.'"[44]

Also in Northern Rhodesia, human population densities had more than a biomedical meaning. They offered ways both to understand and to problematize citemene, the very productive and reliable system of shifting cultivation taken up by hoe cultivators when they entered the area. The Bemba, who engaged in widespread raiding until the end of the nineteenth century, had lived in large, stockaded villages. Once they too took up citemene, a very specific pattern of settlement and land use developed. Citemene cultivators scattered to *mitanda*, the garden huts families lived in during the growing season: by 1904, for example, no villages could be seen in Mpika.[45] In large-circle citemene, the system of the Mambwe and the Bemba, trees are lopped, not felled, and pollarded trunks are left at chest height. Branches are carried for miles to form a large circle, often of about an acre, in a clearing and left to dry in the sun. Burning takes place late in the dry season: too early and the ash would scatter in the wind; too late and the wood stacks would be wet and the burn incomplete. After the branches are burned, the large ash circle is planted with a sequence of crops, starting with finger millet the first year. Burned-over land is sometimes cultivated for as long as five years.[46] Citemene depleted the woodland—burned areas made up from 4 to 10 percent of deforested areas—and the intense heat of the late burning destroyed the forest canopy and retarded the growth of new

43. McKelvey, *Man against Tsetse*, 175–76.

44. Kenneth Bradley, *Once a District Officer* (London: Macmillan, 1966), 69.

45. Henry S. Meebelo, *Reaction to Colonialism: A Prelude to the Politics of Nationalism in Northern Zambia, 1893–1939* (Manchester: Manchester University Press, 1971), 102; Vail, "Ecology and History," 136; Henrietta L. Moore and Megan Vaughan, *Cutting Down Trees: Gender, Nutrition, and Agricultural Change in the Northern Province of Zambia, 1890–1990* (Portsmouth, N.H.: Heinemann, 1994), 10–17.

46. Audrey I. Richards, *Land, Labour and Diet in Northern Rhodesia: An Economic Study of the Bemba Tribe* (Oxford, 1939), 288–304; William Allan, *The African Husbandman* (Edinburgh: Oliver & Boyd, 1965), 67–68.

trees.[47] Nevertheless, it was burning that transformed cut branches into a garden. Burning was the only occasion Richards observed in which the Bemba acted as "one economic unit."[48] Citemene was also a system of great productivity: experiments at the research station in Lunzuwa compared yields from Mambwe citemene fields and Mambwe hoed mounds: from 1935 to 1940, citemene gardens produced at least three times more finger millet per acre than hoed gardens.[49] The official construction of citimene in the 1930s, of primitive cultivation, performed with an ax, gradually gave way to an official and scientific understanding that citimene was combined with permanent gardens and was both adaptable and productive.[50]

However productive it might have been, citemene was considered an administrative and agricultural nightmare. Whatever it did to forests and ecosystems, it made ordinary Bemba hard to rule and harder to tax. In large-circle citemene, gardens were scattered and temporary, and for much of the year families lived in mitanda. From the early years of colonial rule, mitanda dwellers guarded their independence fiercely: they were "malcontents who renounced the authority of the chiefs and the Boma."[51] Mitanda became sites of new community and social relations for Bemba.[52] In 1906, the British South Africa Company, which then governed Northeastern Rhodesia, banned citemene. Widespread hunger followed. By 1908, the Chitimukulu, the Bemba paramount, complained of his people's starvation and poverty. Administrators complained of a new, menacing attitude of opposition among the Bemba, and expressed some anxieties about the newfound unity of chiefs and commoners— against the boma. Citemene was restored in 1909, and in 1910 administrative units were made smaller to accommodate mitanda.[53]

47. Allan, *African Husbandman*, 75; Moore and Vaughan, *Cutting Down Tress*, 22–37.

48. Richards, *Land, Labour and Diet*, 295–96.

49. Allan, *African Husbandman*, 73.

50. C. G. Trapnell, *The Soils, Vegetation and Agriculture of North-Eastern Rhodesia. Report of the Ecological Survey* (Lusaka: Government Printer, 1943); Moore and Vaughan, *Cutting Down Trees*, 34–42.

51. J. H. W. Sheane, West Awemba native commissioner, quoted in Meebelo, *Reaction to Colonialism*, 103.

52. Bemba children could imitate adult life and its sexual division of labor in mitanda, but were not inscribed with gender until puberty; see Hugo H. Hinfelaar, "Religious Change among Bemba-Speaking Women in Zambia" (Ph.D. diss., University of London, 1989), 164; Moore and Vaughan, *Cutting Down Trees*, 13–15.

53. Meebelo, *Reaction to Colonialism*, 105–6, 114; Moore and Vaughan, *Cutting Down Trees*, 9–15.

Objections to citemene did not cease, but they ceased to be described in administrative terms. The problems with citemene became agricultural, not political: environmental degradation replaced social disintegration. By the late 1930s, a new official line had emerged, claiming that while fly-infested areas had long existed, they had also been uninhabited, but as the security of Pax Britannica went on, villages broke up and smaller villagers formed, and Africans "drifted" into fly areas, just as the bigger villages ceased to function as fly barriers.[54]

The scientific study of African land use and population densities gave expression to colonial anxieties about deforestation, late burning, and Africans' relationship to authority. But colonial anxieties, even those sanctioned by science, were not uniform. The biomedical view was that the greater the population density, the fewer renewable resources, whereas entomologists believed that the greater the population density, the fewer the tsetse flies. Population density statistics were used in Northern Rhodesia in the 1930s to show the damage done by citemene and, sometimes, land alienation. Officials bandied grim figures for population per square mile to proclaim ecological doom, to be sure, but also to participate in scientific discourse. None of the figures so pronounced took male migrancy or environmental variations in the landscape of the plateau into account.[55]

ANIMALS, FLIES, AND OFFICIALS

Throughout the 1920s and 1930s, many officials thought that the low population densities of citemene encouraged garden raiding by elephants, which was said to cause "serious starvation" in Lundazi, for example, starting in 1919, when elephants had first come into the area. In 1922, villages in Luwingu, Lundazi, and Abercorn were said to have no food.[56] Africans were too poorly armed to fight off garden raiders themselves, and after much debate, the district commissioner in Abercorn

54. T. Vaughan Jones, district commissioner, Abercorn, tour report 3, 1938 (NAZ, SEC2/820, Abercorn Tour Reports, 1933–38).
55. Trapnell, *Soils, Vegetation and Agriculture*, 71; Moore and Vaughan, *Cutting Down Trees*, 36, 43–45.
56. Société des Missionnaires d'Afrique, Rome, Diaire de Kapatu, March 1920, 19 July 1922; E. H. L. Poole, native commissioner, Lundazi, 8 January 1923; J. Moffat Thompson, acting district commissioner, Abercorn, "Destruction of Native Crops by Elephants" (27 June 1923); native commissioner, Luwingu, to district commissioner, Kasama, 14 April 1924 (NAZ, RC/659, Protection of Crops from Elephants).

adopted the policy already in place in southwestern Tanganyika and gave a white hunter free license to shoot elephants in inhabited areas.[57] Soon after, many white hunters wrote to the boma requesting employment on Tanganyika Territory terms. Throughout the 1920s, the basic structure of authorized elephant hunting remained the same. A hunter was appointed elephant control officer and was allowed to kill any elephant tracked from garden raiding. To avoid the authorization of ivory harvesting, it was specified that elephants had to be caught in the act or shortly thereafter, but according to Norman Carr's description of elephant control in Nyasaland in the 1920s, this rarely happened. A hunter "went out, as I did, and shot the first elephant he saw with reasonable tusks and called it a garden raider."[58]

The hunter's fee for shooting an elephant was, with variations according to weight, to keep one tusk. The other tusk went to the boma and the meat went to the villagers, distributed in theory according to local hierarchies, but in practice at the discretion of the hunter.[59] The importance of this meat is clear. Audrey Richards provides a compelling description of the meaning of meat to Bemba villagers in 1931. They claimed the meat from an antelope she had shot gave them energy, "not only before the food was digested, but before it was cooked! . . . The next day they went to work early, declaring that their arms were strong."[60] Indeed, 1920s elephant control almost at once became a local source of meat, the sale of which proved almost as profitable for hunters as the sale of ivory. One hunter worked out complex equations by which he might profit most: he would not shoot young elephants; he would keep all tusks under thirty pounds or 35 percent of tusks under fifty pounds, or he would be allowed to sell the meat without a butcher's

57. Moffat Thompson, "Destruction of Native Crops by Elephants." Arming Africans was apparently out of the question; there were not enough working guns for the twenty or thirty affected villages, and there was always the risk that Africans would only wound elephants, which would then go to other gardens; see "Protection of Crops from Elephants" (cited n. 56 above).

58. Norman Carr, The White Impala: The Story of a Game Ranger (London: Collins, 1969), 20.

59. Norman Carr, Luangwa, 21 July 1990; R. W. M. Langham to PC, Kasama, "Elephant Control," 31 October 1936 (NAZ, SEC1/1018, Game Protection of Crops, Northern Province, 1936–38); for hierarchies of meat distribution that show the relationship of elephants to chiefship, see Richards, Land, Labour and Diet, 349, and S. A. Marks, Large Mammals and a Brave People: Subsistence Hunters in Zambia (Seattle: University of Washington Press, 1976), 33.

60. Richards, Land, Labour and Diet, 38–39.

license.[61] Indeed, false reports of raiding, designed to bring a well-armed hunter into an area, were common, and attempts to withdraw hunters or verify complaints were unpopular: chiefs tended to encourage false complaints whenever continual hunger eroded their authority.[62] By the late 1930s, for example, hunters readily acknowledged the pressures on African game rangers: they were subject to "a good deal of temptation" if posted to their own areas and were frequently used by their chiefs as suppliers of meat.[63] Even elephant culling became a food issue, which then seeped into issues of race and propriety. Once a rudimentary Game Department was established, it was loathe to hire African game scouts, because "the villagers with whom they stay are often naturally keener on getting meat than on genuine crop protection," and lobbied for an increase in white rather than African personnel.[64] African game scouts may have seen the situation somewhat differently. According to Norman Carr, "A 'fundi' . . . with tons of meat at his disposal became the most popular man in his community."[65] For these reasons, most conservationists were uneasy about elephant control.

The official emphasis on population densities and deforestation meant that citemene was thought of solely as a system of shifting cultivation. It did not take into account the ways in which citemene engendered relationships with government hunters that could provide valuable sources of meat and prestige for chiefs. Nor did it take into account the late burning that citemene required, and the decrease in *G. morsitans* populations that late burning caused year after year. Not only did late burning destroy the shade tsetses needed, but grass became dense in the burned

61. David Ross, Sakamba Village, to native commissioner, Mporokoso, 19 April 1926 (NAZ, RC/659, Protection of Crops from Elephants). A few years later, Richards thought that many men went to the mines in order to earn enough for a gun and a license (*Land, Labour and Diet*, 348).

62. C. R. S. Pitman, *A Report on a Faunal Survey of Northern Rhodesia with Especial Reference to Game, Elephant Control, and National Parks* (Livingstone: Government Printer, 1934), 74–75; T. S. L. Fox-Pitt, district commissioner, Mpika, tour report 1/1938 (NAZ, SEC2/836, Mpika Tour Reports, 1933–38). A few loyal senior chiefs were allowed to have elephant hunters working directly for them (Richards, *Land, Labour and Diet*, 348; Vernon Brelsford, "The Garden Raider," n.d., NAZ, HM 38, Vernon Brelsford Papers).

63. Abercorn Annual Reports, 1935–37 (NAZ, SEC2/1303); R. W. M. Langham to provincial commissioner, Kasama, 22 November 1937 (NAZ, SEC1/1018, Game Protection of Crops, Northern Province, 1936–38).

64. T. Vaughan-Jones, Game Department, to PCs, Fort Jameson and Kasama, "Notes on the Functioning of Elephant Control, 8 November 1937" (NAZ, SEC1/1018, Game Protection of Crops, Northern Province, 1936–38).

65. Carr, *White Impala*, 50.

areas during the rains, destroying G. *morsitans*'s breeding grounds. Moreover, the barren areas produced by citemene created barriers to tsetse flies.[66] Despite some hints in tour reports, citemene was on the whole not considered a tsetse-control measure. In all probability, this was because sleeping sickness, particularly the variety caused by *T. rhodesiense,* was seen as a cattle disease, the absence of which was best demonstrated when people kept cattle. As a cattle disease, *T. rhodesiense* implied a specific landscape, free of bush and big game, occupied by cultivators and their herds, a paradigm so powerful that scholars and scientists were disinclined to see *T. rhodesiense* in the same terms in which non-cattle-keeping Africans might have seen it.

Game preservation had been under attack for years for causing the spread of sleeping sickness. As early as 1911, a game park bordering Nyasaland and Northeastern Rhodesia—named, appropriately enough, Elephant Marsh—was closed because of missionary complaints about the increase in tsetse flies and sleeping sickness.[67] By the 1930s, game parks created another layer in the either/or paradigms of tsetse control, adding the issue of people versus animals and tsetse to a landscape already mapped by official thinking of cultivation versus tsetse. The landscape that emerged from debates about game preservation and game parks was mandated to house animals for European sensibilities and hunting, rather than those of Africans. Animals in game parks, as in some tsetse-control schemes, became an undifferentiated category of prey in which hunting was racially and technologically specific, although assisted by Africans.[68]

Where did these biomedical ideas that proposed either the destruction of fauna or the destruction of flora come from? The line between African ideas and imperial science was never a sharp divide. Swynnerton's bush-clearing campaigns had originated in Ngoni practices of land use, relations between domestic and wild animals, and authority: in

---

66. My argument here follows James Giblin's use of Ford's arguments about acquired immunity to trypanosomiasis. Africans used bush fires to create wooded areas in which game and tsetse flies thrived; areas were cleared for hoe cultivation by late burning, the fierceness of which destroyed shade trees. Africans and cattle developed and maintained immunological resistance to trypanosomiasis through periodic forays into the tsetse-infested woodland, while farms and homestead remained free of tsetse flies. See James L. Giblin, *The Politics of Environmental Control in Northeastern Tanzania, 1840–1940* (Philadelphia: University of Pennsylvania Press, 1992), 29–34.

67. Vail, "Ecology and History," 146–48; MacKenzie, *Empire of Nature,* 237–38.

68. Roben Mutwira, "Southern Rhodesian Wildlife Policy (1890–1953): A Question of Condoning Game Slaughter?" *J. Southern Afr. Studies* 15, 2 (1989): 255.

Shinyanga, he tried to make them scientific and experimentally sound.[69] The game preservation of tsetse research and reclamation of the 1930s had European as well as African antecedents, however, and these blurred the lines between hunters, conservationists, and scientists. The creation of game parks and game preserves, for example, came out of two contradictory turn-of-the-century motivations: to safeguard the natural world, in manageable proportions, so that the modern world would not lose touch with it, and a desire to subdue that same natural world, regardless of whether or not such actions had any social context. White hunting in Africa had a very different meaning in 1885, for example, than it did in 1935. Early game parks were created to be "unpoliced spots on a map," to be protected from African exploitation. Early colonial game parks were places where African hunting was illegal. They preserved hunting land for foreign hunters—many of whom were museum collectors and scientists as well.[70] In the early years of game preservation, wild animals were not romanticized, white hunting was.[71] Within the next thirty years, game parks became sites in which decreasingly important imperial interests could assert their power against growing biomedical and social lobbies.[72]

BLOOD STORIES

In June 1930, Major Hingston of the Society for the Preservation of the Fauna of the Empire—the ideological wing of the hunting lobby— visited Northern Rhodesia as part of his African tour. Northern Rhodesia was, however, a special concern because it was the only British colony in Africa without a game warden. Without a game warden or national parks, there was nothing to prevent the excessive slaughter of game. Officials agreed, but noted: "All agriculturalists, whether European or native, are equally anxious to prevent game damaging their

69. C. F. M. Swynnerton, "An Experiment in Control of Tsetse-Flies at Shinyanga, Tanganyika Territory," *Bull. Ent. Res.* 15, 4 (1925): 313–63.

70. The quotation is Norman Carr's, Luangwa, 21 July 1990. MacKenzie, *Empire of Nature,* 226–33; Lisa Mighetto, *Wild Animals and American Environmental Ethics* (Tucson: University of Arizona Press, 1991), 94–106, describes how this attitude shifted among American environmentalists in the late 1930s.

71. Haraway, *Primate Visions,* 26–58; Thomas R. Dunlap, *Saving America's Wildlife: Ecology and the American Mind* (Princeton: Princeton University Press, 1988), 98–111. For an unromantic plea to save Africa's vanishing species, see C. R. S. Pitman, *A Game Ranger Takes Stock* (London: T. Nisbett, 1944).

72. See MacKenzie, *Empire of Nature,* 225–56, and Iliffe's scathing nationalist history of the Selous Game Park in *Modern History of Tanganyika,* 201–2.

crops." Hingston proposed that a game department and game parks be established; he dismissed the idea that African nutrition would suffer if African hunting was limited by citing evidence from Uganda and Kenya, and noted that in Tanganyika Territory, Africans were not subject to game laws unless they indulged "in barbarous practices or wholesale slaughter." By March 1931, many officials concurred with the recommendations, which had proposed game parks in areas considered unsuitable for European settlement.[73] Also during the first six months of 1931, and between April and August 1932, C. R. S. Pitman, then game warden of Uganda—which had East Africa's model game department—visited Northern Rhodesia to prepare a report on wildlife there. He traveled 8,000 miles and corresponded with white hunters in twenty-seven districts. He proposed game regulations and licensing quotas, based on his game census, and recommended the creation of an official elephant-control department and game parks from which a "meat-eating armed population" had been removed.[74]

Northern Rhodesia may have been the only British colony in Africa without a game warden, as Hingston noted, but it was also the only British colony where Africans understood "game ranger" to mean vampire. In March 1931—during Pitman's first visit—the provincial commissioner in Kasama District first wrote about *banyama,* a word that combined Swahili and Bemba to mean "people of the game, or meat." That *banyama* (singular, *munyama*) was never elided into its literal Bemba form reveals how both the term and the concept were maintained as a neologism, something foreign and new.

SCIENCE, FLIES, AND LAND

Rumors about banyama seemed "to have arisen from a perverted notion in the Native mind as to the function of the Tanganyika Territory Game Department," which had been so fully recoded and reterritorialized that the banyama were said to consist of "large bands" of Africans under the

---

73. R. B. Hingston to acting chief secretary, Northern Rhodesia, 18 June 1930; acting chief secretary to Lord Passfield, Colonial Office, 21 July 1930; R. B. Hingston, "Report on a Mission to East Africa for the Purpose of Investigating the Most Suitable Methods of Ensuring the Preservation of its Indigenous Fauna, December 1930"; D. Willis, provincial commissioner, Kasama to chief secretary, Livingstone, 7 March 1931; PC's Office, Abercorn, "Memorandum on Hingston Report," 24 March 1931 (NAZ, SEC1/996, Reports on Elephant Control, 1930–31).

74. Pitman, *Report on a Faunal Survey of Northern Rhodesia,* iii, 61–65, 85; secretary for native affairs, Lusaka, minute, 16 March 1935 (NAZ, SEC1/1008). I am grateful to Stuart Marks for this reference.

charge of European officials. These officials wore khaki uniforms and helmets with a badge with a small antelope's horns on it; what the African staff wore was not known. These banyama were said to make their camps in the bush where Africans, "expert in the art of tracking and hiding . . . are sent out to murder any native, male or female, found alone," an official report noted. After killing their victim, the banyama drained his or her blood and, "by making an incision behind the ear, extract a certain portion of the brain. The body is left in the bush, and the blood and brain forwarded to the Medical Department to be used as medicines in hospitals and dispensaries." [75]

The rumor had been circulating in the district for about three years and became particularly intense early in 1931, when Africans returning from Tanganyika's sisal plantations claimed that "the natives of Tanganyika Territory had found effective methods of frustrating the efforts of banyama who were accordingly being sent to Nyasaland and Northern Rhodesia in search of victims, the employers remaining in Tanganyika Territory." [76] It was said that the Tanganyika Territory Game Department aroused suspicion because the game wardens "'do not walk along the paths like normal men, but wander through the bush like outlaws.'" Moreover, the insignia with the buck's head may have reminded many Bemba in Northern Province of witchcraft, as the skull of the buck is often associated with those practices. [77]

As we have already seen, much of this was true. The men of the Tanganyika Territory Game Department did wander through the bush on foot or bicycle. [78] Their purpose was not to hunt Africans but to count

75. Willis, "Report on Banyama" (cited n. 7 above); see also L. H. Gann, *A History of Northern Rhodesia: Early Days to 1953* (London: Chatto & Windus, 1964), 231. The incision behind the ear probably refers to the extraction of lymphatic fluid for the diagnosis of sleeping sickness, while "blood and brain" is Willis' gloss for a much richer Bemba term, *umlopa,* meaning all life-giving fluids, including blood, semen, and vaginal fluids; see Hinfelaar, "Religious Change," 8.

76. Willis, "Report on Banyama" (cited n. 7 above). In Luwingu, it was said that banyama were sent by Europeans working in the Belgian Congo; see S. Hillier, district commissioner, Luwingu, tour 11–25 February 1931 (NAZ, ZA7/4/19, Awemba Tour Reports, 1931).

77. Willis, "Report on Banyama" (cited n. 7 above). According to Richards, "Modern Movement of Witchfinders," 448–51, "horns" was a generic term for charms. Some of the wanderings of banyama and the vulnerability of banyama victims may have alluded to menstruation and menarche, which Bemba often describe as *ukutaba* ("to be moved away from daily life"), *ukuya ku mpepo* ("to go to the coldness of the forest"), and *ukuba mu butanda* ("to live outside the village"); see Hinfelaar, "Religious Change," 4–5.

78. C. F. M. Swynnerton, *Tsetse Flies of East Africa: A First Study of Their Ecology, with a View to Their Control,* Transactions of the Royal Entomological Society of London, vol. 84 (London: The Society, 1936), 12; McKelvey, *Man against Tsetse,* 176.

tsetse flies in units unique to imperial systems of measurement and discipline. Tanganyika Territory's fifteen African fly collectors wore dark blue puttees; Swynnerton's chief fly boy, Saidi Abdullah, wore a brass buffalo head on his pillbox cap. According to T. A. M. Nash, Abdullah was a superb naturalist who knew trees and plants and could track animals. He discovered the species of tsetse fly that was named for Swynnerton. In the Mwanza sleeping-sickness epidemic of 1922, Abdullah ferreted out victims who had been hidden by their relatives; it was said that he took blood smears from corpses.[79] He and many other tsetse researchers, African and European, diagnosed sleeping sickness by taking a sample from lymph glands, hence the "incision behind the ear."

But what did fly boys do to earn this reputation? There is no documentation regarding their actual activities during tsetse control: entomologists and officials tended to write about what they intended to do, not what transpired. In the absence of such data, however, we should not assume that each and every fly collector was overzealous in his performance of his duties. Such an assumption would presume a uniform identification with a job and a regime for which there is no evidence; it would assume that Africans misunderstood, rather than recoded, imperial practices. Indeed, the question of what these men did on the job may not be the best way to approach the complicated and often contradictory origins of vampire rumors. There was probably not a simple correlation between an action and its fantastic representation as banyama; it seems more likely that banyama represented the often puzzling meanings of activities in which counting flies and protecting animals or prohibiting agricultural practices fused.

The association of Tanganyika's Game Department and vampires was specific to the Northern Rhodesia. In August 1931, officials in Morogoro, Tanganyika Territory, identified surveyors as those thought by Africans to drink their blood, a group referred to by the older Swahili terms *cinjacinja* or *mumiani*.[80] It was not until the mid 1930s that whites

---

79. T. A. M. Nash, *Zoo without Bars: A Life in the East African Bush, 1927–32* (Tunbridge Wells: Wayte Binding, 1984), 22; McKelvey, *Man against Tsetse,* 174. It is unlikely that Abdullah took blood smears from dead bodies, since trypanosomiasis advanced enough to cause death would not have been found in the blood, but in the lymphatic tissues.

80. E. E. Hutchins, district officer, Morogoro, "'Mumiani' or 'Chinjachinja,'" (Tanzania National Archives, film no. MF 15, Morogoro District, vol. 1, part A, sheets 25–26, August 1931, but inserted into file marked 1938). I am grateful to Thaddeus Sunseri for this reference.

in Tanganyika began to hear of "Bwana Nyama," the veterinary or game officer who went alone into the bush to look for blood.[81] Although individuals may have been called that during the 1930s, no form of *bwana nyama* took hold as a collective term for vampire in colonial Tanganyika, which remains *mumiani* or *chinja-chinja* to this day.[82]

The Northern Rhodesian rumors continued well into 1932, but there were no other official alarms about their import until 1936. Then it was the tsetse-fly pickets, men stationed on paths to physically remove flies from travelers leaving infested areas. How fly pickets came to be considered a viable method of tsetse control discloses many of the concerns and blind spots of colonial thinking, both about tsetse flies and about African agriculture, in the mid 1930s. The language of tsetse control and the language of citemene control both described a landscape that was either usable or had to be abandoned—the simplified either/or paradigm of Tanganyika's Game Preservation Department, headed by Swynnerton, in the mid 1920s. Where the boundaries between infested and uninfested landscape were violated, or ignored, cattle and people sickened and died. In Northern Rhodesia, some cattle deaths were the result of ambitious attempts at cattle keeping in known tsetse areas, so that when 2,000 head of cattle died in the Luangwa Valley in 1930–31, no one paid much attention. When cattle became infected in the formerly fly-free area of Isoka in 1932, "notoriously bad" African husbandmen were blamed for bringing the disease into the area, and the cattle were left to die.[83] But for European coffee growers in Abercorn—the district of greatest labor migration to Tanganyika—already reeling from a drop in coffee prices, cattle keeping was a necessity. Their industry depended on successful mulching and manuring, and their farms bordered on fly-infested areas, so they needed either to keep their cattle free of sleeping sickness or to import fertilizers.[84] When in 1932 one settler had lost half of his cattle, he blamed the increase in fly numbers on motor transport

81. Fr. H. de Vries, Morogoro, "Superstition in Africa," *Holy Ghost Messenger*, 32 (1936): 67–69. I am grateful to Peter Pels for these notes.

82. David Anthony, "Culture and Society in a Town in Transition: A People's History of Dar es Salaam, 1865–1939" (Ph.D. diss., University of Wisconsin–Madison, 1983), 141–43.

83. A. T. Williams to acting chief secretary for agriculture, Livingstone, 4 August 1932; director, Animal Health, Livingstone, to chief secretary, Livingstone, 6 October 1931 (NAZ, SEC3/525, vol. 1, Tsetse Fly Control, 1926–36).

84. Provincial commissioner, Northern Province to chief secretary, Lusaka, 25 June 1935 (NAZ, SEC3/525, vol. 1, Tsetse Fly Control, 1926–36).

from fly-infested areas. His complaints to the governor met with the stern response that in impoverished times, Abercorn farmers had to accept the risks of having plots in fly areas.[85] After two years of discussion the Abercorn Coffee Growers Association invited Swynnerton, then of the Tanganyika Territory Department of Tsetse Research, Shinyanga, to come and investigate Abercorn—one of the areas suggested by Pitman as an elephant reserve—on his way to a hunting holiday in Nyasaland.[86]

The main work of the survey was done by Swynnerton's two head fly boys, including Saidi Abdullah, who preceded him to Abercorn. Their report was finished at the end of October 1935. It showed that the planters had good reason for alarm: the coffee area was to the west of a "cultivation steppe"—plains and glades that had been grazed bare and hills cut for agriculture, the result of the close settlement of African reserves—that would be an ideal habitat for *G. morsitans,* should it ever reach there. Before Africans were removed into their present reserves, their cultivation had provided a natural barrier to the fly. Because of years of slash-and-burn agriculture, the low trees and dense shrubs were among "the best" example of *miombo* woodlands Swynnerton had ever seen. The regular burnings of grass had maintained semi-open patches, *vipya,* on the ridges and hillsides. The creation of African reserves in 1930 had not only destroyed that barrier, it had provided a good source of food for *G. morsitans.*

It was the relationship of land use to fly feeding and breeding that Swynnerton and his team examined. *G. morsitans* is associated with miombo but cannot survive in "large stretches of homogenous wooding, even if miombo." Instead, it requires miombo-like wooding "in which to lie up when fed and in which to breed" and "glades and dambos interspersing it" that provide good visibility and animal life on which to feed "every two or three days in the late dry season and every dozen days in the wet." Any semi-open country is thus hospitable to *G. morsitans* when interspersed with miombo, but only if it does not cover large stretches of the countryside. The gallery forest of Abercorn covered too large an area to be an ideal habitat for *G. morsitans,* but because buf-

85. Minutes, Abercorn Planters Association, 13 October 1932 (NAZ, SEC3/525, vol. 1, Tsetse Fly Control, 1932–36).

86. Abercorn District AR, 1935–37 (NAZ, SEC2/1303); minutes, Abercorn Coffee Growers Association, 7 January 1935, and meetings of provincial commissioner, Northern Province and ACGA deputation, 25 January 1935 (NAZ, SEC3/525, vol. 1, Tsetse Fly Control, 1932–36).

falo lived there, tsetses could feed at its edges.[87] Given that the landscape was "naturally" appealing to G. *morsitans,* why was sleeping sickness only becoming a serious problem in the early 1930s?

In the "natural" scheme of things, Swynnerton argued, sufficient African population and their burned gardens "would constitute an excellent barrier to tsetse and a measure for tsetse control," however dangerous they were to forests: "[T]setse do not like country that is generally open and do not for some years find very favorable the regrowth of felled miombo."[88] When native reserves were formed in 1930, they created unprecedented population densities, as high as sixteen or twenty per square mile. Although citemene-cultivating Mambwe responded by reducing their citemene and expanding their hoed gardens, the degeneration of the surrounding woodlands was rapid and spectacular.[89] Administrators extolled the virtues of hoed garden crops, but had "no reason to believe," the provincial commissioner wrote in 1933, "that hoeing will become general until the last tree in the Reserve is cut and burnt."[90] But according to Swynnerton, the removal of citemene cultivators into "reserves far from the tsetse" was harmful to the ecology of the region. It "appears to be responsible for such danger as attaches to the present position." The land to the east of Abercorn had been protected by Africans' citemene, but with the Africans gone, "fly advance will be facilitated."

Swynnerton dismissed any move to eradicate wild animals, because new animals would simply move in to to replace them; miombo was a good animal habitat as well. Instead, he suggested that tsetse be controlled by *African* land use, especially citemene. In a powerful argument for citemene as a method of fly control, contrary to all official thinking in the mid 1930s, he claimed that leaving areas fallow and unburned for years at a time would actually cause a retreat in G. *morsitans* popula-

---

87. C. F. M. Swynnerton, "A Late Dry Season Investigation of the Tsetse Problem in the North of the Abercorn District" (29 October 1935, NAZ, SEC3/525, vol. 1). A summary of these ideas was published in "Appendix II: How Forestry May Assist towards the Control of the Tsetse Flies," in R. S. Troup, *Colonial Forest Administration* (London: Oxford University Press, 1940), 339–42.

88. Swynnerton, "Late Dry Season Investigation."

89. Allan, *African Husbandman,* 133; Mambwe hoed gardens tended to support greater population densities than citemene, a fact officials rarely acknowledged in their figures (Moore and Vaughan, *Cutting Down Trees,* 44–45).

90. S. R. Downing, provincial commissioner, Abercorn, tour report no. 1, 1939 (NAZ, SEC2/820, Abercorn Tour Reports, 1933–39).

tions.[91] Tsetses need bare ground to settle on; G. morsitans in particular need visibility and dry ground to breed. When grass is not burned for years at a time, the conditions for fly breeding are destroyed: a grass mat forms and the undergrowth becomes dense and inhospitable. There is no place for G. morsitans to settle or breed. "I have seen no area which is so suited to this measure as in Abercorn," Swynnerton wrote (emphasis in original). Moreover, burning the grass "very early" in the dry season—a method Swynnerton had already used in Southern Rhodesia—"made grass so dense that it proved unfavorable to morsitans." Since Africans in Abercorn did not burn their woodpiles until late in the dry season, he thought that they would support bans on burning at other times during the dry season.[92]

Late burning—burning woodpiles late in the dry season—had been problematized at least as much as citemene itself, as we have seen. Even when officials tolerated citemene, they emphatically opposed late burning. Slash-and-burn systems depend on fire: when it is time to burn the stacked branches, the flames run riot, sweeping through the leaf litter and vegetation nearby. This vegetation would be particularly dense if the ground had been burned early in the dry season. The later in the dry season burning takes places, the dryer the surrounding vegetation, and the hotter and more intense the fire. According to Richards, "The piled-up branches, dry and brittle from three or four months exposure to the sun, crackled and flamed in a moment. . . . Next morning nothing was left but a circular bed of ashes around the blackened trunks of mutilated trees."[93] But late burning, year after year, was held to retard the regrowth of trees, and destroy the forest canopy. The "scientific proof" of burning experiments in the 1930s was offered to show that citemene had only survived because there had not been repeated late burnings. Early burnings—early in the dry season—which were less intense and cooler, allowed trees to regenerate more rapidly.[94] But the intensity of late burning at the end of the dry season produced overgrown ground, its shade cover retarded by fire, early in the rainy season that was inhospitable to G. morsitans; the long-term effects of late burning destroyed areas of

91. Indeed, in the early 1940s, cattle were seen to graze on the fallow gardens near Abercorn during the dry season; see Trapnell, Soils, Vegetation and Agriculture, 41.

92. Swynnerton, "Late Dry Season Investigation"; William Allan, Studies in African Land Usage in Northern Rhodesia, Rhodes-Livingstone papers, no. 15 (Cape Town and New York: Oxford: University Press for the Rhodes-Livingstone Institute, 1949), 85.

93. Richards, Land, Labour and Diet, 295–96.

94. Allan, African Husbandman, 75.

shade that were essential to *G. morsitans's* survival. While Swynnerton argued that the overall patterns of citemene provided natural barriers to tsetse flies,[95] he underestimated the extent to which late burning also prevented tsetse breeding.

Swynnerton's recommendations were sent to the deputy director of agriculture, William Allen. His response was swift and severe: these plans were not really worthwhile and were too expensive "to protect a few Mtungu Road coffee farms."[96] But Abercorn's white farmers persisted, offering their own version of reterritorialization; they proposed early burning over large areas and argued with officials who said that the value of the district's cattle did not warrant drastic ecological or hunting measures. Within a few weeks, the provincial commissioner requested that Lusaka authorize Swynnerton's other recommendations: the resettlement of Africans in areas they had formerly occupied and the use of fly pickets to remove flies from travelers.[97] Pickets immediately became a charged issue. Various planters' association wanted pickets installed at once, as did the medical officer at Abercorn, who wanted pickets on selected paths, to which Africans would be confined.[98]

A month later, the survey botanist of the Tanganyika Territory Department of Tsetse Research, B. D. Burtt, explained how pickets worked and what they were expected to do. Fly pickets were to consist of two Africans in khaki uniforms—"proved to be the most suitable garb" for catching flies—and provided with a hut; their hours should be 7:00 A.M.–5:30 P.M.; "each picket would examine each passing native coming up from Isoka or Mewilo areas" or passing up and down the Abercorn-Mpulungu road; flies caught should be placed in a tube and shown to inspecting officers, who should visit frequently to make sure that the work was being done efficiently; and a record of "the fly take"

95. T. Vaughan Jones, district commissioner, Abercorn, tour report 3, 1938 (NAZ, SEC2/820, Abercorn Tour Reports, 1933–38).
96. William Allan, Department of Agriculture, Mazabuka, to chief secretary, Lusaka, 14 December 1935 (NAZ, SEC3/525, vol. 1).
97. Minutes, Abercorn Planters Association, 10 January 1936 (NAZ, HM61/2/1, Abercorn Planters Association); A. F. B. Glennie, district commissioner, Abercorn, to provincial commissioner, Kasama, 4 February 1936; director, medical services, Lusaka, to chief secretary, Lusaka, 11 February 1936; provincial commissioner, Northern Province, Kasama, to chief secretary, Lusaka, 13 February 1936, NAZ, SEC3/525, v. 1.
98. A. Scott, medical officer, Abercorn, to DMS, Lusaka, 30 March 1936, "Re: Trypanosomas in Abercorn District"; district commissioner, Abercorn, to provincial commissioner, Northern Province Kasama, 14 April 1936 (NAZ, SEC3/523, vol. 1, Sleeping Sickness in Northern Rhodesia, 1929–39).

at each picket should be kept and inspected.[99] Pickets were assigned to the posts nearest their villages in order to simplify rationing procedures, and Africans traveling on picketed paths were to submit to examinations by the pickets and could not "proceed until this has been done to their satisfaction."[100] Such a system may have allowed pickets great latitude in determining who to stop or what "their satisfaction" might require. Nevertheless, fly pickets did not stay on the job very long, and gave notice often.[101]

Pickets began operation in June 1936 and were soon in use throughout the district.[102] They were also soon recoded:

> Curious rumours have become extant concerning the existence of human vampires. These were alleged to prey upon solitary persons come upon in the bush whose blood is conveyed to a white master for the manufacture of pernicious medicines. In 1936 the anti-tsetse operations and the natives armed with nets to take fly off travellers at fly posts furnished fuel for these stories and at one time hindered the efficacy of control measures. Propaganda caused these rumors to die out but they have unexpectedly broken out again in other parts of the district and it is difficult to say what, or to whom, their origin is to be ascribed. Variants of the rumor suggest that Government is itself interested in the taking of blood.[103]

The fly pickets were said to "stupefy their victims, murder them and extract their blood which is an essential ingredient in medicine concocted by the European."[104] It was said that the butterfly nets of the fly pickets could expand to capture a grown man.[105]

99. B. D. Burtt, report to district commissioner, Abercorn, 4 May 1936 (NAZ, SEC3/523, vol. 1).

100. C. R. B. Draper, supervisor, tsetse control, Abercorn, to district officer, Abercorn, 9 December 1936; A. F. B. Glennie, district commissioner, Abercorn, to provincial commissioner, Northern Province, Kasama, "Tsetse Fly Measures in Abercorn," 2 June 1936 (NAZ, SEC3/526, vol. 2, Tsetse Fly Control, Abercorn).

101. C. R. B. Draper, supervisor, tsetse control, Abercorn, to district officer, Abercorn, 12 November 1936 (NAZ, SEC3/526, vol. 2, Tsetse Fly Control, Abercorn).

102. See NAZ, SEC3/525, vol. 3, Tsetse Fly Control, 1936–38. By June 1937, fly pickets were posted to the west of Kasama town (R. B. S. Smith, medical officer, Kasama, to director, Medical Services, Lusaka, 29 June 1937, NAZ, SEC3/527, vol. 3, Trypanosomiasis: Tsetse Fly Control).

103. Northern Province Annual Report, Native Affairs, 1937 (NAZ, SEC2/1297); Abercorn Annual Report, 1935–37 (NAZ, SEC2/1303).

104. A. F. B. Glennie, district commissioner, Abercorn, to provincial commissioner, Northern Province, Kasama, 3 December 1937, Native Customs, etc., "Report on Vampires at Kasama, 1937–38" (NAZ, SEC2/1240); see also NPAR, Native Affairs, 1937.

105. Brelsford, "'Banyama Myth,'" 51.

OFFICIALS, ANIMALS, AND FLIES

What was government doing at this time, to earn such a reputation? Also in June 1936, provincial commissioners met in Lusaka to discuss the implementation of Pitman's recommendations for game parks, a game department, and elephant control by licensed hunters. The PCs liked the idea of a game department, and all suggested ways in which it could be established inexpensively: they could second someone already in service to head it, for example, and employ the African game scouts "already being effectively trained by elephant control officers." Settlers were so keen on the idea of a game department and game preservation that they "had gone so far as to guarantee part of the cost of the establishment of such a Department." PCs neither wanted any Africans moved to create a new reserve, as Pitman recommended, nor wanted to distinguish between amateur and professional hunters' licenses the way other colonies did.[106]

In 1938, a white hunter was accused of being banyama, although the evidence about the accusation is vague. In July 1938, G. Kennedy Jenkins, a cadet, toured part of Mpika District with two goals in mind. First, he planned to preach the control of grass fires and the merits of early burning—a scheme, he wrote, that "must have struck some as revolutionary" but that would protect young trees—and second, he hoped to investigate a "disagreeable encounter" between a white hunter, identified only as Captain Henderson, and local villagers, who thought he was a munyama. Jenkins wanted to find out what had happened and "to dispel the fanciful rumours which made such a incident possible. . . . I made it clear at the outset that my intentions were simply to find out why these stories received credence and to allay the fears they aroused." Yet almost no one in the village would talk to him; villagers seemed to believe that "any confession of complicity in the Captain Henderson incident or even belief in the banyama stories would at once be rewarded with punishment." The only person who spoke of the incident was one of Henderson's porters. Traveling with Henderson had brought him within a few miles of his home, but when he went to find his mother working in her garden, "To his surprise she greeted him with an outburst of maledictions and harangued him for allowing himself to be engaged in so dis-

---

106. PCs conference, June 1936 (NAZ, SEC1/933, Formation of the Game Department, 1936–38).

honorable a project." She ran to her village, where her "grief . . . was calculated to unsettle the minds of her fellow villagers." The villagers did not threaten Henderson, but they did believe he was a munyama and feared "he might conduct his business on their doorsteps."

Despite his belief in Africans' "ingrained appetite for such fancies," Jenkins quickly realized the limits of his investigations and his inability to recode those fantasies into imperial words. "It was impossible to arrive at any very clear conclusions or to discover in what manner the minds of these people had arrived at any such alarming ideas. . . . I doubt whether people with such a curious turn of mind are at all likely to be won over by rational argument," especially as villagers denied any knowledge of banyama beliefs. His solution to such silences was to warn locals that "if harm came to any strangers punishment would not be mediated because the victim was an alleged munyama," in his hope that this might guarantee an end to such incidents.[107]

What did Henderson do? It is impossible to tell from these records; all we can really discern is that he was a sport hunter with an African staff—although in Northern Rhodesia amateur hunting had the same status, and the same appearance, as elephant control in the late 1930s. But just as banyama accusations did not emerge from the specific deeds of "fly boys" they did not emerge from official or sportsmen's acts. The extractive power of Europeans—whether taxation, migrancy, poorly paid fly pickets, or the creation of new reserves—was in the air: banyama accusations were leveled at figures in a specific locale because of local issues and concerns.

Banyama rumors related to hunting and tsetse control seem to have died out after 1939. There were few banyama scares during World War II, most of which were anticipated by officials.[108] Wartime economies reduced administrative staff and curtailed activities not directly related to the war effort; W. V. Brelsford, DO, Chinsali, noticed a decline in banyama accusations when the Game and Tsetse Fly Control Departments were not working. According to Brelsford, Unwin Moffatt, the agricultural officer at Abercorn, told how in 1939,

---

107. G. Kennedy Jenkins, cadet, tour report 6, 1938 (NAZ, SEC2/837, Mpika Tour Reports, 1938–40, extracted in NAZ, SEC2/429, Native Affairs: Banyama).

108. A visiting parasitologist whose research included taking blood and skin samples was forbidden to go to "any area of northern province for some considerable time to come" (G. Howe, provincial commissioner, Northern Province, Kasama, to chief secretary, Lusaka, 27 March 1944, NAZ, SEC2/429, Native Affairs: Banyama).

accompanied by one or two Tsetse Fly Catchers, he went to speak to a group of African men resting by a stream. The whole group rushed off into the bush abandoning all their loads and possessions. Unwin Moffatt, a descendant of David Livingstone, whose father was a famous missionary and whose two brothers were administrative officers, all well known to the Africans of the area, had been stationed in Abercorn for many years and he was universally liked by Africans. But even the appearance of a familiar and trusted man did nothing to banish the panic raised by the sight of those little white Banyama nets.[109]

I have combined Jenkins's self-conscious account and Moffatt's unreflexive one to make a text. As such, it raises another question: were officials feared because they were considered banyama or were they considered banyama because of their individual association with anti-citemene policies? But that question is read off my text; it is not necessarily one that Africans in Northern Rhodesia in the late 1930s would have worried about: the very question imposes a distinction between tsetse control, early burning, and banyama that individuals in the region may not have made. Indeed, such ambiguity may be a hidden strength of documentary evidence, however. I think it is unlikely that oral interviews conducted in Mpika today, for example, could uncover whether or not Africans believed in the late 1930s that white hunting was emblematic of official disdain for citemene as a form of tsetse control. Even if such a viewpoint could be extracted from personal memories and narratives, such evidence might obscure the ways in which banyama rumors blended and disputed the issues of African and European ideas about disease and agriculture. The very layers of meaning that make some oral accounts so rich might, in this particular instance, decontextualize the ideas and concerns these rumors contained. Just as villagers refused to speak about banyama to Jenkins and many other officials, individuals do not speak to me; I can identify neither speakers, believers, nor nonbelievers. However, without individual African voices, I may nonetheless be able to listen to general anxieties and concerns. Using only archival sources, I lose a great deal of meaning, of African specificity, of who believed what and possibly even why, but I gain the complexities and confusions of and about agriculture and science, late burning, and blood in a colonial situation. The archive reveals not only its own confusions and contradictions but the inability of colonialists to locate their practices completely in imperial rather than African terms.

109. Jenkins cited n. 107 above; Brelsford, "'Banyama Myth,'" 51.

CHAPTER 8

Citizenship
and Censorship

Politics, Newspapers, and
"a Stupefier of Several Women"
in Kampala in the 1950s

This chapter is about news and current events—how they are spoken about, written about, and sometimes not written about, and the play between these. It is about how men and women in postwar Uganda talked about what happened (and what did not happen and what was not said to have happened) and how that talking has been theorized by oral historians. Because many of my sources are, in fact, African newspapers, I want to theorize how Africans read them. This chapter discusses oral and written accounts of the trial of Juma Kasolo, a despised agent of *bazimamoto* in Kampala, which coincided with the events leading up to the deportation of the Kabaka of Buganda. It shows how the two stories, oral and written, and oral and unwritten, might comment on each other. I argue that the formulaic elements in a local vampire story straddle oral and written media and became a way to talk about current affairs. This chapter is about how different stories were reported or not reported in different media—which made the newspapers, and which newspapers, and which were primarily part of oral testimonies—and how citizens—ordinary and official—interpreted these stories.

VAMPIRES, POLITICS, AND THE COLONIAL SITUATION

It is possible to interpret the vampire accusations and vampire riots of the 1940s and 1950s as an additional idiom with which the grievances of the postwar era were articulated. Charges that white mine managers ate an African strike leader at the beginnings of Katanga labor protests of 1943, a riot at the Mombasa fire station a few months after the general strike of 1947 (and a week before a tribunal announced what wage increases, if any, might be granted), and death threats against government broadcasters said to sap the will of Northern Rhodesians who opposed the Central African Federation in the early 1950s can all be seen, without too much imagination, as popular expressions of protest.

But is that all they were? Were these expressions of protest merely that—opposition to an existing regime—or did the way in which a well-known belief becomes a cause for public alarm and outrage speak to concerns that were not directed against employers or Europeans, but were part of local struggles, directed at the social and economic tensions and fissures of a particular time and place? This has been the begrudged insight behind many of the fragmentary writings by Europeans about African vampire rumors. In a 1948 letter to Max Marwick, Clyde Mitchell—both were doing anthropological fieldwork in Central Africa for the first time—described vampire beliefs in Nyasaland but wondered why whites were held responsible but black people were accused and attacked by other black people:

> Africans kidnap unsuspecting fellows at the dead of night and cart them off to the Whites who drain their blood to use for their own purposes. For this the Blacks are well and truly paid. The Whites are licensed from the boma to do this and the blood is used to make European medicine. The interesting thing about this is the way in which hostility is directed to the Europeans probably through a misinterpretation of blood transfusion. But the interesting thing is though the Whites are the real villains of the piece, i.e., the prime movers of the crime, the real hostility is directed to the Blacks in their employ. Just how you explain this I don't know. It is hostility directed to those who threaten the integrity of the in-group. Is it that the Whites by reason of their position of authority are father images and are thus above overt hostility? What is it that gives these people this Hamletic make-up of being unable to express their aggression against their oppressors. Recently a policeman was killed in Limbe because he was believed to have been one of *cinjacinja*.[1]

But are the issues here how responsibility for colonial bloodsucking was allocated, or who were accused of such vampirism and attacked for their roles in it? Or are the allocation of responsibility and accusation different things—the first, the clear elucidation of structure, a chain of

---

1. J. Clyde Mitchell, Namwea, Nyasaland, to Max Marwick, 15 September 1948 (J. Clyde Mitchell Papers, Rhodes House, Oxford, RH MSS Afr. s. 1998/7/1).

a command, and accountability, and the second, the naming of the person locals want gone from their immediate environment? Those who
captured Africans and took their blood were not responsible for the
practice; the reasons they did this work were obvious: "If someone
asked you to look for a liter of blood for 50,000/-, would you not do
that?"[2] A man—or woman—working for whatever agency of the colonial state that required the blood "did this for money, they needed the
money, and they could do this kind of work."[3] They might be despised,
but their motivations were not unreasonable: it was a job. The allocation of responsibility was about knowledge, the firm and not uncom-
fortable understanding of how the world worked. Accusation was about
power, and who could use it when and where.

If selling someone to the bazimamoto was not personal and had none
of the personal enmity associated with witchcraft, why were suspected
agents attacked and killed? After World War II, there were a number of
newspaper and anecdotal accounts of violence against those suspected
of taking Africans' blood. Does this mean that vampire accusations increased in violence after 1945 or that the sources with which I study
them changed? This need not be an either/or question, of course. Increased violence was perceived everywhere in East African urban life in
the postwar era, and officials' anticipation of violence made every crowd
a riot, and every mob worthy of police reinforcements. Nevertheless, the
evidence for vampire-related homicides is striking: although there were
a few attacks on Europeans, Africans—many of them policemen or firemen—were attacked, some of them killed, in Mombasa in 1947, in Dar
es Salaam in 1947, 1950, and again in 1959, and in rural Uganda and
rural Tanganyika throughout the early 1950s.[4] Was this, as Mitchell

2. Yonasani Kaggwa, Katwe, Uganda, 27 August 1990. All the interviews cited in this
chapter took place in Uganda unless otherwise noted.

3. Zaina Kachui, Pumwani, Nairobi, 14 June 1976.

4. For information about attacks on Europeans, Michael Macoun, personal communication, 13 March 1990; John Huddletson, interview with author, Kampala, 18 August
1990; Darrell Bates, The Mango and the Palm (London: Rupert Hart-Davis, 1962), 47–
55; "'Witchcraft' Murder of Geologist," Tanganyika Standard, 2 April 1960, 1; "Mumiani Riot: Six Jailed," ibid., 2 June 1960, 5. J. A. K. Leslie, personal communication,
13 March 1990, provided information about attacks on Africans; Alec Smith, Insect Man:
The Fight against Malaria (London: Radcliffe Press, 1993), 72–73; "'Human Vampire'
Story Incites Mombasa Mob's Fire Station Attack," East African Standard, 27 June 1947,
3; Elspeth Huxley, The Sorcerer's Apprentice: A Journey through East Africa (London:
Chatto & Windus, 1948), 23 n; "Sacking of House Began Night Chase" and "Police Askari
Stoned," Tanganyika Standard, 16 February 1959, 1; "29 on Murder Charge after Riot,"
ibid., 20 February 1959, 1; "'Kill Them All' Rioters Roared," ibid., 9 April 1959, 1–3.

suggests, a sublimation of colonial grievances? Did African mobs attack Africans rather than whites in the heat of the riotous moment? Or were these attacks part and parcel of a range of grievances against both the colonial situation and some individual Africans?[5] Were the Africans attacked those who had been despised for years? Were the angry mobs swept away by fears of vampires or were they aware—in varying degrees—that vampire beliefs articulated other fears as well?

But how was the oppressor to be identified as colonialism waned in Uganda? In Buganda—one of several kingdoms in the protectorate's southern, Bantu-speaking half—the relationship between kingdom and colonial state had been uneasy since the official colonial conquest negotiated the legal conditions under which Baganda were to be subject to both the king in his palace at Mengo in Kampala and the Colonial Office in London. The king, the Kabaka, was hereditary, but chiefs and kingdom officials were appointed, based on merit and qualifications determined by British officials: both were accountable to the Lukiiko, the kingdom's parliament, comprising, after significant struggles, a small number of the Kabaka's nominees and twice as many elected chiefs and representatives from each county (*saza*). The Lukiiko was fractious in relationship to the king and the protectorate, the bureaucratic uneasiness matched by the ways in which individual Baganda struggled to be citizens of both states. Many Baganda saw no contradiction in being royalists and modernizers at the same time and sought to move their kingdom to the forefront of colonial politics and those of the world. The frequently repeated anecdote about the young Kabaka's anger at not being given the same royal status as the queen of Tonga at Queen Elizabeth II's coronation was often told to explain the true place of Buganda in the world, or to explain why Baganda might have such pretensions.[6]

The kingdom of Buganda, its politics and its pretensions, troubles Mahmood Mamdani's recent distinction between citizen and subject, non-native and native, as the defining characteristic of all colonial situations. In Africa the non-natives, the urban workers, elites and educated modernizers, were the citizens, empowered by their access to modern in-

---

5. In the heat of the moment, Africans seem to have been very sophisticated in their reckoning of enemies. During the riots in Kampala in 1945, rioters mainly attacked European police officers, not African ones (Uganda Protectorate, *Annual Report on Uganda, 1946* [London: HMSO, 1948], 78).

6. Harold J. Ingrams, *Uganda: A Crisis of Nationhood* (London: HMSO, 1960), 67–68; Mutesa II, Kabaka of Buganda, *Desecration of My Kingdom* (London: Constable, 1967), 117.

stitutions of the state, while Mamdani's natives were maintained in rural Africa by customary law and indirect rule as exemplars of the dark continent.[7] But late colonial policies were so confused that they could barely bifurcate the people they ruled. Colonial officials were so baffled by how to deal with urban workers and rural guerrillas and unruly kings that they frequently reprimanded these groups in the vocabularies of nation, self-government, and citizenship, which the workers, the guerrillas, and the unruly kings—who already understood the principles—then applied in a wider frame.[8] Indeed, in Uganda in 1953, the governor dethroned a king because he would not accept the idea of a unified nation-state. The events in this chapter—including the trial of Juma Kasolo in 1953—describe how colonial officials promoted an idea of citizenship that envisioned responsible Africans capable of self-government in part to stifle an older, "traditional" citizenship in which loyalty, gossip, and ties to the palace not only governed citizens of Buganda, but kept them from harm. Many Baganda themselves had sought ways of transforming the kingdom's citizens from backward Africans to modern ones, but these visions had to do with controlling the flow of information, not making them citizens of a unitary nation-state.

Part of the task of transforming Buganda by Baganda was modernizing the king's subjects, freeing them from custom, superstition, and their old ways. When a group at the royal court, including the Katikiro, the kingdom's prime minister, Martin Luther Nsibirwa, encouraged the widowed queen mother to remarry a commoner in 1941, the popular and chiefly outcry was such that Nsibirwa was asked to resign by the British. Almost fifty years later, Baganda spoke passionately about this. "Don't you see the trouble it caused, that this earth is not at peace?" said Magarita Kalule.[9] The issue was not seen as one of royal blood purity—difficult enough to conceptualize in a polygamous society—but of rank and status. "What if you had a wife and she remarried your houseboy?" asked Joseph Nsubuga.[10] "If you are grown up. . . . and then you hear that your mother is looking around for a boyfriend, wouldn't you feel ashamed?" said Alozius Kironde.[11] Rank and status were not separate

---

7. Mahmood Mamdani, *Citizen and Subject: Contemporary Africa and the Legacy of Late Colonialism* (Princeton: Princeton University Press, 1996).

8. Frederick Cooper, *Decolonization and African Society: The Labor Question in French and British Africa* (Cambridge: Cambridge University Press, 1996).

9. Magarita Kalule, Masanafu, 20 August 1990.

10. Joseph Nsubuga, Kisasi, 22 August 1990.

11. Alozius Kironde, Kasubi, 17 August 1990.

from the fractious politics of the kingdom, however. Six months after Nsibirwa was reinstated as Katikiro after the riots of 1945, he was assassinated.[12]

But the same citizens preserving the hierarchies of rank and heritage were Christians and Muslims, farmers, clerks, and laborers. Their relationship to the kingdom of Buganda, its customs, and the elite who were its government, was anything but one of unmediated loyalty. By the 1940s, a movement had begun among urban and rural traders to change how kingdom and clan officials, groups that had been considerably strengthened during the two regencies of the twentieth century, were elected. A growing trade union movement, demands for representative government in the kingdom, and middlemen's profiteering in coffee and cotton sold abroad led to civil strife in 1945 and again in 1949. Such "disturbances" were commonplace in postwar Africa, but in the polities of southern Uganda, with widespread literacy, many newspapers, and royal and colonial bureaucracies, these disturbances were described in a variety of domains with a variety of narratives. Thus, John Iliffe, writing in 1998, suggested that Baganda populists deliberately spread vampire rumors to fuel the riots.[13] In Busoga, in the 1960s, for example, a chief magistrate warned the anthropologist Lloyd Fallers, "There are two kinds of Basoga: the first loves Busoga, the second loves the protectorate government. The first will tell you one kind of history, the second will tell you another kind."[14]

The different histories were not about who was a citizen and who was not, but about what determined state citizenship, what the qualities of that citizenship should be, and how it was articulated. But both kinds of histories were about motives, fears, and what lay behind colonial policies. Some modernizers among those who spoke of relations with the colonial government admitted that they had once been so naive as to believe that Europeans did take African blood or ate Africans. The same Busoga official quoted above laughed when he told Fallers that in the early 1940s, when he was a young headman taking a petition to the dis-

---

12. Several people insisted that the queen mother was pregnant by Nsibirwa when he engineered her marriage to the commoner Kigozi (Ssimba Jjuko, Bwase, 20 August 1990; Julia Nakibuuka Nalongo, Lubya, 21 August 1990).

13. John Iliffe, *East African Doctors: A History of the Modern Profession* (Cambridge: Cambridge University Press, 1998), 90–91.

14. Lloyd A. Fallers, *Law without Precedent: Legal Ideas in Action in the Courts of Busoga* (Chicago: University of Chicago Press, 1969), 84. For a recent analysis of the "crisis" of 1945 and the strikes that preceded it, see Gardner Thompson, "Colonialism in Crisis: The Uganda Disturbances of 1945," *African Affairs* 91 (1992): 605–29.

trict commissioner's office, he had been fed in a room in the DC's house. "I heard a car outside, and English voices. I didn't understand and thought I was going to be eaten. The messenger called me to the office where the Englishmen were. On my way, I opened my knife in my pocket in case they tried to kill me! When I arrived, I saw only white faces, and I trembled!"[15] Baganda officials were not so amused, and passed their displeasure onto the scholars they spoke to: Paolo Kavuma wrote in his memoirs that the Baganda thought the British "drank blood and killed children because they did not understand what happened in hospitals."[16] David Apter noted that the populist Katikiro Samiri Wamala, who led the struggle against Nsibirwa in 1941, was "the first to reckon with public opinion" but the "public was not particularly well-informed. Common stories were that Europeans drank blood and were vampires (because of efforts to create a blood bank), that mission hospitals killed children (because few maternity cases reached the hospitals until there was difficulty)."[17]

The politics of the kingdoms were as layered and distrustful as those of the colonial government and its subjects. In 1949, there were riots, which Baganda said "were between the kingdom and the people."[18] After months of agitation, the Bataka Party—claiming in the name of clan elders that chiefs and officials had ceased to serve them—called Baganda to come to Mengo "to inform the Kabaka [of] the things that are undermining him and our country." When eight party members were allowed to meet with the Kabaka, he responded to their demands—including the election of chiefs—by citing the 1900 agreement by which Buganda had a special status in the Protectorate. When the police arrived to control the crowd, violence began: 400 officials' huts were burned in Mengo; shops were looted and many people were beaten; outside Kampala, chiefs' cattle were killed. Government broke down for a few days until an additional battalion could come from Kenya. Order was restored, and some reforms were instituted, but the Protectorate advised the kingdom to consider its own role in creating an emergency that it could not itself police.[19]

15. Fallers, *Law*, 83.
16. Paolo Kavuma, *Crisis in Buganda, 1953–55: The Story of the Exile and the Return of the Kabaka, Mutesa II* (London: Rex Collings: 1979), 9.
17. David E. Apter, *The Political Kingdom in Uganda: A Study in Bureaucratic Nationalism* (1961; 2d ed., Princeton: Princeton University Press, 1967), 226.
18. Musoke Kopliamu, Katwe, 22 August 1990.
19. *Uganda Herald*, 27 April and 7 May 1949; Apter, *Political Kingdom*, 256–62; Mutesa II, *Desecration*, 110–11; Uganda Protectorate, *Report of the Commission of En-*

The riots of 1949 and their resolution led to another development. According to Apter, Baganda "efforts . . . to avoid control by the Protectorate government began to assume the proportions of an ideology and mythology. In every gesture, benevolent or not, they saw the threat of control. . . . Baganda and British viewed the intransigence of the other as a cover for hidden motives." [20] During the correspondence and meetings leading up to the deportation of the Kabaka in June 1953, words were read and reread, silences interrogated, and intentions analyzed. A speech in London in June 1953 by the colonial secretary praising the Central African Federation had included a passing reference to the possibility of an East African Federation. The summary in the English-language *East African Standard,* published in Nairobi, was after many retellings interpreted by the Kabaka and the newly reformed Lukiiko to reveal the true goal of British colonialism: that Buganda would lose its autonomy with the independence of Uganda. A subsequent union of Britain's East African territories would devour the kingdom; Uganda's status as a protectorate would leave it as weak and vulnerable as Nyasaland was in the face of the Central African Federation. The new ruler of independent Uganda would be Kenya. That the governor, Andrew Cohen, had come eighteen months before directly from the Colonial Office, where he had been undersecretary for the African colonies, only proved Britain's long-term plans. Only by demanding a separate independence could Buganda subvert these plans. Mutesa II—writing from his second exile, imposed by the president of an independent Uganda—confirmed that this was now his goal, but since two-thirds of the members of the Lukiiko were now elected, to disagree with them would have been to flaunt "the wishes of my people." The Kabaka noted that Cohen could have salvaged the situation had he been willing to abandon his fixation on the idea of "a unitary state of Uganda," which "found no support in the country." Paolo Kavuma, Mutesa II's Katikiro, was to later describe himself as the voice of moderation. What, he recalled asking the Kabaka on 6 November, the day of Kasolo's arrest, did he, the king, consider to be public opinion? "Should we, I asked, regard the crowds which assembled from time to time at Katwe or Wandegeya, two of Kampala's liveliest suburbs, as representing public opinion?" The

---

quiry into the Disturbances in Uganda during April 1949 (Entebbe: Government Printer, 1950), 21–25; Uganda Protectorate, *Annual Report on Uganda, 1949* (London: HMSO, 1950), 4

20. Apter, *Political Kingdom,* 261–62.

Lukiiko asked for a statement that no federation would ever take place in East Africa, and then for a separate independent status for Buganda. Cohen refused, and a nervous Kabaka—trying to balance the demands of anti-royalist parties that nevertheless sought an independent Buganda—went armed to a final meeting with Cohen. But instead of a showdown, the Kabaka's authority was withdrawn, and he was sent to England on 1 December 1953. Although Kavuma had asked that the Luganda press not cover these talks—and only the anti-royalist *Uganda Post* refused—the deportation was headline news.[21] But its greatest power was in the spoken word: when the Kabaka's sister was told of the deportation, she died of shock at once, and when his brother heard of it on the radio in England, he vomited. Ordinary Baganda, reading the story in the newspaper, were only stunned: a student later said that he took a newspaper to a park bench and read it for several minutes before he realized it was upside down.[22]

NEWS, RUMOR, AND NEWSPAPERS

Who was to mediate between the king and the governor, the vampires and the officials, the producers and the middlemen, the trade unionists and the Katikiro, and all their different histories? How could people learn what was really the truth, and who was to make sure information was correctly understood? Before he showed his disdain for Baganda public opinion, David Apter was elegiac about the casual, illiterate citizenship practiced around the Lukiiko in the early 1950s. Men sitting on the low window-frames of the Lukiiko building listening to debates; small groups of men and women discussed the news of the day in the royal enclosure; there was a constant murmur of gossip: "For the Baganda, this was the metropole, not London, not Nairobi . . . Mengo was where the rules of propriety and modernity were laid down." But the whispered, polite citizenship of Buganda masked distrust and suspicion, fueled by how Baganda heard the gossip all around them: "The

21. Mutesa II, *Desecration*, 120–22; Apter, *Political Kingdom*, 276–86; Kavuma, *Crisis*, 22–26; "Buganda Lukiiko Asks for Date to Be Fixed for Independence," *Uganda Herald*, 17 October 1953, 1; "Kabaka Deposed," ibid., 1 December 1953, 1. In colonial Northern Rhodesia, Federation generated intense vampire rumors; see Mwelwa C. Musambachime, "The Impact of Rumor: The Case of the Banyama (Vampire-Men) in Northern Rhodesia, 1930–1964," *Int. J. Afr. Hist. Studies* 21, 2 (1988): 201–15; Peter Fraenkel, *Wayaleshi* (London: Weidenfeld & Nicholson, 1959).

22. Ingrams, *Uganda*, 71; Mutesa II, *Desecration*, 122–23.

Baganda can withhold few secrets from one another." The intimacy that led to gossip made each man "impute motives to his enemies that he feels sure are real." This led to a passion for secrecy that almost always failed, as men in public life attempted to obscure the motives for their public acts.[23] Yet a few years earlier, articles in the Luganda press complained bitterly about the rumors spread by county chiefs and political leaders: "You may hear a big person in the country saying something which does not bear any truth. . . . One wonders why such people are ever given freedom to rule us. . . . This is why members of the National Assembly go astray in their thinking, because of rumors they might have heard." Rumor "shames the nation." "It is the duty of everyone to always ask whoever tells you something to prove what he tells you before accepting it."[24] "If you hear a rumour which you think to be untrue and then you circulate it you become an enemy of the people. What does one lose by being quiet?"[25]

But the question of how to keep Baganda from distorting the truth and telling tales eluded many Baganda, commissions of inquiry, and colonial observers alike. The printed word did not amend the spoken one. When an emergency meeting of the Lukiiko was rumored to be scheduled for late April 1945, county chiefs gathered in Mengo despite a published government announcement that no such meeting was planned.[26]

Moreover, versions of the printed word were available on every street corner in Kampala. In 1945, there were seven vernacular newspapers published in Uganda, including *Matalisi* and *Gambuze,* which had been published in Luganda since the 1920s. After the post-1949 reforms, ten new newspapers were founded by 1954, and only one of the older Luganda papers survived. By the late 1950s, the *Uganda Argus* was the only English-language newspaper available in Kampala. Of the twenty-four other papers, ten were African-owned and financed—sometimes with missionaries' help—and two were owned and financed by Roman Catholic missions; the *Argus*—begun in the mid 1950s, replacing the *Herald,* published three times a week—was partly European-financed, and the remaining eleven newspapers were funded by some government body, either ministries of development, local government, or information agencies. Seven were published monthly and three weekly; only the

---

23. Apter, *Political Kingdom,* 14–18.
24. Young Muganda, "Rumour," *Matalisi,* 4 May 1945, 2, 3, 4.
25. L. L. M. Kasumbo, letter to the editor, *Matalisi,* 24 January 1947, 7.
26. Young Muganda, "Rumour."

Argus was published daily. The newspapers with the largest circulations were in Luganda and owned and financed by Africans: the *African Pilot,* published Monday and Thursday, had a circulation of 12,000, as did *Uganda Eyogera,* published Tuesday and Friday. The *Argus's* circulation was 8,200, and the *East African Standard,* published in Nairobi since the 1920s, was widely read in Uganda. The Luganda *Uganda Post* was published Wednesday and Saturday and had a circulation of 9,000, and the weekly Luganda *Uganda Times* had a circulation of 5,000. The *Uganda Post* and *Uganda Eyogera* were closely allied with political movements—the *Uganda Post* was the organ of the Uganda National Congress, successor to the Uganda African Farmers' Union, which was banned along with other trade unions after 1949, and the *Uganda Eyogera* was founded in 1953 by E. M. K. Mulira and became the mouthpiece of the modernizing Progressive Party, founded in 1955.[27]

What did such circulation figures mean in East Africa in the 1950s? Many chiefs and functionaries stated that they read two newspapers.[28] Purchasing newspapers conferred a certain status: not everyone who carried a newspaper could read. Daniel Sekiraata, quoted later in this chapter, described the business of transporting corpses to their rural homes for burial, in which they were dressed them to look like passengers in cars, in suits, with newspapers placed on their laps. Virtually all newspapers were read by more than one person, and many more were read aloud, translated, summarized, amended, and made fun of by a variety of readers for a variety of audiences. Even newspapers written in languages that required years of schooling to read could be read out loud in a few minutes to illiterates. The crowds in Katwe and Wandegeya might not be newspaper readers, but they knew what newspapers said. Where newspapers were sold without subscription—where all purchases of newspapers were on the street—the need of all but the most intensely subsidized to appeal to popular issues was great: popular stories were in demand.[29] Newspaper reading in Africa is a

27. Apter, *Political Kingdom,* 273–74, 337–40; A. B. K. Kasozi, *The Social Origins of Violence in Uganda, 1964–1985* (Montréal: McGill–Queens University Press, 1994), 49; Louise M. Bourgault, *Mass Media in Sub-Saharan Africa* (Bloomington: Indiana University Press, 1995), 165.

28. Fallers, *Law,* 80.

29. Jeffrey Brooks, "Literacy and Print Media in Russia, 1861–1928," *Communication* 11 (1988): 50–51; Misty L. Bastain, "'Bloodhounds Who Have No Friends': Witchcraft and Locality in the Nigerian Popular Press," in Jean Comaroff and John L. Comaroff, eds., *Modernity and Its Malcontents: Ritual and Power in Postcolonial Africa* (Chicago: University of Chicago Press, 1993), 129–66.

social event: not every reader was a purchaser, as many people read newspapers on the street without buying them and many more read newspapers handed around to friends, neighbors, and kin. Newspapers travel from reader to reader in neighborhood after neighborhood, county after county. As Isabel Hofmeyr has argued, "illiteracy" in Africa is not a monolithic state: Africans need not read to participate in a complex "documentary culture" in which they take—and just as often reject—ideas from written texts.[30] In one of the few ethnographies of African reading ever published, Hortense Powdermaker argues that the intense privacy of reading gives a sense of detached sophistication to readers in a preliterate society. According to a young, educated clerk on the Copperbelt, "In a newspaper you can read and re-read the news, so you can understand it properly. Also, a newspaper keeps a record of what has happened, or has been said, but the wireless only says something once and leaves no record for the future which one can refer to."[31] But such an account obscures the fractious street corner argument and performance that accompanied many newspaper readings. As the following section makes clear, children knew what was in newspapers as much as adults did; newspapers read aloud were public culture, an argumentative citizenship in which a person need not be literate to participate. As Ssekajje Kasirye, quoted below, states, reading and understanding were separate, dependent on local knowledge and context as much as the ability to read words on a page. Indeed, Baganda modernizers sought to replace the contestation around the printed word with an authoritative spoken one. Before he became a newspaper editor E. M. K. Mulira wrote that the rise of private land ownership had helped rumors to go unchecked. When the landlord was chief of an area, he "silenced subversive rumours and not much damage was done," but in recent years, "the peasant and anyone with a piece of strange news is regarded as one of the people-in-the-know" and there is no landlord-chief to correct their misinformation. "Much suffering and suspicion in Uganda is caused by simple misunderstandings—often by the failure of authorities to explain things clearly." A belief in ordinary people's expertise and participation had replaced time-honored hierarchies. Mulira argued that whereas people in towns could be protected from misunderstand-

---

30. Isabel Hofmeyr, "'Wailing for Purity': Oral Studies in Southern African Studies," *African Studies* 54, 2 (1995): 22.

31. Hortense Powdermaker, *Copper Town: The Human Situation on the Rhodesian Copperbelt* (New York: Harper & Row, 1962), 280; for a somewhat different view, see Bourgault, *Mass Media*, 190–95.

ings by writings, speeches, or posters, rural people should receive radio broadcasts, "one of the best ways of combating rumours."[32]

Such concerns reveal how the newspaper-reading public was imagined. Benedict Anderson has argued that for colonial societies, newspapers occupy a certain place in national consciousness. While the first colonial newspapers were simply appendages to the market, giving shipping tables, prices, and carrying advertisements, their presentation of local and colonial news in local languages made the colony an imagined community—linked by social, political, and commercial announcements—for readers. But what gave the colony its national consciousness was not its newspapers but the knowledge among their readers that there were many newspapers, each invoking community through the ordering of a day's or a week's events. That some, elites, would not touch a vernacular newspaper when they could have the week's events summarized by a metropolitan publication and others cared little for the metropolitan newspapers hardly mattered. What turned the published word into ideas about the nation-state was the very process of the refraction of world events into a "specific imagined world of vernacular readers" in which events elsewhere in the colony, the continent, or even Europe would, over time, appear to be similar to events at home. The world's events, reported in a single vernacular newspaper, provided the imagined community of readers with a steady flow of similar events, and it was that similarity that encouraged them to imagine similar processes of nationhood across the huge continents under colonial control.[33] This chapter, and the Baganda modernizers who inform it, argue something very different. First, that well into the 1950s, there were many consciousnesses within African colonies, not all of them formally nationalist. Second, newspapers were not read in isolation from each other; they were taken as a whole, not only by the people, who read many and had many more read to them, but by their editors and reporters, who saw

32. E. M. K. Mulira, *Troubled Uganda* (London: Fabian Colonial Bureau, 1950), 7–10 passim. When radio became widespread in Uganda, it was parodied just as the spoken word was. "Radio Katwe," the popular term for street talk in Kampala (named for the loquacious suburb of Katwe), became a synonym for wild speculation, a way of talking that was beyond accountability, so that no one could object to hearing oneself slandered in a rumor from Radio Katwe (E. M. K. Mulira, Mengo, 13 August 1990).

33. Benedict R. O'G. Anderson, *Imagined Communities: Reflections on the Origin and Spread of Nationalism* (1983; rev. ed. London and New York: Verso, 1991), 61–63. For two views that differ both with Anderson and myself, see Jeffrey Brooks, "Socialist Realism in *Pravda*: Read All About It!" *Slavic Review* 53, 4 (1994): 973–91, and Louise M. Bourgault, "Occult Discourses in the Liberian Press under Sam Doe: 1988–1989," *Alternation* 4, 2 (1997): 186–209.

in one vernacular ordering of events a way to comment on other newspapers, not only those in local languages but those approved by the colonial state and written in English. I am not arguing that newspaper readers did not share an imagined community, however, but I do want to suggest that such communities were not imagined through newspapers, but with newspapers–that print capitalism became one of the ways that people spoke, not only about political events, but about the place of newspapers in structuring a vision of what those events meant. Baganda editors and politicians clearly found the reading public to be too suspicious; they refused to believe that printed words alone could be true. According to Mulira, rumors were "a habit. . . . lazy thinking. You hear a rumor, you believe in it, and then it has become a habit for people, they cannot distinguish between rumor and truth. . . . We are so lazy, when we hear that, it satisfies our mind, and even if you tell people the truth they will not take it because it is easier to believe the rumor. . . . So rumors go on." [34] Officials seem to have articulated this somewhat differently. When Andrew Cohen became governor of Uganda in 1952, he budgeted half a million pounds to community development—"mass education . . . concerned with fostering the spirit of citizenship"—and almost as much money to set up a training center where policemen, seminarians, and estate managers from the Housing Department joined chiefs and community development officers for "the citizenship course" that taught them about "water, health, postal services, wealth, Government, and education. . . . 'And we teach them also,' said the Principal, 'how to read a newspaper.'" [35] But if officials believed that the authority of newspapers could combat the power of the spoken word, they also believed that the silences of newspapers could stop the spread of spoken words.

VILLAINS AND VAMPIRES

According to my informants, vampires were first noted in Uganda in the early to mid 1920s and persisted until independence. In colonial times, there were a few Africans, who often owned cars, who captured other

34. E. M. K. Mulira, Mengo, 13 August 1990.
35. Ingrams, *Uganda*, 32–35. For years before the establishment of community development courses, officials in Kenya had argued that familial and national stability could emerge from men and women educated well enough to read vernacular newspapers and talk about current events; see Luise White, "Separating the Men from the Boys: Constructions of Sexuality, Gender, and Terrorism in Central Kenya, 1939–59," *Int. J. Afr. Hist. Studies* 23, 1 (1990): 1–25.

Africans by subterfuge and drugs and held them prisoner. They either
sold them or extracted their blood over a period of months to sell it to
a person or government department in Entebbe, the capital. These vampires were the bazimamoto, well known long before there was a formal
fire brigade in Kampala. A few informants were at great pains to distinguish whether the bazimamoto were actually the receivers of the blood
or those who secured it for others. The bazimamoto, according to most,
were the people who purchased the blood, not those who did the work
of capture. Individual Africans were named as such in local accounts, as
we shall see. "Kasolo was not bazimamoto but an agent of bazimamoto,
they were different types of people." [36] There was little confusion about
who these people were, however, and no conflation of unscrupulous
men about town with the men said to capture people. When my assistants and I mistakenly asked if these men were agents of the bazimamoto, we were corrected. [37]

Long before his trial in 1953, Kasolo was well known in Kampala's
African suburbs. He was, according to some, a driver by profession, but
most of his income came from his work for the bazimamoto. Kasolo and
others like him did the work of capturing Africans and either delivered
them to the bazimamoto or allowed bazimamoto to come and take
blood from these victims. For older residents of Kampala, people born
before 1915 or 1920, Kasolo was only known because he was "connected to these rumors." [38] According to Magarita Kalule, "You would
just hear of him from a distance." [39] "Yes, Kasolo, they were talking
about him . . . we used to fear him very much because he took people
and sold them and he would use any opportunity," said Julia Nakibuuka Nalongo. [40] Long before the events described in this chapter, he
was despised and fearful of popular reprisals: "When he was traveling
in his car and his car had mechanical problems, he would stay in the car
while it was being repaired," said Samuel Mubiru. [41]

Nevertheless, Kasolo was not the only Kampala man rumored to be
an agent of bazimamoto. Many people, including the editor of *Uganda
Eyogera,* which figures prominently in this chapter, remembered Mika:

36. Julia Nakibuuka Nalongo, Lubya, 21 August 1990.
37. One man, Kabangala, was the source of a number of urban legends, all involving
his ability to outwit and steal from Indian merchants.
38. Nechumbuza Nsumba, Katwe, 20 August 1990; Joseph Nsubuga, Kisasi, 22 August 1990.
39. Magarita Kalule, Masanafu, 20 August 1990.
40. Julia Nakibuuka Nalongo, Lubya, 21 August 1990.
41. Samuel Mubiru, Lubya, 28 August 1990.

He had a big house, and in one room was a big pit, and on the pit there was a mat, and on the mat there was a chair. He would take his friends and say, "You're my special friend, and I want to show you this wonderful thing I have, go into that room and sit on the chair, I'll be right there." The man would go sit on the chair and fall straight into the pit, and then the bazimamoto would come and take his friend.

Several others remembered Kanyeka.[42] Yet none of these men seem to have been arrested, let alone put on trial. Why not? No one doubted that they were personally responsible for many disappearances, but the allocation of such responsibility was not the issue in Kasolo's trial: accusation and its power in local politics were. Kasolo was not accused and arrested because he was more heinous or more responsible than Mika, Kanyeka, or anyone else in 1950s Kampala: he was put on trial because of the conflicts between his neighbors, his accusers, and his interlocutors at that time. The newspaper accounts I cite are part of those conflicts, retold by journalists to these contentious audiences and to each other in those months of 1953. That Kasolo's case was heard, in the matter-of-fact tone reserved for an accused "stupefier of several women" stands in ironic contrast to the political events that, just outside the courtroom doors, galvanized both Mengo, the seat of Buganda's royal government, and the suburb of Katwe in Kampala.

Kasolo was arrested because an angry group of men and women gathered at Kibuye Police Station and demanded that the parish chief of Katwe accompany them to Kasolo's house, where one man had seen his sister, missing for quite a long time.[43] Going to the police for help or to resolve disputes was not common in either Katwe or Mengo in the early 1950s. The rule of law was, if anything, shady. Aiden Southall and Peter Gutkind, who did fieldwork in Kisenyi from January 1953 to March 1954, describe the fluidity with which thieves vanished into an urban landscape in which detectives, informers, and criminals were often the same people, their professional identities much more a matter of who was asking than it was a statement about one's source of income. Blackmail, bribery, and connections to the royal family shaped the apprehension of criminals and recourse to the police. Stories of connection and corruption were commonplace. African beer brewers with relationships to the king's household were never arrested, although hardly any

42. E. M. K. Mulira, Mengo, 13 August 1990; Isaak Bulega, Makarere, 23 August 1990; Ssekajje Kasirye, Kisenyi, 24 August 1990.
43. Testimony of Stanley Kisitu, Sabuwali parish chief of Katwe, "Kasolo's Case Is Very Complicated," *Uganda Eyogera*, 4 December 1953, 1.

brewers were arrested without informers' help. A man caught stealing a bicycle was beaten by a crowd and offered the owner of the bicycle 100/- not to go to the police. The owner demanded 200/-, and the two finally settled on 175/-.[44] Threats of going to court may have had more power than an actual police presence may have mustered. "You policemen are very notorious and I intend to take you to court because you came to my house and took away my wives. I intend to sue over that," Kasolo is quoted as having said when he was arrested at his hiding place.[45]

In the case of Kasolo, the police may have been a last recourse, when rumor and gossip failed to contain the complex bundle of emotions and ideas that Kasolo had come to represent. Kasolo's actual arrest and trial added a degree of rationality to the irrationality of agents and vampires. As such, the trial did not resolve Kasolo's innocence or guilt or anything else; it simply indicates the limits of gossip and rumor as a way of resolving social tensions and crisis.[46] The citizenship of fractious Baganda gossip no longer worked. Indeed, much of the testimony at his trial debated whether or not he was married to two women—and thus raised important questions about the fluidity of urban marriage in Uganda in the 1950s and the stability of households in unstable political situations. Kasolo's lengthy explanation of the difference between his "town marriage" and his Muslim marriage raised the issue of Kiganda specificity and loyalty and played on widespread Baganda ideas that Baganda Muslims were more backward than their Christian counterparts.[47]

During the trial, the parish subchief was chastised by the magistrate for not having searched for more women, or indeed for Kasolo, at the time of the search. According to *Uganda Eyogera:*

> One beautiful-looking girl was found in the house and was immediately escorted to Mengo Police Station. Kasolo at that moment could not be traced.

44. Aiden W. Southall and Peter C. W. Gutkind, *Townsmen in the Making: Kampala and Its Suburbs* (Kampala: East African Institute of Social Research, 1957), 57–65.

45. "Kasolo Is Now in Prison at Njabule," *Uganda Eyogera* 6 November 1953, 1.

46. Barbara Yngvesson, "The Reasonable Man and Unreasonable Gossip: On the Flexibility of (Legal) Concepts and the Elasticity of (Legal) Time," in P. H. Gulliver, ed., *Cross-Examinations: Essays in Honor of Max Gluckman* (Leiden: E. J. Brill, 1978), 133–54; Max Marwick, "The Social Context of Cewa Witch Beliefs," *Africa* 22, 2 (1952): 120–35.

47. "Kasolo Fought in Court: His Case Will Get a Ruling Today," *Uganda Eyogera,* 27 November 1953, 1; Apter, *Political Kingdom,* 16–17; T. W. Gee, "A Century of Mohammedan Influence in Buganda, 1852–1951," *Uganda Journal* 22, 2 (1958): 129–50; Felice Carter, "The Education of African Muslims in Uganda," *Uganda Journal* 29, 2 (1965): 193–99.

When the police searched again, they came upon five women who had been hidden in one room and it was believed they had been forced into that room.

A lot of people turned up at Kasolo's home, to see for themselves the women whose skin had turned pale and who were being kept in Kasolo's sitting room then. These five women who had been accustomed to darkness for a long time found it difficult to face the light.

These women were dressed up in different kinds of clothes . . . the police said they were going to accuse Kasolo of the abduction of people.

Two of the women ran away almost at once, and one simply vanishes from newspaper accounts. "From that day the whole town was full of rumor saying that Kasolo was a stupefier of several women. This is the talk today."[48]

These two sentences should trouble the distinction between rumor and news; the talk of the town was no less reportable than who was found in Kasolo's sitting room. But this may not be as much a comment on the Luganda press as on our own modern distinction between published "news" and spoken "rumor"—the idea that the printed word contains a degree of credibility and reliability that widespread accusation and gossip does not. Men and women in colonial Uganda may not have subscribed to or even recognized this distinction. The distinctions between varieties of orally transmitted information that contain in the telling an evaluation of reliability might include several gradations of fact and fiction.[49] Gossip is communication that plays on, and creates, ties of intimacy: it is not by definition either reliable or unreliable. Nevertheless, the story of Kasolo did not appear in the *Uganda Herald*. While it is unlikely that the raid on a Katwe house would have made the English-language press in Kampala, the sentencings of various thieves did make third- and fourth-page news there. Kasolo's trial, however, coincided with the events leading up to the deportation of the Kabaka. Reports of these events were censored by the kingdom's court: Paolo Kavuma, Katikiro of Buganda, asked newspaper reporters not to publish the Lukiiko's letter rejecting federation—because the governor wanted to discuss it in England first—and only the *Herald* and the *Uganda Post* dissented.[50] Yet what can newspaper censorship mean in

48. "In Kasolo's House, Pale Coloured Women Were Recovered," *Uganda Eyogera*, 11 September 1953, 1. All translations from *Uganda Eyogera* were done by Fred Bukulu and Godfrey Kigozi.

49. Clay Ramsay, *The Ideology of the Great Fear: The Soissonnais in 1789* (Baltimore: Johns Hopkins University Press, 1992), 131–40.

50. Kavuma, *Crisis*, 24, 39.

a place where ties to the palace were common and constant, where Baganda gossiped and, if anything, overinterpreted that gossip, and where printed newspapers were not thought to contain truth? Newspaper censorship did not censor news; it simply made it more oral than it would otherwise have been. Indeed, the oral may have been more easily censored than the written. One man explained that he could not remember the song that criticized Buganda bureaucrats for the queen mother's remarriage because the king had banned it.[51] It is possible that the events of late 1953 may have increased newspaper readership, with Baganda seeking to read the silences and omissions around the royal turmoil, and some newspapers seeking increasingly popular stories with which to sell copies.

How was calling Kasolo a "stupifier" of popular interest? In Kampala bazimamoto stories, trapping Africans with drugs, in particular chloroform, was a common element. In the context of the newspaper story, "stupefier" was synonymous for a number of readers with "agent of bazimamoto." The impact of chloroform on captives was gendered, as we have seen. Women reported being silenced by it and men claimed it made them unable to walk. When Kasolo was found hiding two months later in the house of a "free woman" near his own, police surrounded the house. According to the newspaper account, he described himself the way one of his captives might have done: "Kasolo refused to come out saying that he felt muscle pain and therefore could not walk except if he was carried by police. He was therefore carried out of the house and dragged to Mengo Police Station."[52]

In the pages that follow I attempt to distinguish which parts of the Kasolo story were being told before his arrest and which parts began to be told as a result of the newspaper accounts of his arrest and trial. This will not reveal which parts of the story are part of an essentially oral, popular culture, but it will show how parts of the story were used in print media and in talk about Kasolo after his arrest. African historians have long sought a pure, uncontaminated orality that reveals an African past, with African cosmologies and African ideas. But as many of the people quoted in this book suggest, there is little point in seeking an orality that is free of the written; stories traveled between the two media, and speakers used elements from written and oral versions of a story to depict urban life, their own memories, and the colonial situa-

51. Gregory Sseluwagi, Lubya, 28 August 1990.
52. "Kasolo Is Now in Prison at Njabule" (cited n. 45 above).

tion. The question is not which elements of bazimamoto stories reside in which medium but how people thoughtfully used each medium to reconstruct a past that had meaning to them.[53] The citizenship of urban Uganda was not a passive act: Africans analyzed events by open discussion and disagreement. In recalling Kasolo's arrest and trial, they were telling stories about authority in Buganda.

The lines between oral and written are not hard and fast, of course. Newspaper allusions to bazimamoto played off the oral genre. Thus, whether or not Kasolo could actually walk is probably not important. The way Kasolo talked about his own legs during the trial played on a number of characteristics and tropes about the victims of bazimamoto. One of the things recalled frequently in oral accounts of Kasolo was that he tied rags onto his legs to get out of one legal obligation or another. "He used to tie a rotten rag on his leg, to pretend he was mad, so he would not have to pay tax," recalled Ahmed Kiziri.[54] Sapiriya Kasule, who came to Kampala in 1947, when he was twenty-five, denied that Kasolo abducted people, but allowed that he could not walk. When asked if it was true that Kasolo was arrested with "some people in his house," he replied: "But it was not like that, he was not arrested with some people as has been said, but he was involved in those riots [1949] and was beaten terribly and only escaped with his legs fractured."[55] Given the intensity of violence in Katwe and Mengo during the disturbances—the editor of *Matalisi,* for example, was beaten outside his office—this seems likely.[56]

And Kasolo played on these tropes, or at least the newspaper reporters did. When he was arraigned, he said: "I am Juma Kasolo . . . I am jobless and have been so ever since. . . . My legs have become paralysed." He asked not to have to stand trial because he was so ill and was sent for a medical examination. "When Kasolo reached Mulago almost all the patients and indeed the entire population on Mulago Hill gathered around him to see who Kasolo was." The doctor examined him and found him fit enough to stand trial.[57] Ten days later,

> Kasolo, in a cruel voice, complained that the judge was not listening to him. It was very sad to see that since he had been taken to prison he had not been given any food. He asked how the court expected him to answer his charges

53. See Hofmeyr, "'Wailing for Purity,'" 16–31.
54. Ahmed Kiziri, Katwe, 20 August 1990.
55. Sapiriya Kasule, Kisenyi, 28 August 1990.
56. *Uganda Herald,* 7 May 1949.
57. "Kasolo Fought in Court" (cited n. 47 above).

when he was so hungry. . . . In fact he asked the judge how he would feel if
had not taken food for two days and whether the judge would have been able
to listen to this case in such a condition.[58]

The stories and complaints men and women tell in a courtroom are not
always those most advantageous to their cases. The images and "facts"
and narratives with which defendants tell their stories may have multiple
audiences, in and out of the courtroom—and when writing from newspaper accounts of courtroom testimony, this is almost always the case—
rather than merely the judge and jury.[59]

The newspaper account of Kasolo's trial had a profound impact. In
some of the oral accounts quoted below, people talked about what was
in the newspaper. But does this mean that people took newspaper accounts more seriously than they did neighborhood gossip? Many African historians have worried that written texts simply drive oral versions
of events out of existence. According to these scholars, writing deforms
earlier understandings of the past and submerges the pure material of
oral transmission.[60] In the early 1970s, David Henige went so far as to
coin the term "feedback" to show that Africans took written accounts
of the past and often incorporated them into oral versions, making
them less than reliable. Worse, Africans sometimes took concepts from
the world of writing and relocated oral historical information in those
frameworks.[61] Such concerns tended to make Africans' oral traditions
impersonal and apolitical: written versions of the past were used, of
course, but because they were useful in an argument, or an interview.
The reasons to show one's knowledge of written materials were varied;
they sometimes had to do with presenting one's sophistication rather
than one's history.[62] Anxieties about feedback ignored one important

58. "Kasolo's Case Is Very Complicated" (cited n. 43 above).
59. See Lucie E. White, "Subordination, Rhetorical Survival Skills, and Sunday Shoes:
Notes on the Hearing of Mrs. G.," in Katharine T. Bartlett and Roseanne Kennedy, eds.,
Feminist Legal Theory (Boulder, Colo.: Westview Press, 1991), 404–28.
60. David Henige, "'The Disease of Writing': Ganda and Nyoro Kinglists in a Newly
Literate World," in Joseph C. Miller, ed., *The African Past Speaks: Essays on Oral Tradition and History* (Hamden, Conn.: Archon Books, 1980), 240–61; Jan Vansina, *Oral Tradition as History* (Madison: University of Wisconsin Press, 1985), 42–45.
61. David P. Henige, "'Disease of Writing'"; id., "The Problem of Feedback in Oral
Tradition: Four Examples from the Fante Coastlands," *J. African History* 14, 2 (1973):
223–35. In the past fifteen years, however, the concept has been resuscitated only to be
attacked; see Justin Willis, "Feedback as a 'Problem' in Oral History: An Example from
Bonde," *History in Africa* 20 (1993): 353–60.
62. This is, of course, true of oral materials as well; see Ben G. Blount, "Agreeing to
Disagree on Genealogy: A Luo Sociology of Knowledge," in Sanchez and Blount, eds.,
Sociocultural Dimensions of Language Use, 117–35 (New York: Academic Press, 1975).

point—in orality, like electronic music, feedback was manipulated for a specific impact. Indeed, in Kampala, it would seem that knowing what was in a newspaper demonstrated something, whether or not one had actually read the paper or not. George Ggingo, for example, who was thirteen at the time of Kasolo's trial, said:

> We read in the newspaper that somebody was caught when he was keeping people illegally . . . so the man was taken to court and his victims were six girls, in the range of ten to twenty-five years. . . . when it was brought out in court . . . they wanted to know where those people came from. So the man was prosecuted and was sentenced to serve six months.[63]

What was the oral version of Kasolo's story? Joseph Nsubuga, born in 1915, spoke with motifs and images that were common to many urban East African vampire stories but with ideas about drugs and consciousness specific to Kampala versions. His description may disclose some of the elements of the story that were specifically oral:

> Kasolo had some victims who managed to escape from his house, whom he had captured, then the people could prove that he was selling people. . . . he was well known, and those who had been there said that he had dug some pits in his house, and he used to cover them with mats, and when you were trying to sit down you would find yourself in the pit, and I think he used some of their drugs, like caliform, as he was keeping them in one room, I think he gave them some drugs to sniff. And they could not get out, but only be unconsciously moving there.[64]

Bibiana Nalwanga, a woman in her sixties, said it simply: "Kasolo was found with victims in his house and he was asked, what are these?"[65] Yonasani Kaggwa, an artisan, began working in Kampala in 1938, when he was twenty. The version he told my assistant and me took the newspaper account and elaborated on it:

> One day the government of Mengo investigated and they found he had some people unconscious in his house, they had their blood sucked from them. Ask anyone, they will tell you this story, ask anyone in Katwe . . . they know this story very well because that person was selling blood . . . Kasolo was arrested with those women, who were his victims . . . and definitely Kasolo was in the business of selling people to the bazimamoto, and he was found red-handed with some people in his house, they were unconscious, or he would give them some body-building food, so they would recover, because he had already sucked blood from them.[66]

63. George W. Ggingo, Kasubi, 15 August 1990.
64. Joseph Nsubuga, Kisasi, 22 August 1990.
65. Bibiana Nalwanga, Bwase, 24 August 1990.
66. Yonasani Kaggwa, Katwe, 27 August 1990.

These accounts suggest that scholars need not fret about feedback
from written to oral texts: rather than worrying about "adulteration"
from written sources, I would argue that oral and written texts coexist.
They coexist in part because they are inseparable, and in part because
what is said and what is published are precisely how people construct
and construe their public culture. A generation of African historians, not
unlike late colonial modernizers, imagined that the written word had
the natural authority to dominate oral accounts, but they were wrong.
Storytellers and newspaper readers in Kampala might each retell the Kasolo story using aspects of the oral and written versions; they elaborate
on written material with oral and on the oral with the written, but one
kind of source does not overwhelm the other. Indeed, in 1990, my assistants and I heard an account of Kasolo from Katwe that did not mention the trial at all. Isaak Bulega, who had been about thirty years old in
1953 said, "Kasolo had a pit in his house, and when you relieved yourself near his house, Kasolo would call you and say, 'Why are you doing
such a thing here?' Then Kasolo would take you inside his house, and
ask you to sit on a mat, which was a trap, and then you would fall into
the pit." [67]

Neighbors in Katwe, born in about 1918, did not necessarily have
more knowledge than newspaper readers, or at least did not speak
with greater specificity than those who did not live near Kasolo. Peter
Kirigwa said Kasolo was "a driver . . . he was looking for money and he
was profiting." [68] Another, Adolf Namatura, said:

> Not only did I hear about him, I saw him . . . Kasolo, he was sucking
> blood. . . . He would capture people and take them to places where they
> would get their blood sucked, and that was his work. We didn't know he was
> taking them, but he was capturing them, and I saw them. When Mutesa II
> reigned, he was taken to Mengo and the town clerk's office for having been
> found with six people in his house, and he was arrested. . . . I saw him with
> my own eyes. [69]

Katwe residents who were born in the early 1930s knew the story
as well. But two younger men, born in 1931 and 1932 respectively, did
not know much about Kasolo, except "people used to fear him very
much . . . he was pretending to be a sick person, that he could not

67. Isaak Bulega, Makere, 20 August 1990.
68. Peter Kirigwa, Katwe, 24 August 1990.
69. Adolf Namutura, Katwe, 24 August 1990.

do anything . . . because he didn't want to pay the graduated tax."[70]
Ssekajje Kasirye, born in 1934, who commuted daily in 1953 between
his home in Entebbe and his job in Katwe, was skeptical about the
rumors:

> He was an intelligent fellow indeed, who was dealing in buying . . . and sell-
> ing old spare parts . . . but there was a rumor that he used to sell people but
> whenever we went to buy things we never saw anybody sold, but he would
> just brag that people said I am selling people, but no one was missing, so it
> was just empty talk. [When Kasolo was arrested] I wasn't old enough so I
> didn't understand it. . . . I was working in Katwe here, and during that time
> that newspaper [*Uganda Eyogera*] existed, and I was old enough to read it,
> but I didn't understand it.[71]

Not resident in Katwe, it is possible that this man missed the local idioms of drugs, and pits, and legs—idioms so well known that no one in
Katwe believed they had to elaborate on them. Or it may be, as the man
himself suggests, that he was too young to understand the references as
older residents might have done. Ahmed Kiziri, who was born in 1935
and lived in Katwe throughout the 1950s, did understand, however: "I
have seen one of their victims. . . . she was one of the five women, she
was still alive when they were found at Kasolo's house but they were
looking like stupid people, and that man, Kasolo, he was the one who
did it!"[72]

Drawing on ideas about the sale of bodies that coincided with the
completion of New Mulago Hospital in 1962 and ideas about the cot-
tage industry of transporting corpses to rural areas for customary burial,[73] younger residents of Katwe, such as Daniel Sekiraata, who was
born in 1940, revised the story of Kasolo's deeds and arrest:

> He was taking some dead bodies to Zaire, which was called Congo then.
> Once he was caught with some dead bodies, and they were four dead bodies,

70. Musoke Kapliamu, Katwe, 22 August 1990; also Christopher Kawoya, Kasubi,
17 August 1990.

71. Ssekajje Kasirye, Kisenyi, 24 August 1990.

72. Ahmed Kiziri, Katwe, 20 August 1990.

73. The big new teaching hospital at Mulago was finally finished in 1962, after being under construction for years; see Margaret MacPherson, *They Built for the Future:
A Chronicle of Makerere University College, 1922–1962* (Cambridge: Cambridge University Press, 1964), 34; Julia Nakibuuka Nalongo, interview cited in n. 37 above. On
transporting corpses home for burial, see David W. Cohen and Atieno Odhiambo, *Burying SM: The Politics of Knowledge and the Sociology of Power in Black Africa* (Portsmouth, N.H.: Heinemann, 1992).

and he used to dress them very like a live person! And he could put them in his car and he was pretending they were people on safari, and he gave them some newspapers to read and he did this several times, but I don't know what he was doing with them or what he got for transporting them.[74]

Beatrice Mukasa, about the same age as Sekiraata, but a more recent immigrant to Katwe, had only heard that Kasolo "used to capture people and drop them in a certain pit."[75] But Gregory Sseluwagi, also born around 1940, who lived outside Kampala had heard about Kasolo in very different ways:

Kasolo, Kasolo, . . . when they had sent some children for something, and sometimes we would understand through those who had survived capture. This would happen especially when you had paid a visit to one of the well-known bazimamoto, because they had some pits in their houses and therefore somebody who had survived capture could tell you the story. They could tell you to be careful, and you were warned not to walk at night, and to take care by Kasolo's homestead and others who were doing the same work.[76]

STORIES AND STRATEGIES

The case of Kasolo—as it was reported in the newspaper and as it was recalled—reveals how the formulaic elements—legs, cars, pits, food, and stupefying drugs—constitute the local construction of a genre that straddled and continues to straddle oral and written sources. And why not? The story of Kasolo was "the talk of the town" and unlike the talk of the king and the governor, it was uncensored by both officials and notions of hierarchy and propriety. Indeed, it was headline news when royal politics were not. Were royal politics simply absent from the trial, which in fact described Kasolo's legs and food and silent women to make vivid the world of bazimamoto never mentioned in the press? If victims believed they had been fed "body-building food" to make them produce more blood, can we read Kasolo's complaint that his jailers failed to feed him as the abductor's story? And did ordinary readers of *Uganda Eyogera* read this complaint and think of the food fed the victims in Kasolo's house?

Such an interpretation explains this chapter but not the trial. The trial may in fact require a more local reading—an understanding of the

74. Daniel Sekiraata, Katwe, 22 August 1990; also Ahmed Kiziri, Katwe, 20 August 1990.
75. Beatrice Mukasa, Katwe, 16 August 1990.
76. Gregory Sseluwagi, Lubya, 28 August 1990.

lower ranks of kingdom politics at a moment of intense crisis. It may be
a story about royal politics told with vampire beliefs. Without such local knowledge—and without a knowledge of what appeared and did
not appear in other Luganda newspapers—I can only point to directions future researchers, better prepared for such tasks than I am, might
wish to use vernacular newspapers to pursue. There is no question that
bureaucratic politics in Buganda had been ferocious for some time. The
populist and anti-Mutesa II lobby seems to have had many supporters
after the reforms of 1949. Factions in and around Mengo must have lis-
tened carefully—attentive as always for the hidden meanings—to the
news that seeped out of the king's meetings with the governor to see how
they might fare in an independent Buganda or a fully colonized one. It
is possible that at any other time, a policeman would have been less willing to respond to a Katwe crowd and search Kasolo's house. But much
of the vehemence and the rage in the trial was between officials. At Kasolo's trial, Stanley Kisitu, parish chief of Katwe, was attacked by the
judge for not having searched for Kasolo in his house.

JUDGE: Since you were told that Kasolo was not there, did you search his bed-
         room to see if he was there?

KISITU: No, I stopped in the sitting room and after the search, I collected all
         the women who had been found in Kasolo's house. . . .

JUDGE: From the evidence you have been giving this court, it seems like you
         have been telling lies. A person of your nature is usually put before the
         law. Therefore I request the court prosecutor to open a case against
         you. Indeed, it would be impossible for a parish chief who was sent
         with a search warrant for searching a home to come back and say it
         was impossible. This is a real lie.[77]

It is quite possible to read this exchange and imagine that the purpose
of the arrest and trial was, in some ways, to get rid of Kisitu rather than
Kasolo. His role in the arrest was in fact unclear. By his own account
"In September . . . I was invited by Sergeant Sebirumbi to go to the
Kibuye Police Station. On my arrival Sebirumbi blew a whistle and some
policemen turned up. These policemen together with their leader were
ordered to go to Kasolo's house in my presence. The group included
women and men who were not from the police."[78] It seems altogether
possible, even without knowing the specific fissures and personalities of
Buganda bureaucratic politics in Kampala's suburbs in the early 1950s,

77. "Kasolo's Case Is Very Complicated" (cited n. 43 above).
78. Ibid.

that one of the reasons Kasolo's case came to trial had to do with the politics around Kisitu. Just as the angry crowed attempted to control Kasolo in ways that gossip no longer could, the judge and some police sought to control Kisitu in ways that gossip no longer could, and in ways that might facilitate a few of the many possible futures suggested by the crisis censored in the nation's newspapers.

CONCLUSIONS

Vampire stories do double duty in this chapter. Ordinary everyday talk about bazimamoto and its agents was a way for men and women in co-lonial Kampala to talk about egregious accumulation, the trials of urban marriage, Islam, political violence, and their own difficulties with be-ing loyal subjects of their king, the Kabaka. Talk about Kasolo the bazi-mamoto's agent engaged with questions of consciousness, chloroform, inhaled drugs, and paralysis that were commonly used to talk about Western biomedicine with vampire stories. But newspaper accounts that alluded to vampire stories, with their detailed descriptions of trials of "well-known stupefiers," provided a forum through which vampires sto-ries were used to comment on the royal politics silenced in the English-language press, while the courts and the press used vampire accusations as a way to discipline local royal officials.

CHAPTER 9

Class Struggle
and Cannibalism

Storytelling and History Writing
on the Copperbelts of Colonial Northern
Rhodesia and the Belgian Congo

This chapter, like several others in this book, posits two distinctive sets of historical materials, one expressed in the vocabulary of blood and abduction and one that we might call conventional, the standard narrative and the facts and figures with which that narrative is proved. This chapter is intended to take the notion of two kinds of histories a step further. It argues that the two sets of materials, which are, as we have seen, different in different places, can be compared across political and cultural boundaries to produce a more comparative history, which can in turn reveal a broader range of African workers' strategies than other sources have done.

JIGSAWS, HOLOGRAMS, AND LABOR HISTORY

This chapter compares vampire stories on the two central African copperbelts, that in the Belgian Congo, where mining was controlled by one company, Union Minière d'Haute Katanga (UMHK), and that on the Northern Rhodesian side of the border, where mining companies—the Anglo-American Corporation and the Rhodesian Selection Trust—competed for labor and profits during the 1930s. Although African laborers, artisans, and hangers-on crisscrossed this border well into the 1940s, working men told different stories of abduction and extraction in both places. The *banyama* who sought their victims around Northern Rhodesia's copper mines took men's blood, but they also captured men's wills. Banyama stories from the Northern Rhodesian Copperbelt produced some terrifying descriptions of how men became workers:

> This story was going around when I arrived at Luanshya in 1935. . . . The Banyama . . . snatch live men and sell their bodies to people who need them. . . . Another story is that the European has a special license from the Government, and he employs natives armed with charms to do his work in secret. These secret agents are never known and they go about at night. Having picked their victim they lure him to a secret spot where they hit him on the head with a "mupila." A "mupila" is said to have a rubber tube full of medicine which steals the man's mind and he even forgets his name and can be taken anywhere.[1]

In colonial Katanga, *batumbula* captured Africans with the same methods found in banyama and *wazimamoto* stories elsewhere, but ate their flesh and did not take their blood. Africans were hired by white men to capture other Africans and give them an injection that made them "dumb." Finally, victims became fat, white or pinkish, and hairy like pigs. Sometimes a special diet transformed the victims into cows. White men then ate them on special occasions like Christmas and New Year.[2] Sometimes these white men worked for Americans. The revolts of the early 1940s—Luluabourg and Katanga—were fueled by rumors of white cannibalism.[3] A Belgian priest, Dom Grégoire Coussement, was said to be a batumbula in Elisabethville. After he was transferred to Kasenga, on the Luapula, in 1943, he was said to kidnap Africans on both sides of the river, imprison them in the belfry of the mission church, and drive them to Elisabethville, where they were killed and eaten.[4]

1. P. K. Kanosa, "Banyama—Copper Belt Myth Terrifies the Foolish," *Mutende* [Lusaka] 38 (1936) (National Archives of Zambia [henceforth cited as NAZ], SEC2/429, Native Affairs: Banyama). Luanshya was the town around Roan Antelope Mine.

2. Rik Ceyssens, "Mutumbula: Mythe de l'opprimé," *Cultures et développement* 7 (1975): 484–95.

3. Bruce S. Fetter, "The Lualabourg Revolt at Elisabethville," *African Historical Studies* 2, 2 (1965): 273; J.-L. Vellut, "Le Katanga industriel en 1944: Malaises et anxiétés dans la société coloniale," in *Le Congo belge durant la Seconde Guerre mondiale* [= *Bijdragen over Belgisch-Congo tijdens de Tweede Wereldoorlog*] (Brussels: Académie royale des sciences d'outre-mer, 1983), 501–3; and John Higginson, "Steam without a Piston Box: Strikes and Popular Unrest in Katanga, 1943–45," *Int. J. Afr. Hist. Studies* 21, 1 (1988): 101–2. Whether these "Americans" were actually thought to be from the United States or whether they were a gloss for ancestors is impossible to tell from the many transcriptions and translations these accounts have undergone. For both possibilities, see George Shepperson, *Myth and Reality in Malawi* (Evanston, Ill.: Northwestern University Press, 1966), and Wyatt MacGaffey, "The West in Congolese Experience," in Philip Curtin, ed., *Africa and the West: Intellectual Responses to European Culture* (Madison: University of Wisconsin Press), 49–74.

4. W. V. Brelsford, "The 'Banyama' Myth," *NADA* 9, 4 (1967): 52.

The next section shows how laborers from Northern Rhodesia worked in Katanga's mining industry well into the 1930s. This raises the question, why, if the men telling the stories were the same, are these stories so different on the two copperbelts? Finding out is not easy. The source materials for both copperbelts have little in common. Even before the 1935 strike on the Northern Rhodesian Copperbelt, officials and missionaries had been concerned about the impact of migrant labor on African society. As we have seen in chapters 6 and 7, officials worried about the moral fiber of migrants—already compromised in their eyes by how they imagined matrilineality—and the vulnerability and privation of women left alone to farm. The Depression had shocked these officials even more, showing them the grim realities of rural poverty as nothing had before: when the world price of copper dropped by almost half, and all but two of Northern Rhodesia's mines closed, many African laborers did not return home. By 1933, the International Missionary Council's Department of Social and Industrial Research, founded in 1930, published the results of its research on Northern Rhodesia's mines, *Modern Industry and the African,* which offered a wealth of evidence with which to reconstruct the lives of copperbelt workers, and how they managed urban life. Of the African workforce at Nkana Mine, 10 to 15 percent had Barclays Bank accounts, for example, and a large number of miners at Roan Antelope Mine ordered blankets and other goods by mail rather than patronize local shopkeepers.[5]

The 1935 strike generated another set of concerns. Typical of the labor protests of the 1930s, African miners had actively and collectively left work, apparently to protest a tax increase, and in the subsequent panic the police shot and killed six Africans and wounded many more at Roan Antelope Mine. Although Africans soon returned to work without incident, officials launched a commission of inquiry that served to inscribe the strike with a level of leadership and organization that their findings disputed. The commission also produced page after page of miners' and managers' testimony about work, remuneration, and relations underground and in the compound.[6] More than dockworkers'

5. Charles W. Coulter, "The Sociological Problem," in J. Merle Davis, ed., *Modern Industry and the African: An Enquiry into the Effect of the Copper Mines of Central Africa upon Native Society and the Work of Christian Missions Made under the Auspices of the Department of Social and Industrial Research of the International Missionary Council* (London: Macmillan, 1933), 59–78.

6. Albert B. K. Matongo, "Popular Culture in a Colonial Society: Another Look at *mbeni* and *kalela* Dances on the Copperbelt, 1930–1960," in Samuel N. Chipungu, ed.,

strikes elsewhere in Africa, the 1935 Copperbelt strike had a profound impact on British imperialism: the anthropology of urbanization was born, as were studies of the conditions of mine labor and urban life. Indeed, the banyama story quoted above comes from a government-run newspaper sold—without much success—on the Northern Rhodesian Copperbelt in the wake of industrial strife. Its editor sought to make it the vehicle by which educated Africans could offer information to their less educated fellows.[7] This particular tension of the reporting of a story by those attempting to prove it wrong informs many of the banyama stories in this chapter. P. K. Kanosa, the author of the quotation above, cautioned that Africans "who have some sort of education" had an obligation to "kill this story," but noted that as long as "ignorant natives continue to arrive on the Copperbelt there will always be people to believe stories like this." [8]

No such sources, let alone uses of storytelling, exist for UMHK in the 1930s. The details of consumption and pleasure that percolate in and out of the Northern Rhodesian material are absent, as far as I can tell, from the Congolese material. Missionaries in Katanga, as we shall see, did not see themselves as opponents of state labor policies. Visitors who had just come from South Africa, such as Margery Perham, were usually impressed by the differences between the two countries. The Belgian government in exile conducted no large-scale investigation of Congolese labor protests of the early 1940s; it was assumed that Belgium's status as an occupied country encouraged African extremism. Northern Rhodesia and the Congo do not have equivalent data; the material presented here cannot, in and of itself, yield a reliable historical comparison: data on African banking on the Rhodesian Copperbelt cannot usefully be compared with travelers' anecdotes about the Congo.

So I ask readers to bear with me and think of this chapter as two kinds of histories at once—the history of the puzzle, in which each and every piece clarifies and completes the picture, and the history of the

---

Guardians in the Time: Experiences of Zambians under Colonial Rule (London: Macmillan, 1992), 180–217. On 1930s labor protests in East and Central Africa, see Frederick Cooper, *On the African Waterfront: Urban Disorder and the Transformation of Work in Colonial Mombasa* (New Haven: Yale University Press, 1987), and Ian Henderson, "Early African Leadership: The Copperbelt Disturbances of 1935 and 1940," *J. Southern Afr. Studies* 2, 1 (1975): 83–97.

7. Rosaleen Smyth, "Propaganda and Politics: The History of *Mutende* during the Second World War," *Zambian J. of History* 1 (1981): 43–60; NAZ, SEC2/1127, Native Newspapers.

8. Kanosa, "Banyama—Copper Belt Myth Terrifies the Foolish."

hologram, in which the image is constructed from the light shed on a fragment. This is a history-writing strategy, a way to get at two different kinds of knowledge at once. The material on consumption and savings on the Northern Rhodesian Copperbelt allows for a detailed examination of how workers regarded their wages and all they contained. There are no comparable data for the Belgian Congo. But there is a level and commonality of description from the Congo that is unlike anything for Northern Rhodesia—descriptions that are so similar that, seen in the same light, they make a hologram, a single image that becomes vivid and three-dimensional when seen through a single, consistent illumination. African miners were not alone in describing the physical transformation that accompanied their sojourns in Katanga. Margery Perham used the metaphor of castration to describe the hospitalized Congolese mine-workers she visited in February 1930. Listening to them "rasping out" responses to a nun, she reflected: "There is something almost ludicrous about it. Ten, five years ago (now, if they had the chance) these men were indulging in tribal warfare, perhaps in torture and cannibalism; now they look as docile and as lifeless as bullocks in a fat-stock show." [9] The barely fictionalized autobiography of a willful Belgian nun in Elisabeth-ville in the late 1930s includes the powerful image of a hospital orderly, sent to sleep off a binge on local brew, eaten by ants: ". . . on the dirt floor was a man-shaped mound of white ants that had eaten Banza clean to the skeleton. Not even a tuft of hair was left on the skull." [10]

Let me argue that the Northern Rhodesian copperbelt is the jigsaw. Between missionaries' studies, testimonies about the 1935 strike, a generation of anthropologists and another generation of labor historians, the data about the Copperbelt in 1930–45 provide a number of "pieces" with which I can reconstruct a picture. The Congolese side is the hologram—whether I recreate an image from Dame Margery, African miners, or former nuns, the image is always the same: Africans are being eaten alive, their shapes transformed, and emasculated. Each of these images is blurred and incomplete. Taken together they do not add up to

---

9. Margery Perham, *African Apprenticeship: An Autobiographical Journey in Southern Africa, 1929* (London: Faber & Faber, 1974), 217.

10. Kathryn Hulme, *The Nun's Story* (Boston: Little, Brown, 1956), 214. Even tales of African cannibalism were revised to be about whites eating blacks. An American medical missionary among the Tatela in the 1920s heard the story of a "pygmy chief" who was "surprised by a visit of the State Commissioner at a time when he happened to have no meat to offer him. He determined not to fail in hospitality to the white man, so he cooked one of his nicest wives to make a feast for his guest" (Janet Miller, *Jungles Preferred* [Boston: Houghton Mifflin, 1931], 102).

the kind of picture one gets from diverse pieces; they add up to something somewhat different, made three-dimensional by the way it is
looked at.

TWO COPPERBELTS, TWO HISTORIES

The history of both copperbelts may have been made into separate colonial and national histories because few historians worked in both
French and English. The history of UMHK has been seen as separate
and distinct from that of the mines on the British side of the border. In
part this has to do with Africanists disinclination to mix the history of
francophone and anglophone regions, and in part it is because the two
histories do not provide a good chronological or comparative fit. Although copper mining in Katanga had begun well before World War I,
copper production on the Northern Rhodesian Copperbelt only began
in the late 1920s, and a few mines were only ready for production when
they had to close due to the Depression. More important, perhaps, was
the fact that labor policies differed in the two colonies. By 1926, before
the first copper mine in colonial Northern Rhodesia was fully opera-
tional, the UMHK had begun to stabilize its labor force. Officially, copper mines in Northern Rhodesia did not encourage a family presence,
but most mines allowed women to settle in compound housing.[11]

Both copperbelts had separate and distinct histories with deep play
between them. They also had separate and distinct historiographies, and

11. James Ferguson, "Mobile Workers, Modernist Narratives: A Critique of the Historiography of Transition on the Zambian Copperbelt," *J. Southern Afr. Studies* 16, 3 and
4 (1990): 385–412, 603–21, notes that although most colonial Copperbelt researchers
asked and answered these and many more questions about long-term lives on the Copperbelt, they nevertheless accepted rhetoric about phases of migrancy and stabilization; see
also George Chauncey, Jr., "The Locus of Reproduction: Women's Labor in the Zambian
Copperbelt, 1927–1953," *J. Southern Afr. Studies* 7, 2 (1981): 135–64; Perham, *African
Apprenticeship*, 233; *Evidence of the Commission Appointed to Enquire into the Disturbances on the Copperbelt of Northern Rhodesia* (Lusaka: Government Printer, 1935)
(hereafter cited as Russell Commission), passim; Jane L. Parpart, *Labour and Capital on
the African Copperbelt* (Philadelphia: Temple University Press, 1983), 36, 47–48; Charles
Perrings, *Black Mineworkers in Central African Industry: Industrial Strategies and the
Evolution of the African Proletariat in the Copperbelt, 1911–1941* (New York: Holmes
& Meier; London: Heinemann, 1979), 82–89. I have argued elsewhere that stabilization is an employers' concept that must be read against the grain; the so-called informal
sector—hangers-on, brewers, and petty criminals—frequently lived in stable, if illegal,
family units beyond the gaze of the mining company and the colonial state; see Luise
White, *The Comforts of Home: Prostitution in Colonial Nairobi* (Chicago: University of
Chicago Press, 1990), 212–17. This chapter argues that both migrancy and stabilization
are historians' concepts that have often obscured the place of bonuses and equipment in
workers' strategies.

the different sources for production and reproduction on both sides of the border have meant that, with few exceptions, the threads that link the two copperbelts have been overlooked, and the fluidity with which African labor penetrated colonial and cultural borders has not been the source with which history was written. It has also meant—incidentally, I think—that employers' categories have dominated the analysis more than was necessary, and that colonial mythologies have survived longer than they might otherwise have done. The idea that labor was stabilized in Katanga, while the copper mines of Northern Rhodesia relied on a system of migrancy has gone unchallenged; there has been a disinclination to look for sources that might suggest what these categories might have meant to the men engaged in mine labor in either place.

Belgian and British copper mines in Central Africa shared labor and managerial expertise from a very early date. In its early years, copper mining in Katanga was dependent on Northern Rhodesian labor and British expertise: until World War I, in fact, the main language in Elisabethville was English.[12] As late as 1929, there were almost 11,000 miners from Northern Rhodesia working for the UMHK, and the most common language spoken in the mines of Katanga was Bemba. In the early 1930s, Northern Rhodesian Africans also seem to have dominated petty trade and artisan labor outside the mining sector in Katanga.[13] The wages paid to Northern Rhodesian workers were the same on both sides of the border, but had a greater purchasing power on the Belgian side. The preference for working in Katanga may have had to do with commodities, not wages.[14] The Depression served to make the border more porous than it had been before. Workers of all races migrated in search of better wages. In 1930, white miners crossed the Congolese border in numbers great enough to alarm Belgian officials, and within a few years, skilled, literate African workers, most of them from Nyasaland, crossed the border from the Congo into Northern Rhodesia after the UMHK reduced the wages for clerks and *capitães*.[15] But it was not only mine workers who crossed the border between Belgian and British Africa. European peddlers and hawkers and a few Indian traders carried

12. Johannes Fabian, ed. and trans., *History from Below: The Vocabulary of Elisabethville by André Yav* (Amsterdam and Philadelphia: John Benjamins, 1990), 76, 157.
13. Bruce Fetter, *The Creation of Elisabethville* (Stanford, Calif.: Hoover Institution, 1976), 130–31; Perrings, *Black Mineworkers*, 102–3.
14. Fetter, *Creation of Elisabethville*, 80–87.
15. Perham, *African Apprenticeship*, 212–13; Perrings, *Black Mineworkers*, 101–2; Ian Henderson, "Early African Leadership: The Copperbelt Disturbances of 1935 and 1940," *J. Southern Afr. Studies* 2, 1 (1975): 86–87.

goods across the border and sold them for less than they could be purchased for at Katanga's newly opened shops. After 1930, African and Greek traders sold dried fish to migrants on both sides of the border.[16] Northern Rhodesian women also crossed the border with ease. In 1938, district officers complained that several hundred women lived in temporary unions in Katanga with men from Kasai: "There is no intention that it should be a proper marriage—it is only a means of getting money and clothing." Parents routinely crossed the border to visit their daughters; "they all admitted that they were going to see what they could get from their 'sons-in-law.'"[17] Some sources suggest that one reason for the 1935 strike was that the Belgians had closed the border to Northern Rhodesian trade and produce the year before, thus making Africans more dependent on income from wage labor than they had hitherto been.[18] Even when the border was officially closed, religious movements, witch-finding movements, and new dance fads crossed the border regularly.[19] These movements must be added to the picture of African labor—the jigsaw puzzle again—that has emerged over the past twenty years, in which African workers' gossip passed on the latest information about the safest working conditions, the best living conditions, the best wages. Such talk sent African workers across cultural and colonial boundaries to work and to make money, where they found themselves in worlds and seams and stopes that had different safety records, different standards of living, and different rates of remuneration.[20] Moreover, such talk placed Africans in worlds and seams and stopes that required different descriptions and different imaginings.

16. Yona Ngalaba Seleti, "Entrepreneurs in Colonial Zambia," in Samuel Chipungu, ed., *Guardians in Their Time: Experiences of Zambians under Colonial Rule* (London: Macmillan, 1992), 147–69.

17. R. L. Moffat, district commissioner, Kawambwa, tour report 1, 1938, "Lukwesa and Kapesa Areas: Rhodesian Women in the Belgian Congo" (NAZ, SEC2/872, Kawambwa Tour Reports, 1933–38).

18. P. W. M. Jelf, district officer, Fort Roseberry, tour report, June 1932 (NAZ, SEC2/888); A. R. Munday, district commissioner, Fort Roseberry, Annual Report on Native Affairs, 1934, and Fort Roseberry Annual Report, 1935–37 (NAZ/SEC2/1302). Charles Perrings, "Consciousness, Conflict and Proletarianization: an Assessment of the 1935 Mineworkers' Strike on the Northern Rhodesian Copperbelt," *J. Southern Afr. Studies* 4, 1 (1977): 40–41; Parpart, *Labor and Capital*, 57; Perrings, *Black Mineworkers*, 114–16.

19. See esp. Sholto Cross, "The Watchtower Movement in South Central Africa, 1908–1945" (Ph.D. diss., Oxford University, 1973), and Karen Fields, *Revival and Rebellion in Central Africa* (Princeton: Princeton University Press, 1985).

20. See, e.g., Charles van Onselen, "Worker Consciousness in Black Miners: Southern Rhodesia, 1900–1920," *J. Afr. History* 14 (1973), and I. R. Phimister, "Origins and Aspects of African Worker Consciousness in Rhodesia," in E. Webster, ed., *Essays in Southern African Labour History* (Johannesburg: Ravan Press, 1979), 47–63.

But given the intensity of travel and association, why are the region's stories about whites who, some way or other, consumed Africans imagined so differently? Is it a matter of storytelling conventions, that a genre of story shaped and set in one place becomes the framework that all future storytellers use? Is there a standard plot in which characters and place-names are inserted? Or are these differences a matter of experience? Is the reality of work and life so different in each place that it can only be described with different narratives? There may not be an either/or answer, of course—stories and imaginings and lives are not such separate domains that they can be rigidly segregated—but the question of whether these differences of detail are about the social construction of narrative or the social construction of experience may reveal far more than is usually discerned from regional studies of the Central African copper industry. I do not argue that banyama and batumbula stories are more important than any other aspect of this region's history, however. My point is that by looking at these stories, historians can examine workers' strategies and experiences more closely than they could with other sources.

The writing strategy of the jigsaw and the hologram notwithstanding, how solid a wall is the divide between storytelling in colonial Katanga and the Northern Rhodesian Copperbelt? Images and clichés did not stay put on one side of a border, unable to cross colonial boundaries. They slipped across, where, based on the evidence I have, some took hold and others did not. Two separate accusations involving priests from the first half of 1932 show how stories might travel without settling. In March 1932—in the midst of intense banyama accusations, many directed at two priests at this mission—the monsignor of Chilubula, the White Fathers' Mission in Kasama District, a major recruitment area for mine labor of both copperbelts, received a letter written in English containing "gross insults not to be repeated" in the mission's daily diary. It was signed "your good roast mutton captivity, imprisonment, and bandages." [21] It hardly matters whether this letter can be demonstrated to be a banyama accusation, although I think it is. The word "bandages" echoes the medical idiom of contemporary banyama accusations. But "roast mutton captivity" does not correspond to blood accusations in Northern Rhodesia either of this time or later. It recalls Congolese stories of captured Africans being made into animals to be consumed.

21. Société des Missionnaires d'Afrique, Rome, Diaire of Chilubula, 12 March 1932.

Two months later, a young priest in the Belgian Congo asked to be sent home. For six months he had been accosted wherever he went by Africans who accused him "of imprisoning women and mistreating children," he said.[22] Imprisoning women was a standard theme of batumbula accusations but harming children was not. Indeed, the Congolese painter Tshibumba recalled that when he was a toddler, in about 1948, his mother was accosted by two batumbula, but they said to each other, in Swahili, "Shouldn't we let her go? She's with a child. We'll let her go."[23] But by the early 1940s, however, kidnapping children was a standard theme of banyama stories in the Kasama District of Northern Rhodesia. One official reported that these kidnapped children were killed on Christmas Day, a theme of Congolese stories absent from Northern Rhodesian ones.[24]

But if the images and clichés of banyama and batumbula crossed boundaries as regularly as they went back, what about individuals, the stock characters of these stories? Did they travel across borders as well? Dom Grégoire appeared in many banyama accusations in colonial Northern Rhodesia. By the time he was transferred to Kasenga, stories about him circulated on both sides of the Luapula River: in Northern Rhodesia, where he was said to be a White Father, Africans claimed that an African man offered the oldest of his wives to Grégoire for the banyama; the priest refused and asked the man to kill the younger one for him.[25] By 1949, stories about "Gregory" involved the crisscrossing of boundaries, conceptual and political. He was said to pay men on behalf of the Belgian government to cross the river and capture Africans in Northern Rhodesia, who would be sold to his mission, said to be Chibondo, where there was a strange building connected to the mission sta-

22. Dom Grégoire Coussement, Elisabethville, to X. L. Neve, 8 May 1932, Archives, Saint Andreas Abbey, Bruges.

23. Quoted in Johannes Fabian, *Remembering the Present: Painting and Popular History in Zaire* (Berkeley and Los Angeles: University of California Press, 1996), 50.

24. Gervas Clay, district commissioner, Isoka District, "Memorandum Concerning 'banyama' and 'mafyeka' with Special Reference to Provincial Commissioner, Kasama's Confidential File on Banyama and to Incidents in Isoka District during the Latter Part of 1943" (NAZ, SEC2/429, Native Affairs: Banyama, 24 January 1944). By the late 1940s, the kidnapping of children was a widespread anxiety on the Copperbelt, and an Ila novelist noted that parents would pay 30/- for a lost child returned to the mine office; this, of course, gave rise to kidnappers taking children simply to be paid the 30/-. See Enoch Kaavu, *Namusiya in the Mines,* trans. from the Ila by R. Nabulgato and C. R. Hopgood (London: Longmans, 1949), 66. I am grateful to Bryan Callahan for bringing this passage to my attention.

25. Brelsford, "'Banyama' Myth," 52.

tion in which captured Africans were killed and their brains eaten. The few victims who were not killed were unable to speak when they were found. Images of dumb captives seem to have stuck in Northern Rhodesian banyama stories, whether bundled with those about Dom Grégoire or not. A headman was forced to leave Northern Rhodesia for the Congo; people insisted that he was banyama, charging that he had captured a man from his own village and when they found the man he could not speak.[26] But not every banyama—or every priest—crossed boundaries. The European called Yengwe on the Copperbelt was said by Africans on the Luapula to have been working with Greek traders in Kasenga and with Belgian plantation owners in the Congo, but only his victims were said to cross the border.[27] In 1944, an administrator in Northern Rhodesia wrote that Africans in the Luapula River valley believed that an Italian priest was the "head" of banyama, "and if he should cross to our side of the river they intended to kill him."[28] Does this mean that stories and rumors and ideas do not diffuse, but that some individuals and objects carry with them bundled traits and associations that do cross borders and rivers? If so, it may be that these images and clichés, the traveling priests and silenced Africans, may reveal regional rather than local concerns.[29] The individuals who became the subject of transnational accusations may have been those who embodied local ideas about colonial policies in the wider regional economy. In other words, Dom Grégoire and the headman were associated with

26. Ian Cunnison's field notes, March 1949. I am grateful to Professor Cunnison for making these available to me.

27. Mwelwa C. Musambachime, "The Impact of Rumor: The Case of Banyama (Vampire Men) in Northern Rhodesia, 1930–1960," *Int. J. Afr. Hist. Studies* 21, 1 (1988): 205–7n.

28. G. Howe, provincial commissioner, Northern Province, to chief secretary, Lusaka, 8 June 1944 (NAZ, SEC1/1072, Survey of Helminthic Diseases; I am grateful to Bryan Callahan for taking notes on this file for me).

29. Not all accusations against individuals spread beyond a locality however. In 1934, in Isoka District, Harold Cartmel-Robinson was accused of collecting blood for banyama when he ordered a smallpox vaccination campaign; see S. R. Denny, "Up and Down the Great North Road" (typescript, 1970, Rhodes House, Oxford, RH MSS Afr. r. 112), 27–28. A year later, he was appointed to the Russell Commission without incident or accusations that survive, but he developed a healthy respect for the relationship between invasive medical procedures and banyama accusations. In 1944, he warned a British parasitologist about his research on the Copperbelt as "the dangers that such tests might be misunderstood is obvious" (H. F. Cartmel-Robinson, acting chief secretary, to provincial commissioner, Western Province, 20 May 1944, NAZ, SEC1/1072, Survey of Helminthic Diseases). S. R. Denny was the editor of *Mutende* who commissioned P. K. Kanosa's "Banyama—Copper Belt Myth Terrifies the Foolish," the essay about the foolishness of banyama quoted earlier in this chapter.

speechlessness because he and speechlessness were associated with Belgian rule. The Italian priest who was considered a banyama who did not cross the Luapula had no such associations. I return to these issues at the end of this chapter, but for now my point is that while parts of stories cross borders, they do not do so as storytelling idioms. Whatever their narrative strengths and appeals, they do not survive in local storytelling unless they reflect local thinking and local experiences.

WORK AND TALK

My question is simple: what is the relationship between the jobs men do and the stories they tell about them? The answer, however, may be complicated: I have no oral material that I collected so as to let Africans reconstruct their workplaces of the past, no "voices." But even with voices, with Africans "speaking for themselves," what kind of picture would I have? The idea that a pure voice can be distilled and disembedded from the struggles of colonial experiences is itself problematic. It argues that colonial African language and thought and imagination were not sullied by the categories and constructs of the oppressors. A clear, pure African voice may be an impractical vehicle for the ambiguities that rested in the relation between underground work and the drinking of African blood. Had I, or anyone else in the 1990s, interviewed African miners about banyama in the 1930s, would the interviews be shaped by the increased control and the intensified supervision of the post-1935 Copperbelt? The complexities and contradictions of a past workplace might best be reconstructed from sources officials did not take seriously, stories considered the domain of "ignorant natives," stories that were in fact handed over to Africans like P. K. Kanosa to debunk.

Let me return to the story Kanosa heard at Luanshya in 1935. Who are these men with licenses and tubes of drugs that can steal another man's mind? I suggest that this is a discussion (as opposed to a description) of the relations of production at Roan Antelope Mine at Luanshya. At Roan Antelope, there were far more flat, scraping stopes than at other mines, and these stopes required more semi-skilled hoist drivers than other mines. More important, because of these flat stopes Roan Antelope required more underground blasting, and therefore more mineworkers with blasting licenses than any other mine in the 1930s. Indeed, in 1934, 34 percent of the underground workforce at Roan Antelope was classified as skilled.[30] At Roan Antelope and Nkana mines, Africans were required to take a training course to get blasting licenses, and 112 obtained licenses by examination in 1934.[31] At Roan Antelope, such a high percentage of skilled workers must have decreased the level of supervision underground, an ideal version of which was set at Nkana at 1 white miner:1 boss boy:16 underground workers.[32]

But what of the term *mupila* and its place in mine labor in Central Africa? *Mupila* is a word for rubber, ball, or football that probably entered Central African languages from Portuguese or possibly French. In the languages of colonial industrialization, Shaba Swahili and Town Bemba, *mupila* came to refer to the qualities of expansion, a quality stressed in usage more than anything to do with resilience. Thus, while throughout the region *kapila* means ball, in northeastern Zambia the same term can be used for the mechanism that inflates balls. On the Copperbelt, *kapila* can refer to miners' boots; in Shaba Swahili, it can mean a pullover sweater. What then do we make of an early 1930s gloss of *mupila* as a white tube of drugs?[33] The use of *pila* means this cannot refer to tablets of medication, whatever their size or shape. It is conceivable that it refers to a syringe, the contents of which do not expand but contract, although no Bemba-speaker I asked had ever heard this usage. More likely, the meaning of *mupila* as a tube of drugs rests on another translation, that of drugs: it probably glosses the Bemba *umuti*, meaning medications or drugs in the sense of any substance taken internally or applied externally for healing purposes. It can thus include bandages—such as those in the salutation of the letter to the monsignor of Chilubula—and splints and poultices. Tubes filled with drugs may well gloss rolls of bandages, which were white and which expanded, the stan-

30. Perrings, *Black Mineworkers*, 111–12.

31. Sidney Bray, assistant inspector of mines, *Evidence,* Russell Commission, 810. He was like many others derisive of the skills of white miners, whom he compared unfavorably to the Africans on the training course. White miners were licensed when they showed they had worked on other mines. Brian Goodwin, a miners' union activist, said it was government policy to allow Africans to sit for blasting licenses in the late 1930s (interview with Jane Parpart, Lusaka, 28 June 1976).

32. E. A. G. Robinson, "The Economic Problem," in J. Merle Davis, ed., *Modern Industry and the African* (London: Macmillan, 1933), 131–226, at 164.

33. On the Copperbelt, Town Bemba included rapidly evolving and often short-lived slang words and temporary meanings; see Mubanga E. Kashoki, "Town Bemba: A Sketch of Its Main Structure," *African Social Research* 13 (1972): 176–83; A. L. Epstein, "Linguistic Innovation and Culture on the Copperbelt," *Southwestern Journal of Anthropology* 15 (1959): 235–53.

dard first aid equipment carried by boss boys throughout the region. Indeed, the possession of bandages identified an African miner under-ground as the boss boy.[34] Men enthralled by mupila may have been cap-tured by boss boys at the very time that blasting licenses fixed the hier-archies of underground work teams. Where most underground mine labor was unskilled, boss boys maintained their position by continually negotiating coercion and consensus. Starting in the mid 1930s, however, blasting licenses may have given them a degree of permanence they otherwise would not have had.

But if the banyama who capture men have many of the attributes of boss boys, what are they doing above ground, and why must they snatch a man's mind to get him to follow them? Such a story seems to have been specific to the Copperbelt. It had little in common with other 1930s ver-sions reported in rural Northern Rhodesia.[35] But an earlier version of Copperbelt banyama stories told of European banyama. "In 1930 thou-sands of Africans . . . left the Copper-belt and fled home to their villages because they believed that white men were going into the compounds and capturing Africans. The method used was to strike an African with a stick of rubber—mupila—which paralysed him, and then throw him into a lorry and drive him off," Thomas Fox-Pitt recalled.[36] The changes between 1930 and 1934 and 1935 might not have had anything to do with the extractive power of mupila or even the uses to which they were put; it had to do with the race of supervisory personnel and skilled la-bor in the copper mines that operated in Northern Rhodesia during the Depression.

In copper mining, the Depression years were 1929 to 1936, with cop-per prices starting to fall in mid 1930 and hitting bottom in 1932. But

34. T. Dunbar Moodie and Vivienne Ndatshe, *Going for Gold: Men, Mines, and Mi-gration* (Berkeley and Los Angeles: University of California Press, 1994), 61–73. Accord-ing to a man describing underground conditions in the 1940s, "If you started as a lasher, you lashed until you finished your contract—unless you assaulted the boss boy and took all those first aid badges and put them on yourself and said 'Hey, lash'" (66–67).

35. See Musambachime, "Impact of Rumor"; Luise White, "Vampire Priests of Cen-tral Africa: African Debates about Labor and Religion in Colonial Northern Zambia," *Comp. Stud. Soc. and Hist.* 35, 4 (1933): 744–70, and "Tsetse Visions: Narratives of Blood and Bugs in Colonial Northern Rhodesia, 1931–39," *J. Afr. History* 36 (1995): 219–45.

36. Thomas Fox-Pitt, "Cannibalism and Christianity" (MS, 1953, Thomas Fox-Pitt Papers, Correspondence, 1952–53, MS 6/5, School of Oriental and African Studies Li-brary, University of London). Fox-Pitt had not been on the Copperbelt in 1930 and re-ported the official understanding of this panic: "[I]t was thought by the authorities that this scare originated from the visits of a feeble minded European youth to the compounds where he frightened women by sticking them with a blind worm."

throughout the 1930s, there were substantial improvements in underground conditions, so that in many mines the conditions in which men worked improved and remuneration for skilled labor increased. As late as 1930, the proportion of skilled workers on both sides of the border was high; at the Roan Antelope Mine, the percentage of labor classified as skilled more than doubled in 1931. This meant that even though starting wages were reduced in most of the mines in the region, skilled wages remained high enough that the average wage bill per shift increased. In Northern Rhodesia, the increase in skilled labor coincided with an improvement in underground efficiency, so that there was a reduction in accidents and mortality, while—as would seem probable during the Depression—turnover was at an all-time low, with workers staying on the job for about sixteen months.[37] By 1935, an underground worker engaged at 22/- could, with overtime and bonuses, earn almost 40/- a month.[38]

But was the man working overtime the same man engaged at 22/-? Did more than one man work on the same ticket and share the month's earnings?[39] Copperbelt workers testifying before the Russell Commission spoke of unemployed Africans living in the compound, men on whom some were eager to blame the 1935 strike. Did these men work a few shifts each month in exchange for accommodation or a portion of a wage? There is probably not enough evidence available to answer this question, but it does provide an additional context for the banyama who could make a man forget his own name. This might refer to the name under which a man worked a few shifts a month.[40] But the man made to forget his name may have been a fleeting trope from Katanga, a part

---

37. Perrings, *Black Mineworkers*, 106 ff.

38. *Evidence*, Russell Commission, passim.

39. Laborers sharing tickets, working alternate days, or changing jobs within a mine under a new name were common problems for mine management in colonial Africa; see Jeff Crisp, "Productivity and Protest: Scientific Management in the Ghanaian Gold Mines, 1947–1956," in Frederick Cooper, ed., *Struggle for the City: Migrant Labor, Capital, and the State in Urban Africa* (Beverly Hills, Calif.: Sage, 1983), 91–129.

40. African names did worry officials in Northern Rhodesia. In 1939, the district officer of Luwingu complained about "the native propensity to call himself by any name he thinks his employer may be able to pronounce." Worse still, African workers called themselves by the name of whatever ancestor they wanted to appease, so it was often impossible to tell from names when family members were related (C. H. Rawstorne, tour report 1/1939, NAZ, SEC2804, Luwingu Tour Reports, 1933–39). Patrick Harris, *Work, Culture, Identity: Migrant Laborers in Mozambique and South Africa, c. 1860–1910* (Portsmouth, N.H.: Heinemann, 1994), 59–60, argues that, like their names at home, the names Africans gave themselves in the workplace had to do with individual identities and affiliations.

of the story best understood by men who had spent some time working in and around Elisabethville. Men with the same name—or even men who chose to be called the same name—claimed a name relationship, a practice that in urban Katanga developed into a bond that was often considered stronger than kinship.[41] There is no reason to have an either/ or interpretation of part of a story about banyama, of course. What is important is to note how part of a story might have different and overlapping meanings to different men, depending on where they had worked.

In Katanga, UMHK's African workforce increased dramatically during the Depression years. In general, each mine had a large core of semi-skilled or skilled workers on contracts supplemented by the number of short-term unskilled employees production processes required. At the same time, the 1920s policy of replacing white skilled labor with black skilled labor was reversed, and the policies of migrancy were applied to white workers. In an attempt to lower skilled wages overall and to take advantage of the decreased mechanization of 1930s mining, a great number of white workers were laid off between 1929 and 1933. But it was usually local white workers who were let go—thus saving UMHK the family wages these men required—and white contract workers from Brussels or London were hired, the cost of whose repatriation was to raise the wage bill per shift.[42] In 1932, more than 80 percent of UMHK's African workforce were on three-year contracts. This percentage declined throughout the 1930s. By 1936, contract laborers were graded according to qualities that had little to do with skills. Each laborer was evaluated on a point system according to personal qualities such as intelligence, dexterity, endurance, and education and according to the re-

41. Fabian, *History from Below*, 154.
42. Perrings, *Black Mineworkers*, 104. Margery Perham's reading of this bungled corporate policy inscribes it with the hope of industrialization and the pride of craftsmanship. She writes of visiting a training workshop in Panda:

I could not help comparing . . . what I had seen of technical instruction in South Africa where the missions try to run workshops to instruct the boys. There is in all of them an atmosphere of unreality, a lack of vitality, because there is no certainty that the boys will be able to continue that work but every certainty that they will never be able to go very far with it. But here I saw genuine apprenticeship, with no limitations upon the native but those inherent in himself. . . . The reason is quite simple. . . . There is no permanent white working class to feel themselves being ousted. The white workmen are imported from Belgium and go back to Belgium.   (*African Apprenticeship*, 223)

In 1955 however the newspaper in Lualabourg complained that the Congo had produced neither a black middle class nor black artisans; see Crawford Young, *Politics in the Congo: Decolonization and Independence* (Madison: University of Wisconsin Press, 1965), 44.

quirements of the job, its hazards, the training it required, and how many others wanted that job. A wage scale was devised according to the personal qualities with which a worker performed his job. Thus, an "indifferent" surface worker with a rating of four on the scale and three years' experience would earn a quarter of what a "very good" worker in the same job with a rating of fourteen on the scale and many more years' experience would. A man stripped of his labor classification could be transferred to an unskilled job in another mine or factory.[43] This rating system disrupted all the fluidity and all the violence by which men advanced through the ranks of mining workforces elsewhere. Not only did it put African advancement more firmly under European control, it undermined stabilization and the camaraderie of a skilled workforce.[44]

Although the number of UMHK workers on long-term contracts decreased slightly during the Depression, the company's involvement in the private lives of those workers increased dramatically. In 1931, UMHK executives asked Dom Grégoire to organize leisure-time activities for their workers who lived in the camp, UMHK's compound: "It would be quite dangerous if this time were to be organized by Africans themselves, but it is likely that organized activities within the camp will be more successful if there is an intermediary between UMHK and the Africans." Dom Grégoire was only too eager to be that intermediary, and within a few years he had introduced scouting, TB clinics, and camp schools that banned the children of Protestant and customary unions.[45]

43. John Higginson, *A Working Class in the Making: Belgian Colonial Labor Policy, Private Enterprise, and the African Mineworker, 1907–1951* (Madison: University of Wisconsin Press, 1989), 130–45, 257; Perrings, *Black Mineworkers*, 123–26. Fetter reports another consumption story about how specialized status—the status that carried supervisory status, better wages, and better housing—was allocated. This was done by the European camp manager. There was "no single set of qualifications . . . established for this position. Thus [a] would-be MOI/S had to find some way of ingratiating himself with his white headmen. Some tried fawning servility while others resorted to black magic. One popular technique was to throw a ritually slaughtered chicken at the white chief's house. Given the social distance between the personnel department and the African miners, this method was as effective an influence as any other, particularly if the white man could find out which African wanted the job badly enough to sacrifice a Sunday dinner!" (*Elisabethville*, 148–49).

44. See Moodie and Ndatshe, *Going for Gold*, passim, and Jeff Guy, "Technology, Ethnicity, and Ideology: Basotho Miners and Shaft Sinking on the South African Gold Mines," *J. Southern Afr. Studies* 14, 2 (1988): 254–70.

45. Dom Grégoire Coussement, letters to his mother, 26 July 1931; to Mgsr. G. C. de Hemptinne, 20 July 1931 and 19 July 1932; to the Foyer social indigène, Elisabethville, 19 October 1935 (Archives, Saint Andreas Abbey, Bruges). Johannes Fabian has suggested that the transformation of African miners in TB hospitals may have been a point of origin for rumors about Africans being fattened (personal communication, 22 March 1992).

Catholic missions, urban and rural, began to medicalize African childbirth as early as the 1920s. Bottle-feeding regimes to shorten birth spacing and thus end polygyny were introduced in UMHK camps in the early
1930s, supported by Dom Grégoire and coerced by Leopold Mottoulle
of the UMHK. The company policy of paying bridewealth in some regions for some workers began in the 1920s as well.[46] It is not possible
to prove that these embodied interventions were translated into batumbula accusations—nor do I think it is necessary to my argument—but
both Catholic priests and white mine supervisors were accused of being batumbula.[47] In several oral batumbula accounts, people describe
embodied sensations—inebriation, full stomachs, full bladders—along
with cheerful recollections of Thursday vaccinations or mine dancing,
while they describe white supervisors eating Africans. A woman complained that men who lived in the camp often went to the Cité—the African settlement outside the camp, and the control of UMHK—to drink
and returned drunk and violent. "One group of batumbula would beat
men up when they found them drunk at night. These men would lead
these men to the house where white men ate human flesh. They never
managed to eat all the flesh so they saved the rest in tins, like corned
beef," said Thérèse Mwadi.[48] According to Kasongo Ngoiy, bodily discipline could protect Africans from batumbula. "People did not go out
at night, at least not after 9 o'clock. If you wanted to go to the W.C.,
you would have to take every precaution to go to the W.C. before that
hour. Whoever dared to go out after 9 o'clock was at the mercy of
batumbula." [49]

And then there is the story of Kanka Jean, the "official leader" of
a pick-and-shovel team at Kolwezi, who disappeared just as UMHK began to dismantle the ticket system early in 1943. His team had been
evaluated by a time-and-motion expert, and he disappeared the night

46. Nancy Rose Hunt, "Negotiated Colonialism: Domesticity, Hygiene, and Birth
Work in the Belgian Congo" (Ph.D. diss., University of Wisconsin–Madison, 1992, 65–
66); id., "'Le bébé en brousse': European Women, African Birth Spacing, and Colonial
Intervention in Breast Feeding in the Belgian Congo," Int. J. Afr. Hist. Studies 21 (1988),
401–32; Fetter, Creation of Elisabethville, 145–46.
47. Ceyssens, "Mutumbula," passim; Dom Grégoire Coussement to Abbot Jean-
Baptiste Neve, Saint Andreas, 10 June 1932.
48. Thérèse Mwadi, Katuba, Lubumbashi, 31 March 1991. This is one of four interviews collected for Bogumil Jewsiewicki in Lubumbashi in 1991 that mention batumbula,
which he graciously gave to me. I only have the sections referring to batumbula, and I
know little about the speakers' personal histories, but it is not clear how much, if at all,
my analysis would change if I knew that one speaker had come to Katanga in 1938, for
example, or whether another had been married twice before she came to live in the camp.
49. Kasongo Ngoiy, Cité Gécamines, 9 January 1991.

before his team was scheduled to compete with a mechanical shovel driver. His fellows refused to believe that he had gone home because of marital problems, as they were told; they went to the compound manager's home to insist that Jean had been taken by batumbula and demand his release.[50] Although John Higginson argues that this incident revisited the issues of the 1941 strike, I suggest something more mundane: Kanka Jean was a boss boy, a man whose considerable authority would vanish if the ticket system was replaced by mechanical tools. Although work stoppages and threats thereof were common in batumbula stories in 1940s Katanga, this disappearance may not be of one man only but of a way of organizing labor and extraction underground. According to Kasongo Ngoiy in the 1940s, "Things changed a little when workers got together and demanded that the compound manager help them find their kidnapped brothers."[51] Without a ticket system, the rankings of semi-skilled workers became infused with new meanings. Moreover, these rankings were temporary and not based on seniority. The new manpower regulations that replaced the ticket system favored some men, but such favoritism had only temporary advantages. Some men were treated well, but they were firmly under European control, described in terms of imprisonment and migrancy. "The captives of batumbula did not eat maize meal. They drank sugar water or they ate sugar cane. The captives who were favored this way became fat and hairy, and were taken to the Hotel Biano, where they were killed and eaten. When there were enough captives, one group was transported to Belgium and another to America."[52]

MIGRANCY, STABILIZATION, AND CLOTHES

This section addresses the differences between the jigsaw and the hologram, the history reconstructed from many different pieces and the history reconstructed from one piece illuminated over and over again. Through banyama and batumbula stories, it reexamines workers' strategies on both copperbelts to problematize some of the ways in which historians have dealt with stabilization and migrancy. The batumbula accounts from the early 1940s preface the strikes of 1941 and 1944 and thus provide a point of comparison with the Northern Rhodesian Cop-

---

50. Higginson, "Steam without a Piston Box," 101–2.
51. Kasongo Ngoiy, Cité Gécamines, 9 January 1991.
52. Joseph Kabila Kiomba Alona, Lubumbashi, 28 March 1991.

perbelt in which the vampire stories of the early 1930s are read through the details provided by missionary writings, the literature of urban anthropology, and the commission of inquiry into the 1935 strike.

In recent years there has been much debate about the nature of migration to and on the Northern Rhodesian—and, indeed, the Zambian—Copperbelt.[53] Despite a colonial and developmentalist description of rural Northern Rhodesia as a classic labor reserve, forty years of scholarship have shown that migrants to the mines of the Copperbelt tended to migrate from mine to mine, or from job to job on the Copperbelt, rather than alternate periods of work with long periods not working at home. I want to shift the terms of this debate somewhat and look at migrancy in and out of Northern Rhodesia in the 1930s and stabilization in the Belgian Congo, not to establish which copper regime was truly migrant and which was truly stabilized, but to examine the reasons why one or the other might have provided workers with a reliable accumulation strategy in the Depression. My argument is that both migrancy and stabilization were employers' categories that when taken up by historians have tended to obscure the various strategies by which workers enhanced the value of their wages. For example, the clothing issued to African workers was not simply symbolic or "smart." Clothing was part of the wage, easily converted to cash or goods valued in and of themselves, and I want to suggest that the wages Africans sought—either as migrants or long-term workers with a family presence—can best be understood in terms of the commodities embedded in those wages.

The wages paid to African miners on the Northern Rhodesian Copperbelt during the Depression are by no means a straightforward issue. Indeed, after recording 800 pages of testimony, the Russell Commission could not decide whether miners had gone on strike in 1935 for higher wages or to protest a tax increase. This was not because workers and mine owners did not know which was which, but because they could not tell which caused the greater hardship. More to the point, "wage" was a pervious category, covering not only the money paid to workers as their regular stipend but bonuses, deductions, tickets, commodities, and clothing. During the Depression, at the latest, Africans in Northern Rhodesia had begun to problematize money both as a medium of exchange and as a token of political authority. As copper mines closed in 1932, there was a shortage of money in the colony, along with wide-

53. See, e.g., Ferguson, "Mobile Workers, Modernist Narratives."

spread rumors that unemployed miners had been promised exemptions for their 1932 taxes.[54] In the Isoka District, returning miners told the district officer that they could not work in Tanganyika Territory "because the white ants had eaten all the money."[55] But on the Copperbelt there were rumors of devalued English coins and the king of England being jailed for taxing his subjects too heavily.[56] The next year, there were rumors of an end to British rule, government by black Americans—bringing American currency with them—and, as South African silver coins were withdrawn from circulation, at least one rural administrative headquarters was said to be closed.[57] Tickets, on the other hand, were things that muddled ideas about time and about money in both Northern Rhodesia and the Congo. Tickets were the method by which the length of service by African laborers was measured: a ticket was a booklet containing thirty slips of paper, each representing a shift, not a day. Wages were paid when each slip or ticket in the booklet had been signed by the ganger in charge; "a contract worked out in months was in practice worked out in tickets," Charles Perrings notes. Margery Perham, admiring the torn-off tickets workers' placed on nails in the Congolese mine office each day, wrote: "At the end of six months the whole book goes on. Then there are a whole series of other labels . . . a blue one for bad work and so a reduction in pay; a yellow one for absence in hospital; a green one for prison, etc. It is possible by looking at a man's nail to see his whole industrial history." As late as the 1960s, Africans in Elisabethville saw these tickets as synonymous with time: they worked for UMHK for "6 or 10 tickets" before returning home.[58] In the 1930s,

54. H. A. Watmore, tour reports, 3/1932 (NAZ, SEC2/835, Tour Reports, Mpika District, 1931–33); see also Keith Hart, "Heads or Tails? Two Sides of the Coin," *Man*, n.s., 21 (1986): 637–56.

55. J. W. Sharratt-Horne, district commissioner, tour report, 6/1932 (NAZ, SEC2/767, Isoka Tour Reports, 1932–33). White ants do eat paper money; see Sharon Hutchinson, "The Cattle of Money and the Cattle of Girls among the Nuer, 1930–1983," *American Ethnologist* 19, 2 (1992): 294–316. Africans worried that the new paper notes would be food for insects, while officials worried about what would happen to the hygiene of paper money carried on African bodies; see Keith Breckenridge, "'Money with Dignity': Migrants, Minelords, and the Cultural Politics of the South African Gold Standard Crisis, 1920–33," *J. Afr. Hist.* 36 (1995): 271–304.

56. Société des Missionnaires d'Afrique, Rome, Diaire de Chilubula, 10, 14, and 24 February 1932.

57. Musambachime, "Impact of Rumor," 204; Annual Report on Native Affairs, Chinsali District, 1935 (NAZ, SEC2/1298, Annual Report on Native Affairs, 1935–37); Shepperson, *Myth and Reality*, 7–15, passim; see also Breckenridge, "'Money with Dignity.'"

58. Perrings, *Black Mineworkers*, xvii; Perham, *African Apprenticeship*, 217–18; Fabian, *History from Below*, 121, 156.

many mines in Northern Rhodesia paid a bonus to Africans who completed their ticket books in a month, and Nkana Mine paid a bonus of 2/6 for every six months' continuous work.[59]

On both copperbelts, commodities, especially clothes, were the subject of uneasy negotiation. Whether boots, leggings, and hard hats were issued free or charged for, they seem to have been regarded quite differently by managers and African workers, for whom they seem to have constituted part of the wage. Certainly, they were converted to cash as often as they were used. In Elisabethville in 1930, Margery Perham heard of a Belgian businessman ruined by the liberal regulations of the Congo. He had provided each of his African workers with a blanket of good quality as required by law. The workers promptly sold them, and when the inspector came, the businessman received a heavy fine for not providing his workers with blankets.[60] In Northern Rhodesia, however, which items of clothing were free and which were deducted from wages, and from which kind of wages, varied from mine to mine. According to the Russell Commission, at Nkana Mine, where well over 80 percent of the workforce earned under 30/- for thirty days' work, there was no bonus, but one hard hat, one blanket, and one pair of boots were issued free. After that, the cost of these items was deducted from wages. Two candles per shift were issued free to underground workers in the early 1930s, but the uses to which they were put and Nkana's solutions to free issues and deductions reveals the extent to which Africans sought to make homes under the conditions their employers called "migrant." Africans tended not to use their candles underground, saving them to light their rooms at night. Enforcing candle use proved difficult, and in 1932, Africans asked if they could have lamps, offering to buy them. "The same light that is supplied to Europeans" was deducted from African wages at 8/6, "voluntarily, for the reason that they have not only got good light underground but can also use them at their houses at night."[61]

At Mufulira, most of the workforce was unskilled and worked above ground in construction. Ninety-five percent of Africans earned under 30/- for thirty shifts, and one hard hat and one waterproof coat were

59. George Wellington Rex Lange, safety officer, Nkana Mine, 20 August 1935 (Russell Commission, *Evidence,* 494).

60. Perham, *African Apprenticeship,* 224.

61. George Wellington Rex Lange, safety officer, Nkana Mine (Russell Commission, *Evidence,* 496).

issued free; boots were compulsory, but miners were charged 10/- for a pair (the Commission noted that they cost Mufulira Mine 15/9) and lamps could be purchased for 8/-. The cost of these items was deducted from thirty days' pay at the rate of no more than 10/-. At Roan Antelope Mine, the system was almost arcane. Just over half the African workforce earned under 30/- per thirty shifts, and 85 percent earned under 40/- per thirty shifts; all workers were issued hard hats free, but they were charged 20/- for boots, 13/- for coats, and 2/6 for leggings. Lamps could be purchased for 7/9. Workers received a bonus of 11/3 for working thirty days, from which the cost of clothing was deducted at the rate of no more than 11/3 per thirty days.[62] Workers could recoup the cost of boots, leggings, and hard hats by thirty days of work for wages. African workers did not necessarily think of this bonus the way their employers did, however. In 1936, miners complained to the visiting Ngoni paramount chief that they were charged for their first issue of clothing.[63] It seemed that African workers considered sequential issues of clothing to be part of their wages. By 1935, Nkana's safety officers ruefully noted that the boots issued African miners were almost at once sent home or sold. The second pair was deducted from their pay.[64] These deductions—20/ for boots and 8/- for lamps at Nkana—were contested; a mineworker from Mufulira said this was a bigger problem than taxes, and the compound manager from Roan Antelope said that Africans frequently said they would prefer the money.[65] But at Roan Antelope Mine, many men seemed to have stayed on the job for the commodities provided there. When output restrictions decreased production at Roan Antelope by one-third in early 1935 and retrenchments threatened semiskilled African workers, desertions were at an all-time low.[66] But what about men who worked short periods at different mines, each time getting a new pair of boots? What about the man who had worked at two mines in eleven years, and then, during the Depression, worked at Mu-

62. Russell Commission, *Report*, 34–37. In these pages, "thirty shifts," "a month," and "a ticket" are used interchangeably.

63. 53. Michael O'Shea, *Missionaries and Miners: A History of the Beginings of the Catholic Church in Zambia with Particular Reference to the Copperbelt* (Ndola: Mission Press, 1986), 255–56.

64. George Wellington Rex Lange, safety officer, Nkana Mine (Russell Commission, *Evidence*, 494–97).

65. James Mutali, Mufulira; Frank Ashton Ayer, Luanshya (Russell Commission, *Evidence*, passim). Ayer did point out that "naturally what everybody would like to have is the money and the clothing too. This is not confined to natives" (711).

66. Perrings, "Consciousness, Conflict, and Proletarianization," 46–47.

292   Part Three

fulira for eight months, then went back to Nchanga for five months, then to Bwana Mkubwa for six months, and then back to Nchanga?[67] Were such migrations within the Copperbelt—the source of academic debates about how stabilized the Copperbelt actually was—to do with wages, retrenchment, or the opportunities of a free issue of boots and candles?

Different mines' amalgamation of free issues, compulsory clothing, and wage labor muddle any apparent difference between the three categories on the Northern Rhodesian Copperbelt. From the evidence of banyama stories, it would seem that these policies naturalized clothing, making it much more a part of African bodies than compulsory dress underground. Thus, in 1931, the Copperbelt rumor was that banyama had white balls, called *mupila,* "and the balls were thrown into the path of the victim, and as the victim came up the banyama spoke to him. If he answered then all his power left him, his clothes fell off, and he no longer had any memory or will."[68] Clothing was not a free issue or a compulsory purchase; it was part of a person, like will or speech or potency, that could be stripped away by the dreadful power of the boss boy. This suggests that commodities do not become commoditized when the waged context in which they are acquired blurs the line between money and commodity.

With substantially less secondary evidence, African ideas about clothing in Katanga can be read in batumbula stories. Vampire stories from elsewhere in East Africa are less concerned with clothing, whether that of the victims or the abductors. At least one Ugandan said it was impossible to say what the bazimamoto were wearing, because they did their work at night. Others said they wore black, or white coats and black trousers. Clothing figures frequently in twentieth-century industrial urban legends and rumors, however. Folklorists have written extensively about the stories of snakes found in the sleeves of department-store coats, of young women abducted from dress shops in France, and of racist slogans sewn into the linings of jackets sold to American youths.[69] All of these are stories about clothing or consumption rather

---

67. Parpart, *Labor and Capital,* 66; see also Russell Commission, *Evidence,* passim.
68. Kanosa, "Banyama—Copper Belt Myth Terrifies the Foolish."
69. See, e.g., Edgar Morin, *Rumor in Orleans,* trans. Peter Green (New York: Random House, 1971); Frederick Koenig, *Rumor in the Marketplace: The Social Psychology of Commercial Hearsay* (Dover, Mass.: Auburn House, 1985), passim; Jean-Noël Kapferer, *Rumors: Uses, Interpretations, and Images,* trans. Bruce Fink (New Brunswick, N.J.: Transaction Publishers, 1990), passim; Gary Alan Fine, *Manufacturing Tales: Sex and Money in Contemporary Legends* (Knoxville: University of Tennessee Press, 1992), 141–

than stories in which something happens to clothing. These narratives animate clothing with relationships, dangers, and risks. They valorize and criticize commodity fetishism with stories of clothing's hidden affiliations. The clothing described below has no such hidden meanings; the relations of production and reproduction are present in it and in what happens to it. The clothing in the batumbula stories below does not depict fetishized commodities that conceal the relations of production; on the contrary, it depicts the processes of wage labor, leisure, and capture. According to the artist Tshibumba, batumbula "wore long black coats and miners hats with lamps"; when they caught someone they took his clothes.[70] A former mineworker recalled that in the 1940s, batumbula "wore hats so they could not be recognized."[71] In Leopoldville in 1960, Africans spoke of *muntu wa mudele,* "the men with the lamp," Europeans who captured Africans and ate them.[72] Again, in the 1960s, batumbula in Katanga were said to wear dirty, slovenly clothes,[73] a wary comment on stabilization and independence. Indeed, if Northern Rhodesian migrancy allowed for several pairs of boots and hats—and the money obtained from reselling them or the loyalties accrued from sending them home—stabilization seems to have left Congolese workers feeling naked and vulnerable, their hats, lamps, and uniforms turned against ordinary miners. Recalling how batumbula captured people in Elisabethville in the 1940s, men and women interviewed in 1991 said "they undressed them and tossed their clothes far away from the place of capture. When people found these clothes the next morning, they knew batumbula had captured someone."[74] "When batumbula kidnap people, they do not come back to pick up the traces. You see clothes thrown on the road," Kasongo Ngoiy claimed.[75]

Why were clothes thrown out on the road such a powerful image that they informed popular paintings and were talked about fifty years later? Karen Hansen has noted that there was a trade in second-hand

---

88; Patricia A. Turner, *I Heard It through the Grapevine: Rumor in African-American Culture* (Berkeley and Los Angeles: University of California Press, 1993), 108–36, 165–79.

70. Fabian, *Remembering,* 49–50.

71. Kasongo Ngoiy, Cité Gécamines, 9 January 1991.

72. M. d'Hertefelt, in discussion of William Friedland, "Some Urban Myths of East Africa," in Allie Dubb, ed., "Myth in Modern Africa" (Proceedings of the 14th Conference of the Rhodes-Livingstone Institute for Social Research, mimeographed, Lusaka, 1960), 146.

73. Ceyssens, "Mutumbula," 489.

74. Moukadi Louis, Katuba III, Lubumbashi, 30 January 1991.

75. Kasongo Ngoiy, Cité Gécamines, 9 January 1991.

clothes from the Belgian Congo to Northern Rhodesia beginning in the 1920s.[76] The existence of such a trade would have made stories of abandoned mounds of clothing all the more chilling, and make the purchasers of such garments seem cynical and monstrous. At the same time there seems to have been a demand for luxury clothing. As early as 1929, White Fathers complained that villages in Northern Rhodesia nearest Katanga had emptied as men sought clothing: "The fashion is hats and white shorts, shoes and stockings." [77] In Elisabethville itself, men needed dress suits for *malinga*—ballroom—dancing. In the domestic workers' history of Elisabethville, written in 1965, men recalled that even in the midst of the Depression, when "everyone suffered a lot from hunger. . . . The big thing was to go to the malinga dance." When a man had work, his friends came to his place "to eat and to clothe themselves." [78] The layers of relationships and layers of clothing may have had a straightforward meaning in the regional economy of both copperbelts, however. A man who had lived in Elisabethville for many years recalled that in shops, clothing was purchased in sterling.[79] Ready-made clothing may have been more than a scarce commodity; it may only have been available to the few who with access to the currencies of British colonies. But what about the clothes available to Congolese workers? Well into the 1960s, domestic servants complained of Belgians' unwillingness to allow Africans to wear shoes on the job.[80] For miners, the clothing issued in the late 1930s and early 1940s was thought by miners to be insufficient for the work required of them. By 1940, underground and factory workers complained bitterly that they were not issued shoes, jackets, or shirts that were sturdy enough to protect them from serious injury. Furnacemen demanded heavy woolen shirts to protect them from burns from flying ash. In November 1941, a few weeks before the first of many wartime strikes, a company official complained that African peddlers, selling mainly clothing, invaded the camps every payday. In strike-torn war years, commodities became disaggregated from miners' wages. John

76. Karen Tranberg Hansen, "Dealing with Used Clothing: *Salaula* and the Construction of Identity in Zambia's Third Republic," *Public Culture* 6 (1994): 503–22, and "Transnational Biographies and Local Meanings: Used Clothing Practices in Lusaka," *J. Southern Afr. Studies* 21, 1 (1995): 131–45.

77. Quoted in O'Shea, *Missionaries*, 272.

78. Fabian, *History from Below*, 107.

79. Mumba Nedi, interviewed in 1966, in Bruce Fetter, field notes, Memorial Library, University of Wisconsin–Madison.

80. Fabian, *History from Below*, passim.

Higginson has noted that the connection between the workers and the peddlers, with its inevitable relations of credit, informality, and multiple currencies, was strengthened by the weakness of the company's relationship to its workers.[81] Africans, however, demanded a return to the bundling of clothing, wages, and stabilization. On 4 December 1941, when wives joined strikers at the central workshop at Panda, they demanded that the company reinstate the incentives it had formerly given women to remain in the camps, mainly sewing machines and cloth.[82]

In the three tense years between the strikes of 1941 and 1944, a number of batumbula accusations terrified European personnel in UMHK camps. But the African men armed with machetes who surrounded the houses of mine supervisors and compound managers did not demand a return of their clothing, but of their wives. Their grievances stemmed from the tensions of a family presence. In January and February 1943 — around the time of Kanka Jean's disappearance — European supervisors and camp directors were threatened. In the camp at Sofwe, men armed with axes and machetes surrounded the manager's house shouting, "You have eaten the woman, you took her by force." [83] In other camps, Europeans required police protection when workers attacked their houses, accusing them of eating missing women.[84] The director of Mwale camp was trapped in his house by workers shouting, "You have taken the wife of our brother, you are not looking for her, but we will finish the whites. You, you think you are allowed to eat this woman? . . . whites will not eat sugar after tomorrow, Monsieur Donnay is finished, he is batumbula, a lion of Europe." [85] Tensions around clothing, embedded in other versions of these stories, were part of the nervous relations around matrimony, property, and the place of UMHK in allocating them. Even the most cautionary tales had clothing in them. Joseph Kabila Kiomba

81. Higginson, *Working Class,* 182–83.

82. Ibid., 189.

83. Donnay, "Note pour Monsieur Deforny, directeur des mines, incidents Sofwe–Mwale, 17 février 1943" (Archives du personnel, Gécamines, Lubumbashi).The threatening African UMHK workers at Sofwe and Mwale used *tu* for "you." For the language used between white managers and African workers, see Higginson, "Steam without a Piston Box." Copies of the memoranda cited in nn. 83, 84, and 85 here were kindly supplied to me by Dr. T. K. Biaya.

84. E. Toussaint, directeur MOI, "Note pour directeur generale, incidents à Mwale, février 1943" (Archives du personnel, Gécamines, Lubumbashi).

85. S. Schammo, Sofwe camp, "Note pour Monsieur Toussaint, directeur department MOI: Rapport sûr événements survenus au camp Mwale la 14/2/43" (Archives du personnel, Gécamines, Lubumbashi).

Alona recalled "that in many arguments between husband and wife, wives are in the habit of packing a suitcase and returning to their parents' home. For batumbula this was an opportunity to capture women who abandoned their husbands late at night."[86]

STORIES AND MIGRANTS

Many of the qualities of batumbula stories appeared in accounts of banyama in the late 1940s in eastern Northern Rhodesia, on the border with colonial Nyasaland. These were, according to the young researcher John Barnes, "people (i.e., Africans) who are employed by Europeans to capture people . . . by touching the captive with a wand, which made the captive invisible and helpless." Sometimes they used a lorry at night: "All the children from the villages run out to see and the *amnyama* who have come in the lorry touch the children with their wands." The children "cannot help getting on the lorry" and are taken away, across the border. Captives were taken to Lilongwe "where they were fed on special foods that make them very fat. Then they are in some cases killed and their blood drunk by the European employers of the amnyama, in other instances their blood is just drained, and eventually they get back to their villages very emaciated." Barnes' informants, many of whom had worked on the Copperbelt, assured him that amnyama also operated there, but they used a "flexible piece of rubber" instead of a wand.[87]

Kamupila or *kampira* (*ka-* is a Bemba prefix meaning diminutive) became synonymous with *banyama* in various places: in Lusaka in the early 1950s, in Broken Hill a few years later, and in Southern Rhodesia in 1960. In Lusaka, *kamupila* was a synonym for *banyama,* and stories similar to the Congolese ones were told using specifically Northern Rhodesian idioms and images. The capture of children that had become a feature of Northern Rhodesian stories in the early 1940s was refined in Lusaka, where kamupila were said to capture children, give them injections that made them docile and dumb, and lead them to a faraway place, where their captors drank their blood. Sometimes, adults were

---

86. Joseph Kabila Kiomba Alona, Lubumbashi, 28 March 1991.
87. John Barnes, Fort Jameson, letter to J. Clyde Mitchell, 10 October 1948 (J. Clyde Mitchell Papers, Rhodes House, Oxford, RH MSS Afr. s. 1998/4/1). In the late 1930s, according to one man, Eustace Njbovu, banyama on the Copperbelt used a twig or branch to make Africans follow them (Kapani, Luangwa, 22 July 1990).

captured, and a rubber ball was forced into their mouths as they were marched off to the Belgian Congo for slave labor.[88] In the ferment of anti-Federation activity in Northern Rhodesia in the early 1950s, rumors circulated that whites had poisoned the sugar sold to Africans, that whites gave away soap that would sap the will of Africans, that tinned meat marked for African consumption was made from human flesh.[89] Officials took extreme action: two clerks who printed a pamphlet warning Africans about the poisoned sugar were tried and sentenced to three years each, while on the Copperbelt the district officer in Kitwe ate a can of meat at a public meeting to show how harmless it was.[90] But stories still circulated: the pro-Federation Capricorn African Society was banyama, and government newscasters—two of whom played guitar and sang in the Central African Broadcast Service's most popular show, the Alec Nkhata Quartet—were banyama as well, reading news that made Africans lose their will.

In 1957, the African Welfare Department in Broken Hill had to confine its youth and boys' club activities to daylight hours because no parents would let their children out at night for fear they would be taken by banyama to their headquarters in the Belgian Congo.[91] A year later, in Fort Jameson, it was said that the White Fathers had chosen their victims in advance and had marked their clothes with "the Sign of the Cross," which was invisible to all but the priests and their African henchmen. When enough victims had been marked, lorries were sent out to the villages, whistles blew, and "victims of the Cross" were "collected."[92] In 1960, in what was then Southern Rhodesia, stories resembling those specific to Katanga far more than those specific to the Copperbelt of Northern Rhodesia were told. Kampira in "a typical district"—according to Brelsford, Fort Victoria—was something that was "alleged to mark miraculously the clothes of people for future slaughter by the cannibals known to exist in the northern territories and

88. Peter Fraenkel, *Wayaleshi* (London: Weidenfeld & Nicholson 1959), 200.

89. Hortense Powdermaker, *Copper Town: The Human Situation on the Rhodesian Copperbelt* (New York: Harper & Row, 1962), 64; Timothy Burke, *Lifebuoy Men, Lux Women, Commodification, Consumption and Cleanliness in Modern Zimbabwe* (Durham, N.C.: Duke University Press, 1996), 161–62; Fraenkel, *Wayaleshi*, 197–200.

90. Fraenkel, *Wayaleshi*, 198; Henry Swanzy, "Quarterly Notes," *African Affairs* 52, 207 (1953): 111.

91. G. R. Brooks, welfare officer to African personnel manager, Rhodesian Broken Hill Development Co., Ltd., 1 January–7 February 1957. I am grateful to Carter Roeber for making these notes available to me.

92. Brelsford, "'Banyama' Myth," 55.

particularly the Belgian Congo." People in the district "believe that a big lorry comes across the country and when it hoots all those who have a mark on their garments will rush to the lorry to be carried away to 'Burumatara'—a mythical land. On arrival there they are injected with a chloroform solution which changes them from human beings to pigs. They are then fattened up prior to slaughter." In Salisbury, the capital, Africans were captured, given injections, loaded onto a Sabena airplane while they were unconscious, and changed into pigs during the flight.[93]

What is migrating here? The stories, the details and the words, the storytellers, or the circumstances that made these good and credible stories? Why do idioms and images that do not take hold fifty miles away from where they are first told take hold a thousand miles away fifteen years later? All of these stories were most likely carried by returning migrants. Why did they tell these stories, in all their variants and power? To entertain or to articulate grievances and animate political analyses? Did a part of the story that was not believed in Mufulira in 1934, for example, find a credible audience in Fort Jameson in 1948?

Such questions may isolate these stories from other parts of speech. Men and women may not repeat rumors so much as they report the hodge-podge of events, ideas, and images they have heard circulating in and out of where they worked. If rumors are narrative attempts to figure out the meanings behind events, postwar Africa was a fertile ground for rumors as the cost of living rose amid stagnant wages and increasing political demands, made both by Africans and colonial powers. In Central Africa, this tension was heightened by the Central African Federation, which was to unite Northern and Southern Rhodesia and Nyasaland into one political unit, making settler control greater in Nyasaland and

93. K. D. Leaver, "The 'Transformation of Men to Meat' Story," Native Affairs Dept. Information Sheet No. 20 (Salisbury, November 1960, National Archives of Zimbabwe, No. 36413); Brelsford, "'Banyama' Myth," 53. "Burumatara" is probably Bula Mutari—"breaker of rocks"—the rueful and ironic Congolese name for the officials of the colonial state. By the 1950s, however, it may have carried another meaning: starting in 1946, new production techniques on the Northern Rhodesian Copperbelt created a new category of skilled white labor—the rockbreaker—who was allowed "a personal boy" underground, an African who carried his equipment and ran his errands; see Charles Perrings, "A Moment in the 'Proletarianization' of the New Middle Class: Race, Value, and the Division of Labour in the Copperbelt, 1946–1966," *JSAS* 17, 2 (1990): 183–213. Pigs, on the other hand, may have had different meanings in the Belgian Congo and Southern Rhodesia. Pigs have long been part of rural rumors in Southern Africa; see Helen Bradford, *A Taste of Freedom: The ICU in Rural South Africa, 1924–1930* (New Haven: Yale University Press, 1987), 212, 218, 225–33, 237–41. I would assume that these are categorically different from the pigs of UMHK folklore.

Northern Rhodesia than it had been before. There is no clearer indication of the distrust felt by Africans during this period than the widespread stories of drugged and ingested Africans, kidnapped children,
poisoned sugar, and dangerous soap. Thus, in this section, I shall not
discuss what these rumors are about—they seem to describe how the
last gasp of colonial control was imagined—but how they come to contain so many elements of 1930s and 1940s Congolese stories that had
not been in widespread use in stories on the Northern Rhodesian Copperbelt during that time.

The question is, who knew the bits and pieces of these stories, whom
did they tell them to, and how did they tell them—which details did they
put into a story? All the evidence above comes from written sources, so
it is impossible to tell who said what, let alone who said what to whom.
A. L. Epstein's study of gossip on the Northern Rhodesian Copperbelt
in the late 1950s shows how people conversed across a number of domains. These conversations did not distinguish between migrant and
countryman, between stabilized worker and new arrival, between wife,
mother, and young man in the context of the urban centers to which
people have come and gone and come again. Epstein heard of an unremarkable (but nonetheless amusing) case of adultery in Ndola from one
of his research assistants, who heard the story from a neighbor. The assistant knew the adulterer because both men played on the same football team. The neighbor had gone to school with the wronged husband,
and they were still close friends. The neighbor had told Epstein's assistant the story when he visited his house while he (the assistant) was en-
tertaining a close friend. Epstein also heard the story from a schoolmate
of the wife's, whom he knew because her husband was a senior clerk and
political activist on the Copperbelt. She, however, had not heard it from
the wife herself but from another woman who had been to the same
school. This woman then told several woman friends and a younger
man from her home area, who had quite a good job in town. Epstein
then heard the story from another research assistant, who had grown up
in the mine compound at Mufulira, where his parents were close friends
of the adulterous wife's parents. This assistant had met the adulterous
man at a boxing match at a boy scouts' jamboree in 1947. But he had
not heard the story from the wife or the adulterer but from the wife's
mother, who lived on the outskirts of Ndola, whom he visited often.
This assistant soon heard the story again from the young man who had
heard it from the wife's schoolmate. The young man had told Epstein's

assistant one night in the beer hall because he himself was involved with a close friend of the wife's, who sometimes let the adulterous couple use her house but feared that her husband would think that her sanctioning such actions would cast doubt on her own fidelity. The young man was quite concerned about the extent of gossip in Ndola, since his activities might easily be disclosed, and complained bitterly about the woman who told him this story and the impact her gossip about adultery had had on his wife.[94]

The issue then is not who tells stories but the number of overlapping ways in which people hear stories in urban situations of great mobility and even more affiliations and loyalties. Childhood, school, sport, home area, new friends, old friends, and relations all provided occasions where news was exchanged; untangling who heard a story first and who passed it on may not be as important as noting that someone who hears news might not be the person to whom it was originally told and may pass it on for different reasons than it was first repeated in their presence. And stories may not be heard the same way by all who listen to them: some may hear about the threat of banyama to their children, others may hear a story about the danger of injections, and still another may hear an explanation for the increased availability of canned meat.

The capture of children and the draining of their blood that emerges so strongly in banyama accusations in Northern Rhodesia's Northern Province in the early 1940s may have been a way to talk about the status of children in households in which some husbands demanded bridewealth and increased control over their children, while others wanted to be able to pawn those children.[95] On the Copperbelt, children had been considered sources of industrial disorder for years. Between 1935 and 1940, officials proposed a variety of plans to send children over ten back to rural areas. These were all unworkable, and officials noted that however much they wanted children gone, parents wanted them residing with them.[96] But in Fort Jameson, the situation might have been different for the patrilineal Ngoni. There the kidnapping of children may have reflected a wider change in the regional economy, and the involvement of children in agricultural labor in neighboring Nyasa-

94. A. L. Epstein, "Gossip, Norms, and Social Network" (1969), in id., *Scenes from African Urban Life* (Edinburgh: Edinburgh University Press, 1992), 88–98.

95. John V. Taylor and Dorothea A. Lehmann, *Christians of the Copperbelt: The Growth of the Church in Northern Rhodesia* (London: SCM Press, 1961), 114–16.

96. O'Shea, *Missionaries*, 283–85.

land.[97] But what of the secretly marked clothing of the late 1950s? Is this a version of the clothing of batumbula stories? I think not. Even though many Ngoni men worked on the mines, and many of them and perhaps a few of their fathers worked in Katanga for a time, stories about cast-off clothing in the workplace do not necessarily diffuse into stories about marked clothing hundreds of miles away. The power of supervisory staff in Katanga, with their hats and dark glasses, to strip their victims of the very clothes that wages and employers provided reveals the anxious place of dress in wage labor. The power of banyama in Fort Jameson fifteen years later to mark clothes and persons with a sign only they could see reveals something both broader and more menacing, the subtle power of the colonial state and the variety of operatives that did its work. These stories made the most sense in both places when they included trucks and rich foods rationed to Africans for the most horrific of motives, just as stories of kidnapping and consumption in 1940s Katanga and late 1950s Southern Rhodesia made the most sense when told with details of injections and canned meat. How stories make sense and how they become credible returns us to the question with which I began this essay: do banyama and batumbula stories describe experiences or do they conform to rules of storytelling? Do they sound like reasonable stories because of how they are told or because of what they are told about?

Stories and experiences, performances and topics are not separate and discrete domains; a story sounded reasonable because it described what Congolese mine workers or Ngoni fathers considered the likely motives of Europeans; rumors contained other proofs—hazardous injections and stolen clothes—that both added credibility to the story and structured it in credible ways.[98] But the issue here is not that people must believe stories to retell them or act on them. They probably do, but how is that belief established—and for how long and in which contexts—by the stories of kidnapping and injections themselves or by how those stories are told?[99] But such a distinction may not be necessary and may not explain why a story becomes widespread and powerful. Instead, ba-

---

97. Shepperson, *Myth and Reality,* 8–9, suggests that the Cholo riots of 1953—anothor banyama incident—began with accusations by children who worked in fruit plantations.

98. Kapferer, *Rumors,* 76–77.

99. I take this point not from folklore but from classics; see Paul Veyne, *Did the Greeks Believe in Their Myths? An Essay on the Constitutive Imagination,* trans. Paula Wissing (Chicago: University of Chicago Press, 1988), 79.

nyama stories function both as rumor and gossip, simultaneously containing contradictions that underscore the wider contradictions in the late colonial project. The details of storytelling reveal the details of experience—the hidden motives of the state, the dreadful importance of clothes, the true meaning of colonial medicine, and the dramatic and contradictory tools with which it is carried out.

Northern Rhodesian rumors about government newscasters in the early 1950s may fuse some of these issues in particularly useful ways. The proposed Central African Federation was opposed by African political organizations in Northern Rhodesia, particularly the African National Congress, led by Harry Nkumbula. It was also opposed with popular distrust that was probably not manipulated by the ANC. If Africans in Northern Rhodesia actually supported Federation, it was generally through membership in the liberal, multiracial, elite Capricorn African Society, originally founded in Southern Rhodesia. This group's members tried to recruit educated Africans in Northern Rhodesia and other British colonies.[100] Although it never had serious status as a political party either for whites or Africans, it did actively support Federation. Africans in the Capricorn Society, or Africans suspected of such membership, were accused of being banyama and police informers as early as 1950.[101]

The association of the Capricorn Society with banyama reached its peak in Lusaka in 1952. This was in part fueled by the play of rumors of drugged food and commodities between the Copperbelt and Lusaka, and in part by the tactics of Capricorn Society members, whom European liberals opposed to Federation accused of terrorizing women and children in the capital with "drunkenness and hooliganism."[102] By the end of the year, fears were such that an ANC meeting in Lusaka passed a resolution condemning the government for "failing to deal with the Vampire men threatening the peace and order . . . of the country." Two months later, Harry Nkumbula wrote to the member of Northern

---

100. The "multi-racial Capricorn Africa Society . . . dispensed hope, cash and cocktails with impartial liberality at meetings from Makerere University in Uganda to the Jameson Hotel lounge in Salisbury," according to a liberal journalist; see John Parker, *Rhodesia—Little White Island* (London: Pitman, 1972), 81.

101. Musambachime, "Impact of Rumor," 211–12. Thomas Fox-Pitt to secretary, Capricorn Society, Lusaka, 26 September 1956 (Thomas Fox-Pitt Papers, Correspondence, 1953–56, School of Oriental and African Studies, University of London Library, PP. MS 5/5).

102. Fraenkel, *Wayaleshi,* 196–99; Fox-Pitt letter cited in preceding note.

Rhodesia's Legislative Council who represented African interests "with regard to the vampiremen incidents it is high time that Government took action." [103]

At the same time, radio announcers were accused of being banyama. According to Peter Fraenkel, the director of the Central African Broadcast Service, the reasoning behind these new accusations was logical: "How could the announcers broadcast 'bad news,' news which displeased Africans, unless they had lost their will-power? How else could they be made to read pro-Federation propaganda on the air?" [104] These accusations have their own histories: one broadcaster was so frightened of being poisoned that he cycled miles to his home village once a week to buy food; another, Edward Kateka, was accused of kidnapping a child and took refuge in a police station; Alick Nkhata, arguably the most influential of Central Africa's influential guitarists, wrote a song about banyama stories, which was well received as a dance tune but made little impact on the rumors. [105] These however are beyond the scope of this chapter. What I want to discuss now is how men whose job it was to tell stories came to be accused of being banyama—of being, in short, something made real by storytelling.

Did every accuser believe these broadcasters were banyama? Did they think they actually sold Africans to whites for their bodies and their blood? Some did. An anonymous letter threatening Nkhata and Kateka contained many of the details and hierarchies of Copperbelt banyama stories: "You people Capricornists," it began, "you are selling your people to Yengwe in Ndola." Although Yengwe/Arthur Davison had died in 1951, the court interpreter explained to the judge that he was a European who lived in Ndola who supposedly bought Africans and sold them to the Congo to be eaten. "[Y]ou wanted to kill Nkumbula you even received revolvers from your Minister the General President of the Capricornists . . . you are all civil servants . . . you are the people pretending to become maneaters, *kamupila*," the letter claimed. The colonial state's response was swift, but perhaps not what Nkumbula had in

<hr>

103. S. E. Wilmer, "Northern Rhodesian African Opposition to the Federation" (BA thesis, Oxford University, 1973, quoted in Musambachime, "Impact of Rumor," 212). "Vampire men" is the English translation of *banyama* that appears in documentary sources after 1931; whether this was an English term used by African politicians in the late 1950s or an official translation I cannot tell.

104. Fraenkel, *Wayaleshi*, 202.

105. Ibid., 202–7.

mind: handwriting samples were sent to police in Livingstone and South Africa, who examined 200 of these before they found the culprit, a twenty-year-old office worker from Western Province. He claimed that he had only wanted to warn the broadcasters. The magistrate observed, "This is not a letter of kindly warning" and sentenced the man to five years' imprisonment.[106]

But others believed the story, rather than the literal existence of banyama and Yengwe. According to Nkhata, "My best friends are afraid to come see me . . . I am quite alone. They don't even greet me in the street. They cross over to the other side to avoid me. It is not that they believe this nonsense, but they're afraid. They think they too will be accused if they are seen with me." Another announcer complained that he could not fathom the reason for this accusation: "Why us? . . . They've always trusted us. I know they've mistrusted other departments, but then people like the Forestry officers do bully them to stop cutting wood. But we, we've always been popular. We bring them education and entertainment and we don't even ask a license-fee. Why pick on us now?"[107]

What did cause these accusations? Was it the general panic, the men themselves, the stories newscasters told on the air or the way they told these stories? Would Federation described, however favorably, with reference to injections or lorries have been as suspicious, while Federation described as a negotiated political process aroused fear? Given the evidence available—banyama accusations filtered through so many layers of European translation and summary that the narrative is lost—I cannot say what kind of stories were told about banyama, much less about the kind of stories newscasters told. But the experience of Alick Nkhata in concert, performing a song that joked about banyama, supports the view that it was the work that was suspicious, not the man. Nkhata and his quartet performed in the midst of the most aggressive banyama accusations: "A large audience turned up, paid their entrance fee and applauded his amusing songs about modern town-life. . . . The new song

106. "Five Years for African Who Threatened to Kill Broadcasters," *Central African Post* [Lusaka], 27 January 1953; Musambachime, "Impact of Rumor," 204n; Fraenkel, *Wayaleshi*, 203.

107. Fraenkel, *Wayaleshi*, 203–4. The Central African Broadcasting Service asked the same question, and in January 1953, it started publishing profiles of its African announcers, although Peter Fraenkel told me that this was planned before the rumors became widespread (interview, 16 March 1992). See "Nkhata and His Quartet," *African Listener* 13 (January 1953): 15, and "A Quiet Man with a Guitar," *African Listener* 14 (February 1953): 6.

about vampire-men went down fairly well and caused some laughter." But during a break Nkhata went outside, and members of the audience standing there shrieked and ran away.[108]

Nkhata the broadcaster might have been thought banyama, but Nkhata the guitarist was not. The song itself named Kateka, named the Information Department, but included none of the details of head banyama, injections, and fattening captivities that made banyama stories powerful and immediate. Nkhata's song discredited banyama stories because they were false, not because of what they were about. "Who is Nyama? / Nobody knows him / Some say it is Kateka / Who works for the Information Department / There are no Vampiremen / Do not scare people." [109] The experiences, real or imagined, of marked clothes, stolen children, dangerous injections, and fattened captivities were absent from a song that only reprimanded African ideas. It may not have been frightening because it contained no evidence of banyama.

A banyama or batumbula story that travels, that carries words and ideas hundreds of miles across borders for many years, is told with experiences. Without those experiences, however compressed and cryptic they might be, it is just another song—another example of educated Africans' condescending advice, perhaps the reason for the audience's laughter. These experiences did not need to have the same meaning to all who heard the story and repeated it, but their presence in a narrative, told with injections and marked clothes, rather than any specific storytelling conventions, made it a banyama story.

---

108. Fraenkel, *Wayaleshi*, 205.
109. Quoted in Musambachime, "Impact of Rumor," 213.

CHAPTER 10

Conclusions

I began this book by asserting that vampire stories could be used like any other historical source. But in several chapters I have argued that vampire stories offer a better, clearer, more analytical picture of the colonial experience than other sources do. Did I just become more self-confident as I wrote, or did I in fact manage to use these stories to illuminate new areas of inquiry, to articulate concerns and connections that other sources had simply glossed? Do vampire stories actually make for a more thorough reconstruction of the past, or do they simply add another layer of interpretation to already known histories?

Historians should, I think, find vampire stories good to write about, just as the people quoted in this book found vampires good to talk about. They make for better, more comprehensive histories. As chapter 1 argues, vampires themselves are revealing beings: a separate race of bloodsucking creatures, living among humans on fluids that they extract from human bodies; vampires mark a way in which relations of race, of bodies, and of tools of extraction can be debated, theorized, and explained. No vampire stands alone. The incorporation of vampire stories in any historical reconstruction allows for a description of these debates. And that description alone should generate a more nuanced reconstruction of the past. The reconstruction does not come from vampire stories alone, but rather from how those stories feed off the other stories through which a past is known. The vampire stories that prostitutes told in colonial Nairobi, for example, did not change the way I thought about the history of that city,[1] but they did allow me to access changing ideas about gender and culture, about menstruation and property and its transmission in colonial times. In other places, vampire stories offer insights that can help historians rethink and recontextualize local histories: vampire and batumbula stories ground the place of free issues of clothing in the wages paid on the copperbelts of colonial Northern Rhodesia and the Belgian Congo and suggest a way of thinking about migrancy as a workers' strategy. Here the details of vampire stories transform conventional wisdoms; stories of bloodsucking and cannibalism in which clothes play a prominent part illustrate what was significant about work, what was seen as remuneration, and which strategies—and which form of engagement, in which mine—could increase a wage that was partly commodified.

But the problem of this book has never been vampire stories, but history writing. The stories, as I wrote early on, are fine, worth taking at face value as few other texts are. Historical reconstruction is somewhat more ambiguous and complex, and it does not emerge full-blown from the deployment of good stories. Some of the issues that have recently troubled historians—are we writing truth, or stories? is history constituted by facts, or by many narratives?—are themselves troubled by vampire stories. The line between fact and story, indistinct as it is for most historians, is made concrete by people who believe that some agency of the colonial state captured Africans and took their blood. Vampires are a story, but belief in vampires is a fact, just as the attacks on fire stations in Mombasa, policemen in colonial Nyasaland, and prospectors in Tanganyika are facts. The imaginary makes the real, just as it makes more imaginings: it is the inclusion of both that gives depth to historical analyses, and, if not some certainty, at least solid grounds on which to assess motivations, causes, and ideas.

In February 1959, Nusula Bua was convicted in a Kampala court for offering to sell a man to the fire brigade. A fireman testified that he had met Bua a few days before; Bua had said he had a man he wanted to sell to the fire brigade for 1,500/- and asked the fireman to help him. Bua's defense was that he had taken his friend Alubino Ongon to the fire station to help him find a job. Once there, he was offered 1,500/- for the man, and was waiting for the money when he was arrested. Ongon gave

1. See Luise White, *The Comforts of Home: Prostitution in Colonial Nairobi* (Chicago: University of Chicago Press, 1990).

evidence that Bua had told him he would help him find a job. It was only when he was taken to the fire station that he realized he was being offered for sale.[2] The firemaster, a European, joked about the event: 1,500/-, he said, "works out to about Shs. 12/ a pound, including bone, for the rather skinny Alubino Ongon. Turkeys are cheaper."[3] There is little reason to try to find out which, if any, of these statements is true. Even if that were a viable line of inquiry, it would have disembedded each statement from its own context—the belief in bloodsucking firemen, the ways that white employers played with and off this belief, and the vulnerability of job seekers and their dependence on networks and acquaintances to find work. All of these statements together make a vampire story and vampire actions. It is the several contexts within a vampire story, those contradictions bound within a rumor, that offer historians a space in which ideas and beliefs and motivations come together.

Such a sense of context might unfix academic concerns about whose history should be studied. At some point or other in their careers, most historians—of Africa, of Europe, wherever—have been reprimanded for studying the ordinary, the small, and the insignificant, because it detracts from the larger narrative of tragedies and triumphs that shaped the respective histories of colonies and empires. The same criticism has been applied to those who study the exotic or the extraordinary. Such complaints, however, arise more from historiographic traditions than from specific subjects of historical inquiry. The idea that history must record a national biography, and must provide an explanation for the evils and ills of a nation or a region, is an integral part of the discipline.[4]

2. "Three Years for Attempt to Sell Man," *Uganda Argus,* 16 February 1959, 5.

3. W. V. Brelsford, "The 'Banyama' Myth," *NADA* 9, 4 (1967): 54. Brelsford heard this story at the 14th Conference of the Rhodes-Livingstone Institute for Social Research, the proceedings of which were published as Allie Dubb, ed., "Myth in Modern Africa" (Lusaka, 1960, mimeographed).

4. For African studies, see Bernard Magubane, "A Critical Look at the Indices Used in the Study of Social Change in Central Africa," *Current Anthropology* 12, 4–5 (1971): 419–31; Terence O. Ranger, *Dance and Society in Eastern Africa* (Berkeley and Los Angeles: University of California Press, 1975), 4; Albert B. K. Matongo, "Popular Culture in Colonial Society: Another Look at *mbeni* and *kalela* Dances on the Copperbelt, 1930–1960," in Samuel N. Chipungu, *Guardians in Their Time: The Experiences of Zambians under Colonial Rule* (London: Macmillan, 1992), 180–217; and Luise White, "The Traffic in Heads: Bodies, Borders, and the Articulation of Regional Histories," *J. Southern Afr. Studies* 23, 2 (1997): 225–38. For colonial studies in general, and a masterful statement of the problem, see Gyandendra Pandey, "In Defense of the Fragment: Writing about Hindu-Muslim Riots in India Today," *Representations* 37 (1992): 27–55.

But it is important, especially at this time in academic life, to turn this idea on its head: the biography of a nation (or region, or locality) can be done by historicizing the ills and evils historians wish to exorcise. I would argue that the issue is not what one studies, but how one studies it. The issue may be expressed most clearly as one of how a historical subject is constituted, not as a subject but as a historical project, with which sources and kinds of evidence.[5] The ordinary (or the extraordinary) does not exist separate from the material and the political. The anecdote about Nusula Bua, repeated as a whole story, demonstrates a range of colonial predicaments in late 1950s Uganda. It provides its own overlapping contexts. Whether it is labeled a fragment, trivial, exotic, or supernatural, it contains these different interpretations within it. It is only by the incorporation of these different interpretations that the ordinary and the extraordinary can be historicized.

I have tried to respect the many different interpretations of vampire stories in this book. Each chapter in parts 2 and 3 has argued that a set of vampire stories—taken together either by locality or theme—can be interpreted to tell us a history we did not already know. This raises another question of concern to historians at the end of this century: are vampires a good historical source in and of themselves, or are they simply so slippery and fluid that I have recast them into the dominant concerns of African historians of the past two decades, labor, medicine, and nationalism? Is any history written with vampire stories a valid use of vampires? Is any representation of vampires—themselves a representation—acceptable?

There is too much at stake to let vampire stories be interpreted without close attention to time and place. There are right ways and wrong ways to write history with vampire stories. It is not that vampires are not really wonderful historical evidence in and of themselves, and if historians had nothing else, they would be a good place to start, but history is not written from one kind of evidence. Evidence is situated, lying in relation to other evidence. The chapters in parts 2 and 3 have used vampire stories in relation to other kinds of evidence to do the work of his-

5. See esp. Christopher Browning, "German Memory, Judicial Interrogation, and Historical Reconstruction: Writing Perpetuator History from Postwar Testimony," in Saul Friedlander, ed., *Probing the Limits of Representation: Nazisim and the "Final Solution"* (Cambridge, Mass.: Harvard University Press, 1992), 22–36. Browning reflects on the complications of using captured German documents that were the basis of prosecutions in war crimes tribunals to write a history of ordinary soldiers and their discipline in Poland. How can we use such evidence in such different ways and not suggest that any interpretation is valid?

torical reconstruction. Vampire stories from Uganda, for example, say too much about chloroform to ignore the place of inhaled drugs in ideas about colonial intervention. Vampire stories from colonial Northern Rhodesia are told with the changing techniques of tsetse-fly control. Such stories describe colonial intervention and the ways in which insect-borne diseases were considered part of that intervention. A number of chapters in this book posit two kinds of history—one in letters of blood and one in something more stable, like pathogens, high politics, missionary medicine, or the historiography of migrant labor—not because of any implicit love of binaries on my part, but because it allows me to work through the relationship between different kinds of evidence as I reconstruct the past with that evidence.

Recent struggles about history and history writing may have made evidence, fact, and truth much more solid categories than they ever were before. It is easy to forget, in the heat of argument, how transient evidence, fact, and truth have historically been, and how regularly they have been replaced by new and equally replaceable facts. More to the point, historians' struggles have obscured the way evidence has been deployed and the multiple, overlapping uses to which it had been put long before historians' came to use it. There is no dividing line between evidence and its interpretation; primary and secondary sources are not cast-iron categories. What historians call evidence, or facts, are interpretations of events written down or spoken by others. What historians find—or hear in an interview—was interpreted in many ways before it became "evidence." Thus, the evidence employed to find witches is evidence of a peasant culture when used in later centuries. The evidence against a "well-known stupefier" in Kampala was used to get rid of a low-level chief during a moment of intense royal crisis. The evidence officials wrote to demonstrate the depths of African superstition is used in this book to revise the history of sleeping-sickness control and the meaning of shifting cultivation. And that evidence—in courts, in official reports, as heard by inquisitors—was not produced passively. People interpreted what they saw, what they heard, what someone else had heard, to make personal narratives. Think of Zebede Oyoyo taking a well-known story about the Nairobi fire department and remaking it as his own anecdote about his years as a railway worker in Nairobi. His account of his near capture and escape, used twice in this book to make different points, is both a personal construction and an interpretation. This well-known story, which Oyoyo had been telling for years, best expressed his ideas about his experiences in Nairobi wage labor.

This does not make eyewitness testimony any less or any more reliable, as this book asserts. Eyewitness testimony has an authority because it grounds the history based on it in first-person accounts. It reflects the vision of participants, whether or not it is completely accurate. Eyewitness testimony does not have some pure or unmediated status, which any historian with a penchant for theory deforms. Eyewitness testimony has already been mediated, as people decide what to say or write and how to say—or write—it. The stories individual eyewitnesses appropriate and pass off as their own make the social worlds of circulating stories personal and intimate: the process offers a context that describes what eyewitnesses saw and experienced as they understood it. This process is how people interpret what happened to them; it is the way they describe it. And it is this process that should make historians reflect on our own project and those of the people we write about. Interpretations have been made before we come to an interview or an archive, and it is those multiple interpretations that result in what we call evidence.

So does this mean that any interpretation is acceptable? Hardly. It means that interpretations have to be made with care and caution, not because they are risky in and of themselves, but because interpretations build on so many layers of interpretation that they have to be well grounded or they topple over. This should perhaps be more obvious to people who write about, and with, rumor and narrative than to those who write about diplomatic history, for example, or who use census data or wills. Stories and rumors are produced in the cultural conflicts of local life; they mark ways to talk about the conflicts and contradictions that gave them meaning and power. These conflicts and their meaning can only be reconstructed if the stories are grounded in relation to other evidence, other interpretations, other stories. It is not that vampire stories are such a different kind of evidence that this is any truer of them than of any other kind of evidence, but vampire stories make more connections than other kinds of evidence do. The force with which vampire stories insert themselves into domains of power and regions of the body makes this point clearly: other kinds of evidence are not so invasive; they do not reveal the same breadth and depth of daily life and thought.

Bibliography

ARCHIVAL SOURCES

KENYA NATIONAL ARCHIVES, NAIROBI

Provincial Commissioner, Coast Province, annual reports
Provincial Commissioner, Nairobi, Nairobi Municipal Council Minutes,
   1933–35
Provincial Commissioner, Nairobi District, annual reports, 1936–39

LONDON SCHOOL OF ECONOMICS, UNIVERSITY OF LONDON

Audrey Richards papers

NATIONAL ARCHIVES OF ZAMBIA, LUSAKA

Secretariat Papers, Formation of Game Department
Secretariat Papers, Native Affairs: Banyama
Secretariat Papers, Native Customs
Secretariat Papers, Sleeping Sickness in Northern Rhodesia
Abercorn District reports, 1932–39
Isoka District reports, 1932–39
Kasama District reports, 1931–39
Kawambwa District reports, 1932–40
Luwingu District reports, 1931–39
Mpika District Reports, 1931–39
Mporokoso District Reports, 1935–40
Mweru-Luapula Provincial reports, 1933–35
Fort Roseberry/Mansa District reports, 1932–40

RHODES HOUSE, OXFORD

R. S. F. Hennessey, Elspeth Huxley, Harold Makinder, and J. Clyde Mitchell Papers

SAINT ANDREAS ABBEY, BRUGES

Grégoire Coussement and G. C. de Hemptinne Papers

SCHOOL OF ORIENTAL AND AFRICAN STUDIES, UNIVERSITY OF LONDON

Thomas Fox-Pitt Papers

UNIVERSITY LIBRARY, UNIVERSITY OF BIRMINGHAM

Société des Missionnaires d'Afrique, Church Missionary Society Archives Mission diaries: Chilubula, Chifubwe-Ipusukilo, Ipusukilo, Ilondola, Mulilansalo, Kapatu, Kayambi, and St. Mary's

WELLCOME INSTITUTE FOR THE HISTORY OF MEDICINE, LONDON

David Bruce, Edward Aneurian Lewis, and Sir William Leishman Collected Papers

PUBLISHED BOOKS AND ARTICLES

Abrahams, Roger D. "A Performance-Centered Approach to Gossip." *Man*, n.s., 5, 2 (1970): 290–301.

Adas, Michael. *Machines as the Measures of Men: Science, Technology, and the Ideologies of Western Dominance*. Ithaca, N.Y.: Cornell University Press, 1989.

Allan, William. *Studies in African Land Usage in Northern Rhodesia*. Rhodes-Livingstone Papers, no.15. Cape Town and New York: Oxford: University Press for the Rhodes-Livingstone Institute, 1949.

———. *The African Husbandman*. Edinburgh: Oliver & Boyd, 1965. Reprint. Westport, Conn.: Greenwood Press, 1977.

Allen, Barbara. "'The Image on Glass': Technology, Tradition, and the Emergence of Folklore." *Western Folklore* 41 (1982): 85–103.

Alverson, Hoyt. *Mind in the Heart of Darkness: Value and Self-Identity among the Tswana of Southern Africa*. New Haven: Yale University Press, 1979.

Akyeampong, Emmanuel. *Drink, Power and Cultural Change: A Social History of Alcohol in Ghana, c. 1880 to Recent Times*. Portsmouth, N.H.: Heinemann, 1996.

Ambler, Charles H. *Kenyan Communities in the Age of Imperialism*. New Haven: Yale University Press, 1987.

———. "Alcohol, Racial Segregation, and Popular Politics in Northern Rhodesia." *Journal of African History* 31, 2 (1990): 295–313.

Anderson, David. "Depression, Dust Bowl, Demography and Drought: The Colonial State and Soil Conservation in East Africa in the 1930s." *African Affairs* 83, 322 (1984): 321–43.

Anderson, Warwick. "'Where Every Prospect Pleases and Only Man Is Vile': Laboratory Medicine as Colonial Discourse." *Critical Inquiry* 18 (1992): 506–28.

Apter, David E. *The Political Kingdom in Uganda: A Study in Bureaucratic Nationalism.* Princeton: Princeton University Press, 1961. 2d ed., 1967.

Arata, Steven D. "The Occidental Tourist: *Dracula* and the Anxiety of Reverse Colonialism." *Victorian Studies* 33, 4 (1990): 621–45.

Ardell, K. "In Teso Country." *Mission Hospital* [formerly *Mercy and Truth*] 31, 350 (1927): 60–63.

Ardener, Edwin. "Witchcraft, Economics and the Continuity of Belief." In Douglas, ed., *Witchcraft Confessions and Accusations.* London: Tavistock, 1970.

Arens, W. *The Man-Eating Myth: Anthropology and Anthrophagy.* New York: Oxford University Press, 1979.

Arnold, David. *Colonizing the Body: State Medicine and Epidemic Disease in Nineteenth-Century India.* Berkeley and Los Angeles: University of California Press, 1993.

Atieno-Odhiambo, E. S. [Atieno Odhiambo]. "'Seek Ye First the Economic Kingdom': A History of the Luo Thrift and Trading Corporation (LUTOCO), 1945–56." *Hadith* 5 (1975): 221–60.

———. "The Movement of Ideas: A Case Study of Intellectual Responses to Colonialism among the Ligunua Peasants." *Hadith* 6 (1976): 163–80.

Atkins, Keletso E. "'Kaffir Time': Preindustrial Temporal Concepts and Labor Discipline in Nineteenth-Century Natal." *Journal of African History* 29, 2 (1988): 229–44.

Auerbach, Nina. *Our Vampires, Ourselves.* Chicago: University of Chicago Press, 1995.

Auslander, Mark. "'Open the Wombs!' The Symbolic Politics of Modern Ngoni Witchfinding." In Comaroff and Comaroff, eds., *Modernity and Its Malcontents,* 167–92. Chicago: University of Chicago Press, 1993.

Baker, E. C. "Mumiani." *Tanganyika Notes and Records* 21 (1946): 108–9.

Banage, W. B., W. N. Byarugaba, and J. D. Goodman. "The Embalasassa (*Riopa fernandi*): A Story of Real and Mythical Zoology." *Uganda Journal* 36 (1972): 67–72.

Barber, Karin. "Popular Reactions to the Petro-Naira." *Journal of Modern African Studies* 20, 3 (1982): 431–50.

———. *I Could Speak Until Tomorrow: Oriki, Women, and the Past in a Yoruba Town.* Washington, D.C.: Smithsonian Institution Press, 1991.

Barber, Paul. *Vampires, Burial and Death: Folklore and Reality.* New Haven: Yale University Press, 1988.

Barrios de Chungara, Domitila. With Moema Viezzer. *Si me permiten hablar. Let me speak!: Testimony of Domitila, a Woman of the Bolivian Mines.* Translated by Victoria Ortiz. New York: Monthly Review Press, 1978.

Bartlett, Katherine, and Roseanne Kennedy, eds. *Feminist Legal Theory.* Boulder, CO: Westview Press, 1991.

Bastain, Misty L. " 'Bloodhounds Who Have No Friends': Witchcraft and Locality in the Nigerian Popular Press." In Comaroff and Comaroff, eds., *Modernity and Its Malcontents,* 129–66. Chicago: University of Chicago Press, 1993.

Bates, Darrell. *The Mango and the Palm.* London: Rupert Hart-Davis, 1962.

Bates, Robert. "The Agrarian Origins of Mau Mau: A Structural Account." *Agricultural History* 61, 1 (1987): 52–71.

Beattie, J. M. "The Blood Pact in Bunyoro." *African Studies* 17, 4 (1958): 198–203.

Beck, Ann. "The Problems of British Medical Administration in East Africa between 1900 and 1930." *Bulletin of the History of Medicine* 36 (1962): 275–83.

Beer, Gillian. *Darwin's Plots: Evolutionary Narrative in Darwin, George Eliot, and Nineteenth-Century Fiction.* Boston: Routledge & Kegan Paul, 1983.

Beidelman, T. O. "The Blood Covenant and the Concept of Blood in Ukaguru." *Africa* 33, 4 (1963): 321–62.

———, "Witchcraft in Ukaguru." In Middleton and Winter, eds., *Witchcraft and Sorcery in East Africa,* 57–98. London: Routledge & Kegan Paul, 1963.

———. "Myth, Legend, and Oral History: A Kaguru Traditional Text." *Anthropos* 65, 5 (1970): 74–97.

———. *Colonial Evangelism: A Socio-Historical Study of an East African Mission at the Grassroots.* Bloomington: Indiana University Press, 1982.

———. *Moral Imagination and Kaguru Modes of Thought.* Washington, D.C.: Smithsonian Institution Press, 1993.

———. *The Cool Knife: Imagery of Gender, Sexuality, and Moral Imagination in Kaguru Initiation Ritual.* Washington, D.C.: Smithsonian Institution Press, 1997.

Beinart, William. "Soil Erosion, Conservation, and Ideas about Development: a Southern African Exploration." *Journal of Southern African Studies* 11, 1 (1986): 52–83.

Belasco, Warren James. *Americans on the Road: From Autocamp to Motel, 1910–1945.* Cambridge, Mass.: MIT Press, 1981.

Bickford-Smith, Vivian. *Ethnic Pride and Racial Prejudice in Victorian Cape Town: Group Identity and Social Practice.* Cambridge: Cambridge University Press, 1995.

Birkett, Dea. "The 'White Woman's Burden' in the 'White Man's Grave': The Introduction of British Nurses in Colonial West Africa." In Margaret Strobel and Nupur Chaudhuri, eds., *Western Women and Imperialism,* 177–88. Bloomington: Indiana University Press, 1992.

Bledsoe, Caroline H., and Monica F. Goubard. "The Reinterpretation of Western Pharmaceuticals among the Mende of Sierra Leone." *Social Science and Medicine* 21, 3 (1985): 275–82.

Blount, Ben G. "Agreeing to Disagree on Genealogy: A Luo Sociology of Knowledge." In Sanchez and Blount, eds., *Sociocultural Dimensions of Language Use,* 117–35. New York: Academic Press, 1975.

Boase, A. J. "Reminiscences of Surgery in Uganda." *East African Medical Journal* 31 (1954): 200–204.

Bond, Dr. A. "A Record of Medical Work at Toro." *Mercy and Truth* 11, 129 (September 1907): 273–75.

Bond, Mrs. Aston. "Medical Work at Toro" *Mercy and Truth* 16, 189 (1912): 305–9.

Bonner, P. L. "Family, Crime, and Political Consciousness on the East Rand, 1939–1955." *Journal of Southern African Studies* 14, 3 (1988): 393–420.

Bourdieu, Pierre. "The Attitude of the Algerian Peasant toward Time." In Pitt-Rivers, ed., *Mediterranean Countrymen*, 55–72. Paris: Mouton, 1963.

Bourgault, Louise Manon. *Mass Media in Sub-Saharan Africa*. Bloomington: Indiana University Press, 1995.

———. "Occult Discourses in the Liberian Press under Sam Doe: 1988–1989." *Alternation* 4, 2 (1997): 186–209.

Bove, Joseph R., et al. *Practical Blood Transfusion*. Boston: Little, Brown, 1969.

Bozzoli, Belinda, with the assistance of Mmanthi Nkotsoe. *Women of Phokeng: Consciousness, Life Strategy, and Migrancy in South Africa*. Portsmouth, N.H.: Heinemann, 1991.

Bradford, Helen. *A Taste of Freedom: The ICU in Rural South Africa, 1924–1930*. New Haven: Yale University Press, 1987. Johannesburg: Ravan Press, 1988.

Bradley, Kenneth. *Once a District Officer*. London: Macmillan, 1966.

Bravman, William. *Making Ethnic Ways: Communities and Their Transformations in Taita, Kenya, 1800–1950*. Portsmouth, N.H.: Heinemann, 1998.

Breckenridge, Keith. "'Money with Dignity': Migrants, Minelords, and the Cultural Politics of the South African Gold Standard Crisis, 1920–33." *Journal of African History* 36 (1995): 271–304.

Brelsford, W. V. *Generation of Men: The European Pioneers of Northern Rhodesia*. Salisbury: Stuart, Manning for the Northern Rhodesia Society, 1966.

———. "The 'Banyama' Myth." *NADA* 9, 4 (1967): 49–68.

Brewster, D. A. "A Day at the Dispensary at Ng'ora." *Mission Hospital* 31, 350 (1927): 89–90.

Briggs, Charles L. *Learning How to Ask: A Sociolinguistic Appraisal of the Role of the Interview in Social Science Research*. Cambridge: Cambridge University Press, 1986.

Briggs, Charles L., and Richard Bauman. "Genre, Intertextuality, and Social Power." *Journal of Linguistic Anthropology* 2, 2 (1992): 131–72.

Brooks, Jeffrey. "Literacy and Print Media in Russia, 1861–1928," *Communication* 11 (1988): 48–62.

———. "Socialist Realism in Pravda: Read All About It!" *Slavic Review* 53, 4 (1994): 973–91.

Browning, Christopher. "German Memory, Judicial Interrogation, and Historical Reconstruction: Writing Perpetuator History from Postwar Testimony." In Friedlander, ed., *Probing the Limits of Representation*, 22–36. Cambridge, Mass.: Harvard University Press, 1992.

Buckley, Thomas, and Alma Gottlieb, eds. *Blood Magic: The Anthropology of Menstruation*. Berkeley and Los Angeles: University of California Press, 1988.

Bujra, Janet M. "Women 'Entrepreneurs' of Early Nairobi." *Canadian Journal of African Studies* 9, 2 (1975): 213–34.

Burawoy, Michael. *The Color of Class on the Copper Mines: From African Advancement to Zambianization*. Lusaka: Institute of African Studies, 1972.

Burke, Timothy. *Lifebuoy Men, Lux Women: Commodification, Consumption and Cleanliness in Modern Zimbabwe*. Durham, N.C.: Duke University Press, 1996.

Burnham, John C. *How Superstition Won and Science Lost: Popularizing Science and Health in the United States*. New Brunswick, N.J.: Rutgers University Press, 1987.

Bustin, Edouard. "Government Policy toward African Cult Movements: The Case of Katanga." In Mark Karp, ed., *African Dimensions: Essays in Honor of William O. Brown*, 110–25. Boston University Papers in African History. Boston: African Studies Center, Boston University, 1975.

Bynum, Caroline Walker. "Women Mystics and the Eucharistic Devotion in the Twentieth Century." *Women's Studies* 11 (1984): 179–214.

———. "The Body of Christ in the Later Middle Ages: A Reply to Leo Steinberg." *Renaissance Quarterly* 39, 3 (1986): 399–439.

———. *Holy Feast and Holy Fast: The Religious Significance of Food to Medieval Women*. Berkeley and Los Angeles: University of California Press, 1987.

———. "Material Continuity, Personal Survival, and the Resurrection of the Body: A Scholastic Discussion in Medieval and Modern Contexts." In *Fragmentation and Redemption: Essays on Gender and the Human Body in Medieval Religion*, 239–97. Cambridge: Zone Books, 1991.

Callahan, Bryan T. "'Veni, VD, Vici'? Reassessing the Ila Syphilis Epidemic, 1900–1963." *Journal of Southern African Studies* 23, 3 (1997): 421–40.

Canning, Kathleen. "Feminist History and the Linguistic Turn: Historicizing Discourse and Experience." In Barbara Laslett et al., eds., *History and Theory: Feminist Research, Debates and Contestations*, 416–52. Chicago: University of Chicago Press, 1997.

Carr, Norman. *The White Impala: The Story of a Game Ranger*. London: Collins, 1969.

Carter, Felice. "The Education of African Muslims in Uganda." *Uganda Journal* 29, 2 (1965): 193–99.

Ceyssens, Rik. "Mutumbula: Mythe de l'opprimé." *Cultures et développement* 7 (1975): 483–536.

Chakrabarty, Dipesh. "Conditions for Knowledge of Working Class Conditions: Employers, Government and the Jute Workers of Calcutta, 1890–1940." *Subaltern Studies* (Delhi) 2 (1983): 259–310.

———. "Postcoloniality and the Artifice of History: Who Speaks for 'Indian' Pasts?" *Representations* 37 (1992): 1–26.

Chandler, James, Arnold I. Davidson, and Harry Harootunian, eds. *Questions of Evidence: Proof, Practice and Persuasion across the Disciplines*. Chicago: University of Chicago Press, 1994.

Channock, Martin. *Law, Custom and Social Order: The Colonial Experience in Zambia and Malawi*. Cambridge: Cambridge University Press, 1983.

Chauncey, George, Jr. "The Locus of Reproduction: Women's Labor in the Zambian Copperbelt, 1927–1953." *Journal of Southern African Studies* 7, 2 (1981): 135–64.

Chilube, A. "The Clash between Modern and Indigenous Medicine." *Makerere Medical Journal* 9 (1965): 33–38.

Chipungu, Samuel N., ed. *Guardians in Their Time: The Experiences of Zambians under Colonial Rule.* London: Macmillan, 1992.

Clercq, Auguste de. *Dictionnaire Luba, Luba-Français.* Leopoldville: Missions de sheut, 1936.

Clifford, James, and George Marcus, eds. *Writing Culture: The Poetics and Politics of Ethnography.* Berkeley and Los Angeles: University of California Press, 1986.

Cohen, David William. "The Undefining of Oral Tradition." *Ethnohistory* 36, 1 (1989): 6–18.

Cohen, David William, and Atieno Odhiambo [E. S. Atieno-Odhiambo]. *Siaya: The Historical Anthropology of an African Landscape.* London: James Currey, 1989.

———. *Burying SM: The Politics of Knowledge and the Sociology of Power in Black Africa.* Portsmouth, N.H.: Heinemann, 1992.

Cohn, Norman R. C. *Europe's Inner Demons: An Inquiry Inspired by the Great Witch Hunt.* New York: Basic Books. 1975.

Coleman, William. *Yellow Fever in the North: The Methods of Early Epidemiology.* Madison: University of Wisconsin Press, 1987.

Comaroff, Jean. "Bodily Reform as Historical Practice: The Semantics of Resistance in Modern South Africa." *International Journal of Psychology* 20 (1985): 541–67.

Comaroff, Jean, and John L. Comaroff, "Goodly Beasts, Beastly Goods: Cattle and Commodities in a South African Context." *American Ethnologist* 17, 2 (1990): 196–214.

———. *Of Revelation and Revolution.* Vol. 1: *Christianity, Colonialism, and Consciousness in South Africa.* Chicago: University of Chicago Press, 1991.

———. *Ethnography and the Historical Imagination.* Boulder, Colo.: Westview Press, 1992.

———, eds. *Modernity and Its Malcontents: Ritual and Power in Postcolonial Africa.* Chicago: University of Chicago Press, 1993.

———. *Of Revelation and Revolution.* Vol. 2: *The Dialectics of Modernity on a South African Frontier.* Chicago: University of Chicago Press, 1997.

Comaroff, John L. "Images of Empire, Contests of Conscience: Models of Colonial Domination in South Africa." In Cooper and Stoler, eds., *Tensions of Empire,* 163–97. Berkeley and Los Angeles: University of California Press, 1997.

Cook, Sir Albert R. *Uganda Memories (1887–1940).* Kampala: Uganda Society, 1945.

Cooper, Frederick. *From Slaves to Squatters: Plantation Labor in Zanzibar and Coastal Kenya, 1890–1925.* New Haven: Yale University Press, 1980.

———, ed. *Struggle for the City: Migrant Labor, Capital and the State in Urban Africa.* Beverly Hills, Calif.: Sage, 1983.

————. *On the African Waterfront: Urban Disorder and the Transformation of Work in Mombasa.* New Haven: Yale University Press, 1987.

————. *Decolonization and African Society: The Labor Question in French and British Africa.* Cambridge: Cambridge University Press, 1996.

Cooper, Frederick, and Ann Laura Stoler, eds. *Tensions of Empire: Colonial Cultures in a Bourgeois World.* Berkeley and Los Angeles: University of California Press, 1997.

Copjec, Joan. "Vampires, Breast-Feeding, and Anxiety." *October* 58 (1991): 25–43.

Coplan, David B. *In the Time of Cannibals: The Word Music of South Africa's Basuto Migrants.* Chicago: University of Chicago Press, 1994.

Corbin, Alain. *The Village of Cannibals: Rage and Murder in France, 1870.* Translated by Arthur Goldhammer. Cambridge, Mass.: Harvard University Press, 1992.

Coulter, Charles. "The Sociological Problem." In Davis, ed., *Modern Industry and the African,* 59–78. London: Macmillan, 1933.

Creehan, Kate. *The Factured Community: Landscapes of Power and Gender in Rural Zambia.* Berkeley and Los Angeles: University of California Press, 1997.

Crisp, Jeff. "Productivity and Protest: Scientific Management in the Ghanaian Gold Mines, 1947–1956." In Cooper, ed., *Struggle for the City,* 91–129. Beverly Hills, Calif.: Sage, 1983.

Cunningham, Clark E. "Thai 'Injection Doctors': Antibiotic Mediators." *Social Science and Medicine* 4, 1 (1970): 1–24.

Cunnison, Ian. *History on the Luapula: An Essay on the Historical Notions of a Central African Tribe.* Rhodes-Livingstone Papers, no. 21. Cape Town and New York: G. Cumberlege, Oxford University Press, for the Rhodes-Livingstone Institute, 1951.

Davies, J. N. P. "The History of Syphilis in Uganda." *Bulletin of the World Health Organization* 15 (1956): 1041–55.

————. "The Development of 'Scientific' Medicine in the African Kingdom of Bunyoro-Kitara." *Medical History* 3, 1 (1959): 47–57.

————. "The Cause of Sleeping Sickness: Entebbe 1902–03." *E. A. Medical J.* 39, 3 and 4 (1962): 81–99, 145–60.

————. "Informed Speculation on the Cause of Sleeping Sickness, 1898–1903." *Medical History* 12 (1968): 200–204.

Davis, J. Merle, ed. *Modern Industry and the African: An Enquiry into the Effect of the Copper Mines of Central Africa upon Native Society and the Work of Christian Missions Made under the Auspices of the Department of Social and Industrial Research of the International Missionary Council.* London: Macmillan, 1933. 2d ed. with a new introd. by Robert I. Rotberg. New York: A. M. Kelley, 1968.

Davis, Natalie Zemon. *The Return of Martin Guerre.* Cambridge, Mass.: Harvard University Press, 1983.

————. "On the Lame," *American Historical Review* 93 (1988): 572–603.

Davison, Jean, and the Women of Mutira. *Voices from Mutira: Lives of Rural Gikuyu Women.* Boulder, Colo.: Lynne Rienner, 1989.

"Dawa ya Sindano." *East African Medical Journal* 28, 11 (1951): 476.

Dawson, Marc H. "The 1920s Anti-Yaws Campaigns and Colonial Medical Policy in Kenya." *International Journal of African Historical Studies* 20, 3 (1987): 220–40.

———. "Socioeconomic Change and Disease: Smallpox in Colonial Kenya, 1880–1920." In Feierman and Janzen, eds., *The Social Basis for Health and Healing in Africa*, 90–103. Berkeley and Los Angeles: University of California Press, 1992.

Delaporte, François. *The History of Yellow Fever: An Essay on the Birth of Tropical Medicine.* Translated by Arthur Goldhammer. Cambridge, Mass.: MIT Press, 1991. Originally published as *Histoire de la fièvre jaune: Naissance de la médecine tropicale* (Paris: Payot, 1989).

di Leonardo, Micaela. "Oral History as Ethnographic Encounter." *Oral History Review* 15 (1987): 1–20.

———, ed. *Gender at the Crossroads of Knowledge: Feminist Anthropology in the Postmodern Era.* Berkeley and Los Angeles: University of California Press, 1991

Dotson, Lorraine. "Marvelous Facts and Miraculous Evidence." In *Questions of Evidence*, ed. Chandler, et al., 243–74. Chicago: University of Chicago Press, 1994.

Douglas, Mary. *Purity and Danger: An Analysis of the Concepts of Pollution and Taboo.* New York: Praeger; London: Routledge & Kegan Paul, 1966.

———, ed. *Witchcraft Confessions and Accusations.* London: Tavistock, 1970.

Downs, Laura Lee. "If 'Woman' Is Just an Empty Category, Then Why Am I Afraid to Walk Alone at Night? Identity Politics Meets the Postmodern Subject." *Comparative Studies in Society and History* 35, 2 (1993): 414–37.

Dresser, Norine. *American Vampires: Fans, Victims and Practitioners.* New York: Norton, 1989.

Dubb, Allie, ed. "Myth in Modern Africa." Fourteenth Conference Proceedings of the Rhodes-Livingstone Institute for Social Research. Lusaka, 1960. Mimeographed.

Dundes, Alan, ed. *The Blood Libel Legend: A Casebook in Anti-Semitic Folklore.* Madison: University of Wisconsin Press, 1991.

———. "The Ritual Murder or Blood Libel Legend: A Study in Anti-Semitic Victimization through Projective Inversion." In *The Blood Libel Legend*, ed. Dundes, 336–78. Madison: University of Wisconsin Press, 1991.

Dunlap, Thomas R. *Saving America's Wildlife: Ecology and the American Mind.* Princeton: Princeton University Press, 1988.

Ebling, Walter. *Subtropical Entomology.* San Francisco: Western Agriculture Publishing House, 1949.

Ellis, Bill. "De Legendis Urbis: Modern Legends in Ancient Rome." *Journal of American Folklore* 96, 380 (1983): 200–210.

Engels, Dagmar, and Shula Marks, eds. *Contesting Colonial Hegemony: State and Society in India and Africa.* London: I. B. Taurus, 1994.

Epstein, A. L. *Politics in an Urban African Community.* Manchester: Manchester University Press for the Rhodes-Livingstone Institute, 1958.

———. "Linguistic Innovation and Culture on the Copperbelt." *Southwestern Journal of Anthropology* 15 (1959): 235–53.

———. "Unconscious Factors in Response to Social Crisis: A Case Study from Central Africa." *Psychoanalytic Study of Society* 8 (1979): 3–39.

———. *Scenes from African Urban Life.* Edinburgh: Edinburgh University Press, 1992.

———. "Gossip, Norms, and Social Networks" (1969). In id., *Scenes from African Urban Life,* 88–99. Edinburgh: Edinburgh University Press, 1992.

———. "Response to Social Crisis: Aspects of Oral Aggression in Central Africa." In id., *Scenes from African Urban Life,* 158–207. Edinburgh: Edinburgh University Press, 1992.

Evans, A. J. "The Ila V.D. Campaign." *Rhodes-Livingstone Journal* 9 (1944): 39–46.

Evans-Pritchard, E. E. "Zande Blood Brotherhood." *Africa* 6, 4 (1933): 469–501.

———. *Witchcraft, Oracles and Magic among the Azande.* Oxford: Clarendon Press, 1937.

Fabian, Johannes. *Time and the Other: How Anthropology Makes Its Object.* New York: Columbia University Press, 1983.

———. *Language and Colonial Power: The Appropriation of Swahili in the Former Belgian Congo, 1880–1938.* Cambridge: Cambridge University Press, 1986.

———, ed. and trans. *History from Below: The Vocabulary of Elisabethville by André Yav: Texts, Translations, and Interpretive Essay.* With assistance from Kalundi Mango and linguistic notes by W. Schicho. Amsterdam and Philadelphia: John Benjamins, 1990.

———. *Remembering the Present: Painting and Popular History in Zaire.* Berkeley and Los Angeles: University of California Press, 1996.

Fair, Laura. "Identity, Difference, and Dance: Female Initiation in Zanzibar, 1890–1930." *Frontiers: A Journal of Women's Studies* 17, 3 (1996): 146–72.

———. "Kickin' It: Leisure, Politics, and Football in Zanzibar, 1900s–1950s." *Africa* 67, 2 (1997): 224–51.

———. "Dressing Up: Clothing, Class and Gender in Post-Abolition Zanzibar." *Journal of African History* 39, 1 (1998): 63–94.

Fallers, Lloyd A. *Law without Precedent: Legal Ideas in Action in the Courts of Colonial Busoga.* Chicago: University of Chicago Press, 1969.

Fanon, Frantz. *The Wretched of the Earth.* Translated by Constance Farrington. New York: Grove Press, 1963.

———. *Studies in a Dying Colonialism.* New York: Grove Press, 1965.

Farge, Arlette, and Jacques Revel. *The Vanishing Children of Paris: Rumor and Politics before the French Revolution.* Translated by Claudia Miéville. Cambridge, Mass.: Harvard University Press, 1991.

Farley, John. *Bilharzia: A History of Imperial Tropical Medicine.* Cambridge: Cambridge University Press, 1991.

Farmer, Paul. "Bad Blood, Spoiled Milk: Bodily Fluids as Moral Barometers in Rural Haiti." *American Ethnologist* 15, 1 (1988): 62–83.

Favret-Saada, Jeanne. *Deadly Words: Witchcraft in the Bocage.* Translated by Catherine Cullen. Cambridge: Cambridge University Press, 1980.

Feeley-Harnik, Gillian. *The Lord's Table: Eucharist and Passover in Early Christianity.* Philadelphia: University of Pennsylvania Press, 1981.

Feierman, Steven. "Change in African Theraputic Systems." *Social Science and Medicine* 13B (1979): 277–84.

———. "Struggles for Control: The Social Roots of Health and Healing in Modern Africa." *African Studies Rev.* 28, 2–3 (1982): 73–148.

———. *Peasant Intellectuals: History and Anthropology in Tanzania.* Madison: University of Wisconsin Press, 1990.

Feierman, Steven, and John Janzen, eds. *The Social Basis for Health and Healing in Africa.* Berkeley and Los Angeles: University of California Press, 1992.

Feinblatt, Henry M. *Transfusion of Blood.* New York: Macmillan, 1926.

Ferguson, James, "Mobile Workers, Modernist Narratives: A Critique of the Historiography of Transition on the Zambian Copperbelt." *Journal of Southern African Studies* 16, 3 and 4 (1990): 385–412, 603–21.

Ferguson, Robert. "Story and Transcription in the Trial of John Brown." *Yale Journal of Law and the Humanities* 6, 1 (1994): 37–73.

Festinger, Leon, et al. "A Study of Rumor: Its Origins and Spread." *Human Relations* 1 (1948): 464–86.

Fetter, Bruce S. "The Lualabourg Revolt at Elisabethville." *African Historical Studies* 2, 2 (1965): 269–87.

———. *The Creation of Elisabethville.* Stanford: Hoover Institution Press, 1976.

Fields, Karen E. *Revival and Rebellion in Colonial Central Africa.* Princeton: Princeton University Press, 1985. Reprint. Portsmouth, N.H.: Heinemann, 1997.

Fine, Gary Alan. "The Kentucky Fried Rat: Legends and Modern Society." *Journal of the Folklore Institute* 17, 2–3 (1980): 235–48.

———. *Manufacturing Tales: Sex and Money in Contemporary Legends.* Knoxville: University of Tennessee Press, 1992.

Finlay, Robert. "The Refashioning of Martin Guerre." *American Historical Review* 93 (1988): 552–71.

Foster, Stephan William. *The Past Is Another Country: Representation, Historical Consciousness, and Resistance in the Blue Ridge.* Berkeley and Los Angeles: University of California Press, 1988.

Ford, John. *The Role of Trypanosomiasis in African Ecology: A Study of the Tsetse Fly Problem.* Oxford: Oxford University Press, 1971.

Foucault, Michel. *The History of Sexuality.* Translated by Robert Hurley. Vol. 1: *An Introduction.* New York: Pantheon Books, 1978. Vol. 2: *The Use of Pleasure.* New York: Random House, 1985. Vol. 3: *The Care of the Self.* New York: Pantheon Books, 1986. Originally published in 3 vols. as *Histoire de la sexualité* (Paris: Gallimard, 1976–84).

Fraenkel, Peter. *Wayaleshi.* London: Weidenfeld & Nicholson, 1959.

Friedland, William. "Some Urban Myths of East Africa." In "Myth in Modern Africa," ed. Dubb, 140–53.

Friedlander, Saul, ed. *Probing the Limits of Representation: Nazism and the "Final Solution."* Cambridge, Mass.: Harvard University Press, 1992.

Fry, Gladys-Marie. *Night Riders in Black Folk History.* Knoxville: University of Tennessee Press, 1975.

Gabriel, Frère. *Dictionnaire Tshiluba-Français*. Brussels: Librairie Albert de Witt, n.d. [1948].

Gal, Susan. "Between Speech and Silence: The Problematics of Research on Language and Gender." In di Leonardo, ed., *Gender at the Crossroads of Knowledge*, 175–200. Berkeley and Los Angeles: University of California Press, 1991.

Galaty, John G. "'The Eye That Wants a Person, Where Can It Not See?': Inclusion, Exclusion, and Boundary Shifters in Maasai Identity." In Thomas Spear and Richard Waller, eds., *Being Maasai*, 174–94. London: James Currey, 1993.

Gann, Lewis H. *A History of Northern Rhodesia: Early Days to 1953*. London: Chatto & Windus, 1964. New York: Humanities Press, 1969.

Gee, T. W. "A Century of Mohammedan Influence in Buganda, 1852–1951." *Uganda Journal* 22, 2 (1958): 129–50.

Geertz, Clifford. "Thick Description: Toward an Interpretative Theory of Culture." In id., *The Interpretation of Cultures*. New York: Basic Books, 1973.

Geiger, Susan. "Women's Life Histories: Content and Method." *Signs: Journal of Women in Culture and Society* 11, 2 (1986): 334–51.

———. "What's So Feminist about Women's Oral History?" *Journal of Women's History* 2, 1 (1990): 169–80.

———. *TANU Women: Gender, Culture and the Making of Tanganyikan Nationalism*. Portsmouth, N.H.: Heinemann, 1997.

Gengenbach, Heidi. "Historical Truth and Life Narratives: A Reply to Kirk Hoppe." *International Journal of African Historical Studies* 27, 3 (1994): 619–27.

Geschiere, Peter. *The Modernity of Witchcraft: Politics and the Occult in Postcolonial Africa*. Charlottesville: University Press of Virigina, 1997.

Giblin, James. "Trypanosomias Control in African History: An Evaded Issue?" *Journal of African History* 31 (1990): 59–70.

———. *The Politics of Environmental Control in Northeast Tanzania, 1840–1940*. Philadelphia: University of Pennsylvania Press, 1992.

Ginzburg, Carlo. *Nightbattles: Witchcraft and Agrarian Cults in the Sixteenth and Seventeenth Centuries*. Translated by John and Anne Tedeschi. New York: Penguin Books, 1983.

———. *Clues, Myths and Historical Method*. Translated by John and Anne Tedeschi. Baltimore: Johns Hopkins University Press, 1988.

———. *Ecstasies: Deciphering the Witches' Sabbath*. Translated by Raymond Rosenthal. New York: Pantheon Books, 1991.

Gintzburger, Alphonse. "Accommodation to Poverty: The Case of Malagasy Peasant Communities." *Cahiers d'études africaines* 92, 23–4 (1983): 419–42.

Glover, David. *Vampires, Mummies, and Liberals: Bram Stoker and the Politics of Popular Fiction*. Durham, N.C.: Duke University Press, 1996.

Gluckman, Max. "Gossip and Scandal." *Current Anthropology* 4, 3 (1963): 307–16.

———, ed. *The Allocation of Responsibility*. Manchester: Manchester University Press, 1972.

Goldthrope, J. E. "Attitudes to the Census and Vital Registration in East Africa." *Population Studies* 2 (1952): 163–71.

Goodchild, R. S. T. "News from Kabale." *Mission Hospital* 40, 461 (1936): 137–40.

Goody, Jack, and Joan Buckley. "Inheritance and Women's Labour in Africa." *Africa* 43, 2 (1973): 108–20.

Gottlieb, Alma. "A Critical Appraisal of Theories of Menstrual Symbolism." In Buckley and Gottlieb, eds., *Blood Magic,* 3–40. Berkeley and Los Angeles: University of California Press, 1988.

Greendyke, Robert M. *Introduction to Blood Banking.* Garden City, N.Y.: Medical Examination Publishing Co., 1980.

Gudeman, Stephen. *Economics and Culture.* London: Routledge, 1986.

Guha, Ranajit. "The Prose of Counter-Insurgency." *Subaltern Studies* (Oxford) 2 (1983): 1–42.

Gussman, Boris. *Out in the Mid-Day Sun.* London: George Allen & Unwin, 1963.

Guy, Jeff. "Technology, Ethnicity, and Ideology: Basotho Miners and Shaft Sinking on the South African Gold Mines," *Journal of Southern African Studies* 14, 2 (1988): 254–70.

Guyer, Jane I. "Female Farming in Anthropology and African History." In di Leonardo, ed., *Gender at the Crossroads of Knowledge,* 257–77.

Hamilton, C. A. "Ideology and Oral History: Listening to Voices from Below." *History in Africa* 14 (1987): 57–85.

Hannerz, Ulf. "Gossip, Networks and Culture in a Black American Ghetto." *Ethnos* 32 (1967): 35–60.

Hansen, Karen Tranberg. *Distant Companions: Servants and Employers in Zambia, 1900–1985.* Ithaca, N.Y.: Cornell University Press, 1989.

———, ed. *African Encounters with Domesticity.* New Brunswick, N.J.: Rutgers University Press, 1992.

———. "Dealing with Used Clothing: *Salaula* and the Construction of Identity in Zambia's Third Republic." *Public Culture* 6 (1994): 503–22.

———. "Transnational Biographies and Local Meanings: Used Clothing Practices in Lusaka." *Journal of Southern African Studies* 21, 1 (1995): 131–45.

Haraway, Donna. *Primate Visions: Gender, Race, and Nature in the World of Science.* London: Routledge, 1989.

Harris, Patrick. *Work, Culture, Identity: Migrant Laborers in Mozambique and South Africa, c. 1860–1910.* Portsmouth, N.H.: Heinemann, 1994.

Harris, Olivia. "The Earth and the State: The Sources and the Meanings of Money in North Potosi, Bolivia." In Parry and Bloch, eds., *Money and the Morality of Exchange,* 229–41. Cambridge: Cambridge University Press, 1989.

Harwich, Christopher. *Red Dust: Memories of the Uganda Police, 1935–1955.* Introduction by H. H. the Kabaka of Buganda. London: V. Stuart, 1961.

Hart, Keith. "Heads or Tails? Two Sides of the Coin." *Man,* n.s., 21 (1986): 637–56.

Haviland, John Beard. *Gossip, Reputation and Knowledge in Zincantan.* Chicago: University of Chicago Press, 1977.

Hay, Margaret Jean. "Women as Owners, Occupants, and Managers of Property in Colonial Western Kenya."In id. and Marcia Wright, eds., *African Women and the Law: Historical Perspectives*, 110–23. Boston University Papers in African History, 7. Boston: African Studies Center, Boston University, 1982.

Headrick, Daniel R. *The Tools of Empire: Technology and European Imperialism in the Nineteenth Century*. New York: Oxford University Press, 1981.

———. *Tentacles of Progress: Technology Transfer in the Age of Imperialism, 1850–1940*. Oxford: Oxford University Press, 1988.

Henderson, Ian. "Early African Leadership: The Copperbelt Disturbances of 1935 and 1940." *Journal of Southern African Studies* 2, 1 (1975): 80–97.

Henige, David P. "The Problem of Feedback in Oral Tradition: Four Examples from the Fante Coastlands." *Journal of African History* 14, 2 (1973): 223–35.

———. *The Chronology of Oral Tradition: Quest for a Chimera*. Oxford: Oxford University Press, 1974.

———. "'The Disease of Writing': Ganda and Nyoro Kinglists in a Newly Literate World." In Miller, ed., *The African Past Speaks*, 240–61. Hampden, Conn.: Archon Books, 1980.

Herbert, Eugenia W. "Smallpox Inoculation in Africa." *Journal of African History* 16, 4 (1975): 539–59.

Heusch, Luc de. *The Drunken King, or, The Origin of the State*. Translated by Roy Willis. Bloomington: Indiana University Press, 1982. Originally published as *Le roi ivre, ou, L'origine de l'État: Mythes et rites bantous*. (Paris: Gallimard, 1972).

Hevia, James L. "The Archive State and the Fear of Pollution: From the Opium Wars to Fu Manchu." *Cultural Studies* 12, 2 (1998): 234–64.

Hills, Denis. *Rebel People*. London: George Allen & Unwin, 1978.

Higginson, John. "Steam without a Piston Box: Strikes and Popular Unrest in Katanga, 1943–45." *International Journal African Historical Studies* 21, 1 (1988): 90–111.

———. *A Working Class in the Making: Belgian Colonial Labor Policy, Private Enterprise, and the African Mineworker*. Madison: University of Wisconsin Press, 1989.

Hobson, Dick. *Showtime: The Agricultural and Commercial Society of Zambia*. Lusaka: Agricultural and Commercial Society of Zambia, 1979.

Hoch, E. *Bemba Pocket Dictionary: Bemba-English and English-Bemba*. Abercorn and Kipalapala: White Fathers Press, 1960.

Hofmeyr, Isabel. *"We Spend Our Years as a Tale That Is Told": Oral Historical Narratives in a South African Chiefdom*. Portsmouth, N.H.: Heinemann, 1994.

———. "'Wailing for Purity': Oral Studies in Southern African Studies." *African Studies* 52, 4 (1995): 16–31.

Holmes, Colin. "The Ritual Murder Accusation in Britain." In Dundes, ed., *The Blood Libel Legend*, 99–134. Madison: University of Wisconsin Press, 1991.

Hoppe, Kirk. "Whose Life Is It Anyway? The Issue of Representation in Personal Narratives." *International Journal of African Historical Studies* 26, 3 (1993): 623–36.

Holt, Thomas. "Experience and the Politics of Intellectual Inquiry." In James Chandler, Arnold I. Davidson, and Harry Harootunian, eds., *Questions of Evidence: Proof, Practice and Persuasian,* 388–94. Chicago: University of Chicago Press, 1994.

Hsia, R. Po-chia. *The Myth of Ritual Murder: Jews and Magic in Reformation Germany.* New Haven: Yale University Press, 1988.

———. *Trent 1475: Stories of a Ritual Murder Trial.* New Haven: Yale University Press, 1992.

Hulme, Kathryn. *The Nun's Story.* Boston: Little, Brown, 1956.

Hunt, Nancy Rose. "'Le bébé en brousse': European Women, Birth Spacing, and Colonial Intervention in Breast Feeding in the Belgian Congo." *International Journal of African Historical Studies* 21, 3 (1988): 401–32.

———. "Noise over Camouflaged Polygyny: Colonial Marriage Taxation and a Woman Naming Crisis in Belgian Africa." *Journal of African History* 32, 3 (1991): 471–95.

———. "Colonial Fairy Tales and the Knife and Fork Doctrine in the Heart of Africa." In Hansen, ed., *African Encounters with Domesticity,* 143–66. New Brunswick, N.J.: Rutgers University Press, 1992.

———. *A Colonial Lexicon of Birth Ritual, Medicalization and Mobility in the Congo.* Durham, N.C.: Duke University Press, 1999.

Hutchinson, Sharon. "The Cattle of Money and the Cattle of Girls among the Nuer, 1939–1983." *American Ethnologist* 19, 2 (1992): 294–316.

Huxley, Elspeth. *The Sorcerer's Apprentice: A Journey through East Africa.* London: Chatto & Windus, 1948.

Iliffe, John. *A Modern History of Tanganyika.* Cambridge: Cambridge University Press, 1979.

———. *East African Doctors: A History of the Modern Profession.* Cambridge: Cambridge University Press, 1998.

Ingrams, Harold J. *Uganda: A Crisis of Nationhood.* London: HMSO, 1960.

Inter-Territorial Language Committee for the East African Dependencies. *Standard Swahili-English Dictionary.* Oxford: Oxford University Press, 1942.

Ipenburg, Arie N. *Lubwa: The Presbyterian Mission and the Eastern Bemba.* Lusaka: Teresianium Press, 1984.

Irvine, Judith T., and Jane H. Hill, eds. *Responsibility and Evidence in Oral Discourse.* Cambridge: Cambridge University Press, 1992.

Jack, Rupert. "Tsetse Fly and Big Game in Southern Rhodesia." *Bull. Entomological Res.* 1 (1914): 97–110.

Jakobson, Roman. "On Linguistic Aspects of Translation." In Rueben A. Bower, ed., *On Translation,* 232–39. Cambridge, Mass.: Harvard University Press, 1959.

Janmohammed, J. K. "African Laborers in Mombasa, c. 1895–1940." *Hadith* 5 (1972): 156–79.

Janzen, John, and William Akinstall. *The Quest for Therapy in Lower Zaire.* Berkeley and Los Angeles: University of California Press, 1978.

Johnson, Donald M. "The 'Phantom Anesthetist' of Mattoon: A Field Study in Mass Hysteria." *Journal of Abnormal and Social Psychology* 40 (1945): 175–86.

Jordanova, Ludmilla, ed. *Languages of Nature: Critical Essays on Science and Literature.* London: Free Association Books, 1986.

————. *Sexual Visions: Images of Gender in Science and Medicine in the Nineteenth and Twentieth Centuries.* Madison: University of Wisconsin Press, 1989.

Joyce, Patrick, ed. *The Historical Meanings of Work.* Cambridge: Cambridge University Press, 1987.

Kaavu, Enoch. *Namusiya on the Mines.* Translated from Ila by R. Nabulgato and C. R. Hopgood. London: Longmans, 1949.

Kanfer, Stefan. *The Last Empire: De Beers, Diamonds and the World.* New York: Farrar, Straus & Giroux, 1993.

Kapferer, Jean-Noël. *Rumors: Uses, Interpretations, and Images.* New Brunswick, N.J.: Transaction Publishers, 1990. Originally published as *Rumeurs: Le plus vieux média du monde* (Paris: Seuil, 1987).

Karp, Ivan. *Fields of Change among the Iteso of Kenya.* London: Routledge & Kegan Paul, 1978.

————. "New Guinea Models in the African Savannah." *Africa* 48, 1 (1978): 1–16.

————. "Beer Drinking and Social Experience in an African Society: An Essay in Formal Sociology." In Karp and Bird, eds., *Explorations in African Systems of Thought,* 83–118. Bloomington: Indiana University Press, 1980.

————. "Laughter at Marriage: Subversion in Performance." In David Parkin and David Nyamwaya, eds., *The Transformation of African Marriage,* 137–54. Manchester: Manchester University Press, 1987.

————. "Other Cultures in Museum Perspective." In Karp and Levine, eds., *Exhibiting Cultures,* 373–85. Washington, D.C.: Smithsonian Institution Press, 1991.

Karp, Ivan, and Charles S. Bird, eds. *Explorations in African Systems of Thought.* Bloomington: Indiana University Press, 1980.

Karp, Ivan, and Steven D. Levine, eds. *Exhibiting Cultures: The Poetics and Politics of Museum Displays.* Washington, D.C.: Smithsonian Institution Press, 1991.

Kashoki, Mubanga E. "Town Bemba: A Sketch of Its Main Structure." *African Social Research* 3 (1972): 176–83.

Kasozi, A. B. K. *The Social Origins of Violence in Uganda, 1964–1985.* Montréal: McGill-Queen's University Press, 1994.

Kavuma, Paulo. *Crisis in Buganda, 1953–55: The Story of the Exile and the Return of the Kabaka, Mutesa II.* London: Rex Collings, 1979.

Keegan, Tim. *Facing the Storm: Portraits of Black Lives in Rural South Africa.* London: Zed Books, 1988.

Kennedy, Dane. *Islands of White: Settler Society and Culture in Kenya and Southern Rhodesia.* Durham, N.C.: Duke University Press, 1987.

Kershaw, Greet [Gretha Kershaw]. *Mau Mau from Below*. Athens: Ohio University Press; Oxford: James Currey, 1997.

Klaniczay, Gábor. *The Uses of Supernatural Power: The Transformation of Popular Religion in Medieval and Early Modern Europe*. Translated by Susan Singerman. Princeton, Princeton University Press, 1990.

Koenig, Frederick. *Rumor in the Marketplace: The Social Psychology of Commercial Hearsay*. Dover, Mass.: Auburn House, 1985.

Krapf, Rev. Dr. L. *A Dictionary of the Swahili Language*. London: Trubner, 1882.

Kratz, Corinne A. "Are the Okiek Really Maasai? or Kipsigis? or Kikuyu?" *Cahiers d'études africains* 79, 20 (1981): 355–85.

———. "'We've Always Done it Like This': 'Tradition' and 'Innovation' in Okiek Ceremonies." *Comparative Studies in Society and History* 34, 3 (1993): 30–65.

———. *Affecting Performance: Meaning, Movement, and Experience in Okiek Women's Initiation*. Washington, D.C.: Smithsonian Institution Press, 1994.

LaFontaine, Jean S. "The Ritualization of Women's Life-Crises in Bugisu." In id., ed., *The Interpretation of Ritual: Essays in Honor of A. I. Richards*, 156–86. London, Tavistock, 1972.

Lambkin, F. J. "An Outbreak of Syphilis on Virgin Soil: Notes on Syphilis in the Uganda Protectorate," In Power and Murphy, *A System of Syphilis*, 2: 339–54. London: Oxford University Press, 1914.

Lan, David. *Guns and Rain: Guerillas and Spirit Mediums in Zimbabwe*. London: James Currey, 1985.

Landau, Paul S. *The Realm of the Word: Language, Gender, and Christianity in a South African Kingdom*. Portsmouth, N.H.: Heinemann, 1995.

———. "Explaining Surgical Evangelism in Colonial Southern Africa: Teeth, Pain, and Faith." *Journal of African History* 37 (1996): 261–81.

Larson, Pier M. "'Capacities and Modes of Thought': Intellectual Engagement and Subaltern Hegemony in the Early History of Malagasy Christianity." *American Historical Review* 102, 4 (1997): 969–1002.

Law, Robin. "How Truly Traditional Is Our Traditional History? The Case of Samuel Johnson and the Recording of Yoruba Oral History." *History in Africa* 11 (1984): 180–202.

Leakey, L. S. B. *The Southern Kikuyu before 1903*. 3 vols. New York: Academic Press, 1977.

Leakey, R. A. B. "At Work in Toro Hospital." *Mission Hospital* 33 (1929): 152–54.

Lefebvre, Georges. *The Great Fear of 1789: Rural Panic in Revolutionary France*. Translated by Joan White. New York: Pantheon Books, 1973. Reprint, Princeton, N.J. : Princeton University Press, 1982.

Lennihan, Louise. "Rights in Men and Rights in Land: Slavery, Labor, and Smallholder Agriculture in Northern Nigeria." *Slavery and Abolition* 3, 2 (1982): 111–39.

Lienhardt, Godfrey. "Some Notions of Witchcraft among the Dinka," *Africa* 21, 4 (1951): 303–18.

Lienhardt, Peter. "The Interpretation of Rumour." In J. H. Beattie and R. G. Lienhardt, eds., *Studies in Social Anthropology: Essays in Memory of E. E. Evans-Pritchard by His Former Oxford Colleagues,* 105–31. Oxford: Clarendon Press, 1975.

Lonsdale, John. "The Moral Economy of Mau Mau: Wealth, Poverty, and Civic Virtue in Kikuyu Political Thought." In id. and Bruce Berman, *Unhappy Valley: Conflict in Kenya and Africa,* bk. 2, "Violence and Ethnicity," 315–504. Athens: Ohio University Press, 1992.

———. "The Prayers of Waiyaki: The Uses of the Kikuyu Past." In David Anderson and Douglas H. Johnson, eds., *Revealing Prophets: Prophecy in East African History,* 240–91. London: James Currey, 1995.

Louis, [Sister] M. *Love is the Answer (The Story of Mother Kevin).* Paterson, N.J.: Saint Anthony's Guild, 1964.

Lubeck, Paul. "Petroleum and Proletarianization." *African Economic History* 18 (1989): 99–112.

Lyons, Maryinez. "From Death Camps to *Cordon Sanitaire:* The Development of Sleeping Sickness Policy in the Uele District of the Belgian Congo." *Journal of African History* 26 (1985): 69–91.

———. *The Colonial Disease: Sleeping Sickness and the Social History of Zaire, 1890–1939.* Cambridge: Cambridge University Press, 1992.

———. "The Power to Heal: African Medical Auxiliaries in Colonial Belgian Congo." In Engels and Marks, eds., *Contesting Colonial Hegemony,* 202–23. London: I. B. Taurus, 1994.

MacGaffey, Wyatt. "The West in Congolese Experience." In Philip Curtin, ed., *Africa and the West: Intellectual Responses to European Culture,* 49–74. Madison: University of Wisconsin Press, 1972.

MacKenzie, Fiona. "Local Initiatives and National Policy: Gender and Agricultural Change in Murang'a District, Kenya." *Canadian Journal of African Studies* 20, 3 (1986): 377–401.

———. "Land and Territory: the Interface between Two Systems of Land Tenure, Murang'a District." *Africa* 59, 1 (1989): 91–109.

MacKenzie, John. *The Empire of Nature: Hunting, Conservation and British Imperialism.* Manchester: Manchester University Press, 1988.

———, ed. *Imperialism and the Natural World.* Manchester: Manchester University Press, 1990.

MacLeod, Roy, and Milton Lewis, eds. *Disease, Medicine and Empire: Perspectives on Western Medicine and the Experience of European Expansion.* London: Routledge, 1988.

MacPhearson, Margaret. *They Built for the Future: A Chronicle of Makarere University College, 1922–1962.* Cambridge: Cambridge University Press, 1964.

Madan, A. C. *English-Swahili Dictionary.* Oxford: Oxford University Press, 1902.

Magubane, Bernard. "A Critical Look at the Indices Used in the Study of Social Change in Central Africa." *Current Anthropology* 12, 4–5 (1971): 419–31.

Mair, L. P. *An African People in the Twentieth Century.* London: Routledge and Sons, 1934.

Malkki, Liisa M. *Purity and Exile: Violence, Memory, and National Cosmology among Hutu Refugees in Tanzania.* Chicago: University of Chicago Press, 1995.

Mamdani, Mahmood. *Citizen and Subject: Contemporary Africa and the Legacy of Late Colonialism.* Princeton: Princeton University Press, 1996.

Mani, Lata. "Contentious Traditions: The Debate over Sati in Colonial India." *Cultural Critique* 7 (1987): 119–56.

Marks, Shula. *"Not Either an Experimental Doll": The Separate Worlds of Three South African Women.* Bloomington: Indiana University Press, 1988.

———. *Divided Sisterhood: The South African Nursing Profession and the Making of Apartheid.* Johannesburg: University of Witwatersrand Press, 1995.

Marks, Stuart A. *Large Mammals and a Brave People: Subsistence Hunters in Zambia.* Seattle: University of Washington Press, 1976.

Martin, Phyllis. *Leisure and Society in Colonial Brazzaville.* Cambridge: Cambridge University Press, 1995.

Marwick, Max. "The Social Context of Cewa Witch Beliefs." *Africa* 22, 2 (1952): 120–35.

Marx, Karl. *Capital: A Critique of Political Economy.* Vol. 1. 1867. Harmondsworth: Penguin Books, 1976.

Matongo, Albert B. K. "Popular Culture in a Colonial Society: Another Look at *mbeni* and *kalela* Dances on the Copperbelt, 1930–1960." In Chipungu, ed., *Guardians in Their Time,* 180–217. London: Macmillan, 1992.

Matossian, Mary Kilbourne. *Poisons of the Past: Molds, Epidemics and History.* New Haven: Yale University Press, 1989.

Matsuda, Matt K. *The Memory of the Modern.* Oxford: Oxford University Press, 1996.

Mbilinyi, Marjorie. "Runaway Wives in Colonial Tanganyika: Forced Labour and Forced Marriage in Rungwe District, 1919–1951." *International Journal of the Sociology of Law* 16 (1988): 1–29.

———. "'I'd Have Been a Man': Politics and the Labor Process in Producing Personal Narratives." In Personal Narratives Group, ed., *Interpreting Women's Lives,* 204–27. Bloomington: Indiana University Press, 1989.

McCarl, Robert. *The District of Columbia Fire Fighters' Project: A Case Study in Occupational Folklore.* Washington, D.C.: Smithsonian Institution Press, 1985.

McKelvey, John J., Jr. *Man against Tsetse: Struggle for Africa.* Ithaca, N.Y.: Cornell University Press, 1973.

Meebelo, Henry S. *Reaction to Colonialism: A Prelude to the Politics of Independence in Northern Zambia, 1893–1939.* Manchester: Manchester University Press, 1971.

Merry, Sally Engel. "Rethinking Gossip and Scandal." In Donald Black, ed., *Toward a General Theory of Social Control,* vol. 1, *The Fundamentals,* 277–301. New York: Academic Press, 1984.

Michel, J.-M. "Why Do People Like Medicines? A Perspective from Africa." *Lancet* 210, 1 (1985): 209–11.

Middleton, John, and E. H. Winter, eds. *Witchcraft and Sorcery in East Africa.* London: Routledge & Kegan Paul, 1963.

―――. *Lugbara Religion: Ritual and Authority among an East African People.* 1960. Washington, D.C.: Smithsonian Institution Press, 1987.

Miers, Suzanne, and Richard Roberts, eds. *The End of Slavery in Africa.* Madison: University of Wisconsin Press, 1988.

Miescher, Stephan F. "Of Documents and Litigants: Disputes of Inheritance in Abetifi—a Town in Colonial Ghana." *Journal of Legal Pluralism* 39 (1997): 81–119.

Mighetto, Lisa. *Wild Animals and American Environmental Ethics.* Tucson: University of Arizona Press, 1991.

Miller, Janet. *Jungles Preferred.* Boston: Houghton Mifflin, 1931.

Miller, Joseph, ed. *The African Past Speaks: Essays on Oral Tradition and History.* Hampden, Conn.: Archon Books, 1980.

Mitchell, Timothy. *Colonizing Egypt.* Berkeley and Los Angeles: University of California Press, 1991.

Moodie, T. Dunbar, and Vivienne Ndatshe. *Going for Gold: Men, Mines, and Migration.* Berkeley and Los Angeles: University of California Press, 1994.

Moore, Henrietta L. *Space, Text, and Gender: An Anthropological Study of the Marakwet of Kenya.* Cambridge: Cambridge University Press, 1986.

Moore, Henrietta L., and Megan Vaughan, *Cutting Down Trees: Gender, Nutrition, and Agricultural Change in the Northern Province of Zambia, 1890–1990.* Portsmouth, N.H.: Heinemann, 1994.

Moore, Sally Falk. "Selection for Failure in a Small Social Field: Ritual Concord and Fraternal Strife among the Chagga, Kilimanjaro, 1968–1969." In id. and Barbara Meyerhoff, eds., *Symbol and Politics in Communal Ideology,* 109–44. Ithaca, N.Y.: Cornell University Press, 1975.

Moorehouse, F. H. "The Marxist Theory of the Labour Aristocracy." *Social History* 3, 1 (1978): 50–66.

―――. "The 'Work' Ethic and 'Leisure' Activity: The Hot Rod in Post-War America." In Joyce, *The Historical Meanings of Work,* 233–54. Cambridge: Cambridge University Press, 1987.

Moretti, Franco. *Signs Taken for Wonders: Essays in the Sociology of Literary Forms.* Translated by Susan Fischer, David Fragacs, and David Miller. London: Verso, 1983.

Morin, Edgar, Bernard Paillard, Evelyne Burguière, Claude Capulier, Suzanne de Lusignan et al. *Rumour in Orleans.* Translated by Peter Green. New York: Pantheon Books; London: Blond, 1971. Originally published as *La rumeur d'Orléans* (Paris: Seuil, 1969).

Morrow, Sean. "'On the Side of the Robbed': R. J. B. Moore, Missionary on the Copperbelt, 1933–1941." *Journal of Religion in Africa* 19, 3 (1989): 238–53.

Mottram, Eric. *Blood on the Nash Ambassador: Investigations into American Popular Culture.* London: Hutchinson, 1983.

Mudimbe, V. Y. *Parables and Fables: Exegesis, Textuality and Politics in Central Africa.* Madison: University of Wisconsin Press, 1991.

Mulira, E. M. K. *Troubled Uganda.* London: Fabian Colonial Bureau, 1950.

Mullen, Patrick B. "Modern Legend and Rumor Theory." *Journal of the Folklore Institute* 9 (1972): 95–102.

Muriuki, Godfrey. *A History of the Kikuyu, 1500–1900.* Nairobi: Oxford University Press, 1974.

Murray, Margaret. *The Witch Cult in Western Europe.* Oxford: Clarendon Press, 1921.

Musambachime, Mwelwa C. "The Social and Economic Effects of Sleeping Sickness in Mweru-Luapula, 1906–22." *African Economic History* 10 (1981): 151–73.

———. "The Impact of Rumor: The Case of the Banyama (Vampire-Men) in Northern Rhodesia, 1930–1964." *International Journal of African Historical Studies* 21, 2 (1988): 201–15.

Musisi, Nakanyike. "Women, 'Elite Polygyny,' and Buganda State Formation." *Signs: Journal of Women in Culture and Society* 16, 4 (1991): 750–68.

Mutesa II, Kabaka of Buganda. *Desecration of My Kingdom.* London: Constable, 1967.

Mutwira, Roben. "Southern Rhodesian Wildlife Policy (1890–1953): A Question of Condoning Game Slaughter." *Journal of Southern African Studies* 15, 4 (1989): 248–61.

Myerhoff, Barbara. *Number Our Days.* New York: Dutton, 1978.

Nadel, S. F. "Witchcraft in Four African Societies." *American Anthropologist* 54, 1 (1952): 18–29.

"Nkhata and His Quartet." *African Listener* 13 (January 1953): 15.

Nash, June. "The Devil in Bolivia's Nationalized Tin Mines." *Science and Society* 36, 2 (1972): 220–36.

Nash, T. A. M. "A Contribution to the Bionomics of *Glossina morsitans*." *Bull. Ent. Res.* 21, 2 (1930): 200–208.

———. *Zoo without Bars: A Life in the East African Bush, 1927–1932.* Tunbridge Wells: Wayte Binding, 1984.

Nasson, Bill. "The War of Abraham Essau, 1899–1901: Myth, Martyrdom and Folk Memory from Calvinia, South Africa." *African Affairs* 87, 347 (1988): 239–65.

Needham, Rodney. "Blood, Thunder and the Mockery of Animals." *Sociologus* 14, 2 (1964): 136–49.

Nelson, Cary, and Lawrence Grossberg, eds. *Marxism and the Interpretation of Culture.* Urbana: University of Illinois Press, 1988.

Nettleson, Sarah. "Protecting a Vulnerable Margin: Towards an Analysis of How the Mouth Came to be Separated from the Body." *Sociology of Health and Illness* 10, 2 (1988): 156–69.

Odhiambo, Atieno E. S [E. S. Atieno-Odhiambo; Atieno Odhiambo]. "The Movement of Ideas: A Case Study of Intellectual Responses to Colonialism among the Ligunua Peasants." In Bethwell A. Ogot, ed., *History and Social Change in East Africa.* Hadith 6 (1976): 163–80.

Obbo, Christine. "Dominant Male Ideology and Female Options: Three East African Case Studies." *Africa* 46, 4 (1976): 371–88.

Oboler, Regina Smith. "Is the Female Husband a Man? Woman/Woman Marriage among the Nandi of Kenya." *Ethnology* 19, 1 (1980): 69–88.

Okeyo, Achola Pala. "Daughters of the Lakes and Rivers: Colonization and Land Rights of Luo Women." In Mona Etienne and Eleanor Leacock, eds., *Women and Colonization: Anthropological Perspectives*, 186–213. New York: Praeger, 1980.

Okoth-Ogendo, H. W. O. "Some Issues of Theory in the Study of Land Tenure Relations in African Agriculture." *Africa* 59, 1 (1989): 6–17.

Oliver, Roland. *In the Realms of Gold*. Madison: University of Wisconsin Press, 1997.

Oliver-Smith, Anthony. "The Pistaco: Institutionalized Fear in the Peruvian Highlands." *Journal of American Folklore* 82, 326 (1969): 363–75.

O'Shea, Michael. *Missionaries and Miners: A History of the Beginnings of the Catholic Church in Zambia with Particular Reference to the Copperbelt*. Ndola: Mission Press, 1986.

Packard, Randall M. "Social Change and the History of Misfortune among the Bashu of Zaire." In Karp and Bird, *Explorations in African Systems of Thought*, 237–66. Bloomington: Indiana University Press, 1980.

———. *White Plague, Black Labor: Tuberculosis and the Political Economy of Health and Disease in South Africa*. Berkeley and Los Angeles: University of California Press, 1989.

———. "The Invention of the 'Tropical Worker': Medical Research and the Quest for Central African Labor on the South African Gold Mines, 1903–36." *Journal of African History* 34, 2 (1993): 271–92.

Paine, Robert. "What is Gossip About? An Alternative Hypothesis." *Man*, n.s., 2, 2 (1967): 278–85.

Pandey, Gyandendra. "In Defense of the Fragment: Writing about Hindu-Muslim Riots in India Today." *Representations* 37 (1992): 27–55.

Parker, John. *Rhodesia—Little White Island*. Foreword by Sir Roy Welensky. London: Pitman, 1972.

Parpart, Jane L. *Labor and Capital on the African Copperbelt*. Philadelphia: Temple University Press, 1983.

———. "Sexuality and Power on the Zambian Copperbelt, 1926–54." In Norman R. Bennett, ed., *Discovering the African Past: Essays in Honor of Daniel F. McCall*, 57–64. Boston University Papers in African History, 8. Boston: African Studies Center, Boston University, 1987.

Parry, Jonathan, and Maurice Bloch, eds. *Money and the Morality of Exchange*. Cambridge: Cambridge University Press, 1989.

Peires, Jeff. "The Legend of Fenner Solomon." In Belinda Bozzoli, ed., *Class, Community and Conflict: South African Perspectives*. Johannesburg, Ravan Press, 1987.

Pels, Peter. "Mumiani: The White Vampire. A Neo-Diffusionist Analysis of Rumour." *Ethnofoor* 5, 1–2 (1995): 165–87.

Perham, Margery Freda, Dame. *African Apprenticeship: An Autobiographical*

Journey in Southern Africa, 1929. New York: Africana Pub. Co.; London: Faber & Faber, 1974.

Perrings, Charles. "Consciousness, Conflict, and Proletarianization: An Assessment of the 1935 Mineworkers' Strike on the Northern Rhodesian Copperbelt." *Journal of Southern African Studies* 4, 1 (1977): 36–52.

———. *Black Mineworkers in Central African Industry: Industrial Strategies and the Evolution of the African Proletariat in the Copperbelt, 1911–1941.* New York: Holmes & Meier; London: Heinemann, 1979.

———. "A Moment of 'Proletarianization' of the New Middle Class: Race, Value, and Division of Labour on the Copperbelt, 1946–1966." *Journal of Southern African Studies* 17, 2 (1990): 183–213.

Personal Narratives Group, ed. *Interpreting Women's Lives: Feminist Theory and Personal Narratives.* Bloomington, Indiana University Press, 1989.

Philips, Susan U. "Evidentiary Standards and American Trials: Just the Facts." In Hill and Irvine, eds., *Responsibility and Evidence in Oral Discourse,* 248–59. Cambridge, Cambridge University Press, 1992.

Phimister, I. R. "The 'Spanish' Influenza Epidemic of 1918 and Its Impact on the Southern Rhodesian Mining Industry." *Central African Journal of Medicine* 19, 7 (1973): 136–48.

———. "Origins and Aspects of Worker Consciousness in Rhodesia." In E. Webster, ed., *Southern African Labour History,* 47–63. Johannesburg, Ravan Press, 1979.

———. "Discourse and the Discipline of Historical Context: Conservation and Ideas about Development in Southern Rhodesia, 1930–1950." *Journal of Southern African Studies* 12, 2 (1986): 263–75.

Pitman, C. R. S. *A Report on a Faunal Survey of Northern Rhodesia with Especial Reference to Game, Elephant Control, and National Parks.* Livingstone: Government Printer, 1934.

———. *A Game Warden Takes Stock.* London: T. Nisbett, 1942.

Pitt-Rivers, Julian Alfred, ed. *Mediterranean Countrymen: Essays in the Social Anthropology of the Mediterranean.* Paris: Mouton, 1963.

Poovey, Mary. *Uneven Developments: The Ideological Work of Gender in Mid-Victorian England.* Chicago: University of Chicago Press, 1986.

Portelli, Alessandro. *The Death of Luigi Trastulli and Other Stories: Form and Meaning in Oral History.* Albany: State University of New York Press, 1991.

———. *The Battle of Valle Guilia: Oral History and the Art of Dialogue.* Madison: University of Wisconsin Press, 1997.

Powdermaker, Hortense. *Copper Town: The Human Situation on the Rhodesian Copperbelt.* New York: Harper & Row, 1962.

Power, D'Arcy, and J. Keogh Murphy, eds. *A System of Syphilis.* 14 vols. London: Oxford University Press, 1914.

Prakash, Gyan. "Writing Post-Orientalist Histories of the Third World: Perspectives from Indian Historiography." *Comparative Studies in Society and History* 32, 2 (1990): 383–408.

Price, Richard. *Alabi's World.* Baltimore: Johns Hopkins University Press, 1990.

Prins, Gwyn. "But What Was the Disease? The Present State of Health and Healing in African Studies." *Past and Present* 124 (1989): 150–79.

"A Quiet Man with a Guitar." *African Listener* 14 (February 1953): 6.

Rabinbach, Anson. *The Human Motor: Energy, Fatigue, and the Origins of Modernity*. Berkeley and Los Angeles: University of California Press, 1992.

Radway, Janice. *Reading the Romance: Women, Patriarchy, and Popular Literature*. Chapel Hill: University of North Carolina Press, 1984.

Ranger, Terence O. *Dance and Society in Eastern Africa, 1890–1970: The Beni Ngoma*. Berkeley and Los Angeles: University of California Press, 1975.

———. "Godly Medicine: The Ambiguities of Mission Medicine in Southeast Tanzania, 1900–1945." *Social Science and Medicine* 15B (1981): 259–68.

———. "Taking Hold of the Land: Holy Places and Pilgrimages in Twentieth-Century Zimbabwe." *Past and Present* 117 (1987): 159–90.

Ranger, T. O., and Paul Slack, eds. *Epidemics and Ideas: Essays in the Historical Perception of Pestilence*. Cambridge, Cambridge University Press, 1992.

Ransford, Oliver. *"Bid the Sickness Cease": Disease in the History of Black Africa*. London: J. Murray, 1983.

Ray, Benjamin. *Myth, Ritual and Kingship in Buganda*. Oxford: Oxford University Press, 1991.

Reid, Donald. *Paris Sewers and Sewermen: Realities and Representations*. Cambridge, Mass.: Harvard University Press, 1991.

Richards, Audrey I. "Mother-Right among the Central Bantu." In E. E. Evans-Pritchard, ed., *Essays Presented to C. G. Seligman*, 268–80. 1934. Reprint. Westport, Conn.: Negro Universities Press, 1970.

———. "A Modern Movement of Witchfinders." *Africa* 8, 4 (1935): 439–51.

———. *Land, Labour and Diet in Northern Rhodesia: An Economic Study of the Bemba Tribe*. Oxford: Oxford University Press, 1939.

———. *Chisungu: A Girl's Initiation Ritual among the Bemba of Zambia*. London and New York: Routledge, 1982.

Roberts, Andrew. *A History of the Bemba: Political Growth and Change in North-eastern Zambia before 1900*. Madison: University of Wisconsin Press, 1973.

Robertson, Claire E. "In Pursuit of Life Histories: The Problem of Bias." *Frontiers* 7, 2 (1983): 63–69.

———. *"Trouble Showed Me the Way": Women, Men and Trade in the Nairobi Area, 1890–1990*. Bloomington: Indiana University Press, 1997.

Rodwell, Edward. *Coast Causerie 2: Columns from the Mombasa Times*. Nairobi: Heinemann, 1973.

Robinson, E. G. A. "The Economic Problem." In Davis, ed., *Modern Industry and the African*, 131–226. London: Macmillan, 1933.

Rogers, Peter. "The British and the Kikuyu 1890–1905: A Reassessment." *Journal of African History* 20, 2 (1979): 255–69.

Roles, N. C. "Tribal Surgery in East Africa during the Nineteenth Century, Part 2—Therapeutic Surgery." *East African Medical Journal* 44, 1 (1967): 20–32.

Roper, Lyndal. *Oedipus and the Devil: Sexuality and Religion in Early Modern Europe*. London: Routledge, 1994.

Roscoe, John. *The Baganda: An Account of Their Customs and Beliefs*. London: Macmillan, 1911.

Rosaldo, Renato. "From the Door of His Tent: The Fieldworker and the Inquisitor." In Clifford and Marcus, eds., *Writing Culture*, 77–97. Berkeley and Los Angeles: University of California Press, 1986.

Rysman, Alexander. "How Gossip Became a Woman." *Communication* 27, 1 (1977): 173–80.

Sabean, David W. *Power in the Blood: Popular Culture and Village Discourse in Early Modern Germany*. Cambridge: Cambridge University Press, 1984.

Sacleux, Charles. *Dictionnaire Swahili-Français*. Paris: Institut d'ethnologie, 1941.

Sanchez, Mary, and Ben G. Blount, eds. *Sociocultural Dimensions of Language Use*. New York: Academic Press, 1975.

Sanderson, Stewart. "The Folklore of the Motor-Car." *Folklore* 80 (1969): 235–44.

Santino, Jack. "'Flew the Ocean in a Plane': An Investigation of Airline Occupational Narrative." *Journal of the Folklore Institute* 15, 3 (1978): 202–12.

———. "Miles of Smiles, Years of Struggle: The Negotiation of Black Occupational Identity through the Personal Experience Narrative." *Journal American Folklore* 96, 382 (1983): 394–412.

———. "Occupational Ghostlore: Social Context and the Expression of Belief." *Journal American Folklore* 101, 400 (1988): 207–18.

Scarnecchia, Timothy. "Poor Women and Nationalist Politics: Alliances and Fissures in the Formation of a Nationalist Movement in Salisbury, Rhodesia 1950–56." *Journal of African History* 37, 3 (1996): 283–310.

Scobie, Alastair. *Murder for Magic: Witchcraft in Africa*. London: Cassell, 1965.

Scheper-Hughes, Nancy. *Death Without Weeping: The Violence of Everyday Life in Brazil*. Berkeley and Los Angeles: University of California Press, 1992.

Schoffeleers, Mathew. "Folk Christology in Africa: The Dialectics of the Nganga Paradigm." *Journal of Religion in Africa*, 19, 2 (1988): 157–83.

Schofield, A. T. "Some Patients at Toro." *Mission Hospital* 31, 353 (1927): 135–37.

Scott, Joan W. "The Evidence of Experience." *Critical Inquiry* 17 (1991): 773–97.

———. "A Rejoinder to Thomas Holt." In Chandler, Davidson, and Harootunian, eds., *Questions of Evidence*, 397–400. Chicago: University of Chicago Press, 1994.

Scully, Pamela. *Liberating the Family? Gender and British Slave Emancipation in the Rural Western Cape, South Africa, 1823–1853*. Portsmouth, N.H.: Heinemann, 1997.

Semkubuge, Simon. "The Work of an African Medical Officer." *Uganda Teachers Journal* 1 (1939): 99–101.

Seleti, Yona Ngakaba. "Entrepreneurs in Colonial Zambia." In Chipungu, ed., *Guardians in Their Time*, 147–69. London: Macmillan, 1992.

Seltzer, Mark. *Bodies and Machines*. New York, Routledge, 1992.

Shaw, Carolyn Martin. *Colonial Inscriptions: Race, Sex, and Class in Kenya*. Minneapolis: University of Minnesota Press, 1995.

Shepperson, George. *Myth and Reality in Malawi*. Evanston, Ill.: Northwestern University Press, 1966.

Shibutani, Tamotsu. *Improvised News: A Sociological Study of Rumor*. Indianapolis: Bobbs-Merrill, 1966.

Showers, Kate B. "Soil Erosion in the Kingdom of Lesotho: Origins and Colonial Response." *Journal of Southern African Studies* 15, 2 (1989): 263–86.

Shostak, Marjorie. *Nisa—the Life and Words of a !Kung Woman*. Cambridge, Mass.: Harvard University Press, 1983.

———. "'What the Wind Won't Take Away': The Genesis of *Nisa—the Life and Words of a !Kung Woman*." In Personal Narratives Group, ed., *Interpreting Women's Lives*, 228–40. Bloomington: Indiana University Press, 1989.

Shuman, Amy. "'Get Outa My Face': Entitlement and Authoritative Discourse." In Hill and Irvine, eds., *Responsibility and Evidence in Oral Discourse*, 135–60. Cambridge: Cambridge University Press, 1992.

Smith, Alec. *Insect Man: The Fight against Malaria*. London: Radcliffe Press, 1993.

Smith, Mary. *Baba of Karo: A Woman of the Muslim Hausa*. 1954. Reprint. New Haven: Yale University Press, 1980.

Smyth, Rosaleen. "Propaganda and Politics: The History of *Mutende* during the Second World War." *Zambian Journal of History* 1 (1981): 43–60.

Société des Missionnaires d'Afrique. *Rapports annuels*. Algiers: Maison-Carrée, 1923–49.

Sorrenson, M. P. K. *Land Reform in Kikuyu Country*. Nairobi: Oxford University Press, 1967.

Southall, Aiden, and Peter C. W. Gutkind. *Townsmen in the Making: Kampala and Its Suburbs*. Kampala: East African Institute of Social Research, 1957.

Spacks, Patricia. *Gossip*. New York: Knopf, 1985.

Spear, Thomas, and Richard Waller, eds. *Being Maasai*. London: James Currey, 1993.

Spivak, Gayatri Chakrobarty. "The Rani of Sanir: An Essay on Reading the Archives." *History and Theory* 24 (1985): 247–72.

———. "Can the Subaltern Speak?" In Nelson and Grossberg, eds., *Marxism and the Interpretation of Culture*, 271–313. Urbana: University of Illinois Press, 1988.

Stallybrass, Peter, and Alon White, *The Politics and Poetics of Transgression*. Ithaca, N.Y.: Cornell University Press, 1986.

Stamp, Patricia. "Kikuyu Women's Self-Help Groups." In Claire Robertson and Iris Berger, eds., *Women and Class in Africa*, 27–44. New York: Holmes & Meier, 1986.

Steere, Edward. *A Handbook of the Swahili Language, as Spoken at Zanzibar*. London: Bell & Daldy, 1870. 3d ed. rev. A. C. Madan. London: Society for the Promotion of Christian Knowledge, 1884.

Stevenson, John Allen. "A Vampire in the Mirror: The Sexuality of Dracula." *PMLA* 103, 2 (1988): 139–49.

Stoler, Ann Laura. "Rethinking Colonial Categories: European Communities and the Boundaries of Rule." *Comparative Studies in Society and History* 31, 1 (1989): 134–61.

———. "'In Cold Blood': Hierarchies of Credibility and the Politics of Colonial Narratives." *Representations* 37 (1992): 140–89.

———. *Race and the Education of Desire: Foucault's History of Sexuality and the Colonial Order of Things.* Durham, N.C.: Duke University Press, 1995.

Strobel, Margaret. *Muslim Women in Mombasa, 1890–1975.* New Haven: Yale University Press, 1979.

Strobel, Margaret, and Sarah Mirzah. *Three Swahili Women.* Bloomington: Indiana University Press, 1989. Published in Swahili as *Wanawake watatu wa Kiswahili: Hadithi za maisha kutoka Mombasa, Kenya* (Bloomington: Indiana University Press, 1991).

Strobel, Margaret, and Nupur Chaudhuri, eds. *Western Women and Imperialism: Complicity and Resistance.* Bloomington: Indiana University Press, 1992.

Szwed, John F. "Gossip, Drinking and Social Control in a Newfoundland Parish." *Ethnology* 5 (1966): 434–45.

Summers, Carol. "Intimate Colonialism: The Imperial Production of Reproduction in Uganda, 1907–25." *Signs: Journal of Women in Culture and Society* 16 (1991): 787–807.

Sutton, J. E. G. "Becoming Maasailand." In Thomas Spear and Richard Waller, eds., *Being Maasai,* 19–60. London: James Currey, 1993.

Swynnerton, C. F. M. "An Examination of the Tsetse Problem in North Mossurise, Portuguese East Africa." *Bull. Ent. Res.* 11 (1921): 304–30.

———. "An Experiment in Control of Tsetse-Flies at Shinyanga, Tanganyika Territory." *Bull. Ent. Res.* 15, 4 (1925): 313–63.

———. *The Tsetse Flies of East Africa: A First Study of Their Ecology, with a View to Their Control.* With a preface by W. Ormsby-Gore. Transactions of the Royal Entomological Society of London, vol. 84. London: The Society, 1936.

———. "Appendix II: How Forestry May Assist Towards the Control of the Tsetse Flies." In R. S. Troup, *Colonial Forest Administration,* 339–42. London: Oxford University Press, 1940.

Taussig, Michael. *The Devil and Commodity Fetishism in South America.* Chapel Hill: University of North Carolina Press, 1980.

———. *Shamanism, Colonialism, and the Wild Man: A Study in Terror and Healing.* Chicago: University of Chicago Press, 1987.

Taylor, Christopher C. *Milk, Honey, and Money: Changing Concepts in Rwandan Healing.* Washington, D.C.: Smithsonian Institution Press, 1992.

Taylor, John V., and Dorothea A. Lehmann, *Christians of the Copperbelt: The Growth of the Church in Northern Rhodesia.* London: SCM Press, 1961.

Thomas, Lynn M. "*Ngaitana* (I will circumcise myself): The Gender and Generational Politics of the 1956 Ban on Clitoridectomy in Meru, Kenya." *Gender and History* 8, 3 (1996): 338–63.

———. "Imperial Concerns and 'Women's Affairs': State Efforts to Regulate Clitoridectomy and Eradicate Abortion in Meru, Kenya, c. 1910–1950." *Journal African History* 39, 1 (1998): 121–46.

Thompson, E. P. "Time, Work Discipline, and Industrial Capitalism." *Past and Present* 38 (1968): 56–97.

Thompson, Gardner. "Colonialism in Crisis: the Uganda Disturbances of 1945." *African Affairs* 91 (1992): 605–29.

Thrift, Nigel. "Owners' Time and Own Time: The Making of Capitalist Time Consciousness, 1300–1880." *Lund Studies in Geography,* ser. B, 48 (1981): 56–84.

Timpson, Katherine, and A. R. Cook. "Mengo Hospital." *Mercy and Truth* 2, 13 (January 1898): 10–14.

Timpson, Kate. "Notes from a Nurse at Mengo." *Mercy and Truth* 3, 34 (October 1899): 244–46.

———. "Patients and Nurse at Mengo." *Mercy and Truth* 3, 36 (December 1899): 287–91.

Tonkin, Elizabeth. *Narrating Our Pasts: The Social Construction of Oral History.* Cambridge: Cambridge University Press, 1992.

Trant, Hope. *Not Merrion Square: Anecdotes of a Woman's Medical Career in Africa.* Toronto: Thornhill Press, 1970.

Trapnell, C. G. *The Soils, Vegetation and Agriculture of North-Eastern Rhodesia: Report of the Ecological Survey.* Lusaka: Government Printer, 1943.

Trouillot, Michel-Rolf. *Silencing the Past: Power and the Production of History.* Boston: Beacon Press, 1995.

Turnbull, Colin. *The Lonely African.* New York: Simon & Schuster, 1962.

Turner, Patricia A. "Church's Fried Chicken and the Klan: A Rhetorical Analysis of Rumor in the Black Community." *Western Folklore* 46, 4 (1987): 294–306.

———. *I Heard It through the Grapevine: Rumor in African-American Culture.* Berkeley and Los Angeles: University of California Press, 1993.

Turner, Victor. *The Forest of Symbols: Aspects of Ndembu Ritual.* Ithaca, N.Y.: Cornell University Press, 1967.

Turshen, Meredeth. *The Political Ecology of Disease in Tanzania.* New Brunswick, N.J.: Rutgers University Press, 1984.

Vail, Leroy. "Ecology and History: the Example of Eastern Zambia." *Journal of Southern African Studies* 3 (1977): 138–55.

———, ed. *The Creation of Tribalism in Southern Africa.* Berkeley and Los Angeles: University of California Press, 1989.

Vail, Leroy, and Landeg White. *Power and the Praise Poem: Southern African Voices in History.* Charlottesville: University Press of Virginia, 1991.

van Binsbergen, Wim M. J. *Religious Change in Zambia.* London: Kegan Paul, 1981.

van Onselen, Charles. "Worker Consciousness in Black Miners: Southern Rhodesia, 1900–1920." *Journal of African History* 14 (1973): 352–70.

———. "Race and Class in the South African Countryside: Cultural Osmosis and Social Relations in the Sharecropping Economy of the South-Western Transvaal, 1900–1950." *American Historical Review* 95, 1 (1990): 99–123.

———. "The Reconstruction of a Rural Life from Oral Testimony: Critical Notes on the Methodology in the Study of a Black South African Sharecropper." *Journal of Peasant Studies,* 20, 3 (1993): 494–514.

———. *The Seed Is Mine: The Life of Kas Maine, a South African Sharecropper, 1894–1985.* New York: Hill & Wang, 1996.

Vansina, Jan. *Oral Tradition: A Study in Historical Methodology*. 1961. Translated by H. M. Wright. Chicago: Aldine, 1965.

———. "Les mouvements religieux Kuba (Kasai) à l'époque coloniale." *Études d'histoire africaine* 2 (1971): 155–87.

———. *Oral Tradition as History*. Madison: University of Wisconsin Press, 1985.

———. "Memory and Oral Tradition." In Miller, ed., *The African Past Speaks*, 262–79. Hampden, Conn.: Archon Books. 1980.

Vaughan, Megan. *Curing Their Ills: Colonial Power and African Illness*. Stanford: Stanford University Press, 1991.

———. "Syphilis in Colonial East and Central Africa: The Social Construction of an Epidemic." In Ranger and Slack, eds., *Epidemics and Ideas*, 269–302. Cambridge: Cambridge University Press, 1992.

———. "Healing and Curing: Issues in the Social History and Anthropology of Medicine in Africa." *Social History of Medicine* 7, 2 (1994): 283–95.

———. "Health and Hegemony: Representation of Disease and the Creation of a Colonial Subject in Nyasaland." In Engels and Marks, eds., *Contesting Colonial Hegemony*, 173–201. London: I. B. Taurus, 1994.

Vellut, Jean-Luc. "La Katanga industriel en 1944: Malaises et anxiétés dans la société coloniale." In *Le Congo belge durant la Seconde Guerre mondiale* [= *Bijdragen over Belgisch-Congo tijdens de Tweede Wereldoorlog*], 493–556. Brussels: Académie royale des sciences d'outre-mer, 1983.

Veyne, Paul. *Did the Greeks Believe in their Myths? An Essay in Constitutive Imagination*. Translated by Paula Wissing. Chicago, University of Chicago Press, 1990. Originally published as *Les grecs ont-ils cru à leurs mythes? Essai sur l'imagination constituante* (Paris: Seuil, 1983).

Wachanga, H. K. *The Swords of Kirinyaga: The Fight for Land and Freedom*. Edited by Robert Whittier. Nairobi: Kenya Literature Bureau, 1975.

Waite, Gloria. "Public Health in Pre-Colonial East Central Africa." *Social Science and Medicine* 24, 3 (1987): 197–208.

Walkowitz, Judith R. *City of Dreadful Delight: Narratives of Sexual Danger in Late Victorian London*. Chicago: University of Chicago Press, 1992.

Waller, Richard. "Tsetse Fly in Western Narok, Kenya." *Journal African History* 31, 1 (1990): 71–90.

Watchel, Nathan. *Gods and Vampires: Return to Chipaya*. Translated by Carol Volk. Chicago: University of Chicago Press, 1994.

Waterman, Christopher A. "'Our Tradition Is a Very Modern Tradition': Popular Music and the Construction of Pan-Yoruba Identity." *Ethnomusicology* 34, 3 (1990): 367–79.

Weiss, Brad. "Plastic Teeth Extraction: The Iconography of Haya Gastro-Sexual Affliction." *American Ethnologist* 19, 3 (1992): 538–52.

———. *The Making and Unmaking of the Haya Lived World: Consumption, Commoditization, and Everyday Practice*. Durham, N.C.: Duke University Press, 1996.

West, Michael O. "'Equal Rights for All Civilized Men': Elite Africans and the Quest for 'European' Liquor in Colonial Zimbabwe." *International Review of Social History* 37, 3 (1992): 376–97.

White Fathers. *The White Fathers' Bemba-English Dictionary*. Rev. ed. Cape Town: Longmans, Green for Northern Rhodesia and Nyasaland Joint Publications Bureau, 1954.

White, Hayden. *Tropics of Discourse: Essays in Cultural Criticism*. Baltimore: Johns Hopkins University Press, 1988.

White, Lucie E. "Subordination, Rhetorical Survival Skills, and Sunday Shoes: Notes on the Hearing of Mrs. G." In Katharine Bartlett and Roseanne Kennedy, eds., *Feminist Legal Theory*, 404–28. Boulder, Colo.: Westview Press, 1991.

White, Luise. "Bodily Fluids and Usufruct: Controlling Property in Nairobi, 1919–1939." *Canadian Journal of African Studies* 24, 3 (1990): 418–38.

———. *The Comforts of Home: Prostitution in Colonial Nairobi*. Chicago: University of Chicago Press, 1990.

———. "Separating the Men from the Boys: Constructions of Sexuality, Gender and Terrorism in Central Kenya, 1939–59." *International Journal of African Historical Studies* 23, 1 (1990): 1–25.

———. "Cars Out of Place: Vampires, Technology and Labor in East and Central Africa." *Representations* 43 (1993): 27–50. Reprinted in Cooper and Stoler, eds., *Tensions of Empire*, 436–60. Berkeley and Los Angeles: University of California Press, 1997.

———. "Vampire Priests of Central Africa: African Debates about Labor and Religion in Colonial Northern Zambia." *Comparative Studies in Society and History* 35, 4 (1993): 744–70.

———. "Alien Nation: Race in Space." *Transition* 63 (1994): 24–33.

———. "Between Gluckman and Foucault: Historicizing Rumor and Gossip." *Social Dynamics* 20, 1 (1994): 75–92.

———. "Blood Brotherhood Revisited: Kinship, Relationship and the Body in East and Central Africa." *Africa* 64, 3 (1994): 359–72.

———. " 'Firemen Do Not Buy People': Media, Villains and Vampires in Kampala in the 1950s." *Passages* 8 (1994): 11, 16–17.

———. " 'They Could Make Their Victims Dull': Genders and Genres, Fantasies and Cures in Colonial Southern Uganda." *American Historical Review* 100, 5 (1995): 1379–1402.

———. "Tsetse Visions: Narratives of Blood and Bugs in Colonial Northern Zambia." *Journal African History* 36, 2 (1995): 219–45.

———. "Silence and Subjectivity (A Position Paper)." In Susan Hardy Aiken et al., eds., *Making Worlds: Gender, Metaphor and Materiality*, 243–51. Tucson: University of Arizona Press, 1997.

———. "The Traffic in Heads: Bodies, Borders, and the Articulation of Regional Histories." *Journal of Southern African Studies* 23, 2 (1997): 225–38.

Wiener, Alexander S. *Blood Groups and Blood Transfusion*. Baltimore: Stratton Medical Books, 1939.

Wildenthal, Lora. "Race, Gender, and Citizenship in the German Colonial Empire." In Cooper and Stoler, eds., *Tensions of Empire*, 263–83. Berkeley and Los Angeles: University of California Press, 1997.

Wilkinson, John. "The Origin of Infectious Disease in East Africa, with Special

Reference to the Kikuyu People." *East African Medical Journal* 34, 10 (1957): 542–55.

Williams, Rosalind. *Notes on the Underground: An Essay on Technology, Society, and the Imagination.* Cambridge, Mass.: MIT Press, 1992.

Williams, F. Lukyn, "Blood Brotherhood in Ankole (*Omukago*)." *Uganda Journal* 2, 1 (1934): 33–41.0

Willis, Justin. "Feedback as a 'Problem' in Oral History: An Example from Bonde." *History in Africa* 20 (1993): 353–60.

———. "The Two Lives of Mpamizo: Understanding Dissonance in Oral History." *History in Africa* 23 (1996): 319–32.

Wilson, Monica Hunter. "Witch Beliefs and Social Structure." *American Journal of Sociology* 41, 4 (1951): 307–13.

Worboys, Michael. "Manson, Ross, and Colonial Medical Policy: Tropical Medicine in London and Liverpool, 1899–1914." In MacLeod and Lewis, eds., *Disease, Medicine, and Empire,* 21–37. London: Routledge, 1988.

Yerkovitch, Sandy. "Gossiping as a Way of Speaking." *Journal of Communication* 27 (1977): 192–200.

Yngvesson, Barbara. "The Reasonable Man and Unreasonable Gossip: on the Flexibility of (Legal) Concepts and the Elasticity of (Legal) Time." In P. H. Gulliver, ed., *Cross-Examinations: Essays in Honor of Max Gluckman,* 133–54. Leiden: E. J. Brill, 1978.

Young, Crawford. *Politics in the Congo: Decolonization and Independence.* Madison: University of Wisconsin Press, 1965.

OFFICIAL DOCUMENTS

Commission Appointed to Enquire into the Disturbances on the Copperbelt of Northern Rhodesia [Russell Commission]. *Report* and *Evidence.* Lusaka: Government Printer, 1935.

Interdepartmental Committee on Sleeping Sickness. *Report.* Cd. 7349. London: HMSO, 1914.

Kenya Colony and Protectorate. *Report on Native Affairs, 1939–47.* London: HMSO, 1948.

Kenya Land Commission. *Evidence* and *Memoranda.* 3 vols. London: HMSO, 1934.

May, Alward. *Report on Sleeping Sickness in Northern Rhodesia to February 1912.* Livingstone: Government Printer, 1912.

Uganda Protectorate. *Annual Report on Uganda.* Various years. London: HMSO.

———. *Report of the Commission of Enquiry into the Disturbances in Uganda during April 1949.* Entebbe: Government Printer, 1950.

UNPUBLISHED MATERIALS

Anthony, David. "Culture and Society in a Town in Transition: A People's History of Dar es Salaam, 1865–1939." Ph.D. diss., University of Wisconsin–Madison, 1983.

Bianco, Barbara A. "The Historical Anthropology of a Mission Hospital in Pokot, Kenya." Ph.D. diss., New York University, 1992.

Bledsoe, Caroline H. "Side-Stepping the Postpartum Taboo: Mende Cultural Perceptions of Tinned Milk in Sierra Leone." MS.

Bujra, Janet M. "Pumwani: The Politics of Property." Report for the Social Science Research Council, United Kingdom. Mimeographed, 1972.

Cross, John Sholto. "The Watchtower Movement in South Central Africa, 1908–1945." Ph.D. diss., Oxford University, 1973.

Hinfelaar, Hugo H. "Religious Change among Bemba-Speaking Women in Zambia." Ph.D. diss., University of London, 1989.

Hunt, Nancy Rose. "Negotiated Colonialism: Domesticity, Hygiene, and Birth Work in the Belgian Congo." Ph.D. diss., University of Wisconsin–Madison, 1992.

Garvey, Brian. "The Development of the White Fathers' Mission among the Bemba-Speaking Peoples, 1891–1964." Ph.D. diss., University of London, 1974.

Kershaw, Gretha [Greet]. "The Land Is the People: A Study in Kikuyu Social Organization in Historical Perspective." Ph.D. diss., University of Chicago, 1972.

Leaver, K. D. "The 'Transformation of Men to Meat' Story." Native Affairs Department Information Sheet No. 20 (Salisbury, November 1960). National Archives of Zimbabwe, No. 36413.

Miescher, Stephan. "Becoming a Man in Kwawu: Gender, Law, Personhood and the Construction of Masculinities in Colonial Ghana, 1875–1957." Ph.D. diss., Northwestern University, 1997.

Thomas, Lynn M. "Regulating Reproduction: Men, Women and the State in Kenya, 1920–1970." Ph.D. diss., University of Michigan, 1997.

Swantz, Lloyd William. "The Role of the Medicine Man among the Zaramo of Dar es Salaam." Ph.D. diss., University of Dar es Salaam, 1972.

White, Luise. "The Needle and the State: The Making of Un-National Sovereignty." Paper presented to workshop on Immunization and the Social Sciences. Delhi, India, 15–17 January 1997.

Worboys, Michael. "Science and British Colonial Imperialism, 1895–1940." Ph.D. diss., Sussex University, 1979.

Zeller, Diane. "The Establishment of Western Medicine in Buganda." Ph.D. diss., Columbia University, 1972.

Credits

The following chapters are revised versions of materials published elsewhere:

Chapter 2: "Between Gluckman and Foucault: Historicizing Rumor and Gossip," *Social Dynamics* 20, no. 1 (1994): 75–92. Reprinted by permission.

Chapter 3: " 'They Could Make Their Victims Dull': Genders and Genres, Fantasies and Cures in Colonial Southern Uganda," *American Historical Review* 100, no. 5 (1995): 1379–1402. Reprinted by permission.

Chapter 4: "Cars out of Place: Vampires, Technology, and Labor in East and Central Africa," *Representations* 43 (1993): 27–50. Also in Frederick Cooper and Ann Laura Stoler, eds., *Tensions of Empire: Colonial Societies in a Bourgeois World* (Berkeley: University of California Press, 1997), 436–60. Reprinted by permission.

Chapter 5: "Bodily Fluids and Usufruct: Controlling Property in Nairobi, 1919–1939," *Canadian Journal of African Studies* 24, no. 3 (1990): 418–38. Reprinted by permission.

Chapter 6: "Vampire Priests of Central Africa. Or, African Debates about Labor and Religion in Colonial Northern Zambia," *Comparative Studies in Society and History* 35, no. 4 (1993): 744–70. Reprinted by permission.

Chapter 7: "Tsetse Visions: Narratives of Blood and Bugs in Colonial Northern Zambia, 1931–37," *Journal of African History* 36, no. 2 (1995): 219–45. Reprinted by permission.

Chapter 8: " 'Firemen Do Not Buy People': Media, Villains, and Vampires in Kampala in the 1950s," *Passages* 8 (September 1994): 11, 16–17. Reprinted by permission.

Index

Abdullah, Saidi, 232, 234

Abrahams, Roger, 61

Allen, William, 237

anesthesia, 104–5, 117–18, 157, 238, 260–62. *See also* chloroform

Anderson, Benedict, 254

animals: classification of, 217–18; hunting of, 216–17, 225–29, 230–31, 237–41; and land, 213–19; as object of scientific study, 219–25, 234–39; as predators, 12; protection of, 229–30, 233–34; as sacrifice, 14. *See also* elephants

Apter, David, 248, 249, 250

archives: colonial, 208–41; and reading of, 209–10, 212–13, 241; and rumors in, 210–12

Ardener, Edwin, 21

automobiles, 127–30; in folklore outside of Africa, 132–33; in vampire stories, 127–30, 134–35

bandages, 106, 113–18, 157, 278–79; and mine labor, 280–82. *See also* chloroform

banyama, 12, 181–83, 189–90, 194–95, 197–98, 203–4, 206–7, 229–33, 238–42, 270, 272, 277–78, 280–82, 287, 292, 296–305

Barber, Karin, 81

Barnes, John, 296

batumbula, 12–13, 15–16, 65, 183, 270, 273–74, 278–80, 286–87, 292–99

bazimamoto, 11–12, 108–12, 113–20, 137–46, 255–68, 308–9

Beidelman, T. O., 33, 110

Belgian Congo, 15–16, 83, 177–78, 206–7, 272, 280–87, 293–95. *See also* Union Minière d'Haute Katanga

Bemba: agriculture of, 223–25; and blood, concept of, 192–95, 199; elephant raiding among, 226–27; matrilineality among, 195, 199, 203; money, uses of, 198–201; witchcraft among, 190–91, 206, 212, 231–32

Benedictines, 183, 278–79, 285–86; confusions over, 183–88. *See also* Coussement, Grégoire, Dom

blood: as affiliation, system of, 158–63, 171–73; circulation of, 14–15, 116–17; and cure for European diseases, 4, 105–7; definition of, 14–15; as drink, 195; and fluids, 14, 125, 196; as gendered fluid, 125; loss of and death, 116–17, 125, 157; loss of and impotence, 117, 128; of menstruation, 165–66, 173–74; as metaphor for money, 125; as natural history, 151, 155; and red ink, confused with, 196; and red wine, confused with, 111n, 196; and semen, as opposite of, 160; transfusion of, 16–17, 107–8

347

Text: 10/13 Sabon
Display: Sabon
Composition: G&S Typesetters, Inc.
Printing and binding: Maple-Vail Book Manufacturing Group

Text: 10/13 Sabon
Display: Sabon
Compositor: 1:66 Typesetting, Inc.
Printer and binder: Maple-Vail Book Manufacturing Group